Manna Café and Bakery Cookbook

A Memoir of Two Businesses, a Community, and the Food That Connected Them

Barb Pratzel

Little Creek Press®

5341 Sunny Ridge Road

Mineral Point, Wisconsin 53565

Editing: Terese Allen, Michelle Wildgen, Shannon Booth

Cover Illustration: Julia Taylor

Interior Illustrations: Emily Ranney

Book Design and Project Coordination:

Little Creek Press

Second Edition

May 2024

Printed in Wisconsin, United States of America

For more information or to order books:

www.littlecreekpress.com

Library of Congress Control Number: 2021916525

ISBN-13: 978-1-955656-70-2

This book is dedicated to Michael.
We walked every step of this journey together,
from the turkey skin at Gordon Commons to the last
Manna bialy in our freezer. Truly this adventure,
in all its particulars, would not have happened
without you, nor meant as much.

It is also dedicated to the countless people behind
the piles of e-mails, Facebook posts, cards, and letters
I received after Manna Café closed. People who
had a memory to share, a favorite recipe, or a
reflection on what Manna meant to them.
Your words live on in these pages.

Table of Contents

Recipes by Section

Breakfast/Brunch

Lunch

Soup

Bakery

Jewish Fridays

How-To Recipe Support

Dear Reader,

Welcome!

I am delighted you are here, on the first page of this memoir/cookbook, though also a touch sad that we are not together, sipping lattes and catching up on life at Manna Cafe's sparkly cobalt blue countertop.

Once, I was a professional writer who loved to cook and eat. Then I became a professional cook who occasionally got to revisit my love of words, writing whimsical menus or sassy employee manuals. Now, I have the honor to bring my two passions together.

This cookbook arose from a pressing need to feed a community—not only literally, with thirty-five years' worth of beloved recipes, but spiritually as well, after the pandemic stopped us in our tracks. Manna had been a living, pulsating, dynamic center of food and socializing, and overnight it evaporated. Yet so much more was lost than a slice of quiche or a Cupkopf. There are recipes, and lots of them, but this is also a memoir—the story of how two unassuming businesses evolved into community hubs and the life lessons we as owners learned along the way. It is about two people growing up in two vastly different food worlds, whose early years together laid a unique groundwork for a future in food and hospitality.

The recipes in this book are for everyone, from novice cooks to experienced professionals and from longstanding customers to first-time readers. They evolved in a from-scratch kitchen and cover the gamut from "easy-peasy" to "plan ahead a bit" to "oy vey—is that really what I need to do to have my favorite quiche?" And while I have worked hard to make every recipe clear and concise, you may encounter some that seem to be, well, a lot of work. But keep reading! Where needed, I have included ample detail—sometimes clarity requires verbosity—and careful instruction to help you master certain techniques. It is my hope that, from the simplest pancake to the most complicated pastry dough, the words will carry you through to success. Nothing in this book is hard—much is downright easy. Everything is delicious.

If you were a Manna regular, I hope that in some small way, cooking these recipes and reading the stories will not only bring you a great meal but also transport you back to a place, a feeling, a memory. And to the uninitiated reader—please join us at the table!

Barb

Foreword

Manna Cafe was the heart of the north side.

It all started with the food—hands down. Manna was the best bakery in Madison. One can't do it justice with words; ink is a poor substitute for heavy cream and butter.

Manna Cafe quickly became a culinary destination, putting the north side on the map as people flocked to grab morning buns, pumpkin chocolate chip muffins, scones, rugelach, and those chocolate croissants adorned with a sweet cursive "M." Not to mention the bread—corn tzizel rye, braided challah on Friday. And the quiche! When in doubt, always buy extra to take home. Enjoying a leisurely cafe au lait with tiny flakes of something delicious tumbling onto your lap—this was how Manna drew us in. It's safe to say I'm about 10% Manna food in terms of body weight.

Not only was Manna the reason you lived for weekend mornings, but it became the place to catch up with an old friend. It was the spot you brought your future in-laws on the morning of your wedding. The bakery that met daily cravings when you were pregnant. The friendly, reassuring restaurant you suggested when you need ed to impress an important client over lunch. The cozy cafe where you tucked in for a hot cocoa by the fire while your kids enjoyed a cookie, blessedly calm for a few minutes. Manna was all those things to me, and more.

"Manna" certainly describes the heavenly fare they served us, day after day. Yet it also describes the emotional and physical comfort of being in that cheery place, with its generous staff and playful decor. It met all our needs. In 2011, when it felt like our community was being pulled apart by political battles at the capitol, Manna put signs of solidarity in the window, cheekily naming specials for notorious local figures. They made it clear that everyone was welcome for food, mimosas, conversation, and connection. It was more about building community than it was political.

When Barb asked me to write the foreword, she mentioned that this cookbook would also be a "story of bringing people together over food and what it means to be this sort of a community." That's what mattered most to her and Mike, reflecting their goals as a business and as people, and it was obvious to all of us the minute we walked in the door. That's why, shortly after I was elected to the State Assembly, Mike and Barb graciously agreed to let me host regular "Coffees with Kelda" at Manna Cafe, offering me a table to come together with my constituents, a place for them to share their thoughts, ideas, and concerns with me and each other. They even put my sign in the window, welcoming the public into our gatherings. These community conversations are, to this day, the thing I cherish most from my time in the Assembly.

I believe the welcoming atmosphere, unique to Manna, empowered people to speak to strangers about what was meaningful to them—personal tragedies or challenging experiences that they wanted to turn into something positive by way of legislation. Who wouldn't feel more at ease discussing politics over a rustic cherry tart and an earl grey tea rather than in some meeting room in a library basement?

Sharing good food and earnest company, we were empowered.

Every north sider loved Manna cafe, and those unlucky people who didn't live nearby often found reasons to drive down North Sherman Avenue so they could get that juicy brisket sandwich with melted cheese curds. Having such a gathering place, a place where you would be happy with anything on the menu, was a real point of "north side pride." Manna was the default place to go for a meal or a treat or to meet anyone—any excuse to get close to that pastry case and close to each other in the process.

Now that Manna is gone, I find myself dreaming of some beloved dish, imagining the first bite of perfect breakfast nachos or their garlicky green salad. So many of us are still mourning the loss of this extraordinary place over a year later. There are plenty of restaurants with great food in Madison. Small businesses that don't mind standing up for what's right and cafes with kind staff and a strong dose of community spirit. But there was only one Manna Cafe, and those of us who got to be part of that journey, by way of our stomachs and our hearts, are enriched by the experiences we had there.

For all of us who loved this special place, my hope is that this book helps us recreate these culinary treasures (to the best of our abilities!) and that as we bake, we honor the Pratzels for their gifts to our community by resurrecting the joy, camaraderie, and love that kept us coming back together to the miraculous Manna Cafe.

—Kelda Roys, Wisconsin State Senator

Preface

When a dish or tidbit of food moved my father, he would slip a taste into my mouth and watch me closely, anticipating my reaction. At first, it was his special oatmeal creation, rich with milk and butter. It came, steaming, with a scoop of vanilla ice cream as a sweet, cool, unexpected counterpoint. Later he might offer me coquilles St. Jacques—scallops luxuriating in a creamy white sauce—or a morsel of his Sarah Bernhardt pastry, a beautiful confection of glazed chocolate ganache perched atop a tiny French macaron. Today, still, I can see the look of expectation on his face, the gloss in his eyes, as he awaited my approval. My father was not a natural hugger, nor one to express genuine sentiment. These brief food exchanges were the best way he knew to say the words I might otherwise long to hear, and my nod of approval was practically a familial exchange of vows. In fact, when I cooked something he found particularly exceptional, he would say, "Barbara, will you marry me?"

My dad's love of food was eclipsed only by his endearing ego, which followed him into every room. Dad—Dr. Spaet or occasionally Ted to everyone else—was a man of heft, humor, and gusto. He expected hearty laughs to follow his constant patter of off-color jokes and always needed to be right—to win. Though always a good sport, he was fiercely competitive, playing Scrabble for money because points were just not enough. He loved subjecting people, including my friends, to little tests, unaware that the test recipients were more likely intimidated than enthusiastic. One summer break, my friend Marc, a piano major, visited my home. My father, himself a classical music and opera aficionado, spirited Marc away to his study, where he played one obscure composition after another, waiting for Marc to identify the composers. I was appalled at the time, but now I realize his face must have held that same giddy look of expectation, the hope that Marc would enjoy this moment with him, as though he had been offering up not a passage of Chopin, but a succulent mouthful of slow-braised beef brisket, dripping with sauce.

Good food brought my father a visceral pleasure, which he unfailingly and unapologetically expressed with a series of trumpeting sneezes. No one ever said so aloud, but dinner hosts were mortified if my father did not sneeze after a meal. When Dad was courting two women as potential second wives after my mother's death, one of them, Diana, hosted a party in his honor, surrounding the dinner table with dignitaries from my father's professional circle of research hematologists and a few family members. Nary a sneeze was heard that evening, ominous in its absence—I believe the raw clam dish was the nail in the coffin. But candidate number two, Mona, knew just how to elicit a series of mighty sneezes, and this, among other reasons, helped win his hand in eternal culinary bliss. Diana might have taken solace, though, in knowing her pumpkin chiffon pie became a family favorite, much later appearing in our business and ultimately in our customers' Thanksgiving celebrations.

I could make my father sneeze, and as I reflect on my years spent in the professional food world running a bed and breakfast, a catering business, and a small café, I realize that this achievement was my first badge of culinary pride. I am aware that during my years in business, every maple syrup-drenched oatmeal pancake, every warm mouthful of chocolate chunk cinnamon streusel coffeecake, every delicate matzo ball was meant to make a cafe full of neighbors, friends, and family sneeze in eighty-part harmony. As a restaurateur, I stood in my father's shoes, offering up a taste of the perfect scrambled egg, its creamy, custardy curds resulting from slow, patient stirring on low heat, with threads of cheddar cheese running throughout like veins of gold. Now I was the one watching expectantly as customers or the staff looked up and nodded their approval, for I had inherited my father's gastronomic genes.

Even as I followed the path set out for me in an educated and acculturated upbringing, claimed a major and pursued a degree, I cooked and baked, and sought out like-minded people. I discovered a world of grateful eaters beyond the doors of my childhood home. While my father had ignited my drive to bring joy with food, my friends and coworkers encouraged me to take my cooking to a professional level. In time, I would find my way to first one and then another small business, both of which gave voice to my culinary passions.

My husband Mike and I opened our first business, The Collins House Bed and Breakfast, as an outlet to cook for small groups of people and to welcome travelers to Madison with the comforts of home—flannel sheets, plates of cookies, hearty breakfasts. I might cook for two or four people at a time, serving them and relishing their immediate enjoyment and feedback. Manna Cafe continued The Collins House spirit in the form of a small neighborhood cafe. Manna opened as a restaurant in the neighborhood I called home, but it quickly became a home itself, abuzz with life. Here I had the opportunity to share with a larger audience the homey but elegant foods upon which the B&B and catering were based. By recreating an atmosphere of warmth and hospitality, we also invited our customers to join a larger experience than just the food alone.

Mike and I originally envisioned a happy melting pot of local neighborhood folks, but the business rather quickly and organically evolved into its own small community, becoming a magnet that drew customers from all over the city and beyond. People came for the food but returned with astonishing regularity because of the close-knit, familial environment that embraced every customer. People came to celebrate birthdays, promotions, graduations. They came to feel better after a round of chemotherapy, or to cozy up on a purple couch by the fireplace, reading. Children came for the giant muffins, leaving a trail of crumbs in their wake, and seniors came trailing wisdom and good humor. And they all sneezed in their own special ways—sometimes loudly, with a hug or a heartfelt "thank you," sometimes in a whisper, with one last wistful look toward the bakery case before heading out.

The Collins House had grown and flourished, and when its time came, we distilled its essence into a cafe. Manna, in turn, grew and flourished until 2020, when her life (like so many of her kind) was unexpectedly cut short by the virus's rippling effects. The grief was palpable. Our e-mail inbox and Facebook page overflowed with staff memories, customer stories of why they came, and what Manna meant to them. There was a hole in our community both physically and spiritually, and we joined both customers and staff in mourning the loss of something that had nourished us together all these years. The COVID-19 ending was abrupt, brutal—not the Hollywood ending we had in mind. We needed a more meaningful closure to the cafe and to our life's focus.

Over the years, people had encouraged me to write a cookbook, and I would nod obligingly, though with little appetite for such a daunting project. But in Manna's final weeks, the background cookbook chatter became more audible, and seemingly overnight, the idea went from an amusing rainy day project to a deeply meaningful and pressing imperative. I could barely wait to get started. Years earlier, I had been a professional writer but had set that career aside to cultivate two food-centric businesses. The cookbook would not only let me come full circle professionally, but it would provide the perfect coda—a celebration of life.

My father never had a chance to try my scrambled eggs, but oh how I wish he could have. I have a vision in my mind of his almost childlike pleasure at that moment—it is the vision that inspired my dreams and brought us all together. He would savor the mouthful, maybe ask for another bite, and then we would play a game of Scrabble.

PART I:

A Tale of Two Businesses

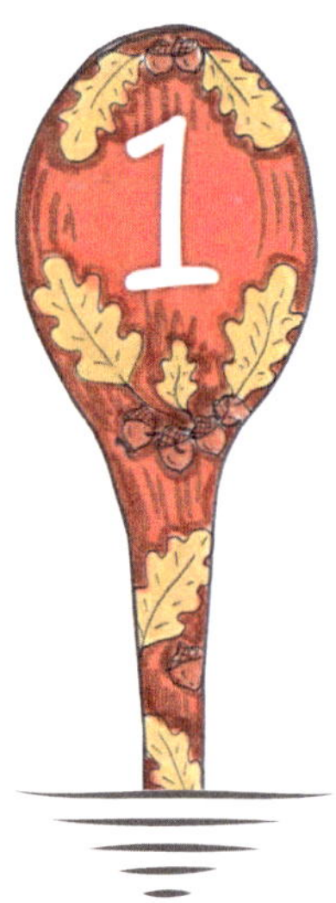

Introductions All Around

For one last time, Mike pulled the little chain—*ka-chink, ka-chink*—and the rainbow neon "Open" sign, shaped like a steaming cup of coffee, blinked cheerfully to life. Outside the cafe, customers were already politely arranged along the orderly duct-tape line we had created, one swatch every six feet, all the way to the street. They filed in, barely recognizable behind their colorful array of masks (though by then, we had even come to know our customers by their masks). No one knew quite what to say because no one was prepared for this to be the last day, when they would say, "Good morning, Mike (or Hannah or Allyson)," or ask for their regular iced mocha and sunrise muffin, one last time. This cafe had become so much a part of their own lives' fabric that its nonexistence the next day was unfathomable. Only four months before, there were long waits for tables, and customers wedged themselves between one another, laughing and jabbering between mouthfuls of sticky buns, waiting to hear their names called. Now, only six people were allowed in at a time, and the tables that once seated groups of two, or six, or fourteen were repurposed as barriers to social contact. It was like adding salt to the wound. Maybe it was really April Fools' Day. Maybe we were pulling *their* chains.

For fifteen years, Manna Cafe and Bakery had embodied what Ray Oldenburg termed society's "Third Place," a space outside of home or work where people gathered with friends for a social experience—a community hangout where both food and camaraderie nurtured the soul.[1] Manna was the first stop on the daily commute, a pause for that morning cup of joe and Danish, when the stoplights were still blinking yellow, and the rising sun cast a pink glow over our peaceful northside Madison neighborhood. And it was the last stop at the end of the workday, where you might pop in to see if that two-berry pie you'd been dreaming about all afternoon was still waiting. For the twelve hours in between, it was a space teeming with life. Manna was situated unassumingly in the corner of a dreary strip mall. Yet, once through the glass doors of the front vestibule, an unexpected world came into vivid, colorful focus: bakery cases beckoned with an array of pastries and fresh breads, baristas hollered out drink orders, staff scuttled this way and that with ample plates of food, and everywhere people were huddled in purposeful conversation.

Manna was where the Scrabble ladies spent hours lost in friendly competition, where authors wrote spy novels, and protesters gathered after an emotional day at the capitol. Teens fresh out of classes did their homework over hot cocoa, and teachers graded papers. Friends consoled friends on the couch by the fireplace, in the back room, over the comfort of a peanut butter ripple cookie. Every week without fail, a large group of neighborhood retirees huddled over coffee and muffins, arguing politics or making travel plans. Manna was the home of The Collins House oatmeal pancakes, fragrant and wholesome and glossy with Wisconsin maple syrup, and Jewish pastries whose names you couldn't pronounce—rugelach and hamantaschen and bialys—but whose cultural origins subconsciously warmed your experience. And it was the place where, as the years passed, lives intertwined. Regulars came to watch our staff performances in local theater, staff dog sat for vacationing customers, and we all attended one another's weddings and funerals. The crisp lines of employee/customer blurred a bit, and friendships blossomed.

Our first business, The Collins House Bed and Breakfast in downtown Madison, was a third place of a different sort, where people gathered from all over the world, the country, and the state. Overnight guests stayed for many reasons: to celebrate weddings, attend Art Fair on the Square, interview at the university, or visit their children. They came to the B&B for the lake views, the historic architecture, the warm welcome, and, especially, the food. Of course, food was the raison d'être for the business in the first place—fresh baked goods upon arrival, deep dark chocolates at bedtime, and an ample breakfast plate to fuel the day. Guests returned over and over to both Madison and The Collins House. More than a handful moved here and became our close friends. We raised children together, formed cooking groups, and catered a multitude of life events.

[1] *While coffeehouses are traditionally thought of as Third Places, many other businesses perform the same function, including hair salons, gyms, or community centers. Ray Oldenburg has written several enlightening books worth a read for people who live the Third Place life. I suggest* The Great Good Place: Cafes, Coffee Shops, Bookstores, Bars, Hair Salons, and Other Hangouts at the Heart of a Community *or* Celebrating the Third Place: Inspiring Stories About the "Great Good Places" at the Heart of Our Communities.

Mike and I introduced travelers to the city we had come to love during our early years together, taking ownership of this special town as so many do. We loved watching people parade around the farmer's market with a child on their shoulders and a sheepdog in a red wagon or sitting in iconic orange, yellow, or green chairs on the Memorial Union Terrace and watching a bedazzling array of sunsets over Lake Mendota. During our student years, L'Etoile Restaurant founder Odessa Piper opened our hearts to rustic, French-influenced food—simply conceived, locally sourced, and skillfully prepared—that helped redefine the food scene for decades to come, and shaped our food sensibilities for a lifetime.

For twenty years at the B&B, we cultivated principles of food service and hospitality, employee management, atmosphere and aesthetic. Most importantly, we learned that by thinking of the business as a lifestyle, rather than as "work," we were freed up to enjoy its daily rhythms. This outlook made our business lives feel integrated into our identities rather than a job to be done. We also learned that by pretending to *be* our customers from time to time, seeing what they saw, we gained insights that helped inform our smallest and largest decisions. Over the years, a business model evolved that reflected this way of life.

Together, Collins House and Manna Cafe tell a story of family values, community spirit, and the love of good pancakes. The Collins House set the stage for Manna's sense of hospitality and the importance of thinking of staff as a kind of family. It provided a starting menu of items—the oatcakes, the triple fudge brownies, the spinach swirl scramble—that brought people running back for nearly thirty-five years. The threads between the two businesses were both tangible: Manna's plate rail recreated from The Collins House oak dining room or the host stand that had once displayed our guest register and restaurant menus, and intangible: the value of human interactions in a business environment, the commitment to serve the neighborhood that defined us, and us them, and the binding power of a bowl of potato nachos, set in the center of a table with extra forks for sharing.

But that all came later. Before Manna and The Collins House were born, two people met at the UW, fell in love with Madison and each other, and worked and played and ate together for a number of years, all while pursuing their chosen career paths of writing and marketing research. Food played a leading role in their story, but not a professional one, until a trip to San Francisco changed their future.

Beginnings

Mike and I met two weeks into our freshman year at UW-Madison, in September 1974. Our meeting was, fittingly, over burgers and chili at Gordon Commons, our dorm cafeteria, and from that early moment, food bound us together. In the dorms, Mike made mac and cheese in a little orange hot pot meant for boiling water, and I cooked dinners using two off-to-college gifts from my big sister Linda: an avocado green electric skillet, and *The Campus Cookbook* by Moira Hodgson, a groovy little volume with a pot brownie recipe thrillingly tucked within. Dorm friends would follow their noses to where we were cooking in the common room, and our reputation took root. These forays led to more ambitious dinner parties and later to entertaining professor friends in our very first $165 per month off-campus rental, where we learned some early and important cooking lessons the hard way: always set a bowl underneath your sieve before straining the stock you simmered for six hours, or it will disappear with shocking finality down the drain; always check labels on boxes because baking soda not only doesn't thicken a stir fry but makes it inedible; and never, ever use a 1960s Hoover canister-style vacuum cleaner to suck up hot cream of broccoli soup, after dropping the pot and splashing the professor's wife's white maternity outfit.

My parents' alma mater was UW-Madison, although I was born and raised in a suburb of New York City. Ours was a household of "gourmet" cooking from the books of Craig Claiborne, Julia Child, and Paul Prudhomme, among many. The family rated every recipe my father made as "Excellent" or "Company" or, less encouragingly, "OK." My mom, a Madison native, contributed her 1928 copies of the original *Settlement Cookbook* and *The Joy of Cooking*, both of which are notated in her feminine, red-penciled script. I have these cookbooks still, covers gone and pages brown and brittle, hanging precariously. But from them all, I cooked many a recipe for my children.

My dad's food sensibility was reflected in the writings of Calvin Trillin, whose classic *Alice, Let's Eat* was as close to a bible as our Jewish household ever got. He applauded authenticity and shunned pretension. At restaurants, I had to ask permission to order shrimp, my favorite food, not because of its price, but because my father had to deem the chef capable of cooking shrimp properly, and the answer was usually "no." So imagine my elation when I experienced my first smorgasbord at age eleven and asked if I could have any of the shrimp piled irresistibly into a giant copper cauldron. My father looked me in the eye and said gravely, but with a mocking gleam, "Barbara, you can eat as much as you want." The joy of this memory was not so much the shrimp itself but the "yes," a word my father used sparingly. To this day, I make food choices based on an assessment—fair or unfair—of a kitchen's capabilities. I chafe at restaurants whose menus offer spaghetti Bolognese and General Tso's chicken side by side, even though both might be delicious. (My dad would say, "If you want Italian, go to an Italian restaurant. If you want Chinese,...")

My father, ever the scientist, taught me precise cooking techniques and the value of food as a means to reach a person's heart. Perhaps it was the only way he really knew, for he had difficulty communicating emotions; I saw him cry but once in his life, and it was over a dog. From my dad, I learned how to sear beef properly. ("Use higher heat! Your pieces of meat are too close! Barbara!" His scolding was a roar in my ears, which echoes still.) From my midwestern mom, I learned the joy of comfort food made with understated care. My father disallowed meat loaf or tuna casserole on his plate, so Mom reserved these as treats for us kids when he traveled. The tuna casserole, in particular, lives on in our family as the ultimate soul food. Every year on my sister's birthday, some of the family members make my mom's version of a tuna casserole—more like a rich sauce of French origins—serve it over broad noodles with a side of broccoli, and share photos of the meal on Facebook, in memory of them both.

Each year my doctor-father hosted The Lab Party for his research staff, his food-obsessed way of saying thank you. Both parents fussed over the event for a week, preparing an oddball spread of idiosyncratic must-haves including classic Jewish chopped liver, decidedly unkosher clam dip, a mid-century lime-ginger ale Jell-O mold probably made to slither about the plate and fill in the cracks, and more ambitious and elegant classics like boeuf bourguignon, meant to impress. My sister Linda and I were forbidden from attending the party, but we'd pick the leftovers clean at breakfast the next day. For years, my pleas to contribute were not taken seriously, but when I was maybe sixteen, my father bestowed upon me his ultimate expression of trust— he allowed me to help cook for the Lab Party. My father set the bar high in every aspect of his life. Whether I observed his professional achievements from afar or absorbed his cooking lessons in our kitchens, I gained a lifelong inner resolve to achieve those high standards myself and expect the same from those around me.

It was taken for granted that we children would go to college, following in our brilliant father's footsteps and living a professional, preferably scientific, life. And so, I found my way to the University of Wisconsin in Madison, subconsciously aiming to please my father by heading myself to vet school. But as always, he knew me better than I knew myself, suggesting that I really ought to be a writer. ("Are you kidding?" I'd ask, not quite sure where he'd gotten that notion. "Barbara," he would respond, in his self-assured, prescient voice, "would I kid you?")

And sure enough, sophomore year, a traumatic encounter with a bunny experiment jolted me out of the laboratory and into a degree in journalism.

Mike was born into a giant mixing bowl of yeast, flour, and sugar, his cheeks kneaded by loving Jewish aunts, his behind patted into perfect little rolls. His family's business, Pratzel's Bakery in St. Louis, was an iconic kosher Jewish bakery with roots in the shtetls of Russia, whose bagels, corn tzizel rye bread, gooey butter cake, and famous chocolate cupcakes drew a huge St. Louis clientele, including a loyal following of the city's older

Jewish population. Its four retail locations were always busy, and the bakery wholesaled its products to many area grocers, synagogues, and delis.

Everyone in the family was connected to the bakery in one way or another. Uncle Nate managed the business and was the resident cake decorator. Uncle Aaron worked the graveyard shift, managing orders and doling out free bagels to the nearby Washington University students who wandered in hungry. And Mike's father, Grandpa Al, made the deliveries. In his younger days, Mike drove around with his father, meeting people and soaking in the lessons of Al-style customer service. Grandpa Al was a schmoozer, lingering at stops to yuck it up with his friends and always throwing in an extra loaf of bread or bag of bagels, a practice that frustrated Uncle Nate's business sense, but which was just Al's way. Every time our family visited St. Louis, Grandpa Al would send us off with a giant box filled with whatever was on hand. "Here, take this, take this..." he would say, all the while stuffing twenty-dollar bills into my kids' pockets and smiling ear to ear.

Pratzel's Bakery was still thriving when my children were young. The kids would wander the floury floors on our family visits and marvel at bread mixing bowls so large they could climb in. Always, they hoped to stumble upon a rack of freshly glazed cupcakes. Those cupcakes were a signature recipe we yearned to share at Manna but which, alas, was lost to the ages. In fact, Pratzel's chocolate cupcake was memorialized in Manna's Cupkopf, created as a nod to the distant original.

Heading off to college at UW-Madison, Mike's original plan was to earn a business degree, then return to St. Louis to help run the bakery. And while his years and experiences during college altered his path, the desire to own and run a business coursed strongly in his blood. Mike's dad had worked into his nineties. Until his late retirement, he spent every day keeping his delivery route going (with Mike's sister Sandy at the wheel as his designated driver!), continuing to the end to nurture his customers. Mike, equipped with the same strong work ethic and his father's generous smile, often gave customers a cookie or an extra bialy in the spirit of friendship and encouraged staff to do likewise.

Marvelous Madison

From the moment my North Central Airlines flight opened its hatch at Madison's Truax Field on a warm August evening in 1974, I was smitten by kindnesses one rarely experiences in New York. First, it was the nice lady beside me on the plane who felt sorry for me because I cried my way from La Guardia to Milwaukee—a bundle of leaving-home emotions—and who graciously offered me a ride to the dorms. Then it was Marc, the piano major-to-be and my first real acquaintance in town, who found me lost on a street corner looking for Bascom Hill. He was too nice to point out that I was practically standing at the foot of it. Later that week, Marc introduced me to his roommate, Mike, from St. Louis. But the clincher was a Madison Metro bus driver. When I boarded the first bus I saw to get to the local Red Cross, the driver smiled apologetically and explained that while his bus did not go there, the one up ahead did. He then radioed that driver to wait for me. Clearly, I wasn't in New York anymore but instead had arrived in a kind-hearted city where expansive lakes dominated the landscape, the capitol dome sparkled in the night sky, and people stopped to smell the roses with you. My new home filled me with a warmth my native home lacked. Within days, I was suffused with an ethos that would inform my future. One day it would become my mission—my career—to be that kind stranger myself and awaken in my out-of-town B&B guests that same joyous sense of this city.

Madison was, and is, a city coveted for its confluence of features. Above all, it was an idyllic setting for a lively and varied community life. Two of its four lakes, one fifteen square miles and the other five square miles, dominated the city's center. Between them lay a narrow isthmus onto which the capitol and most downtown businesses were endearingly squashed. The lakes brought year-round recreation and more than a hint of beauty. A shaded dirt path hugged Lake Mendota behind campus, serenely leading walkers and joggers to Picnic Point, a scenic, wooded peninsula jutting out into the lake. (Picnic Point is where a certain two young lovers spent a frigid November night in sleeping bags, illicitly concealed under a web of branches, sharing bologna sandwiches and potato chips from a local market. Lake Mendota teems with sailboats and crew teams in summer, and in winter freezes so solidly that the same couple was inspired to cross it on foot, until, about one-thirtieth of the way across, the thunderous cracking sounds of shifting ice sent them scampering back to shore.)

The state capitol, perched majestically atop Madison's highest point, offered a front-row seat to the state's political hub, including a newly elected, progressive mayor and a city council invested in nudging the city toward a more cosmopolitan image. This was Madison before the Monona Terrace Convention Center was built, before Epic Systems was a business dominatrix, and before the restaurant scene was so saturated with hip new establishments that employers were looking under rocks to find the rare line cook. In the 1970s, Madison was bubbling with potential.

While the capitol dominated Madison's skyline, as prescribed by the Capitol View Preservation Ordinance,*[2] State Street personified the downtown. Eight blocks of local, eclectic businesses and international eateries ran from the capitol to the beginning of campus. A handcrafted leather accessories store, an incense-perfumed metaphysical bookstore, an expansive head shop, two bike shops, and a fledgling employee-owned pharmacy were interspersed with ethnic restaurants and clothing boutiques. From the

[2]*This ordinance, in essence, prohibits buildings within one mile of the state capitol from being taller than the capitol itself or from obstructing the view of the building from the major arteries leading to it.*

west end of State Street came the UW students, frivolous and carefree and bursting with potential. At the capitol end, smartly dressed business people, state employees, lobbyists, and senators spilled forth for lunch breaks and fresh air. And threaded throughout were parents, potheads, colorful street musicians, and hopeful artists, all grooving to the vibe.

Where State Street ended, the campus began. Here over fifty thousand students and faculty filled their days with academia. On football Saturdays, a sea of Bucky Badger red pulsed through the streets, bringing general midwestern cheer and campus pride to the town. The Memorial Union's sprawling Lake Mendota terrace was a melting pot of tourists, students, and Madisonians, all lost in conversation and draft beer against a backdrop of blue skies and glittering water. Stately old brick and limestone buildings harkened back to earlier eras when warfarin was discovered by my uncle Carl Link, the Forestry Department helped solve the Lindbergh baby kidnapping/murder, and Harry Harlow—assisted by my then-student father—made rhesus monkeys a household name.

Mike and I arrived in Madison during a defining moment in the city's history. In the 1970s, this bustling college town was on the verge of a makeover that would reverberate into the next century. Paul Soglin became mayor for the first time, helping solidify Madison's progressive, activist face. The Pail and Shovel Party, on the UW campus, elected Leon Varjian as its president, setting into motion a series of campus pranks still joyously relived every year, including the sudden overnight appearance of over one thousand plastic flamingos on Bascom Hill, and the materializing of the Statue of Liberty's upper half, rising—or sinking, if you are a pessimist—from the frozen expanse of Lake Mendota. In 1974, State Street, once a two-lane trafficked road, became a pedestrian mall, and out of our dorm room windows, we watched University Square materialize, a campus shopping mall home to the original Paisan's restaurant, and a premonition of campus construction to come. By the decade's end, Epic Systems was born, a fledgling medical software company that would grow from one employee to over ten thousand and help alter the landscape of Madison's modern business community. In 1990, still only about thirty employees strong, Epic became one of our early and regular corporate catering customers.

During this renaissance, two remarkable openings shaped Madison's food scene. In an effort to bring farm foods to city eaters, the Dane County Farmers' Market opened around the Capitol Square in 1972, introducing to Madison the now widely-regarded farm-to-table concept. The market began with five vendors, but within several years it had grown exponentially. Today we think back wistfully on a time when we could circumnavigate the state capitol at a clip, filling our tote bags with a week's worth of fresh produce. Instead, today's wildly popular market is more like rush hour in Los Angeles.

Also, in 1972, Ovens of Brittany (aka, The Ovens) restaurant and its more casual sister, the Baker's Rooms, opened their doors to lines of curious, hungry Madisonians eager to experience authentic, casual French-inspired food and pastries prepared from scratch. Now customers had new expectations for the flakiness of a croissant. They discovered the Ovens' distinct cheesecake, baked more like a pie in a hearty ground nut crust and finished with a thick layer of dark chocolate ganache. My favorite was the Guthrie bun, a savory brioche roll with baked-in slices of roast beef, served with a tiny pitcher of sauce to be poured into the bun's tiny steam hole. Just as Chez Panisse in Berkeley (1971) brought to life the tenets of farm-to-table dining using fresh, locally sourced, organic ingredients, and the Moosewood Restaurant in Ithaca, New York, (1973) created a restaurant whose focus was excellent vegetarian cuisine, The Ovens would lead the way locally to fresh ideas about food and dining out.

The Ovens of Brittany was a game-changing restaurant, and the trickle-down of its bakery sensibilities influenced many subsequent businesses. Most famously, the restaurant originated the morning bun, later renamed the Brittany bun, aka sticky bun in Manna-speak. That bun was the essence of rustic simplicity, yet its crafting required considerable technique. Many-layered croissant dough is rolled up with cinnamon sugar, baked to puffy, flaky perfection, then be-glittered with more sugar. When Mike and I were working on our business plans and core values, our experiences as Ovens' customers helped guide our thinking. At Collins House, we employed a former Ovens pastry chef, and a one-time Ovens baker crafted our Manna sticky bun. An Ovens reference on a resume was pure gold.

We spent a decade exploring the nooks and crannies of the Madison food scene, spending far too many of our hard-earned dollars from cleaning dorm rooms and shelving library books on a memorable cross-section of old-style eateries, many of which would shortly be swallowed up by "progress." Some, like Parthenon Gyros on State Street or Dotty Dumpling's Dowry, withstood the explosive growth and changing tastes of the coming years, still serving up their classic fare to our children's children. Others have been lost to history: Ella's Deli, with its jolly carousel and array of toys meant to distract restless children so their parents could enjoy a meal; Mildred's hippie-dippie ambiance and earthy pita-based sandwiches; The Donut Factory, our go-to for fresh-from-the-fryer donuts at two in the morning, and even the revered Ovens.

Perhaps closest to my heart was Rennebohm's, a classic old-fashioned drugstore replete with original tile floors, a soda fountain, and a long lunch counter ruled by soda jerks. As an undergraduate in 1938, my father was a Rennie's soda jerk. Years later, I found myself in the very same restaurant, working my *New York Times* Sunday crossword puzzles, sipping the very egg creams my father crafted for me at home, a drink that made a cameo appearance at Manna.

While Madison's modern food era was coming to life, I was unknowingly laying the groundwork for the role I would someday play in it. After college and before The Collins

House, working as a writer/editor, I baked compulsively in my free time just for the love of it and because baking was such a great catharsis for the stress of a workday. I brought much of this bakery to my coworkers and friends because I didn't want to eat it all myself, and everyone was always so happy to get it. I fed them white chocolate cashew bars or double fudge cookies, and they fed me encouragement. "You should be a baker someday," they said. "You should do this for a living."

By the end of the 1970s, Madison had become home. We were now married, with a puppy, home, and careers. For six fervent years, we had absorbed the best of Madison, not yet knowing that we would pay that enthusiasm forward for the rest of our lives.

The Butterfly Effect

Two years after our backyard wedding in the suburbs of New York City, it was time for a real honeymoon. We chose San Francisco—I couldn't say why—for a road trip adventure, the first of many. Our friend Claire showed us an intriguing newspaper article on bed and breakfasts in the area, and never having heard of them before, we thought we might give them a gander. I suppose we liked the idea of having something a little offbeat to call our honeymoon. From the listings, we chose a place called, somewhat unremarkably, the Union Street Inn.

Just in time for my birthday, in September 1980, Mike and I set off in our trusty red, manual-transmission Chevette with black cardboard lining, AM/FM radio, and a set of brakes that kept us alive through the San Francisco hills, but almost not through the Rockies. After three days, two state park campgrounds, and one escape from what can only be described as a mosquito plague of Passover proportions at the Great Salt Lake, we arrived in San Francisco tired, hungry, dirty, and ready to luxuriate in a little belated marital bliss.

The Union Street Inn is a three-story Victorian building tucked unobtrusively between similar dwellings in the middle of—you guessed it—Union Street. We climbed the steep stairs to an unimposing entrance, which revealed nothing of the building's inner secrets, and rang the bell. While it is possible that a human being opened the door, all I can recall is a big, bouncy, hospitable golden retriever, filling the door frame with slobbery, throw-my-ball-now energy. And that was all we needed. Mike and I are both dog people, having left two at home while we gallivanted cross country, and the idea of a dog as host was thrilling. We recognized immediately that this was not a customary hotel experience. We felt instantly at home, and at that moment in each of us, I am sure, the seed of our future together as innkeepers was sown, however subconsciously. We were going to be B&B hosts, and Tigger, our own people-loving dog back home, would someday join us as canine greeter.

Once past the dog, the inn unfolded before us as one gracious room after another: a parlor for breakfast, a secret garden in the back, and several guest rooms whose colors were bold and whose amenities were soft and enveloping. Our room had a view of the garden and a king bed with a plush, scarlet comforter. Swaddled in its velvety folds, we planned our San Francisco activities, including exploring the boutique neighborhood around our inn.

Helen, the owner and host, served fabulous flaky croissants from a local patisserie with a side of homemade kiwi jam and freshly brewed coffee. In time, we would find ourselves disappointed with the idea of a continental breakfast at a B&B. Not only did we think of breakfast as a more substantial meal, and the reflection of an innkeeper's care and creativity, but opting for muffins and orange juice over a full home-cooked meal felt beside the point of the B&B promise and allure. Most B&Bs would eventually rise to this occasion as well. Full breakfasts became as competitive as free Wi-Fi. But during our virginal B&B experience, we found that breakfast charming, and the entire visit a novel vision of the future. Later, when we were innkeepers, guests would tell horror stories about their first B&Bs and how they almost never stayed in one again. We had chosen Union Street Inn, and that choice changed our lives. It might have gone differently.

The San Francisco visit itself was a richer experience because of our B&B stay, and the wealth of recommendations offered by hosts who were themselves passionate about their city. We found our way to restaurants that suited us and local neighborhood sights we might have missed. Each night, exhausted from a day of exploration, we were made whole again by delicious bedding, a peaceful garden, and staff genuinely curious about our day's adventures.

Our most serendipitous find was a small boutique chocolatier called Cocolat, not far from the Union Street Inn, owned and run by the famous and fabulous Alice Medrich. One afternoon, we happened into her shop, bewitched by the various chocolate creations displayed in glass cases and on trays before us—elegant and enticing in their crafting, yet unpretentious in their presentation. We shared a giant chocolate truffle, deep and dark, infused with liqueur and melting to the touch, and were awakened to a mind-altering chocolate experience that would lead to our first signature product.

The drive home through the Rockies, golden aspens shimmering in the fall sunshine, and the monotonous highways of Kansas gave us ample road time for reflection and planning. Wouldn't a bed and breakfast be fun? What a great way to cook and serve food in a more or less one-on-one context and share our beloved city with visitors eager to soak in all that is Madison. We could do it! We were nice, we were smart, we were ... naive—but in a good way. Neither of us had been through hotel or culinary school nor worked a day in the hospitality industry. But the concept seemed reasonable. Out-of-town guests were regular people, like your friends; you just hadn't met them yet. So by the time we arrived back to our wiggly-waggly pups and unpacked the last of our California cache, we had hatched a plan.

In the next few years our vacations began to revolve around B&Bs, and travel took on a new meaning. We stayed at the Red Fox Inn in Virginia, an old stone building outside of DC with a fireplace in every room, which sometimes set off all the smoke detectors, invariably when you were sound asleep. The Doe Run Inn near Berea, Kentucky, served a traditional Southern breakfast on a long wooden porch overlooking a stream. The biscuits alone were worth a return visit, much like the magnetic draw of our own future oatmeal pancakes. And at a secluded B&B in Santa Fe, the innkeeper's passion for astronomy translated to a tour of the stars, including a view of the Space Station drifting by.[3]

Each B&B had a story to tell us, a lesson to be learned, and we used our stays to help lay the groundwork for our future. For example, we learned that we did not like being told that breakfast was served promptly at eight (Mike loves to sleep in—his idea of early rising begins at around 10 a.m.), and we preferred the privacy and convenience of our own bathroom. We loved the added touches of homemade food treats and missed them when they were absent. We preferred innkeepers who liked to engage with us and share their favorite hike or roadside stand to the ones who left a list of the local chain restaurants in the lobby. We marveled at clever bathroom fixtures and turned our noses up at frilly curtains. Visit by visit, the vision of our own inn came into focus.

It took us several years to wrap our heads around the idea of being business owners. The Union Street Inn experience had awakened in us a latent desire that drew from our passion for living in Madison, cooking and eating with friends. Before we had been exposed to B&Bs, we had not thought much about doing something professional with our food interests. Now we were visiting homes for sale and boning up on what it meant to run a B&B. We had zero innkeeping experience but a basketful of belief in ourselves and our vision. Both Mike and I had profoundly different upbringings that nonetheless brought us similar desires—to find joy in serving people and cook and feed people comfort food from the heart. As the business took shape, these goals came into focus.

[3]*A couple of decades later, a small-world connection to this inn found its way to Manna in the most surprising and rewarding of ways. One of the inn's guests had been served our oatmeal pancakes, a recipe we had once shared with the Santa Fe innkeepers over breakfast in their outdoor garden. Innkeepers are always eager to swap stories and recipes. The Santa Fe innkeepers told him the story of how they had come by the recipe. Now visiting Madison, he paid Manna a visit to share the story of how he found his way to us and to rustle up another plate of oatcakes.*

The Collins House Bed and Breakfast: Welcome to Madison

One sunny spring day, Mike and I went for a walk and passed a beautiful brick home in our neighborhood with a "For Lease" sign posted out front. Intrigued, we walked around back, drawn to the home's idyllic lakefront location, and watched Lake Mendota sloshing along an open length of shoreline. We peered through grime-crusted windows at the empty interior, wooed by the stunning wood floors and elegant spaces, despite their neglected condition. And we pondered our luck at finding such a home so close to the capitol, downtown, and the university. Everything about this place spoke to what would be important in our business, especially its location, and what would best reflect our sensibilities. Clinching the deal was the plaque at the home's entrance porch, designating its National Landmark Status.[4]

It was April 1984 when we first stumbled upon the dilapidated red brick home that would become The Collins House, and there was nary a B&B in Madison. Within a few years, several would open, but at the time, the concept was as new to Madison as it had been to us on our San Francisco tour of discovery. Certainly, the state had its share, including the Old Rittenhouse in Bayfield and the White Gull Inn in Door County. But the industry was in its relative infancy. In the next decade, B&Bs, country inns, and boutique hotels would pop up in every corner of the country, becoming the chic way to travel. The defining features of a B&B—welcoming hospitality from local hosts in a small setting, with breakfast included—would help redefine what it meant to travel.

During the next sixteen months, we developed a business plan and submitted a proposal for the B&B to the City of Madison, the building's owners. It was a long and winding road through city bureaucracy. Staffers and some alderpeople were initially skeptical, for they knew almost nothing about B&Bs—how to regulate them or what being landlords to one might entail. And we were competing against a proposal for the safer option of more office space, submitted by a known developer with considerable clout

[4]*The plaque designating the historical status of the house refers to it as The Collins House. The original owner of the home was William Collins. He and his brother C.C. Collins (who also built a home, since torn down, on the opposite corner) were both lumber executives. We named our B&B to recognize the building's significance and were honored and delighted to host a ninetieth birthday party for Kay, one of the six siblings who grew up in the home. She and her sister Dorothy generously shared their memories of early Madison, sledding down Gorham Street and having their photo taken by a door-to-door photographer, posing with a goat cart. Next door was the old Lincoln School building, soon to be a twenty-eight-unit apartment. I later discovered my mom had attended grade school there in the 1920s.*

and a shining portfolio in historic preservation. Mike and I were virtual unknowns—a married couple not yet thirty, with no track record and zero industry experience. But we persevered with considerable support from the neighborhood, and an occasional coffee cake or plate of cookies along the way helped to illustrate our vision. By August 1985 the keys were in our hands. Off the diving board we leapt.

The rundown but beautiful home turned out to be so much more than we had bargained for. The building was listed on the National Register of Historic Places as a classic example of the Prairie School style of architecture. It was built in 1911 by turn-of-the-century architects Louis Claude and Edward Starck, local practitioners of the style introduced by their more famous contemporary, Frank Lloyd Wright. Prairie School is a style characterized by horizontal lines; open floor plans where rooms flow organically from one to the next; warm, inviting interiors; and plenty of windows that bring the outdoors inside, making it part of the living experience. We had happened into this particular building accidentally. Still, the discovery of the Prairie School architecture was fortuitous, as it offered us a lifelong metaphor for openness and hospitality and helped us articulate what was important in a business setting. We laboriously removed decades of detritus during the renovation, revealing the elegant and inviting home as it had once been.

Because we were eligible for historic preservation tax credits if we opened our doors before 1985 ended, we had a mere five months—from August 1 until December 31 of that year—to move in, renovate the house, and host our first guest. The Collins House had been vacant for more than six years, and for the preceding several decades had been used as office space. It had suffered considerable weather damage, and its architectural character had been obscured by false ceilings, fluorescent light fixtures, and industrial carpeting. Tar had been poured over the slightly sagged wood floor in the living room, and a carpet hid the ugly scar. Paint peeled and crumbled from the lake-facing walls. The quarter-sawn oak paneling and beamed ceilings in the dining room were caked with years of grime, and layers of wallpaper and paint hid the original stencil designs. In addition to the renovation, we had to furnish 4,600 square feet of space, including five guest rooms; learn how to take reservations; set up an accounting system; choose our dishes, shampoos, sheets, and coffee supplier; build a kitchen; get our licensing; test a hundred muffin varieties; and still find time in the day to walk the dog and breathe.

On day one of the renovation, Matt, my general contractor, handed me a sledgehammer. I had the ceremonial job of knocking the first hole into a false wall to start the project rolling. It was frightening and exhilarating, being given permission to do damage, knowing it was damage that would bring good. I raised the unwieldy tool with trepidation, and with one wimpy, tentative swing, set the project in motion. In time, I would learn to hammer away with confidence.

It took a proverbial village to raise this inn. Friends stripped wallpaper and painted walls. We had no running water and had to fill spray canisters from Lake Mendota to moisten the wallpaper. However, the sprayers' nozzles would clog with algae. The only available lights were fluorescents, hanging by wires from the ceiling, tilted this way and that to help us see. One room had to be repainted in a different color when we realized that using the fluorescents in this way gave a false perception of hue. The local neighborhood association rallied behind our proposal, and several alderpeople helped break through city red tape, initially to help win city council approval for our plans and later to ensure that we could cook a full breakfast or cater a small wedding. Our building crew and architect, Ed Linville, who specialized in Prairie School designs, strove to honor the authentic restoration of a home that had served for so many years as office space, following city guidelines for renovating homes with landmark status.

By the time December 27 rolled around, we had a bare-bones bed and breakfast we could open for business, with beds to sleep in and some pictures on the walls. Our first guests arrived—honeymooners, of all people, holding only the highest of expectations and unsuspecting that we still had not caught our breath from the whirlwind of renovation. We cooked them breakfast from our tiny efficiency on the third floor, as the kitchen was still under construction, and for months afterward continued to run laps up and down those two flights of steps. With merely seconds to spare, we had managed to qualify for the preservation tax credits. Now all we needed to do was run our new business—whatever that would turn out to be.

Finding Our Mojo

Our decision to open The Collins House had altered our life stories permanently. For starters, we gave up every penny of our savings accounts, our house, my job, and the lifestyle we had led up until then, and moved forward on pure faith. There would be life on the other side of the black hole we had dived into, but what it would look like was anybody's guess. The day we were handed the key to the place was exhilarating, to be sure—a victory even—but it was also scary as hell. The months of renovation and business development gave us a period of creativity and occupied us thoroughly, in some ways distracting us from the idea that one day soon, we'd have to fulfill our promises of great food and warm hospitality. It was the difference between the pregnancy—where you can pick baby names, decorate a nursery, and party hearty at your baby shower—and then actually having the baby.

With the renovation more or less behind us, we turned our attention to the dream itself.

If we were going to run a business together, especially a hospitality business whose success hinged on compassionate human interactions, we'd best get along with each other. No bickering in front of the guests, which is not an easy feat for even the happiest of married couples. The first years of our lives together had been lived out in classic American fashion, with separate careers by day, shared activities after hours, including late night racquetball tournaments followed by chocolate chip pancake binges at IHOP, his and hers softball leagues, traveling, and of course, lots of cooking and eating. Abruptly, though, we were thrown together in the workplace, and our every waking hour, more or less, was spent figuring out how to agree on nearly everything. The idea of being spouses and business partners may, on the surface, have a certain romantic appeal, but most people don't see a marital business as the path to marital bliss, especially when the two people are as different as Mike and I are. Yet, it was the differences that helped pave the path for success.

Mike was a business major, and I wrote stories. Mike grew up in a family-owned bakery, playing with bread dough and folding up bakery boxes after school. I was raised by a research hematologist, who taught me how to diagnose leukemia at age twelve, reading slides on my own laboratory microscope. He was a St. Louis Cardinals fanatic, and I got lost in crossword puzzles. And yet, it was our differences that allowed us to travel this road as a team. Mike had just enough formal education in the business world, combined with his experience growing up in the bakery, that he was drawn to contracts, spreadsheets, assets, and payroll like a second language. But when I heard these words, my mind instantly turned to thoughts of horseback riding or what to cook for dinner. The idea of running the business side of things made me want to bolt. Instead, I loved to plan menus, make perfect hospital corners, rearrange the furniture, and orchestrate complicated catered affairs—the fun stuff. I did not research credit card processors, and he didn't manage the staff. In short, we each had our roles and heaps of respect for what the other spouse did—relieved, in fact, that there was someone to do what we each found intolerable. And we both shared the triumphs and sorrows of our days over big bowls of spaghetti carbonara.

Often, we were asked what sort of an inn we owned, and our sound-bite response said it all: we offered "down-to-earth elegance," an apt description for both the B&B and the catering, which began in earnest about a year after opening. Mike and I are both pretty easygoing, fuss-free people. I often think of myself as a woulda-been-hippie, if only I had been born a few years earlier. And Mike lived for the day he no longer had to wear a tie. At the inn we hung out in jeans and flannel shirts, setting the tone for comfort without pretense. And we encouraged guests to kick back and put their feet up on the coffee table or join us to watch a movie. Breakfasts were served on stoneware that was hand-crafted and rustic, yet stylish. At formal catered events, too, we mostly eschewed black and white in favor of ecru and khaki and avoided the formality of white table linens and crystal. Instead, guests would find cream-colored cloths as a backdrop for platters of carved roast chicken with an array of chutneys or cornucopia baskets spilling forth bite-sized chunks of artisan Wisconsin cheeses, nuts, and fresh berries.

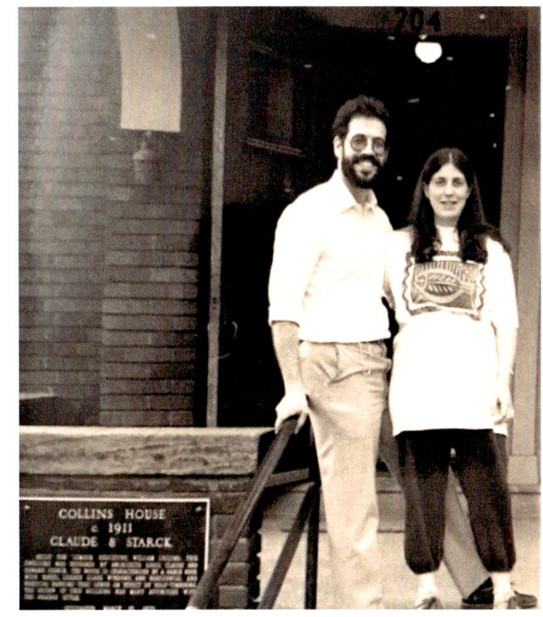

Collins House circa 1989, with baby on the way.

We liked visitors to feel at home from the moment they stepped inside. The Collins House's warm interior provided the backdrop, like a theater whose set defines a play's mood and context, but here the food was the star. It began with fresh home-baked treats, set out each afternoon near the entrance. Returning guests might glance that way in Pavlovian anticipation to find a carefully arranged pyramid of Mexican wedding cakes dusted with a light snowfall of confectioner's sugar, or irregularly shaped nuggets of flourless chocolate cake—leftovers from cutting out heart-shaped pastries—stacked haphazardly like kindling and drizzled generously with chocolate ganache. The latter was a playful mess we enjoyed creating behind the scenes because somehow, a pile of cuttings tasted better than a perfect cutout, or at least had no calories. Serving up the kitchen scraps conveyed our lack of formality and encouraged our guests to feel like one of us.

At the Union Street Inn, a hospitable golden retriever had been partially responsible for us being here at all. Tigger, our gentle dog now in her middle years, loved playing the role of greeter, and most of our guests loved her, but as innkeepers, we learned that not everyone loves dogs—being greeted by an over-eager shepherd-husky can be an intimidating way to start your stay! Mostly, though, Tigger helped set the tone for a laid-back atmosphere, and after she died, we gladly welcomed our guests' well-behaved canine pals.

After a tour of the first floor, guests were brought to their room, where an Alice Medrich-inspired chocolate truffle, maybe amaretto-almond or brandy Alexander, awaited. In the years after the San Francisco trip, I had practiced the demanding and time-consuming techniques of crafting chocolate truffles. I made them for friends, holidays, dinner parties, and for fun. When Collins House opened, I made them for guests—a treat on their pillow upon check-in, which set the stage for our particular brand of hospitality and helped define our destination as a food haven. It was our way of saying, "You are a queen…" The next day, we served an ample and homey breakfast that added, "…but no need to be formal."

The hook for breakfast was the aroma of coffee, brewed from freshly ground beans, drifting invisibly up the wide oak staircase and under the doors before even one soul had arisen. I had the full attention of hungry guests at the breakfast table and loved to pamper them with oatmeal pancakes, swirly roulades with a mushroom and Swiss filling, or a wineglass parfait of homemade granola, yogurt, and fresh berries. A scramble was rarely just a scramble, but a hearty layering of eggs, a fresh tomato-basil sauce, crunchy bacon, and parmesan cheese. Accompanied by slices of fragrant marzipan Danish and fat bunches of purple grapes atop thin slices of sweet cantaloupe, our breakfasts were fit for royalty.

At first, the inn was just a playground for cooking, entertaining, and meeting new people. It began as fun, with a lot of mistakes, and learning from the mistakes became part of the fun. The early months were spent ironing out all the lumps and bumps that came from not knowing any better. Who knew every room should have its own phone (we learned that *really* fast, from our well-meaning but frustrated business guests who, like us, still lived in prehistoric times, and relied on land lines; early on, we did not have a good sense of who our clientele would be), or that people actually expected that their beds would be made up for them while they were out (what were we thinking)? What were we supposed to do with the "no-shows?" (Take credit card info up front, for confirmation purposes.) Our first winter, Mike felt certain he could easily snow blow our eight-car parking with his tiny Toro. After a couple of hours blowing the same snow around in circles, we hired a plowing service. Learning the ropes was fun and often a bit embarrassing, but by conquering one obstacle after another we gained our innkeeping education—and the stories to tell our grandchildren—on the job.

The solutions to these early-on problems were easy enough: buy phones, make beds, hold guests accountable with credit card confirmation. But occasionally, the challenges seemed insurmountable, and over the years, we had a few doozies. Sometimes, bad stuff happens. Sometimes, you can't imagine anything worse. But, we learned the hard way that even your worst nightmare has a reasonable solution, though you might have to search for it.

Once, I double-booked an entire weekend for two wedding parties—all the guest rooms, with onsite weddings and receptions for both. I only discovered the error (or inadvertency, as we would euphemistically call it) when one of the two parties—the one that somehow did not appear in our reservation system—called about three months before the big day to start the wedding planning. "Let me call you back in just a bit," I said reassuringly, barely masking my panic. Although we now had some problem-solving experience under our belts, we had no idea how to correct this dreadful mistake. It felt unsolvable. So I turned to the experts, in this case well-known, long-time innkeepers at another Wisconsin B&B, who'd been down that road and back a time or two. They cheerfully and reassuringly suggested that we present both parties with the dilemma and provide a choice for each to consider. One party could keep the weekend, while the other party would choose a new weekend and, in return, receive a catered reception free of charge. As it turned out, each did have a different preference, and we slunk off in grateful relief. Sure, we were embarrassed and out a buck or two. But we had turned a potential disaster into a positive for all parties involved, including, ironically, the outcome of good publicity. Instead of being bad-mouthed for careless management, we were praised for providing a creative and agreeable solution.

Some years later, the hot water heater died on the Friday afternoon of Labor Day weekend, when we also had an on-site wedding with all the rooms rented. A plumber spent the entire weekend tracking down a replacement and installing it. So what to do with our understandably irritable wedding guests who had a wedding to prepare for? We arranged for them to take their showers in their friends' rooms at a nearby hotel. During the event, we had to hand-wash all the dishes with water boiled on the stove. But the night passed, and then it was the next day, and now it is but a good yarn.

Stuff happens, stuff resolves, and we move on. Everything, even the scariest thing, has a solution. These early crises laid the groundwork for embracing future incidents with a certain calmness, not just in business but also in life. My father was right, as he always was: this too shall pass.

A vacation was never just a vacation once we became innkeepers. We loved to stay at inns wherever we traveled, both as R&R and as an opportunity to learn more about ourselves—a luxurious and delicious education. By slipping into our own guests' shoes, we experienced the inn as if through their eyes. In time, I would formalize this somewhat intuitive approach to self-reflection.

Some observations led directly to changes at The Collins House. At one inn, the hosts provided each room with a crisply organized notebook of information, including B&B protocols and resources, favorite hikes, and restaurant recommendations. We hadn't done that yet, preferring to talk with our guests in person rather than leave information anonymously. Yet now, we saw the value of not having to ask. It was a small detail that could complement our style, not replace it, thus greatly improving our overall service. In fact, the idea of "not having to ask" later became a dominant theme at Manna, where staying ahead of customer needs became a driving force. Creating a resource book gave me a meaningful way to flex my writing muscles.

Other times, we reaffirmed our own choices by experiencing the opposite. At some B&Bs, innkeepers disappeared to parts unknown once we had been checked in, and we were left in limbo. Sure, we could call their cell number if our toilet was backed up or if we wanted directions to a restaurant, but the message was loud and clear: "I am reachable if you need me, but I have my own life to lead." Part of the reason we chose B&Bs over hotels in the first place was the promise of meeting with local people who could bring their destinations to life as knowledgeable, passionate insiders, much as we did with Madison. In our minds, the avoidance of guest interaction defied the whole B&B experience. We were thus encouraged to be all the more available at our own inn—not in peoples' faces, but present, warm, and at the ready. From six in the morning until ten at night, an innkeeper was always available, poised to recommend a good running path, brew up a fresh pot of decaf, or make a new friend.

By pretending to be my own customer, I learned a valuable lesson about myself: I don't smile enough. I am not a naturally smiley person, although I never quite understood how the happiness or bemusement I felt on the inside could appear as sullen or sleepy on the outside. I knew it was a job requirement, though, and made my best effort to do so. But one day, I must have failed to smile, and not long after, a reviewer took note of the unfriendly reception from one of the owners. I was both mortified and, once again, reminded that innkeepers, and hospitality workers in general, are expected to be "on" 24/7.

Sometime after this incident, I picked up a valuable strategy from an innkeeper's journal: smile before answering the phone. Evidently, I was not the only un-smiley innkeeper around. Customers can hear if you've just had a spat with your husband or dropped a plate of eggs on the floor or had a complaint about the smoke detector going off every time the guest took a shower. Your phone voice would be that person's first impression of your business. But by pasting on a smile, however false, before answering, that fake grin filters out the attitude and warms the customer's experience. It works! And it is a universal concept, going beyond the phone line and out into the big scary world of interpersonal communication.

One Collins House couple seemed to devote their every waking moment to finding something that annoyed them. The room had a draft. Why hadn't we offered to help them with their bags? Was there dairy in the pancakes? The faucets seemed kind of squeaky. Nothing seemed to please them, and the edge in their voices, the lack of smiles on their faces, conveyed an understated dissatisfaction with our inn, with us. We spent the weekend in a constant state of unease, awaiting some new insult at every turn. But when the time came for checkout, the couple gushed about their weekend and said they could not wait to return. Off they went, oblivious to their baffling demeanor, and we turned to one another in disbelief. How could two people seem so unhappy yet be just the opposite? They did return, again and again, each time expressing their litany of complaints as though they were chatting about the weather. These whiny people ultimately became loyal regulars, and over time, we got it—this was just the way they were. Like with the smile I tried so hard to wear, this couple was completely oblivious that their constant low-level complaining translated to major dissatisfaction. It must have not even been noteworthy to them.

So each morning, we put on our innkeeper masks, which helped us make it through a day of overcooked eggs, under-answered phones, rooms that were overheated, or sheets that were wrinkly. The key was to think of every whine and whimper not as an annoyance or a personal affront but a call to action. *Thank goodness they spoke up,* I would smile to myself, *or else how would I have known that something, however minor, needed attention?* Later at Manna, when the occasional unhappy customer had an employee close to tears, I coached the staff person to think of the encounter as a learning moment, not a punch in the gut, and reminded them that this too would pass.

An Innkeeper's Life

It is said that if a B&B owner can stay open for three years, then he or she will make it in the world of innkeeping. Those who don't get that far generally cave to the unanticipated elements that chafe at their lifestyle—the daily grind of cleaning, the need to be "on" twenty-four-seven, and the feeling of infringement on personal space. The biggest complaint I can remember hearing from fellow innkeepers, especially newbies, was that they felt their privacy had been invaded by guests looking at their pictures, sitting in their favorite chairs, opening their drawers. This is why some B&B owners can seem aloof. They need to turn off the interactions to feel the space is still their own. Our solution was to carve out a small third-floor efficiency room, where we kept our personal items, photos, or knickknacks. But the entire first floor was a common space. Even after we moved out of the inn to raise our family, we never thought of the guests as invading our privacy. Rather, we felt lucky we were able to share such a beautiful space with so many visitors. Framing our thinking about the inn as a lifestyle choice made everything associated with it feel more organic and less invasive.

A second major stumbling point for innkeepers is the drive to be successful financially—not just to turn a profit but to have a life-sustaining and self-sufficient business. And, of course, without making a profit, a business won't survive. As long as we ensured the business's health, like giving me a regular paycheck, we worked hard not to compromise our choices just to add nickels to our bottom line. Once, an innkeeper proudly shared with us a technique she used to help minimize her costs. She counted the number of grapes that went into her fruit cups because she had read how much the airlines had saved annually using this tactic. In my imagination, I pictured a Collins House breakfast plate being set before an appreciative guest with its bountiful fruit component, which often included a fat clump of glistening grapes. Counting grapes was not how I thought about my business, because my priorities lay with the experience. In the end, we paid the bills and got the paychecks, and the rest was the happiness that came from keeping the clump.

Not all novice innkeepers embrace the relentless mundaneness of the daily routine, but I soon discovered I loved the rhythms of Collins House life. There is a certain catharsis to being alone in a kitchen in the wee hours, baking chocolate cherry muffins, sautéing onions and market mushrooms, turning fresh summer melons into a martini glass full of colorful balls with a raspberry garnish. Serving breakfast to guests was the day's greatest pleasure. After breakfast came me-time, the window in my day when the guests had vanished, the dishes were cleared, and the occasional phone call punctuated the quietude. Afternoons were for cleaning rooms, running laundry, and baking—always baking—for the tea-time treat needed to be readied. Evenings were generally family time. As a rule, guests were especially social at breakfast but more self-absorbed come nightfall, a symbiosis we were grateful to have.

The Collins House kitchen became my playground, initially for breakfast dishes and bakery, and later for the growing catering business. In the commercial basement kitchen that served both the inn and the catering, I mastered techniques of egg cookery, puff pastry, and quiche production. Only muffins whose crumb was soft and moist made it to a plate. The breakfast sausage was crafted in-house, so its flavors and spices were fresh, not preservative-laden. We challenged ourselves to create mouth-watering presentations, simple but elegant, not fussy or overthought. Guests, hoping for those oatcakes or omelets bursting with chorizo, potato, and green chile filling, returned with regularity.

Our location on a lake and near the downtown and campus gave us a built-in, week-round clientele that allowed us to achieve an astonishing annual occupancy rate of about seventy-five percent. Mostly, traffic through the inn consisted of people traveling for regular business or pleasure but who sought an overnight experience not generally found at a hotel. Sometimes it was the charm of a historic property or a place that felt like home. Sometimes it was a desire to see a foreign city through local eyes. And sometimes it was—dare I say it one more time?—the oatcakes.

Weekdays saw a parade of business travelers. The university became our bread and butter, putting up visiting faculty, new job recruits, and vendors. Some departments used us more or less exclusively, and the hosting faculty often morphed into permanent friends or tapped into our catering services. On weekends, the inn came to life with a diverse clientele, including parents of students, anniversary celebrants, marathon runners, and Chicago escapees. Madison was a year-round destination, too, hosting UW football games, March Madness, Taste of Madison, Drum Corp International, and the World Dairy Expo, to name a few. Each of these big-ticket weekends had its regulars who returned year after year, befriending one another and us in the process. Over time, of course, some regulars faded away for whatever reason, and their absence was noticed and mourned.

Over the years, we also hosted a handful of dignitaries and luminaries, including a few Nobel Prize winners, who were very cool by our humble standards, and memorable for the bragging rights they bestowed upon us. And while we were honored and excited that famous and important people had found their way to our little inn, we treated them with the same casualness as any other guest. Surely many of these folks had had their share of the limelight. Chris Van Allsburg signed a copy of *The Polar Express* for my son. Rick Bayless, chef-owner of Chicago's Frontera Grill, among other restaurants, was a most gracious and endearing guest, whose kind and smiling face I see every time I cook the Wisconsin Wild Rice Scramble I served to him. (Remembering what dish you served to a particular guest is not unlike remembering precisely where you were, and what you were doing, when some catastrophe struck—only in a good way.) Jane Goodall kept to herself, mostly. And I will always think of us as having been destined to host Alice Waters, though she ducked out at the last minute, evidently to the solitude and anonymity of a large hotel.

Sometimes though, "famous" translated to "privileged" in ways that were shocking in the moment but became amusing memories nonetheless. One year, a soap opera star and her family rented the entire inn for a family reunion at Christmas. The actress sat at the breakfast table, surreptitiously feeding our inn dog, Tigger (who until then was a well-mannered and respectful girl) a constant stream of eggs, sausage, and muffins. Ever after, Tigger shamelessly helped herself to table scraps, sometimes while other guests were still eating, with a special predilection for licking the butter pat wrappers clean.

Jerry Brown's entourage rented the entire inn during his 1992 run for president. One late night, after we had gone to sleep, the group returned from a day of campaigning, tired and hungry, and proceeded to raid our commercial kitchen, helping themselves to a good bit of food, including several quiches destined for a catered event the following day. If you tackle the quiche recipe included in the book, you will appreciate our challenge in replacing *that* quiche *that* morning. The group then checked themselves out without paying, never to be seen again. Luckily, one of our staffers at the time was active in Jerry Brown's campaign and helped us right this ballsy wrong.

We saw it all. We observed a clandestine affair here, a lonely heart there. One gentleman from South Africa asked us to "find him women." One woman always came to breakfast extra early to make sure she could sit at a square table instead of round to keep her newspaper from slipping off. Honeymooners sprinkled sequins romantically and thoughtlessly about their room (until the day we closed we could not get every sequin out of the braided rug), and parents let their kids sit in the antique bathtubs, drawing pictures on the sides of the tub with ballpoint pens. Once some folks arrived from Chicago with a case of hard liquor and a case of beer. They never left the inn, tipped us ten dollars to bring their delivery pizza to the room, and checked out Sunday morning as quietly as they had arrived, leaving behind the two empty cases of booze. It was a cross-section of humanity, and we had front-row seats.

From Innkeeping to Catering

From the beginning, we knew we wanted to host weddings or other small on-site events. But Mike and I are very much baby-steps people, always wanting to be well grounded in one realm before moving to the next, and this philosophy was never truer than when we introduced catering to the business. It took us nearly a year to dip our toes in, in part because our regular B&B licensing allowed us only to serve breakfasts and only to guests. Getting a fully licensed commercial kitchen had been yet another hump to overcome. But from the get-go, oh, what fun we had. We got to cook and serve food that delighted our customers and their guests and became part of the warm memories at the most joyous moments of their lives. One early such wedding took place on the first anniversary of our opening, December 27, 1986. The fun-loving celebrants rolled up the carpet to dance, stocking-footed, into the wee hours of the morning. The next day at breakfast, the group crowded around the grand oak dining room table—a relic from a famous Wisconsin inn and restaurant—where they gave the breakfast a standing ovation! How humbled and delighted we were to have made such occasions possible and thus encouraged to do more.

For these on-site weddings, bar mitzvahs, birthdays, and graduation parties, we found our niche creating vibrant, dramatic tables of food with colorful fruits spilling forth from crystal bowls; roasted vegetables arranged in swirling patterns, with a sprinkling of Parmesan cheese; trays of dainty, one-bite hors d'oeuvres, from bacon-wrapped, almond-filled dates to tiny carved cucumber cups holding a coil of lox, a dab of sour cream, a dusting of finely minced red onion, and a tiny sprig of dill. This visual approach was as fun to create as it was enticing for the guests, and we rarely neglected this important component of a catered affair. Even plates of cookies and baskets of bread received, at the very least, had a flower with a bit of greenery.

In keeping with our predilection for visual drama, we largely steered clear of the more traditional dinner buffet—endless columns of shiny chafers holding steamy, overcooked dishes. Not only was the table itself less beautiful, with food hidden as if under a plate of armor, but we felt strongly that if we could not maintain a product's integrity to our satisfaction, then we preferred not to serve it at all. This is why later, at Manna, we did not offer scrambled eggs or pancakes as off-site catering options—they simply did not hold well in transit from stovetop to service time. Instead, we featured centerpieces of beautifully roasted and sliced meats or whole poached fish accompanied by interesting sauces, salads, and bite-sized hors d'oeuvres. Many components of these dishes would later resurface as building blocks in the Manna repertoire.

Weekday business meetings soon followed, where we honed our lunch catering skills, testing out new recipes that would also inform Manna's early menus. We learned that 3 1/2 ounces of meat per person was about right for a build-your-own sandwich buffet, and that chicken or turkey was twice as popular as all the other meat choices (unless the group was all men, who liked their beef). We learned that people don't want to return to the office with poppy seeds between their teeth or hints of raw onion on their breath. Also, we learned through these early, on-site experiences that our approach to catering—using our own roasted meats on bread we baked ourselves or serving marzipan bars whose shiny glaze had not yet finished setting—contributed to the success of the meetings. Rather than lunch as an obligatory afterthought, it became part of the experience of the meeting. This shared and memorable repast made the business at hand feel, even if only subconsciously, a bit more pleasurable and thus productive. As we moved out into the larger arena of off-site catering, this home-cooked, freshly-baked mandate became a draw for companies seeking comfort in the less personal environments of their offices. It was as though we were bringing a bit of the Third Place to them.

As eaters ourselves, we were most often drawn to comfort food elevated from its ordinary status, either by excellent preparation or a clever new twist. These personal preferences guided our early catering choices and later the Manna menus. Menu items were created to be recognizable, but just offbeat enough to defy the run-of-the-mill catering genre. For example, we offered several meatball varieties, but each was just a bit unusual: koftas with raisins and almonds in a sauce enlivened with turmeric, cumin, and coriander; Chinese rice-coated pearl balls with a black bean dipping sauce. We seldom served plain old shrimp cocktail, instead talking customers into a far more interesting dish that still fit the bill: cold shrimp in a fresh orange and sesame marinade abundantly displayed like the shrimp of my smorgasbord memory. Ordinary potato salad was brightened by the use of both sweet and white potatoes, lightly dressed with a fresh tarragon vinaigrette. Never too far from home, yet hardly at all like home.

My memory of stepping into the catering arena traces to one particular episode. We had just catered our first off-site party in the home of the president of The State Bar of Wisconsin, and someone from his office wandered our way, asking if we did corporate catering. My partner Jarno and I shared a furtive glance but didn't miss a beat, and in our most self-assured voices, chirped, "Why yes." He then asked us to cater a trial run for a meeting at the State Bar offices. In fact, this would be our first off-site corporate luncheon, and we had no idea what we were getting into. We cooked a beer-braised beef dish accompanied by who-remembers-what, and some fancy dessert bars that must have involved chocolate and a floral garnish. After dressing up in nice clothes for our first-ever delivery, we returned to the inn and waited in anticipation of the verdict. Following several restless hours, the phone rang at last, with the news that The State Bar would like to hire us as their new regular caterer. Jarno and I were giddy with pride and relief. It had been like awaiting the proverbial dad sneeze, and the reward was transcendent.

Yet, we were oblivious to the freight train headed our way. The State Bar alone would order lunch nearly every day, sometimes several different menus each day, and held enormous events for special occasions. From this moment forward we hit the ground running, and we found that once you say yes, you can never say no. Soon, the catering business would be twice as large as that of the inn's, contributing significantly to the groundwork for Manna.

Despite being two decidedly different businesses, the rhythms of catering became interwoven with those of the B&B. Breakfast with the guests gave way to heating soups, slicing meats, and making sure the breads did not overbake. By noon the staff had changed—presto, like Superman—into fresh, clean delivery clothes, scattering about Madison with vanloads of corporate luncheons. Upon return, we would collapse, exhausted, into the renewing comfort of the inn's first-floor space and share a much-needed lunch—usually the delicious scraps and leftovers —before returning to sinks full of dirty dishes. Afternoons were spent attending to a busy prep schedule: caramelizing onions, making marinades, or filling tiny turnovers for weekend parties. By dinnertime, the guests began to trickle back and, the last dish cleaned, the last soup refrigerated, our innkeeper personages returned. Inn guests were often unsuspecting beneficiaries of the catering. Leftover smoked whitefish might be used in an omelet, or re-crisped phyllo pastries filled with a duxelles of wild mushrooms might replace a muffin on the breakfast plate. The inn and the catering lived in symbiotic harmony.

Soon people began asking to make reservations for breakfast "on that lake-facing back porch" or wondering if they could buy some of our sandwiches. Just as my old coworkers had encouraged me to go into business with all the baking, these inquiries got us thinking. How could we make our foods available to a wider audience? Unfortunately, the zoning at Collins House did not allow us to serve food to the public as a restaurant. But it became clear to us that if we ever chose to expand, the customers were waiting.

A Community Takes Root

The seeds of The Collins House's community's character were sown even before our proposal was approved by the city. The Old Market Place Neighborhood Association, strongly committed to downtown preservation and maintaining the neighborhood's family character, worked hard to keep the building from succumbing to yet another use as office space. Once we successfully launched, the inn became a home for the group's monthly potluck meetings that even my preschool kids enjoyed for the endless varieties of pasta salads. Along with our own fledgling family and the staff and guests at the inn, the neighborhood association laid the groundwork for our future as a community nexus.

The Collins House was our first baby, the beginning not just of our family of little businesses but of the notion that your guests and employees could constitute a sort of non-blood family. Three more "children," two humans and one business, would eventually come into our lives, expanding our definition of family into the realm of community. Each component of that family had a different set of driving forces. Our children needed nurturing, upbringing, and moral guidance; our staff needed a happy, rewarding work environment with a paycheck; and our guests and catering customers needed a plate of food to write home about. Along with the many Madisonians who connected to us through the inn and the catering, this network of individuals set the groundwork for the community that Manna became, with Manna providing an important missing link—a public space where everyone could gather, often simultaneously.

Josh was my first child, and in the nine months preceding his birth, he was lulled by the rhythms of our small commercial dishwasher and the monotonous agitations of the washing machine. After he was born, these same noises quieted his months of inexplicable crying, but soon enough, he was in our kitchens, mixing cookies and throwing flour into batches of bread dough. The inn staff cheerfully pitched in to change diapers and walk him in the stroller, and we kept a crib tucked only somewhat inconspicuously into a corner of the dining room. Isaac, soon to be known forever after by the more fitting "Ike," followed a scant three years later, a serene child who was born with his grandfather's wide smile, the polar opposite of his restless and driven older brother.

Despite their differences, both boys absorbed the lessons of small business ownership through their time spent at the inn, and they were an integral part of the guest experience. A regular guest from Iceland brought them a children's picture book about puffins, and sometimes they had the companionship of guests' children. Josh pitched in to serve breakfast or bake the afternoon treats, even helping out at a catering event at age ten, beside himself with pride to be tipped a dime. Ike cleared the tables of plates sticky with maple syrup and scavenged many a piece of dessert, defending his sweet tooth by explaining that he had two stomachs, one just for dessert. Mostly, though, they learned about the grownup world around them through the lens of hospitality—how to smile and be polite, how to pitch in by carrying baggage and folding sheets, how to give your parents a break at the end of a long day. Their adult selves are molded from these experiences.

Collins House employees, like our later Manna employees, were an eclectic bunch, as different from one another as my own sometimes baffling children but united by their love of cooking and serving other people. Many had worked at other Madison restaurants or, like us, were enthusiastic about having food play a starring role in their lives.

Lori was a lay midwife's apprentice, her deeply kind and empathetic demeanor perfectly suited to lending an ear or scrounging up a sandwich for a hungry late-night guest. Deidre crafted cocktails at local restaurants, passionate about the ingredients for a perfect margarita (she spoiled me for life), who shared her love of the local restaurant scene with guests in a way that reflected her own desire to run out, *right now,* for Parthenon's dripping gyros sandwich, or a fat wedge of cherry pie, melty with ice cream, from Nick's. Jody was a research biochemist who moonlighted at the inn, creating recipes and making art out of mounds of vegetables. After a long and productive scientific career, she opened her own catering business. And Adele, though childless, was a gentle mother to guests and staff alike.

The B&B was a novel new workplace for many who loved the hospitality world—an intimate space where coming to work felt more like coming home—no punch clocks, no frenetic kitchens. For some, it was an escape from the intensity or impersonal nature of the corporate world. But once we were accustomed to being paid for what amounted to a chosen lifestyle, it was hard to leave.

There were rarely more than about six or eight people on staff as innkeepers or housekeepers, and while the catering had a few additional staff of its own, it was often the inn staff doing double duty, stretching part-time work into full-time. Owners and staff alike shared all of the work, from cooking and serving breakfasts, to cleaning, to waiting up for late-night check-ins. And while our staff was in their early twenties, and we were in our early thirties, we were all fairly close in age. Although this didn't seem like much at the time, it would, in retrospect, provide us with a better understanding of our work dynamic. They felt very much like contemporaries and friends and less like employees. We all knew what to do without anyone having to be boss.

In our first year, Bob and Marilyn, a couple from Kaneville, Illinois, wandered up to Madison to explore the city and found their way to The Collins House as if by the same fate that led us to the Union Street Inn. The couple fell in love with everything about the city, especially the inn and the restaurant scene. From that first visit forward, it became their habit to visit Madison, staying with us five times each year. Marilyn would pull out her planning calendar each summer and map out their visits. Included in her planning was always, and most importantly, Thanksgiving, the classic "family" holiday that we celebrated at The Collins House by inviting solo staff or guests, thus creating a new motley family of sorts. Mostly everyone cooked, and those who didn't brought wine. Some years we might have thirty people and some years eight. These were always joyous celebrations, unencumbered by the perplexing dynamics that often plague traditional family gatherings.

The couple—Bob with his flowing beard and the latest technological toy and Marilyn with a new craft project in hand—would hang out with the innkeepers and other regular guests, frittering away the morning as if hanging with buddies at the local diner. Soon they befriended local bartenders or waitstaff, making frequent forays to L'Etoile or Deb and Lola's, often joined by Ed and Sally, another couple that regularly visited. Bob and Marilyn were our quintessential guests, and the lives they led at The Collins House helped us better understand the nature of the inn and its role in Madison as a fledgling community in microcosm.

I like to think of 1989 as the "year of the babies," a moment when my life took a sudden jag to the right. We had been running the inn for four years and the catering for three. But we were still without children, and what little social life we had outside of The Collins House revolved around similarly childless friends. Having a new baby can be a shock to the system—your daily routine as well as the trajectory of your life. It so happened that my first child arrived within the same time frame as a series of new inn guests, all of whom were also in the early months of adjusting to life with a baby. We moms bonded over the woes of first-time parenting, and new friendships were forged. That year, an entire social network grew from this unrelated collection of university recruits who chose Madison as their new home. Whatever other role The Collins House played in bringing people together, this one, for me, was most personal and long lasting.

Jim and Wendy Skinner first arrived at the inn during the summer of 1989, when the UW Chemistry Department was courting Jim, and they had their new baby, Colin, in tow. By October, when they returned to house hunt, Josh had been born, and through the language of new mothers and a shared love of cooking for friends, we quickly became close. The Skinners ultimately purchased a Prairie School home of their own as a result of their Collins House experience. Within that "year of the babies," we hosted Joel, Molly, and little Adam; and Denis, Dianne, and baby Seth. A small playgroup evolved and, with the addition of a few other local couples, my social circle was magically redefined. Much like childhood or college friends—the ones you think of as knowing "the real you"—these folks formed the core of our lives with children. One New Year's Eve, we hosted a slumber party at the inn with the idea that if you can't go out to celebrate the holiday because of the babies, then bring the babies and the baby monitors, put the kids to sleep, and have a rowdy party of your own. No designated driver necessary.

Many guests became interwoven into our lives over the years, and many more colored our memories. Manna kept the connections alive, and we were gratified through the years to see all the familiar faces who came in for lunch or to pick up a box of sticky buns. Occasionally a less familiar face would appear at the counter and say, "You guys catered my wedding at The Collins House in 1988. Thank you for the memories."

The Collins House was leased from the City of Madison for twenty years. The city wanted to retain ownership of the building because it was situated in James Madison Park; both were city-owned properties. As our lease neared its end, the building needed considerable repairs beyond the scope of our arrangement with the city. A cantilevered overhang sagged ominously over the front porch, and the entire bank of lake-facing windows needed replacing. While we wanted to continue running the inn, now a landmark business for the community, we had also considered other ways to share our particular style of food and hospitality. The idea of a local neighborhood cafe took hold as the perfect distillation of the best of The Collins House. The story is long and complicated, full of teary drama at every turn. In the end, though, the choice was made for us. The city did not offer the option of a renewed lease, and purchasing the building was cluttered with downsides. While the decision to close the inn at the end of our lease was an unhappy and difficult one, we were thrilled by the creative prospects that lay ahead.

The last year at The Collins House was an emotional roller coaster. Regular guests were notified, and potential weddings were turned away. Repairs and upgrades took a backseat. And as we turned our energies to finding a location for the cafe and began developing the new business, our family time was spread thin. Manna's opening helped soften the blow of closing The Collins House. The two businesses overlapped for three months, leaving us no time to mourn its loss. Instead, Manna demanded so much, so quickly, that we hardly had a moment to catch our breath.

Manna Cafe: Welcome to the North Side

We had moved to Madison's north side in 1994, just before our first child was ready for kindergarten. By that time, we were nearly halfway through The Collins House years and a full eleven years away from Manna's opening. The inn and catering were in full swing, and the idea of a cafe was as yet unborn.

During the first week in our new home, I felt compelled, as usual, to bake something. So I whipped up a batch of brownies, set them still warm on a tray, and wandered out back to introduce myself to my new neighbors. Here I met Helen, the mother of two children about the same age as my kids, and we sat on her porch steps sharing a chocolatey moment that felt, looking back, like the beginning of our own microcosmic community of sorts. Almost instantly, the "corner" of nearby families formed an intimate group of parents and kids. We created reasons to gather for mini food-centric bashes in the sprawling backyards—Fourth of July, Halloween, or no reason at all—with shrimp boils over an open fire, giant cakes shaped like the state capitol, and fireworks on the Fourth, set off by Helen's pyromaniac husband, that sent my kids crying to their rooms. Even at this first encounter, a neighborhood food business became a speck on my horizon. Helen, now on her third brownie, turned to me and said, offhandedly, "Why don't you open up a place?" In time she became my cheerleader, a developer who knew what our neighborhood needed and was not at all shy about nudging us forward.

The north side was brimming with cultural diversity but only just beginning to cultivate its own strong identity. Many other Madison neighborhoods enjoyed the reputation of being go-to destinations, whether for shopping, eating, or just meeting up. The near west side, close to the UW-Madison campus, Edgewood College, and several major hospitals was populated by academics and a large portion of Madison's Jewish population. Its business corridor was defined by Monroe Street, a several-mile-long corridor with intermittent stretches of locally-owned boutique businesses and popular restaurants. Likewise, the near east side, stretching along Lake Monona, was home to young professionals, artisans, and many a street festival. It boasted a somewhat funkier collection of haunts, hangouts, and off-beat stores along Williamson Street and Atwood Avenue. But in my neighborhood, it was not uncommon to hear people talk wistfully about having such places to go to "on this side of town."

In fact, the north side was poised for a small explosion in its own development. The Warner Park Community Center had opened in 1999, and the Northside Planning Council of Madison, established in 1993, was gaining momentum in its far-reaching plans for economic and community development in the area. On the horizon was an incubator commercial kitchen space called FEED Kitchens; a new home for DAIS, a facility offering domestic abuse protection and education services to Dane County; the Northside Farmers' Market; a major bike lane development; and more, all aimed at establishing the north side as a socially conscious, family-friendly destination. A neighborhood cafe might be a potential catalyst in attracting other restaurants and businesses to the area.

Madison's north side had lacked a local cafe/bakery ever since the Ovens of Brittany vacated its spot on Fordem Avenue. In fact, few restaurants were serving this fairly large geographical area. And while the Warner Park Community Center was increasingly becoming a neighborhood Third Place as a social and recreational hub, people also clamored for a gathering place where the food was the draw.

The Collins House had a great run, but as its time drew to an end, a little neighborhood cafe close to home seemed an appealing and logical next step. Here we could funnel twenty years' worth of breakfast traditions, hand-crafted baked goods, and creative catering fare into a place that would reflect the hospitality and small business values that had guided us so far. The Collins House had evolved into a Madison food and B&B landmark, and many of our core friendships had begun there. This new venture, dangling like a proverbial carrot before us, promised a fresh creative outlet, a business close to home that the kids could walk to and be a part of, and a chance to bring our joy of sharing a delicious bite to eat with our northside neighbors.

After months of scouring nearby Sherman Avenue for the perfect site, we found our home in the corner of a nondescript strip mall building, a choice once again driven by location. The cafe would be in the middle of a major northside commuting corridor, and the parking was ample. In April 2005, someone (not me this time) raised a sledgehammer and smashed the first noisy hole in the concrete wall separating the two spaces that would become Manna. This big bash echoed the launch of The Collins House renovation, reminding us of the exhilaration and challenges that lay ahead.

Everything about Manna's design was intended to lay the groundwork for a Third Place experience—a place for neighbors to gather and share social ties over breakfast or lunch or an afternoon bakery snack with a latte. We chose oak woodwork and Prairie School design elements to echo the warm and welcoming ambiance of The Collins House. Front-of-house staff were hired for their outgoing, social personas. The food was familiar, homey, and imaginative, and threads of our Jewish culture were interwoven throughout, including in the fragrant loaves of challah and nourishing, life-affirming bowls of chicken matzo ball soup. When we opened our doors, we had our fingers crossed that what we envisioned would play out as we hoped. Like with the producer and director who toil for years hoping to create to create a great film, it is the critics and the box office who have the final word come opening day.

The timing of our opening was, in hindsight, fortuitous. We opened our doors at a time when many neighborhood projects were in their early planning stages. Manna Cafe instantly became a hub for planners, developers, politicians, and neighbors who needed a table to spread out their drawings or a cozy corner to get to know their constituents. Later, as the north side became increasingly recognized as a great place to raise a family, more restaurants appeared, old strip malls upgraded their outward appearances and lineup of stores, and a well-established food co-op moved in. It was a right-place-at-the-right-time story.

Here We Go Again

We had once again hit the ground running in five short months, this time with twenty years of experience behind us (although how that experience applied remained to be seen). Thoughtful food and down-to-earth hospitality still grounded us, yet our experience on day one at Manna abruptly brought home an unexpected lesson: A restaurant is an entirely different animal from either a B&B or a catering business.

One might think that the catering experiences in particular—serving multiple daily business meetings and parties of up to five hundred people—would have better prepared us for the challenges of a restaurant. They are, after all, both demanding food service operations. Yet two fundamental differences make these operations feel worlds apart. First, a single catered event happens at one time—lunch for fifty at twelve thirty, or a cocktail party for two hundred at five. You spend a couple or more days baking bars, roasting meats, and assembling salads, all at your own pace, so on the day of the event all that remains is final assembly and delivery. It is a lot of work, but it is parsed out over time. Second, for a catered event, your group of 200 people all gets the same menu—the same eight or ten different items, plus a couple of desserts. In a restaurant, rather than feeding a group of a hundred people all at once, you are now serving a hundred people in sets of two or four or eight. And instead of feeding them all the same dishes, they each get to pick from one of maybe twenty five or so choices on your menu (and, guaranteed, each person will make some tiny change to their order: extra cheese, sub avocado for bacon, use egg whites only). You have to prepare each meal to order in ten minutes or less, over and over again. Generally the line cooks prepared from one to eight sets of orders at a time, depending on their size. In contrast to the demands of working on a restaurant line, catering seems downright leisurely.

Day one at The Collins House had been scary, but it was just two guests, one breakfast, and a room to be made up the next morning. On September 1, 2005, when Manna opened, long lines of people greeted us, and they didn't stop coming. We were exhilarated and gratified but scared out of our wits. That day we had eagerly awaited would become a trial by fire and a shock to my easy-going B&B sensibilities. Things were gonna be different!

How do you decide how many turkey clubs or Reubens or any of your other twenty sandwich varieties to prepare for when you've never sold one? What will you do if the soup runs out? The bread? The food disappeared faster than we could blink. There was not so much as a leaf of lettuce to adorn a sandwich by midday, and someone bolted to the grocery store. Next, it was the meats, followed by another dash to the store. The bakery was licked clean. Customers asked about ingredients and allergies, answers we had not yet thought to organize in notebooks for quick reference at the register. The tills ran low on change, and the baristas never once looked up from their steam wands and espresso shots.

To this day, no one who was part of the whirlwind has any idea how we made it through to closing time or what happened between six in the morning and six in the evening. But everyone remembers the crying. When the last customer disappeared and the clock's minute hand had slipped safely past the closing hour, we locked the doors in long-awaited relief, and the floodgates opened. There was not a dry eye in the house, and as much as I might have wanted to set a good example, I cried right along with everyone else. The crew was exhausted but exhilarated and also a bit apprehensive. It was Friday, Labor Day was the following Monday, and we were a melted down pile of humanity. After a fast, furious, and baffling first day in business, Manna reluctantly, though thankfully, closed for the weekend.

It took those next two days to pull up our big boy and girl pants, regroup, and reopen. Having learned so much from our day one ordeal, day two was better, and so was day three until slowly, the fun began to emerge, and we felt once again like our old selves. When Dennis, one of my sales reps and a man who made a living helping restaurants open their doors, saw me holding back tears, he told me like a calm and reassuring sage that it would take about three months for the debris to settle. And indeed, in just that amount of time, cafe life began to feel normal, predictable, fun. We could begin to look up at the people in front of us, engage in conversation, and focus on the human connections rather than the mystery of making a kitchen and a service staff jumble and jive.

In hindsight, that opening day now seems unassuming. Sure, we caromed wildly off the walls the entire time, but in the years to come, that would rank as a quiet business day.

Manna's starting menu, both the bakery lineup and the food menu, was a distillation of B&B and catering favorites—our way of starting this new venture in baby steps. But it also spoke to our new and somewhat different audience. The overarching principle was handcrafted, homey fare elevated somehow, like using the more elegant tenderloin rather than the traditional eye of round, or creating an offbeat sauce like the perky, orange-red romesco, or insisting on home-baked bread. It was a safe way to begin, knowing that the spicy Jamaican chicken that was central to catered sandwich buffets, or oat date scones we had once wholesaled to area coffee shops, already had a devoted following. We made sure we appealed to the less adventuresome eaters with items like tuna melts and turkey clubs, which had no spiciness and were recognizable from the American canon of lunch fare. From here, our menus quickly evolved, with chefs and bakers providing new ideas that kept to this sensibility.

Once past the opening frenzy, and with our customers now knowing what to expect, the days at Manna took on a certain comforting rhythm. Mondays offered a gentle, sleepy start to the week, a respite from the preceding two days of busy brunches. Staff lazed about the cafe, watering plants, straightening crooked pictures, updating the community board, and spending extra time loafing with their favorite customers. The kitchen took stock of their caches and plotted out strategies for the upcoming days, planning specials and reviewing the previous week's ups and downs. From there, the activity crescendoed. Wednesday, somewhat randomly, was a day that larger groups gathered for weekly coffee clutches. On Friday, with the weekend looming, the orders picked up for cakes and quiches and boxes of desserts. Weekend travelers stopped for lunch on their way out of town. By Saturday and Sunday, we were rested and ready, excited for the rush brought on by the challenges of a busy service.

Learning to Parent the Second Child

Neither Mike nor I had waited a table nor worked a cook line nor pulled an espresso shot in our lives. The closest I had come to restaurant work was back in my college years when I cooked bacon in the dorm cafeteria but was relieved of my responsibilities when I refused to leave the bacon limp and flabby per cafeteria standards. Ironically, bacon cooked to crispy deliciousness was later the standard for Manna. We were thus bend-over-backward grateful for the expertise of the folks who got us up and running.

Sure, we brought recipes and menu ideas to the table, but managing a production bakery or cooking on a line was not in our skill set. There were so many things we didn't know we needed—ticket spikes, silverware holders, diaper stations, three sizes of plastic wrap, number ten can openers. We learned at once the important lesson of surrounding ourselves with people who knew what we did not. Our restaurant-savvy staff provided a sound base of hands-on experience—how to roll up silverware packets, how to shimmy through a crowd of customers balancing three plates on each arm. We filled in the spaces by running a compassionate and respectful business. And we learned to lead not by assuming we knew best but by empowering those who did.

During The Collins House years, we had found business insight by traveling to other inns and experiencing them as if standing in the shoes of our own customers. Now, everywhere we traveled, we went out of our way to find locally-owned restaurants, and each provided a useful lesson. We learned that if a restaurant's menu offered enough variety, we wanted to return again and again, but if the menu was overly focused and brief, it would likely be a one-time visit or only for a special occasion. Some places used the same ingredients repeatedly in their menus, in different combinations and lacked variety. We made it a goal to use specialty ingredients no more than twice on a particular menu so that the menu seemed fresh and original. And every time we ate somewhere that used store-bought bread, it reaffirmed our commitment to the fragrant challah or deeply flavorful multigrain or Pratzel's corn tzizel rye. Breads crafted in-house conveyed the importance of bread as cultural markers.

I loved a good bowl of oatmeal, but most restaurants served it as a singular specialty item—apricots and pistachios with notes of cardamom or baked with apples, nuts, and cinnamon. And I came to find that people have wildly different ideas of what constitutes a great bowl of oatmeal. This discovery led to Manna's "Oatmeal as You Like It," a basic starting bowl of steamy steel-cut oats served with brown sugar and sliced bananas on the side. From there, customers could choose from a veritable shopping list of additions, such as different nuts, a dried fruit mix, granola, chocolate chips, fresh berries, maple syrup, a dusting of cinnamon. And it could be rewarmed with milk, soy milk, or oat milk. Each restaurant we visited was no longer just a meal but a place where, for better or worse, we found guidance in our own choices. Eating out would never be the same.

Manna's "customer-shoes" ethos was articulated in a formal statement of our core values, posted on the swinging kitchen door for all staff to see. Mike or I discussed them with each new hire as part of their orientation, conveying to our team members what it meant to them and our business to have people see their responsibilities through the lens of respect, compassion, community, and fun. Every new employee listened for over an hour to the story of Collins House, and our lives together, as a prelude to the Manna experience. The story was heartfelt, deeply meaningful, and I don't think there was an employee who left their orientation unmoved by Mike's teary delivery. It immediately set the stage for our expectation of a people-first work experience at Manna. At the same time, we made it clear that employees were expected to live up to their end of the bargain, abiding by guidelines in our detailed Employee Manual, but that in return we would always have their backs.

Our written core values formalized the principles that had more implicitly guided the actions of our small team at The Collins House. Now, with a much larger staff working in the front-of-house, kitchen, bakery, and dishwashing, it helped bind the group with our particular brand of business philosophy. For example, we articulated the expectation of what we termed "informal yet professional" conduct, encouraging our staff to work with integrity and commitment, all the while dressed in mismatched socks, or flowing boas, or shorts in winter. We particularly eschewed anything that smacked of a corporate feel: no matching aprons, no rehearsed patter ("...and how are those first bites tasting...?"), and especially no annoying upselling. We embraced the notion that if each employee exuded uniqueness, our customers would likewise feel treated as individuals.

We worked hard to convey the customer-shoes notion as a way of life for a cafe employee, to help guide them through a busy day where, at every turn, a lesser customer experience might be lurking. Sometimes, I would find coffee cups steaming hot from the dishwasher but bearing an inner shadow of coffee stains. Instantly I became one of my customers being handed this very cup, and even though the cup was freshly sanitized, all I would see was "dirty." I would intercept these cups and ferret them back for a more thorough cleaning, thus staying one step ahead of customer dissatisfaction. Staff was encouraged to take lunch breaks in the dining room, sitting at a table next to customers. In doing so, they were often rewarded with coos over the creamy plate of scrambled eggs—positive feedback that they might otherwise never hear, and that often made their day. But they might also overhear that a bathroom needed toilet paper, or we had forgotten to add bacon to a sandwich, or any of a myriad of small dissatisfactions that spoke to ways we could be better. I enjoyed watching staff wander about the cafe, swiveling their periscope heads this way and that, seeing what was missing, or dirty, or out of place. Was the cinnamon shaker filled? Were there smudgy children's handprints obscuring the view through the door? What does the customer see, and can I see it first?

Once, an entire staff meeting was devoted to "bakery love," which focused on keeping the bakery case organized, well stocked, condensed as the day's supplies dwindled, and shiny. We all gathered in front of the bakery case and as a group saw what the customer saw: cookies sitting too far back on their pans and not in clear view; cakes whose cut side was facing away, thus obscuring the beautiful inner layers; crumbs scattered messily about, or sticky pie filling left on a shelf. So impactful was this singularly focused meeting that even years later, all a manager need do was utter "bakery love," and a staffer, even one who had not been present at the meeting, would be off and running. We could riff on the term, asking for a little espresso machine love, and everyone knew just what we meant. The experience taught me another important management lesson: meetings with a singular, narrow focus were significantly more fruitful than those with a lengthy agenda.

Of course, you can't catch everything. More than once, a customer wanted to substitute gluten-free bread. Maybe they didn't remember to ask for it when they placed the order. Maybe we didn't hear the request. Maybe we heard it but entered it wrong on the computer, or perhaps the kitchen person didn't read the ticket carefully or read it but forgot. Or they reached for the wrong bread. Whatever! When it got to the customer, it was the wrong bread. The staff person apologized, and the order was remade, only this time we forgot to remove the bacon, as also originally asked. And so on. Not only that, but this general scenario replayed itself twice with the same customer on different visits.

During Manna's early years, I was introduced to the compelling book, *Setting the Table,* by acclaimed New York restaurateur Danny Meyer. He tells a story of excellence in hospitality management, as learned through building his New York City empire of upscale and casual restaurants. And, coincidentally, it turns out that Danny Meyer was raised on Pratzel's corn tzizel rye! Nearly every word resonated with me, and I was grateful that someone had so clearly, and with such good humor, described the type of service and hospitality I practiced but could not as easily articulate. *Setting the Table* became required reading for my front-of-house managers. Sometime after reading the book, we were discussing ways of compensating customers for any small mistake that impacted their experience. Danny Meyer strongly believed that the best solution for smoothing ruffled feathers was to offer freebies—sometimes small and sometimes big, such as free catering for a double-booked wedding—because the end result is generally good publicity instead of bad Yelp reviews. So we added a "Danny Meyer" button to our register, and a similarly titled section on our staff bulletin board, so we could track complimentary gift certificates or free meals resulting from unhappy customers. At day's end, when I reconciled our cash register drawers, I might be saddened to see a line entry titled "Danny Meyer," but I was grateful for the spirit in which our system was developed.

Of course, It was one thing to correct an error, or compensate for a perceived wrong, and another thing entirely to succumb to the sense of entitlement a customer might feel, simply for being a customer, and for believing that he or she is "always right," just by definition. It is a fine line that all service industries walk when ensuring good customer experiences. And while we worked hard to lay the groundwork for success, we drew the line when a customer's unhappiness negatively impacted our well-meaning staff.

Sometimes, people understand, and you give them a free cookie anyway. Sometimes they are less understanding, but offering a free meal on the next visit smooths the ruffles, and they become regulars. And on very rare occasions, they shout obscenities at the people behind the counter while baffled customers look on in embarrassment. The lesson here? It will be tomorrow soon enough.

It was not just the infinite small details that made for good customer experiences. Some of the bigger decisions we faced were more philosophical. A fine line we were forced to navigate, and that challenged our every baby boomer beliefs, was the balance between the need to live in the digital age, and the value of cultivating human interactions, which was so fundamental to Manna's existence. We had grappled with similar issues at Collins House, considering whether to put televisions in every room or deciding, toward the end, whether to prepare the inn for the latest technology since sliced bread. During Manna's construction phase, we were advised to install electrical outlets at regular intervals, so people could keep everything charged and running. Our hesitation arose from the idea that each step toward electronic reliance was one more step away from human connections, something we felt we were struggling to maintain, even as it was crumbling around us. How would Manna's sense of self play out in this era that was anathema to its existence?

Younger generations were born and raised in a cell phone-centric world, where social interactions were through electronic media, and eye contact was through FaceTime. Manna, though, was about talking to people and taking the time in the day to indulge in a bit of small talk. Did we need to modernize every aspect of our operation to stay current? Provide call-in coffee pickup capabilities? Use an expensive, but convenient, delivery service? Speed up our in-house systems so customers could run in and out without stopping to breathe? Of course, that's what it came to anyway, once the pandemic swallowed us whole.

While technology continued its inevitable march forward, replacing conversation with screen time, and distracting customers as they placed their orders, we worked to keep its negative effects at bay by reminding ourselves and our customers that people still come first. Even if we had lines at the bakery case during the breakfast-time rush, we made a habit of having a few friendly words with each customer, slowing down each transaction just a bit, to keep the connections alive. During our busy brunch service, we found gentle tactics to usher squatters—people who sat for hours with a pot of tea and a laptop—to the overstuffed chairs or the counter. Eventually, the squatters learned to respect the importance of a table as a place for eating, and everyone appreciated the efforts. But we made our peace with the modern world and stopped short of pulling the plug on the internet during weekend brunch service. Much as I might have wished otherwise.

A Community Blossoms

Manna was as mom and pop as it gets, with an enormous family reaching from Superior, Wisconsin, to somewhere in Texas, to the backyards of our northside neighbors. Some of that stemmed organically from the nature of a neighborhood-driven cafe and some from how we emphasized and embraced the many variations on the theme of family throughout the business. Much of it, of course, was the food. And sometimes, we were surprised by how even the tiniest corners of our business world became the ties that bound us.

Strangers became customers, customers became regulars, and regulars interconnected with staff and owners. Hundreds of them. Everybody seemed to know everybody, and the days felt familiar not just because of the rhythms of work but also from the ebb and flow of recognizable faces.

Days were frequently characterized by who we saw, who we missed. Buzz and his entourage gathered around the front table in the mornings, holding court. Buzz, as if stuck in a *Groundhog Day* sequel, ordered his not-on-the-menu spinach scramble and coffee. Friends would stop by for a quick laugh, a reassuring hug, a little snitch of someone's cookie. Morning coffee clutches lingered, then dispersed, and the lunch crowds rolled in, a disparate assortment of friends meeting friends, business people talking shop, and neighbors seeing and being seen. Late afternoons would see Joe and Chris talking quietly over crossword puzzles and pie, Joe's eyes always on the lookout for someone's chain to yank. All day long was a colorful parade of people: The Captain pining for his blueberry scone and a touch irritable if it was sold out; Groggy Joe picking up her daily latte, a lip-wrinkling concoction of four espresso shots and twelve flavor shots; Adam, who sat at a corner counter space for hours, earphones humming and computer blinking. So many people.

Every front-of-house (FOH) employee had a handful of favorite customers, and customers became attached to specific staff. ("Is Kurt here today? He's the only one who makes my latte right.") At the epicenter was Shirley, whose role at Manna was core to our self-identity. Shirley first came to Manna early on, when her husband Craig was at the beginning of a long and

Craig and Shirley, with FOHer Nick Johnson.

debilitating disease. Quickly Manna morphed from a stop for a snack, to a comforting place where staff saw to Craig's slowly-changing needs with empathy and respect, and Shirley found friendship and compassion. Craig's condition inevitably worsened, and even after he could no longer come, Shirley continued to stop in for a daily breakfast and to pick up Craig's favorite chocolate chip cookie. Many of our staff attended Craig's celebration of life, and until COVID-19 arrived, Shirley rarely missed her scrambled eggs, crispy bacon, side of greens with dressing on the side, Jasmine tea, and coconut milk latte to go. We all knew the order by heart, but she recited it anyway. If she was feeling chatty, there was always someone eager to join her. If she needed alone time, she found a secluded spot in the back room. At every employee orientation, Mike would show a newly-hired staff person the picture of Craig and Shirley, shown on page 58, and ask, "Why do you think Shirley comes in every day?" His answer pretty much summed us up. "Manna is not just a plate of food in the window, a cozy chair by the fireplace, or an after-work stop for a cookie. It is a place for building relationships. Shirley came to connect with staff, connect with friends, connect with customers, and ultimately to connect with herself." Shirley was Manna's Bob and Marilyn.

The kitchen staff, notorious for preferring to stay hidden, knew the regulars not so much by name as by the specifics on the order tickets: Reuben no bread no meat; scrambled eggs with one whole egg and two egg whites, spinach on the side. Line orders might be called out by a customer's name or an aptly coined soundbite: the Corny Aaron for a Reuben served cold on ungrilled bread, no sauce, cheese, or kraut; the Paleo Benny for a couple on a strict dietary regimen. Sometimes cooks would slip on a clean apron and deliver a plate of food themselves, grateful for a brief respite from the fast-paced line work and the unrelenting heat of ten burners, two ovens, two grills, and a broiler. The *"Oh my gosh, that's beautiful!"* exclamation from the grateful customer would make their day and make the return to the line that much more rewarding.

Some of the regulars found a special place in our hearts, and we in theirs, and many of them also found each other. It was an oft-repeated scenario: two strangers who saw one another frequently enough that they introduced themselves and got lost together in the camaraderie and food. At the memorial service for Lenore, a long-time Manna regular, her friend Carolyn stood and talked at length about their first meeting at Manna and the lifetime friendship that had ensued. We were Lenore's community, her home, her oatmeal cookie fix.

We even had our first Manna baby, Will, born to Jay and Erica, a couple who'd followed us by e-mail when all we had was a website during construction. While many children grew up with Manna as their home away from home, leaving behind a trail of tables sticky with maple syrup, blueberry muffin crumbs, and chess pieces in the potted plants, Will blazed the way. By the age of one, he sat at the counter babbling long sentences in a language only he understood, but from his body language, we knew it was deeply meaningful. We were convinced he'd grow up to be president. Will, his two brothers, and their parents drove across Wisconsin to say goodbye when we closed, completing our little circle of life and offering up a few masked tears and hugs to boot.

Will center stage, with Sean and Spike.

Will, front and center, and the family.

Coffee shops can be a revolving door for service workers, but many of our employees made Manna a home for years. Our turnover was astonishingly low, and even people who had left for purportedly greener grass would return to "the mothership." We were grateful for the stability.

As with Collins House, Mike and I played our roles at Manna as husband and wife, Pop and Mom, but in an entirely new scenario. We had upwards of forty employees, requiring an entirely different approach than managing six to ten people. Also, while the staff at Collins House was similar in age to us, the Manna crew was younger by at least a generation. At Collins House, we were one of the gang and more like siblings or contemporaries. Now we had little in common socially with our employees, who were more like work-children. This added distance to the working relationship, which kept the lines between owners and employees more clearly drawn. Yet, we felt driven to bridge this gap to the extent that we could and cultivate the feel of one giant, diverse family. We just had to work harder.

Most importantly, we made sure we worked the same long hours as staff, doing the same tasks, filling dishwashing shifts when needed, and always taking our lunch breaks last. Three to four days each week, Mike arose at four in the morning for the daily routine he cherished—filling the bakery cases, warming the quiche, gabbing a bit with the bakers as their shifts wound down, calibrating the espresso machine, and poking his nose into every corner of the cafe to make sure the stir sticks were stocked and the chairs were tucked in. I think there was nothing more rewarding for him than setting the stage for a successful launch to our day, so that when he unlocked the doors at six for Paul, who was always patiently waiting, the cafe gently awakened. For the next several hours,

Mike continued to greet customers, bagging up muffins or slicing fresh bread loaves while bantering with the regulars. Other staff opened on other days, but Mike owned the mornings and lived to welcome the early trickle of customers. When new staff were trained for the opening shift, Mike took them under his wing and infused them with his passion for being the first face of Manna's day. Customers and staff alike found a father-like grounding in his presence and commitment, especially knowing that after four early hours at Manna, he had a full-time job awaiting him elsewhere, one he gave equal attention and energy to.

Until they were grown and moved away, our children were regular fixtures at the cafe, working alongside the staff after school and on weekends. They received no special treatment and were expected to follow our lead in putting employees' needs ahead of their own. Even before we opened, Josh and Ike were eager to make an impact on the family business, sitting around the dinner table with us discussing potential business names or helping choose dishware. Josh prepped food and cooked on the kitchen line, ultimately teaching the new breakfast cooks how to scramble eggs, as he had once learned in The Collins House years before. He loved the busyness and the chaos and sometimes announced at the beginning of a busy Sunday line shift, "Bring it on!"

Ike was the ultimate millennial. He didn't want to push a broom or wash a dish, but he wanted to "be there." Soon enough, he found his place, trained as a barista by Jessa, our first FOH manager. He proudly carried the badge that he was "Jessa-trained," checking that the honey bottle had no drips and the napkins were in tidy piles. Even Ike's middle-school sweetheart, the one he married ten years later, cut her work-teeth as a barista, going from an almost inaudible and shy teen to a self-assured leader of new employees. The commitment and joy that our kids exuded at ages fifteen and twelve impacted the staff and customers alike, and helped reinforce the family part of the business. Even ten years after they had left home, they were both hard hit by the decision to close during the pandemic.

The Pratzels were not the only family on the premises. Our first kitchen manager was joined by her sister, and one of our lead bakers worked for a number of years with his wife by his side. Two of the kitchen cooks were married during their tenure with us, and our last kitchen manager, Eric, met his future wife, Lindsey, at Manna seven years before closing. Much of the staff attended their wedding, and we all pitched in with extra shifts so the two could enjoy a honeymoon. Eric

Brandon and Phil get married.

and Lindsey worked tirelessly to keep Manna going up until the last day and echoed our own commitment as a husband-wife team. Finally, there was the wedding of our employee Brandon to his partner Phil. Brandon's parents were estranged from him, and Brandon asked Mike and me to give him away at the wedding, which was held in front of the soapstone fireplace in Manna's back room. Many staff and some customers were in attendance. Everyone in the room shed copious tears. ("Ruined a nice pair of shoes from all the crying," quipped Bialy Joe, Manna's resident deadpan comic.) Rather than discourage office romances, we loved having family working side by side.

Our annual July 4th staff party was a Manna-style version of the Thanksgiving gathering we hosted for guests and employees of The Collins House and a thank you to all for their labors on our behalf. The event was filled with fondly embraced traditions: the annual kickball game on the local driving range (always attended by our Bernese Mountain Dog, who occasionally stole the ball with a gleam in her eye and led a stream of gleeful staff on a wild goose chase between houses); the bottomless martini glasses of way-too-easy-to-drink Bee's Knees cocktails; the huge buffet with anything from blackberry BBQ ribs to barbecued shrimp to spicy mac and cheese, and always Barb's deviled eggs, laboriously finished with garnishes like lox and fresh dill sprigs, or bacon shards and roasted asparagus tips. The party culminated in the local fireworks display, after which Mike or I, as designated drivers, safely shuffled our crew home. The next morning at work, we turned back to the tasks at hand together, renewed.

Taking a break from the annual kickball game, and chasing Moka.

Perhaps the greatest joy I experienced as a metaphorical Manna mom was watching my work-children grow up and take flight in ways that, in my own experience, would have been out of the question. As a teenager in the 1970s, the idea of a college-bound high-schooler taking a year to travel, even a semester off to have a little fun, was unthinkable. Our parents firmly believed that if we didn't go straightaway to college, we were doomed. This philosophy was so deeply ingrained in me that I rode my own kids to do the same. Yet, at Manna, I was awakened to a different story. Here, much of my staff was made up of people in limbo, people who had not yet fully discovered themselves and who would spend a better part of their mid-twenties to early thirties finding their path.

And as I watched their stories unfold, I came to appreciate—even embrace—the value of letting life's experiences wash around you until you understand your place in the world more organically. So many people, I discovered, don't really know at eighteen what they want to be when they grow up.

Kyle was one such individual, and his journey was both gratifying and motivational to the crew who surrounded and supported him. Kyle started at Manna just months into sobriety, an empathetic soul filled with a need for friendship and acceptance. At the time, he had no particular future in mind for himself. Over the course of seven years with us, he learned the joy that comes from helping others in need. He began taking general classes, conquered math, traveled from technical college through graduate school at the UW, and ultimately found a rewarding career in social work. Along the way, he was supported and encouraged by staff and customers alike, assisted with a letter of recommendation here, a few bucks there.

Kyle.

So many of the staff had similar journeys. Kurt, one of our early FOH managers and a transplant from Hurricane Katrina, schmoozed his way through several years of customers before being ready to finish an art history degree. He went on to teach art in high school. Trevor, a barista extraordinaire, spent a few years impressing staff and customers alike with his passion and talent for pulling espresso shots. In time, he came to understand his need to be his own boss and went on to run his own business. And Aaron, nicknamed The Wall because of his imposing stature, whose life's dream was to be a cook in a fire station. He succeeded by sheer determination and encouragement from then Madison Fire Chief Debra Amesqua, whose first Madison encounter was at The Collins House. "Chief's here," someone would holler, and the two would share a few words at the front counter over the chief's plate of oatcakes.

Included in the mix of young folks drifting through was a long line of high school kids, who walked into Manna with their millennial glow, self-absorbed and naive to the ways of the working world. They were a fun-loving and charming bunch, eager for a paycheck and a foot in the door of the grown-up world that lay ahead. They were maybe sixteen years old when they began work with us, and by the time they graduated high school, they had learned so much: how to be kind and empathetic to older adults, how to hustle out five plates of food in one trip, how to work as a

The Wall.

team with respect and leadership, and how to disarm a grumbling customer with grace and a cookie. And, man, could these guys eat! These shy and unassertive children found their voices, hollering out, "Skinny vanilla latte, extra shot extra hot at the counter," like nobody's business. For many, college came next, yet every winter break, and every summer, they gravitated back to Manna, returning to pick up where they had left off.

It was gratifying to have been an incubator of sorts, keeping our little family warm and fed until they took wing and left us. Over thirty years before Manna opened its doors, I had worked as a limited-term employee at the Department of Natural Resources, my first semi-real job, doing mindless clerical work that provided me with my only paycheck at the time (and that also gave me the singular ability to recite the seventy-two Wisconsin counties in alphabetical order, backward). An opportunity arose to take on a position as a science writer and editor, my chosen field. For weeks I struggled with how to break the news to the boss I so deeply respected, for I was racked with guilt and fear about leaving and letting him down. But when the moment came to tell him my news, this kind man laughed. He told me that people would be remiss not to follow their dreams when they had the chance. He had not expected me to stay forever and was genuinely overjoyed that I had found my calling. His jovial encouragement left a deep impression on me about our responsibility as employers to nurture our staff and lay the groundwork for them to find their "forever homes." It was in this spirit that I bid our young achievers farewell when they moved on, smiling to myself as I saw in their worried, apologetic faces my own youthful venture into the world.

Hidden in plain sight at Manna was a somewhat random collection of memorabilia-in-the-making, and the stories they had to tell became, surprisingly, the story of Manna itself. That story begins with the kitties.

In Madison's eclectic history was a small store on State Street called Shakti. Mike shopped there to stock up on incense, while I enjoyed perusing the glass cases brimming with sparkling gemstones. One day a kitty caught my eye. Scattered about the store were tiny wood kitties for sale, no more than a couple of inches tall, except for the tails, which rose grandly behind them, each hand painted in different colors and designs. Smitten by their style, I bought a few to tuck randomly about my new cafe. Immediately, customers remarked about the kitties, asking if they were for sale, which at first they weren't. But interest increased, so I found a wholesale source for them, delighted to learn that they were not only cute but fair trade to boot.

The demand for the kitties was immediate, enthusiastic, ironic. For we were a bakery crafting breads and pies and cupcakes, a brunch and lunch place with creative and appealing menus, and here we were selling hundreds of kitties each month! The kitties started as a novelty, but soon Manna became the place to go for kitties. Over the years, we

Kitties on the march.

heard many a heartwarming kitty story: the grandparents who visited over the holidays and treated each grandchild to a new kitty for their collection; the two women who spent an extra half hour on their occasional visits, inspecting the nooks and crannies of the place for the one kitty that spoke to them; the small children who begged their mothers to buy two this time because they couldn't decide between the purple one with yellow stars and a blue tail or the one that looked like a tiger, only pink. People stumbled upon kitties hidden in the ivy or perched atop a framed picture. Half the fun for us was finding places to tuck the latest batch. I always meant to, but never did, sell them by the litter, lined up in cookie boxes. When we closed, Mike's last official act was taking down the most famous kitty of all—the one our long-time manager Sean had stuck upside down, appearing to hang on, as cats will do, from the ceiling.

The last kitty.

The kitties became a part of our community fabric, touching nearly everyone with a certain sense of endearment and joy, and bridging the generations for the fair price of $3.95 a piece. I'm sure they will be thought of right up there with the oatcakes.

The wooden table spoons spun a similar tale. We had decided early on to take food orders at the counter, then deliver them to people at their tables. And wooden spoons, hand painted with table numbers and anchored in small blocks, became our system. When we opened, the artist-husband of one of our bakers created a collection of stylized numbers that were a source of curiosity and amusement. As these early spoons succumbed to attrition, they were replaced by others. Staff enjoyed designing them, and a couple of times a party was organized around painting new sets. For their dating anniversary of August 22, my son Ike created the number eight, decorated with a soccer theme, and his

Are you dining in today?

girlfriend Ashley made the number twenty two. Each of them painted half of a heart on their spoon so that the two halves together would make a whole heart. (Oh, these two—high school sweethearts! They were married July 1, 2017.) A wooden fork was fashioned to be the number fourteen, and a spoon with a hole in its center became number nine. The bases, too, were part of the fun. We had moved from painted wooden building blocks to clear acrylic bases, and each acrylic base had a themed filling: coffee beans, dreidels, layers of colored lentils, My Little Ponies.

The spoons took on a life of their own. Customers asked for their favorite spoon. Forty-five was bunnies, and two and six were painted as billiard balls. On Sundays, when we hosted the seating, Mike had a bit of fun, assigning number ten to a party of ten, or the number five to a couple celebrating their fifth anniversary. Kids always grabbed the spoon to carry to the table, often more as a plaything than a useful piece of a communication system, and many—even the beloved number twenty-two—were lost forever. During the closing weeks, customers tried to lay claim to the few remaining kitties and hoped we would give out the spoons.

Strewn randomly about the cafe were bits and pieces of our Jewish culture, complementing the Jewish foods that peppered our menus. There was just enough to give the cafe a little seasoning, like salt, to bring out the flavor of our roots, but not so much that you might think the food itself was kosher (although maybe your first hint was the crispy bacon, or treif—Yiddish for unkosher—you'd just polished off). We were proud of our heritage and wanted to share it without making it the central point of the place.

We had strong ties to the Jewish community in Madison, having catered umpteen bar/bat mitzvahs, baby namings, and a bris or two in our time. And while the critical mass of Madison's Jewish population lives on the west side of town, many made their way over to kibitz with Mike and me over a bowl of matzo ball soup. It was another reason naming the cafe Manna felt so right to us. While we both tended toward a more cultural expression of our heritage, the biblical reference to bread mysteriously appearing from the heavens, to sustain the Jews during their forty years of wandering the desert, had a meaningful symbolism. Bread is a core cultural icon, sustaining communities around the world.

A kitty of another language.

For Purim we baked hamantaschen, and during Passover we made matzo brei, and offered matzo throughout the week for the more observant Jews. At Rosh Hashanah, we put apples and honey in everything, and for Hanukkah, we fried up latkes, set out a menorah and lit the candles. Every Friday was Jewish Friday and featured our classic brisket, braided challah loaves, and perhaps the most authentic matzo ball soup I can imagine. The recipes and stories for all of these foods and more are included in the "Jewish Fridays" chapter in the recipe section of this book, and, like the little tchotchkes, tie the threads of our culture to yours.

We were blessed to have two businesses that felt less like jobs than a way of life. We were surrounded and supported by staff whose hard work and commitment were crucial to our success. And we were equally blessed to have such a diverse customer base to join us in these endeavors. Every day, I got to watch people savor a bite of sticky bun French toast dripping with chocolate maple syrup or chomp into a saucy beef brisket sandwich. Occasionally, I would slip into an empty chair at a table full of regulars, and they would turn my way with cheerful surprise, for they knew these moments were rare for me. Sometimes I brought along a bakery creation—maybe a generous wedge of banoffee pie oozing thick caramel, chocolate ganache, and a mountain of bananas—that I had whipped up for fun. I would set the plate and a pile of forks before them, then linger for a few moments to share some chatter and to relish the moment when they savored that first forkful of pie, eyes closed in a moment of personal indulgence. These were the moments that carried my day and made my life. ❤

A room full of magic.

The Cookbook: Welcome Back Home

When you are in the middle of a happy stage of your life, it seems like it will go on forever. At The Collins House, we felt that we would always run an inn until one day we couldn't. Later, Manna connected people from all over Madison, the state, and beyond, becoming a respite, a favorite breakfast haunt, a meeting space, a place of celebration and comfort. Until one day it couldn't.

Manna had been open for nearly fifteen years, seven days a week, save for the occasional holiday. We were open when the blizzards hit, and our only customers were the people who had spent hours shoveling circles around themselves and were grateful for hot cocoa and a muffin, a glowing fire, and a friendly face. We were open on Labor Day and Memorial Day for festive themed breakfasts that generally included a few too many variations of blue and red berries topped with white whipped cream. We were open from before the dawn cracked until the hour of the gloaming, and it was only with the greatest reluctance that we occasionally turned on the "Closed" sign a wee bit early, lest we disappoint a latecomer dashing in for a quick bag of granola.

But there was nothing we could do to stop the spread of COVID-19 into our lives and business. Suddenly the interior space was rearranged to keep customers socially distanced while waiting for to-go food. The tables, once conversation hubs, became barricades keeping us safely, sadly apart. What had been a hustly-bustly business with socializing and human companionship at its core was now a lonely space where bags of food were passed from masked person to masked person, where customers dashed in and out and avoided conversation, and employees stressed about the safety of the workplace. Even when the Public Health Department granted permission to begin opening to twenty-five percent occupancy, we all agreed that we could not in good conscience do so. Those early days of COVID were full of a sense of impending doom.

Last day blues.

On Manna's last day, I sat outdoors with my twenty-eight-year-old son and his wife, passing out peanut butter ripple cookies and kibitzing with the long lines of customers who were here for the last time. I wanted our final day in business to be a happy one—a celebration of life rather than a mourning of our closure. And it was. Everything about it remains a joyous memory. Eric, the kitchen manager, had asked me what menu I would like to serve for this last supper. He was eager to make it the happiest menu I could imagine. So he cooked up all the important favorites, including several varieties of eggs Benedict, and the old tenderloin triumph sandwich, just cuz. Carlos, who had not worked at Manna for a couple of years, came back as a volunteer to cook one last time with his friends on the line. Nick, a one-time front-of-house manager, came for brunch. His oatcakes were the last three we ever made. And while there were tears all around, it was one of the warmest moments of my life.

A cookbook had been on the back burner for years, the book I never really envisioned myself writing until one day I could. A cookbook was the perfect celebration of our two businesses, a way to capture thirty-five years of living and eating a dream. And most important, it was a way to keep alive and share the foods so many came to love. Our customers and inn guests gave us the gift of supporting our businesses, becoming our friends, and sharing in our lives. The cookbook is our gift of thanks, the pandemic's silver lining. ❤

Shad Wenzlaff, extraordinarily regular customer, captured this goodbye photo shortly after Manna closed.

PART II:

The Cookbook

A Prelude to the Recipes

My formative years of childhood and college had been meager preparation for opening The Collins House. Twenty years of running a B&B only hinted at the world of restaurant management. When Manna Cafe closed in 2020, I was completely unprepared for a third career as a cookbook writer. My first years out of college had been spent writing and editing in the scientific community, but a whole book—a memoir yet? I thought I knew how to craft a sentence, even a paragraph, but it did not take long to realize that authoring a book would be a new journey entirely. At this juncture in my life, the challenge of writing a book harkened back to the feat of pulling off a seamless catered event for 500, held on two floors of a law firm, with no oven for heating and no running water, when you're 8 1/2 months pregnant (and those attorneys had expectations)!

There was a bit of masochistic joy in diving off the deep end once again, but this time I was confident I could learn everything I needed along the way. The Collins House and Manna had both shown me how to do this by surrounding myself with those who knew more and knew better, and by persevering. In her book *The Writing Life,* Annie Dillard likened the process of writing to the splitting of a log. To be successful, she pictured in her mind not the act of splitting, but the split log itself. On the days when this project got the better of me, I imagined my readers triumphantly opening their oven doors to reveal a perfect pan of sticky buns or serving up a plate of long-awaited oatcakes to their families. That always pulled me through.

What Sort of a Cookbook Is This?

Much of Manna's food was derived from straightforward recipes, yet many seemingly simple menu items relied on a great deal of technique. Those techniques can be easily mastered with a bit of patience, and bring you great satisfaction in your cooking forays. Even if the most cooking you've ever done is warming up one of our cornmeal raspberry muffins in the microwave, and now you miss that muffin greatly, you'll find that our recipes are approachable. Or maybe you love to bake bread and have years of experience working with the nuances of ambient temperatures, artisan flours, and steam-injection ovens. The breads presented here offer new realms to explore, even though they too are written to be achievable by newcomers. (My husband, Mike, and younger son, Ike, both bread-baking virgins, not only made beautiful loaves from these recipes but discovered in the process that bread baking is not the scary activity it once seemed.) I have worked hard to present straightforward recipes and more challenging techniques to engage cooks of varying skill levels and interests.

Several recipes take time and require close attention to detail. But where would our Manna community have been without the quiche that was a staple for special occasions and celebrations? How could a Manna-centric cookbook not offer up a sticky bun technique? Like the quiche or the matzo ball soup, some recipes are practically a chapter unto themselves because there is so much to say, not just about their preparation, but about what they meant to our customers and us—to the community. But a recipe with lots of words does not mean that it's difficult. Sometimes it simply takes a lot of words to describe on paper what goes pretty quickly once you understand the process. The eggs Benedict, for example, has many components, including hollandaise sauce and poached eggs, each of which requires particular attention to detail and carefully plotted timing. The first time through may seem intimidating, but the next time will be a breeze.

Not every recipe we served at the cafe made the cut, and I apologize for that. No Salted Chocolate Caramel Cake here. Sorry. Morning-After Breakfast Burrito? Oops. There are many reasons why I ended up with this particular collection. Perhaps most importantly, I wanted to balance time-consuming projects and challenging techniques with mandatory favorites, and a core of recipes achievable by most cooks. But if you can't live without something, I am reachable, happy to share, and no longer have any secrets to keep!

It is my hope that this cookbook appeals to a broad range of readers, from faithful former customers who begged me for the recipes to those of you who never came closer to Manna than zipping along I-80 on your way from the Great Salt Lake to the Big Apple. The recipes stand alone. Manna was as much about the experience of human connections as it was about the food, and the stories and lore that accompany the recipes bridge that world.

Barb's Cookbook Logic

The recipes are organized, somewhat untraditionally, to reflect the cafe's various working parts. Manna was a brunch place, a lunch spot, a bakery, and a coffee shop all rolled into one. Each part was distinct, yet each supported and elevated the others. Pratzel's fresh-baked sourdough corn tzizel rye, for instance, was a big contributor to the success of the Reuben sandwich, a lunchtime favorite. A tall, bold slice of lemon cake filled with an abundance of fresh lemon curd was a reminder that every corner of the business—in this case, the corner where gluten-free products lived—was valued equally.

Preceding the main body of recipes is the chapter **"Guidelines and a Bit of Kitchen Wisdom,"** where I share my assumptions about basic ingredients called for in the recipes, and some musings on equipment that has improved my life as a cook, both at home and professionally. I have also included a brief appendix at the end of the book that provides some techniques to support the main body of recipes.

The recipe chapters begin with **"Breakfast/Brunch"** because they're the meals we all woke up to (except for the bakers, who would just be crawling into bed). Manna began serving at 7:30 a.m. (for some even this was too late), and for several hours the entirety of the kitchen's griddle space was devoted to oatcakes, oatcakes, more oatcakes and numerous pans of omelets and scrambles. Several burners were given over solely to poaching eggs, and pans for the fried potato process bogarted half the stove. The breakfast/brunch section of the book presents specific recipes for cherished menu items (yes, the oatcake recipe awaits) and also offers up a good bit of technique on the basics behind the recipes, such as how to poach an egg or cook incredibly creamy scrambled eggs.

"Lunch," an entirely different animal, comes next. Beginning at 11:00 the kitchen took on a new cadence. All the brunch ingredients—bins of cheeses and vegetables, gallons of eggs and leftover batter—were spirited away by staff and replaced by the lunch lineup in the blink of an eye. The grill was transformed into an orchestration of hot sandwiches. Soups simmered silently within arm's reach of the line cooks, and an eclectic assortment of building blocks (Romesco Sauce, Jalapeño Pesto, Caramelized Onions, to name a few) lined the counters and cold stations. This chapter presents the many working parts that comprised lunch. Sandwiches are first deconstructed into building-block recipes, including some meat preparations. They are also presented (reconstructed, really) as the sandwiches that appeared on the menu. You can either make your favorite building-block preparation, such as the Bacon Jam that graced the brisket melt, to use in a sandwich of your invention, or you can look up one of the Manna sandwiches and find a reference to all the parts you need for it. In the lunch chapter, you'll also find recipes for salad accompaniments and many great soups, from the gentle, Carrot Ginger Soup to my favorite soup ever, Mulligatawny.

"From the Bakery" goes right to the core of Manna's sweet and yeasty soul. Our bakery, nestled into its own corner of the kitchens and separate in its operations, was nonetheless intimately connected to the rest of the business, both as support for the kitchen menu and a self-sufficient entity. For some customers, a muffin was not merely a coffee go-with; it was the raison d'être for a stop at the cafe on the way to work. The hand-constructed oak bakery case was a customer's first view inside the door, its warm wood a symbolic thread to The Collins House origins of our bakery lineup. Manna's bakery offerings spanned the day, providing croissants, Danish, muffins, and scones for the morning, and cookies, bars, cakes, and pies for the afternoons. We baked a focused collection of breads to support our sandwiches and offered gluten-free breakfast pastries and desserts that enjoyed a cult-like following. The bakery chapter shares many favorites.

Though we could hardly be considered a Jewish restaurant, every corner of Manna was touched by our Jewishness. Religion aside, there is a strong cultural component to Judaism which expresses itself in food. And many classic Jewish foods—matzo ball soup, challah, or brisket—are homey in a Manna-esque way. These dishes convey a certain sense of family togetherness and values that were also a strong part of the Manna ethos. It felt natural to include them in our offerings, and we were gratified to share them. The final chapter of this book, **"Jewish Fridays: Manna's Culinary Soul,"** is dedicated to our Jewish roots threaded gently in and about the cafe. The recipes are drawn from both the bakery and kitchen and assembled in proud homage to our heritage.

The Making of a Cookbook, One Recipe at a Time

"Of course, you'll have to test all the recipes."

Until Terese Allen mentioned it, I hadn't thought much about recipe testing. Terese is a local cookbook author and food columnist whose many titles include *The Ovens of Brittany Cookbook and The Flavor of Wisconsin: An Informal History of Food and Eating in the Badger State*. I sought her out to be my personal cookbook midwife, and she guided me on all the minutiae of getting a cookbook right, every step of the way. But the recipe-testing mandate, offered as casually as a napkin for barbecue dribbles, caught me off guard.

Recipe testing? I had 150 recipes, and I had made most of them before. I knew they worked quite well at Manna. But they had to work for you! The distance between Point A, a muffin you bought for $2.95, and Point B, a muffin warm from your oven, suddenly felt like a marathon, and I hadn't run the first mile. (I don't even run.)

But Terese knows everything, and I knew pretty much nothing, so I took a closer look. A recipe that makes 100 servings is not the same as one that feeds a family of four. Many of the recipes were just a list of ingredients with no instructions, the implication being that the user ought to know what to do with them. Shortcuts abounded, and some recipes had been so worked and reworked that I had no idea which proportions were actually correct. Above all, I had to be clear and concise so that all the work of putting together these recipes would pay off with a happy cooking experience for the reader. My foodie friend Jim once related the experience of trying a cookbook by a renowned restaurateur, only to find the instructions so confusing that he shoved the cookbook to the back of his bookshelf, never to be thumbed through again. That was most decidedly what I did not want.

So, alongside the many tasks that define the making of a memoir/cookbook (like writing narratives until you've lost your way, going back and forth with a good editor until you find it again; searching for publishers who will get your book out sometime before the next pandemic; tracking down photos from cell phones and scrapbooks; occasionally barking at your husband and bursting into tears), I embarked on the gargantuan process of recipe wrangling. This meant deciding what to include, rewriting every recipe to be consistent in format and scaled for a home kitchen, choosing testers, and managing the process of testing, gathering commentary, retesting, problem-solving. Many recipes had a story behind them, and writing the introductory blurbs became a joyous way of illuminating the big picture. As it turns out, by the time I had finished the process, recipe testing became a sort of silver lining in ways I would never have imagined.

Recipe testing provided a social element during the pandemic, giving me the chance to hobnob and "share food" with an eclectic group of enthusiastic individuals. I reconnected with old friends, including Jody, an extraordinary cook from the early Collins House years, and met many new people, like my son Josh's cook-friend in New York and her mom back here in Madison. Rounding out the collection were family members from Copenhagen to Philadelphia and a bevy of local friends with whom I had eaten many meals. Through a lively e-mail correspondence, driven by the pressing importance of getting these recipes right, we kept ourselves occupied together and with purpose as the months of the pandemic dragged on. If you have to endure a pandemic, write a cookbook.

Cooks of all skill levels provided useful insights. Little things I never thought to specify—dark or light brown sugar? How big is a six-ounce onion? The range of testers' cooking capabilities helped ensure clarity for beginners and provided scientific accuracy where it was important, especially in bread baking. At one end of the spectrum was my son Josh, the trained professional chef and baker, who provided both food wisdom and expert writing critique. At the other was my younger son Ike, the non-cook of the family, who often called me several times in one evening to say, essentially, "Explain it to me like I'm a six-year-old!" In between were an assortment of home cooks whose every question or observation opened a window into how to write something that much better.

I asked testers to document their work with photos, and this request paid off in unexpected ways. Some pictures were simply fun, adding an extra layer to the story: the Labrador retriever ogling a plate of scones; 10 shots of multigrain bread, from unrisen dough to partially eaten loaf; the proud plate of eggs Benedict made by a non-cook for the first time; a tester's wife showing off a bowl of potato salad before the Super Bowl. But there were other benefits. I could see from a picture that something went wrong (that's not how the cookie looked at Manna) or that I had not been explicit enough in my instructions (that glaze is way too thick). The pictures told a story that testers might not have thought to articulate, but were worth a thousand words.

Collins House and Manna had satisfied my need to be creative, grow personally and professionally, and work with like-minded people in a team fashion. Writing the cookbook satisfied the same desire, and the testers became my new team, my new family. Everyone was motivated to do their part to make this project successful, and the group's enthusiasm and commitment were palpable.

One hundred and fifty or so recipes were divided amongst 18 people, and two testers tested each one, sometimes once more (and in one case, once more ... and then again!).

All except one recipe. Mike and I had made this one recipe so many times, and we joked that we could do it blindfolded. No tester could add anything to the oatcake recipe, so we saved it just for you.

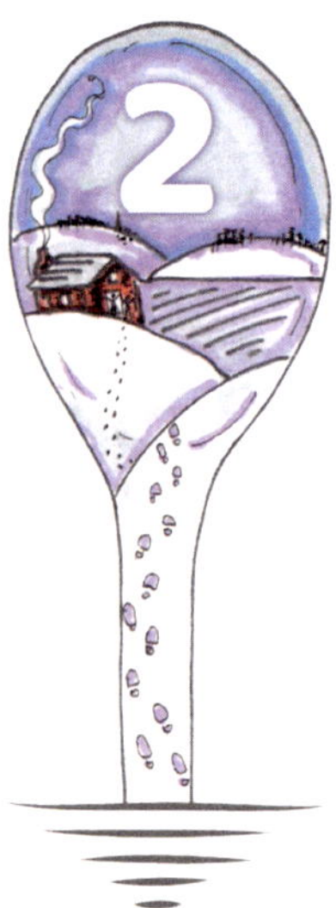

Guidelines and a Bit of Kitchen Wisdom

The first time you make a recipe, read it through from start to finish. This applies to quick and easy recipes just as much as multi-part, all-day affairs and to familiar as well as first-time preparations. Know what is coming so that you are prepared from the outset. Sometimes what separates one version of a recipe from another is a detail in the technique, and overlooking that detail might make all the difference in the outcome.

Every cookbook (or cook) does things a bit differently, so there is no one way to think about cooking. I want you to have great success with these recipes, so this brief chapter shares the assumptions I make with ingredients and equipment recommendations that will make your cooking life a happy one.

Ingredient Assumptions

Unless otherwise specified:

- **Butter:** Always use unsalted for cooking or baking. Since most recipes call for salt, using salted butter adds more, and likely too much, salt.
- **Milk:** Choose whole or 2%.
- **Eggs:** All recipes assume large eggs.
- **Salt:** I use iodized table salt in the recipes here, but if you only have kosher salt, use about twice as much as the table salt measure calls for.
- **Flour:** As a general rule, use all-purpose unbleached white flour. Most but not all breads will call for bread flour, and gluten-free recipes specify which flours to use.
- **Sugar:** Refers to granulated white sugar. Any other sugar will be specified.
- **Brown sugar:** Either light or dark brown sugar will work in any of the recipes that call for it.
- **Onions:** Standard yellow onions have a standard onion flavor and are what I assume you would choose for the recipes here. If red onions are needed, the recipe will say so. But if you are cooking the onions, pretty much any onion you have on hand will work.
- **Vegetable oil:** My choice for a general cooking and baking oil is the neutrally flavored, healthier canola oil, which comes from a single source. Generic vegetable oils are generally blended from many sources and are less predictable in their stovetop heating behavior. If the recipe requires olive oil, it will say so.

Equipment I Love

There is a lot of kitchen gadgetry in this world, and much of it is narrowly focused and single-use. After decades of professional baking and cooking, I've acquired a few truly useful, versatile, or well-crafted products with multiple uses. An offset spatula, for example, will spread batter in a pan or refried beans over your burrito very nicely. Some equipment will make your life so much easier that you'll want to cook again and again, just to use it. I use my immersion blender to puree everything from soup to salsa without having much to clean up afterward, and with its whisk attachment, I can efficiently whip a single egg white. And some, like jumbo muffin pans, are necessary if you want to tackle sticky buns but will also open up other possibilities, such as individual crustless quiche for that bridal shower you are planning.

Sheet Pan vs. Cookie Sheet

A half-sheet pan—hereafter referred to as a "sheet pan"—measures 18 x 13 inches and is a perfect pan all around. (It's half the size of a professional, full-sized sheet pan, which is too large for home ovens.) It has about one-inch high shallow sides, allowing it to be used for baking shallow cake layers or stirring granola without making a mess. It is also ideal for sheet pan meals, an efficient and modern approach for cooking one-dish dinners.

Cookie sheets, by contrast, have one raised side for grasping, but the other sides are flat, allowing cookies to slide off. This feature is convenient for cookies but limits the pan's uses. Also, they tend to be less sturdy and poorer conductors of heat. I strongly prefer the more versatile sheet pan and refer to it throughout the recipes.

Jumbo Muffin Pan

All our muffin recipes are scaled for a home-sized muffin pan, which ends up being roughly one-third the size of the large Manna muffins. But the sticky buns do best in a jumbo muffin tin (the recipe is written for that size pan), and I encourage you to find one. You want a nonstick pan whose individual cups hold eight ounces. They come six or twelve cups to a pan, so if you get the smaller size, be sure to get two. I keep one 12-cup tin in my repertoire and appreciate its versatility.

Parchment Liner

Not to be confused with waxed paper, parchment paper pan liners are a cook's best friend. They protect your pan, minimize cleaning, and have a reliable nonstick surface for all sorts of cooking and baking. You can buy parchment in rolls, but it is best in flat sheets, which sit nicely on your pan without re-coil. You can cut them to fit any shape or size of pan, and in many situations, you can use them repeatedly.

Cast-Iron Griddle (and other cast iron cookware)

Cast iron is a seemingly old-fashioned cooking medium that reminds me of the expression, "They just don't make things like they used to." A well-seasoned cast-iron pan provides one of the best cooking surfaces I know. It distributes and maintains even heat beautifully, providing an excellent sear to meat or deep crispness to hash browns, as no other pan does. And cast iron is ideal for pancake making. Sure, it's heavy and requires a bit of love to keep the surface in tip-top cooking condition (e.g., using non-abrasive cleaning techniques, lightly heating and oiling the surface after washing), but it gives back so much.

Dedicated Nonstick Egg Pan

Nonstick cookware is pervasive in American households, yet it is often misunderstood. It is a fragile item requiring special care. Metal spatulas easily mar these pans, and abrasives and repeated dishwasher use can quickly ruin their pristine surfaces. Of course, even the best-cared-for pans will ultimately suffer from repeated exposure to high temperatures and the need to be washed, but they will last a long time with good care. If you cook eggs frequently, a dedicated nonstick pan will be a welcome addition to your equipment repertoire. After cooking, all you need to do is wipe it out with a damp dishcloth and hang it back up. Don't stack it, don't use soap or abrasives, and don't cook anything else in it.

Immersion Blender

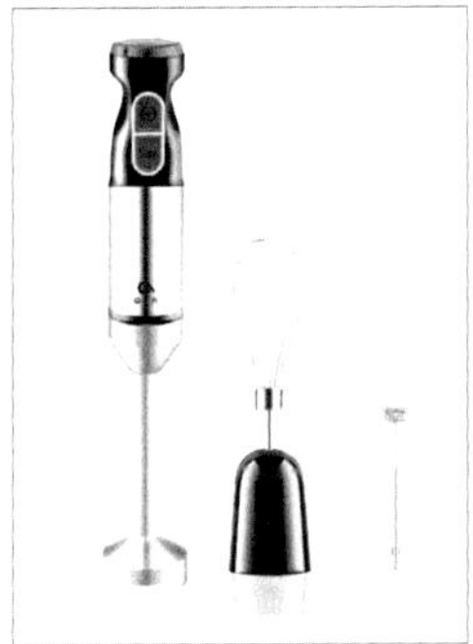

Manna had an immersion blender the size of a Great Dane, one so loud that cooks were instructed to use it only in the farthest depths of the kitchen, and only after calling out "loud noise" so as not to frighten people out of their wits! It was terrific at whirring up to 60 cups of creamy soup or a ginormous batch of House Dressing, but the ones made for home cooks are even better, if for no other reason than you can talk and whir at the same time. I do not usually drop names, but I love my Cuisinart immersion blender, with its array of useful attachments.

At its most basic, an immersion blender has a pureeing blade at the end of a handle, which can be directly inserted into bowls or pots, and does an efficient job of pureeing the contents in a short amount of time. You can just plug it in and puree away, saving the nuisance and mess of transferring sloppy hot soup to a blender and back again. My immersion blender also has a small food processor bowl and a whisk attachment. The tiny food processor works wonders for chopping up small quantities of things, like garlic cloves, nuts, or small-batch pestos. The whisk attachment is ideal for beating heavy cream or egg whites, and it does the work in no time! I cannot emphasize enough how this multi-purpose home tool will improve your cooking experience.

Scale

Measuring by weight is more accurate than by volume. For example, depending on how packed it is, one cup of flour may weigh more or less than another. But eight ounces of flour is always eight ounces of flour. Scales are inexpensive, and once you start using one in cooking, you will find yourself relying on it. A scale that measures up to five pounds is a good starting size.

High-Heat Spatula

This marvelous invention lets you cook over high heat on a stovetop without your spatula melting, burning, or otherwise losing its integrity. Its rubber composition lets it bend to the pan's contours, thus reaching every nook and cranny. Rubbermaid makes the best high-heat spatula I have found. It is rugged, and it will last a long time and get the job done. These spatulas come in varied sizes. We keep a couple of each size around at all times, including tiny ones that get the last splootch of mustard from a narrow-rimmed jar.

Offset Spatula

An offset spatula is a metal spatula. It comes in different lengths, and I recommend having one short and one long. You will find multiple uses for this handy spatula, the most important of which is spreading batter in a pan. It makes the task effortless and graceful.

Portioning Scoops

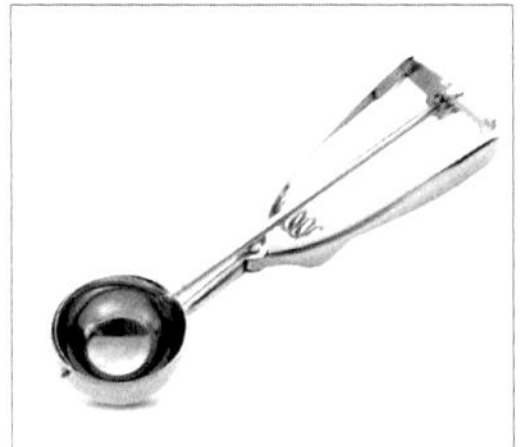

One of my pet peeves about recipes is how you are instructed to portion out the dough by "one heaping teaspoon," "a large scoop," "a walnut-sized ball." Phooey. Not only does everyone have a different sense of what each of these descriptions might mean, but the recipe yields may not be accurate.

I love using scoops and recommend owning a few. They come in many sizes, make portioning easy and relatively mess-free (the dough pops right out), and they provide consistency, giving your products a more uniform look.

Scoop size designations vary. My small scoop, good for cookies, has a 1 1/3-ounce capacity, the equivalent of three scant tablespoons. I suggest getting three sizes and then working with each to find your happy portion for whatever you are making—meatballs, scones, pancakes—by making your portions consistently round, scant, or perfectly flat with the scoop.

Bench Scrapers (aka Dough Cutters) and Bowl Scrapers (aka Dough Scrapers)

The terminology is confusing, but these two tools, while sharing some qualities, are distinct. Both serve useful purposes.

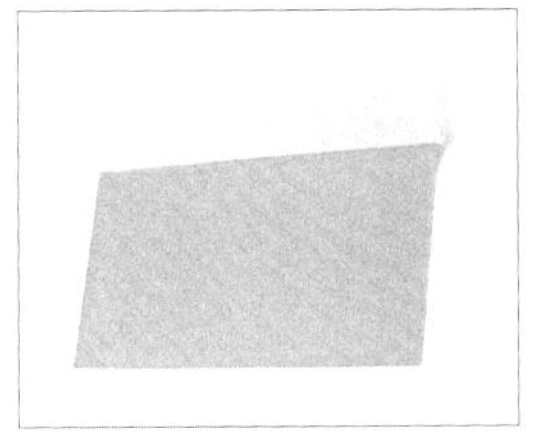

A bench scraper (aka dough cutter) is a sturdy rectangular metal scraping tool with a wooden or plastic handle. It is used in professional kitchens to portion bread dough (hence the term "dough cutter") but an even more important use is to scrape counters clean of grungy debris, thus saving you the added annoyance of sponges gummy with tiny dough blobs that just won't let go.

A bowl scraper (aka dough scraper), on the other hand, is a flexible plastic device about the same size as a bench scraper, with a beveled edge that cleans out rounded bowls nicely. It curves with the bowl as you use it, also helping to avoid the sponge grunge. (If you attend a restaurant show, you can get these by the handful for free!)

Safety Grater

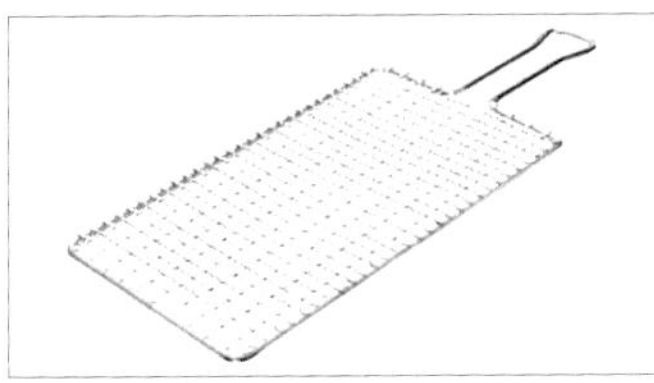

I don't know why more people don't know about this simple, unassuming kitchen contraption. We had one handed down from our family. When it broke, and I needed a new one, I did not even know what to call it. It took hours of searching until I finally located one (and then I bought six)!

A safety grater is a rectangular metal frame, about 3 x 6 inches, with a handle at one end. It holds a wire grillwork with little square holes. My favorite use for it is coarsely chopping soft foods with ease, like hard-boiled eggs and avocados for guacamole, to name a couple. It also acts as a good screen for straining.

Microplane

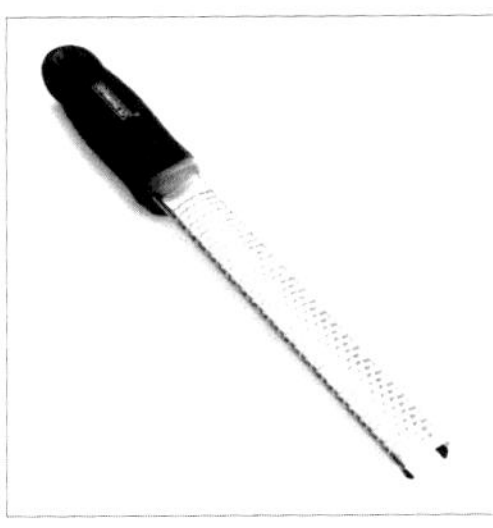

This versatile tool is like a long knife whose blade has been replaced by a skinny grater with tiny holes. It makes easy work of zesting limes, finely grating Parmesan cheese, mincing garlic and ginger, and otherwise providing a finely grated ingredient that no other tool can replicate.

A Key to Recipe Timing/Effort

I am not a huge fan of specifying how long each recipe will take because time is rather elastic, and each cook approaches each task differently. Nonetheless, it is handy to know what you are up against, so I offer the following guidelines:

Start to finish in less than a half hour

Start to finish within an hour, give or take

Hands-on time less than an hour (additional cooking or chilling times involved—read through before beginning)

Project Alert! May require multiple stages or overnight preparations—read through before proceeding

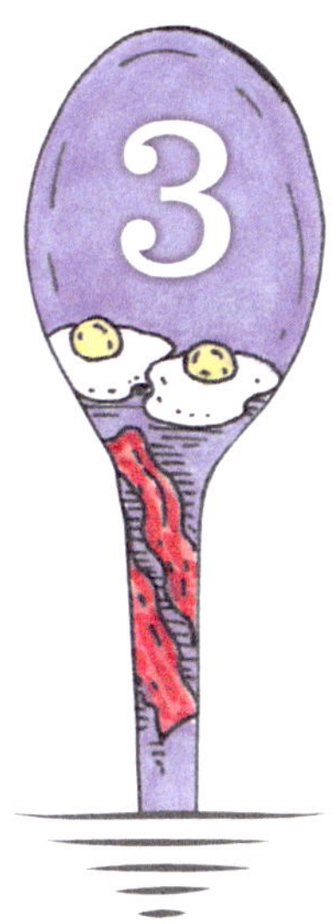

Breakfast/Brunch

On the weekends, Manna felt like a destination vacation, where crowds of happy people gathered in the best of weekend social spirits. Customers came to celebrate or just meet up, and the place pulsed with a vibrant energy. For many, brunch was a special occasion—the indulgent finale to the workweek and a time reserved for living it up a bit. Thus, our weekend brunch menu—an elevated and lengthier version of our regular weekday breakfast menu—was designed to underscore the special place that "brunch" has in our hearts. We added Eggs Benedict, Potato Nachos, Lemon Love Pancakes, even Bialys, thus giving the weekends a more distinct character.

At 7:30 a.m. on Saturday and Sunday, the official brunch starting time, tickets were already backlogged on the kitchen line. Within the hour, both the kitchen and front-of-house (FOH) were staffed with seven people each and our well-oiled system kicked into high gear. The adrenaline floated us through to the end of service at 2 p.m. when we all, as if hearing a timer, came to a hungry and exhausted halt. We were tired, hot, grumpy maybe, but supremely proud of accomplishing another busy service. Nearly every customer made a change to the menu description, and keeping it all straight, accurate, and on time felt akin to a Cirque du Soleil performance. To the audience it looked easy, but to the performers it was a precarious balance.

Saturdays and Sundays were festive for FOH staff despite the waits, the crowds, and the frenetic pace. The moment we unlocked the door, the cafe began to fill with people who had been sitting in their cars waiting for this moment. At first, the pressure was on the barista, and soon there was a rhythm to the clamor of steaming milk and grinding coffee, as the first stage of Manna's day was set in motion. From here, the day crescendoed into a well-choreographed dance, with orders printing to the kitchen, bakery tucked into bags or boxes, drink orders shouted out, and plates of food sailing to tables balanced precariously on arms. The phone rang, the timers clanged, and every staff member knew exactly where to be at any given minute. It was pretty to watch if you knew what you were looking for.

In the kitchen, a 10-burner stove was filled from end to end, front to back, with pots and pans, and a line of cooks shuffled them rapidly about, sweating from the constant glow of burner flames and oven heat. The stove was flanked on either side by two grills, and hovering over it all was the red-hot salamander, or broiler, where many a dish was finished with crisp edges or a molten topping. And everywhere, on counters and in cold stations, was a surround-sound array of ingredients and building blocks within reach. Expediters, maestro-like, orchestrated the timely production and pinpoint timing of the brunch dishes. They knew how long it took to poach an egg to medium soft relative to how long it took for French toast to fully cook through, along with 25 other things simultaneously. Expediting a weekend brunch was not for the faint of heart! Bathroom breaks were carefully timed in between pans of eggs, and lucky was the cook who could slip in a quick smoke. While the dining room hummed with chatter and laughter, the kitchen ramped up to machine mode, turning out dish after dish in rapid-fire style, never looking up, never breathing, it seemed, for six straight hours of intensity. (And yet, for machines, they sure laughed a lot!)

For customers, there was a certain exuberance in coming, not just for the food but the scene. Scrums of millennials gathered in groups of seven or ten or fifteen to yak for hours. Families arrived bearing packages in a rainbow of colors to celebrate birthdays or a passed bar exam. These larger groups were oblivious to their surroundings, absorbed in their own camaraderie. Yet they were balanced out by the many parties of two or three who marveled at the hubbub while sipping mochas, hoping their food would be delivered next. A parade of onesies and twosomes stood patiently (or sometimes less patiently) in line to grab a coffee and a pastry and then make their quick escape, meanwhile schmoozing with staff or friends they'd bumped into. Any remaining space was filled by people waiting for a table, enjoying a latte and muffin "hors d'oeuvre."

At the confluence of all this vibrant activity, of course, was the food. It's what brought us all together and gave us a common language. It was the gently warmed sticky bun, or a steaming maple butter latte, aswirl with a foamy barista valentine. It was glistening eggs and lustrous hollandaise, a generous wedge of quiche whose filling oozed plate-ward. It was the extra order of golden oatcakes in the center of the table for everyone to share, because even though there was more food than anyone could eat, you could not not have the oatcakes. And it was whatever they were having at the next table—which you would order next time. The food connected people to people, making them one.

Here, then, are the breakfast/brunch recipes. I hope they warm your weekend gatherings and bring you a delicious plate of nostalgia.

Scrambled Eggs

I have a pocket full of heroes and heroines who comprise my collection of role models, and Julia Child—smart, funny, larger than life—is at the top of the heap. It all began one morning back in The Collins House years, when I randomly cracked open one of her books to the chapter on scrambled eggs. I had never much cared for scrambled eggs, so dry and unremarkable, but here I found that it needn't be so. Perfect scrambled eggs are creamy, custardy, fully cooked curds without a wisp of dryness. The texture tricks you into thinking they are richer than an egg alone, but they are just that—a humble egg coaxed into its most luxurious form.

Once Manna began serving breakfast, scrambled eggs became my obsession. Every egg cook went through a little Barb demonstration, watching me cook and then tasting the final results. I would undercook, overcook, and properly cook the eggs in two sets, one with no salt and one with salt added. The cooks first tasted mouthfuls of "regular" eggs, and then a mouthful of eggs made the "Julia" (and thus "Barb") way. I would watch with anticipation for the telltale gleam of delight in their eyes and the knowing nod as they experienced their moment of epiphany. Julia eggs make people happy, and helping people learn how to make these eggs is my all-time favorite cooking activity. It is like teaching a child to ride a bike, watching them discover a new skill that will empower them and bring joy for a lifetime.

For years, I had my little training session with every new cook. Then Carrie, the kitchen manager, cultivated their skills until they were ready to cook for customers. Carrie held the bar high and relentlessly rejected scrambles that even I might let pass on a busy day with a 45-minute wait for food. She turned my passion into a system, making scrambled eggs one of Manna's prized dishes. Mastering the Julia scramble was a badge of honor.

Anyone can do the same with a little patience. And once you master an excellent dish of eggs, they become a palette for creative brunch recipes. A few of our favorites are included here, but have fun with your own ideas. This is a slow-cook process and, done right, yields scrambled egg bliss. Your goal is eggs that have medium-sized, creamy curds with no dryness or sponginess. They will be rich and heavenly. Expect the cooking to take from five to eight minutes.

LIFE-ALTERING LOW-AND-SLOW SCRAMBLED EGGS

Makes 4 servings

 Start to finish in less than a half hour

This technique uses a lot of words, but it is not difficult at all—you'll catch on after a couple of run-throughs and from then on will never need to consult the recipe again.

A serving size for scrambled eggs can be two or three eggs, depending on your appetite. (At Manna, we used three eggs per person.) If you are cooking for yourself, use your smallest sauté pan (about 6 inches is good). If you are cooking for a crowd, use a big one. Adjust the salt and butter accordingly.

While cheese is an optional ingredient in basic scrambled eggs, most of Manna's scrambles incorporated it. For more elaborate additional variations, check out the recipes on the following pages.

A final note: Scrambled eggs turn out their Sunday best if they are cooked alone in the pan. If you add eggs to a pan full of other items, you will get a fine plate of food, but the eggs will interact with the other ingredients in a way that will detract from their ability to finish their proper cooking in peace. As with the cheese, I mostly prefer to add other ingredients toward the end of the cooking. So sauté your onions and asparagus (or whatever) in a separate pan, and stir them in at the end with the cheese. Bon appetit!

---

8 eggs

1/4 teaspoon salt

1 tablespoon butter

1/2 to 3/4 cup grated cheese of your choice (optional)

---

1. Beat the eggs and salt together well, leaving no white showing. Heat an 8-inch sauté pan over medium-low heat for 3 minutes. Add butter to the pan. It should lightly sizzle and foam. Swirl the pan to coat the bottom and sides with the butter. Add eggs to the pan and reduce the heat to low.
2. As soon as the eggs show the first hint of beginning to cook, stir them with a heat-resistant rubber spatula by scraping the spatula across the bottom of the pan and folding the thin layer of cooked egg into the remaining wet egg. In the beginning, this will just be occasionally, but the cooking will quickly crescendo, and you will stir and fold with increasing frequency. The goal is to mix cooked eggs with not-yet-cooked eggs so they stay moist and creamy and the developing curds or clumps do not dry out. Every 5 to 10

seconds, fold newly cooked eggs upward from the bottom of the pan. Toward the end of cooking, stir almost constantly. This last stage goes very quickly. If you stir too often, your curds will be tiny and dainty, but if you do not stir often enough, the eggs will overcook rather than become custardy. Do not be tempted to turn your heat up, though.

3. Just before the eggs are done, there will be a bit of uncooked wetness around the formed curds. If you want to add cheese to your eggs, do so now. By stirring cheese in just before the eggs are finished, you get distinct rivulets of melty goodness. If you stir in cheese too early, it blends with the fabric of the egg, becoming less noticeable both in flavor and appearance. Once you add the cheese, stir constantly. In about 10 seconds or less, the last bit of raw eggs will finish cooking. Immediately remove them from the pan to a plate, lest they continue to cook in the heat of the pan. Perfect scrambled eggs will look creamy and glossy, like a thick chocolate glaze that is no longer viscous but has not yet fully dried. If the eggs are mostly done but still have some wet, runny areas, they are not quite there. Admittedly, it is a fine line and perhaps the most challenging moment to master.

CREAMY TOMATO BASIL SCRAMBLE WITH BACON AND PARMESAN ("THE PARM")

Makes 4 generous servings

 Start to finish within an hour, give or take

This is perhaps my favorite egg creation, which I especially enjoy making on a summer morning, when my backyard vegetable garden is begging to be harvested. Scrambled eggs are topped with a sauce of fresh tomatoes, basil and cream. Crunchy bits of bacon and Parmesan gratings adorn the top. The plate is vibrant with orange, yellow, and a splash of green. It is a jamboree for the senses.

Though basil is in the recipe title, you can substitute any fresh herb you love. Also, depending on how generous you are with the sauce, there will likely be leftovers. It freezes well for a rainy day.

Tomato Basil Sauce

1 tablespoon butter

1 small onion (about 4 ounces), finely chopped

2 large fresh market tomatoes (about 1 pound), diced to 3/4 inch

2 tablespoons sherry or brandy

1/2 cup heavy cream

1/4 cup gently packed fresh basil, cut into a chiffonade (small, very thin juliennes)

Salt and pepper to taste

For the Eggs

8 eggs beaten, with 1/4 teaspoon salt

1/2 cup or so excellent quality, finely grated Parmesan cheese, divided

8 strips crisp-cooked bacon, crumbled

Optional (but encouraged) garnish:

4 basil leaves

8 heirloom cherry tomatoes, halved

---

1. Heat a medium sauté pan over medium heat. When hot, add butter and let it melt, then add onions and sauté for about 10 minutes until golden brown. Add tomatoes, turn up the heat and cook, stirring occasionally, until most of the moisture is gone.
2. Add sherry or brandy and let simmer a few minutes to cook out the alcohol. Add cream and simmer for about 5 to 7 minutes until the cream is reduced by half and the mixture has thickened. Remove from heat and stir in basil and seasonings to taste.
3. Prepare the Scrambled Eggs (pages 88-89). Just before the eggs are done, stir in about 1/4 cup of the Parmesan cheese.
4. To serve, spoon tomato topping decoratively over the eggs (allow 1/4 to 1/3 cup per serving). Top with crumbled bacon and shower with more Parmesan. Garnish with whole basil leaves and cherry tomatoes halves, if desired.

WISCONSIN WILD RICE SCRAMBLE

Makes 4 servings

 Hands-on time less than an hour (additional cooking or chilling times involved—read through before beginning)

The Ojibwe, or Chippewa, people have long resided in the northernmost parts of the Midwest, Wisconsin included, and Canada. They referred to themselves as Anishinaabe, meaning "original person." This dish is a nod to people native to our state and some of the ingredients they harvested, which, in addition to wild rice and mushrooms, included cranberries, bison, corn, beans, squash, maple syrup, and more.

This scramble, adapted from a recipe found in a Native Peoples magazine, became an instant Collins House favorite and later a Manna staple. It is earthy and satisfying, one of our few eggy menu items without cheese. Shiitake mushrooms are not native to Wisconsin's Northwoods, but I like their pronounced flavor and creamy consistency. You could substitute any mushrooms, including ones that you yourself have foraged. Fresh corn off the cob would be a classy addition.

At the core of this recipe is a mix of wild rice, scallions, and sautéed mushrooms, which freezes well and is therefore convenient to make in larger batches. For each serving you will use 1/2 cup of the wild rice mix, 1/4 of the scrambled eggs, and some freshly cooked bacon. The eggs in this dish need not be scrambled perfectly, as described in the scrambled egg recipe. The abundance of wild rice in the concoction is the focus of this dish. The wild rice mix can be eaten as is, without adding eggs, and also works well as a frittata filling (page 97).

Wild Rice Mix

1/2 cup wild rice (not a blend)

1 1/4 cups water

1/4 teaspoon salt

4 ounces shiitake mushrooms, de-stemmed and sliced

1/2 tablespoon butter

2 scallions, thinly sliced

To Finish the Dish

1 tablespoon butter

8 eggs beaten with 1/4 teaspoon salt

1/2 pound bacon, diced, cooked until crisp, and drained

---

1. Place wild rice in a pot with the water and salt, and bring to a boil. Cover, reduce heat to its lowest setting, and time for 1 hour. Turn off heat and drain out extra water, if any. Let cool.

2. Sauté the mushrooms in 1/2 tablespoon butter until tender, and all liquid has cooked off. Add mushrooms and scallions to the cooked wild rice and mix well. This mix can be used immediately or frozen for future use.

3. For the final preparation, heat a large sauté pan over medium heat. When hot, add 1 tablespoon butter. When the butter is melted, add the wild rice mixture to the pan and stir-fry for 1 minute to heat ingredients through. Pour eggs into the pan and cook, stirring often. Do not overcook the eggs or let them get hard. Stir in the bacon at the very end, and serve immediately.

SPINACH SWIRL SCRAMBLE

Makes 4 servings

 Start to finish in less than a half hour

Each time we wanted to update old menus, we walked a precarious tightrope. There was a balance between safe old standbys that customers would not let go of and sexy new entrees that perked their imaginations. You couldn't please everyone.

The Spinach Swirl Scramble had graced our menus long enough (we thought), and many new entrees were out there awaiting their turn. But when we dropped it from our printed menus, we were met with such an outcry that we had to resort to our secret solution. We included it on our computer system, referring to it as our "Secret Santa" button, so that when people asked if we could still make this for them, we said, "Of course!" And meanwhile, precious real estate on our printed menus was given over to other items.

The Spinach Swirl Scramble was one of our simplest yet most requested recipes. My father used to turn up his nose at recipes whose ingredient list was too long, not because he was lazy, but because he was philosophically against the idea that "bigger is better." Maybe he was right.

---

1 tablespoon butter

2 tablespoons Caramelized Onions (pages 156-157)

1 cup packed fresh spinach, stems removed, leaves finely julienned

8 eggs beaten with 1/4 teaspoon salt

1 cup grated pepper Jack cheese

---

1. In an 8-inch sauté pan, melt 1 tablespoon butter over medium-low heat. Add in caramelized onions and break them up with a rubber spatula to distribute them around the pan. Add spinach to the pan and cook, stirring constantly, until it has wilted.

2. Add beaten eggs to the pan, reduce heat to low and cook per the technique described on pages 88-89. Just before the eggs are done, stir in the cheese. Remove from heat and serve.

GRANDPA AL'S SCRAMBLE

Makes 4 generous servings

Start to finish in less than a half hour

The proud grandpa pictured here—Mike's father, Josh's "Grandpa Al" and Pratzel's Bakery delivery man into his 90s—loved breakfast (Denny's was a favorite). He lived the St. Louis Jewish life, eating lox on Pratzel's bagels, catering bar mitzvahs and weddings with a glorious array of sweets (including their famous mini cupcakes), and kibitzing with his old codger buddies. We created this scramble in his honor.

Bagels, or if you have been ambitious, Bialys (page 314) or Corn Tzizel Rye (page 312), make the ideal toast.

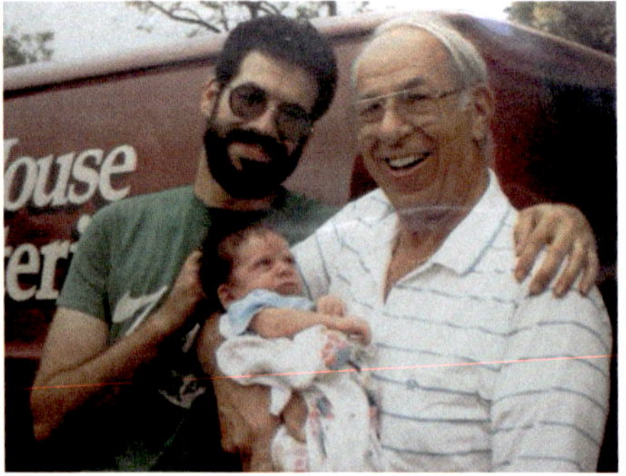

Three generations of Pratzel's. Grandpa Al, Mike and Josh.

---

1 tablespoon butter, plus another 1 tablespoon for the eggs

1/2 cup diced onions

2 ounces excellent Nova lox, cut in thin strips

8 eggs beaten with 1/4 teaspoon salt

2 ounces cream cheese (1/4 package), softened and cut into 1/2-inch bits

1 tablespoon minced fresh dill

Whole dill sprigs for garnish

---

1. In a small sauté pan, melt 1 tablespoon of the butter over medium heat. Add onions and cook, stirring, until they begin to turn golden brown and translucent, about 8 minutes. Lower the heat a bit if necessary. When the onions are done, turn off the heat and add the lox to the pan to gently warm it.
2. Slow-scramble the eggs following the directions on pages 88-89. Just before the eggs are done, scatter the cream cheese blobs over the eggs and stir in, letting them melt. Remove the pan from the heat and stir in onions, lox, and minced dill. Serve garnished with sprigs of fresh dill.

"THE IKE" SCRAMBLE

Makes 4 servings

 Start to finish in less than a half hour

A boy and his kitchen.

Ike was 13 years old when Manna opened. He did a stint as a griddle cook in the kitchen. For a time, he even did the expediting. And let me tell you, there is nothing more gratifying for a 13-year-old boy than to be one of the guys in a testosterone-driven kitchen! He was good at it, but when he looks back on that time now, he shakes his head in disbelief that he had ever managed the ticket orders after we had transformed into a crazy-busy brunch place. Ironically, Ike was a capable restaurant cook, but at home, his idea of cooking was Hot Pockets with a side of cottage cheese.

Ike created this scramble, which would be a fitting centerpiece at a St. Patty's Day breakfast. He was extremely particular about the details, especially the 1/4-inch dice size, which was meant to provide a confetti-like appearance in the eggs. When he returned to Manna during his college years, Ike would complain about how the dice size had crept upwards. "They're not the same," he'd whine. Kids! (Below, finely diced refers to 1/4 inch or smaller.)

---

1 1/4 cups finely diced red potatoes

1 tablespoon vegetable oil

Salt and pepper

3 ounces corned beef (about 3/4 cup), fat trimmed off, finely diced

1/2 cup finely diced sweet red pepper

2 scallions, trimmed, thinly sliced

2 tablespoons butter, divided

8 eggs beaten with 1/4 teaspoon salt

1 1/2 cups grated pepper Jack cheese

---

1. Preheat the oven to 425 degrees. Toss potatoes in the vegetable oil and season lightly with salt and pepper. Place potatoes in an 8 x 8-inch baking pan lined with aluminum foil and roast for about 10 minutes, until cooked through and golden and crisp around the edges. Let cool.
2. In a large sauté pan, melt 1 tablespoon butter over medium heat, and sauté red pepper until softened. Add in potatoes, corned beef, and scallions and sauté together briefly. Set aside.
3. In a separate pan, cook the eggs using the technique described on pages 88-89. Just before the eggs are done, stir in cheese, then the corned beef mix. Remove from heat, and serve.

Frittata Wars

Frittatas are a big, bold, open-faced omelet whose filling is worked into the eggs as they cook. Topped with cheese and finished in the broiler, they emerge with crisp brown edges and a melty, bubbly center. They fill up a whole plate and thus provide a bit of drama when delivered to hungry diners.

For many years running, Manna featured a special frittata for weekend brunches. Part of the fun was the friendly, competitive creation of these specials by two unlikely buddies, Carlos and Michael. Carlos was a soft-spoken, gentle man who had a strong work ethic and did his job with excellence. Michael shared his values and lived up to the Carlos standard, but in a way that was, shall we say, more talkative. Michael had something to say about everything. Where Carlos showed his frustrations with subtle body language, Michael nattered on to anyone within earshot. They both had great respect for one another, and their opposite energies and ideas stoked a friendly frittata feud for which our customers were an unknowing focus group.

Each week, Michael and Carlos took turns creating the weekend special, and each week we looked up the day's sales to confirm which frittata sold best. The reward for this showdown was bragging rights for these two passionate cooks and customers always on the lookout for the next best creation.

Frittatas are all about the technique, which is described in the recipe that follows. I've also offered a number of the weekend specials, just to give you some ideas.

Far left, Michael. Far right, Carlos. Carrie and Sean.

FESTIVAL ITALIAN SAUSAGE FRITTATA

Makes 1 personal-size frittata

 Start to finish in less than a half hour

This frittata was a regular on our menus, rather than one of the many weekend special varieties, but it gives you the technique for creating any frittata in the Manna way. Named for the aromatic, street vendor-style sandwich dripping with fried peppers and onions, it summons to mind summer strolls through the Art Fair on the Square. Steel drums pulse from the side streets, the sun is hot, the beer is icy cold, and this sandwich has caught your attention.

As a frittata, the classic sandwich becomes something a bit more genteel—easier to eat and easier on the laundry. You can double or triple the recipe if you like, using a larger pan, then cut the finished frittata into wedges for serving.

---

1 tablespoon olive oil

1/3 cup cooked Italian sausage (either links halved and sliced 1/4-inch thick or crumbled bulk sausage)

1/3 cup sliced onion

1/3 cup sliced sweet red pepper

A tiny pinch of dried red pepper flakes

3 eggs beaten with a generous pinch of salt

1/3 cup grated Monterey Jack cheese

2 tablespoons grated Parmesan cheese

---

1. Turn on a broiler to have ready for use. Adjust the oven rack to be close to the top.
2. Add olive oil to a 6-inch nonstick skillet, and heat over medium heat. Add onions and peppers to the pan and sauté, stirring often until vegetables are soft and beginning to brown. Add cooked sausage to the pan along with red pepper flakes and cook to heat through.
3. Add eggs to the pan and turn the heat down to medium-low. Continue to cook, stirring with a spatula, as you would for scrambled eggs. When the eggs are about 3/4 of the way cooked, use a spatula to flatten them on top and against the sides of the pan.
4. Poke divots into the eggs at intervals, where the cheese will puddle into little pockets. Sprinkle the two cheeses lightly over the eggs.
5. Place the pan into the broiler (keep the handle facing out) and let the cheese melt until bubbly and beginning to brown. The edges of the frittata may become a little crisp as well.
6. Slide frittata onto a plate and serve.

Frittata Wars Favorites

At Manna, the frittata fillings tended to revolve around holidays or special events. For Father's Day, we might do something meaty and hearty. On New Year's Eve, special ingredients like shrimp and shiitakes might make an appearance. And for Bastille Day, a fine ham with brie and summer herbs seemed appropriate. Here are a few frittata combos from the Manna memory lane using the techniques on page 97.

- **Ground Hog's Day:** braised pork shoulder, roasted poblano peppers, sautéed yellow onion, garlic-roasted cherry tomatoes, and habanero cheddar cheese
- **Carlos's Country:** chorizo sausage, black beans, potatoes, roasted poblano peppers, and Monterey Jack cheese
- **Butternut Fall Behind (for Daylight Savings Time):** roasted butternut squash, mushrooms, leeks, bacon, and Havarti cheese
- **Lumberjack:** sliced beef sirloin, bacon, potatoes, red onion, sweet red pepper, and cheddar cheese
- **Go Pack Go Tailgate:** beer-cooked brats, roasted potatoes, caramelized cabbage, scallions, and plenty of cheese curds dotted about
- **My Big Fat Greek Frittata:** sausage, mushrooms, roasted red peppers, artichoke quarters, and feta cheese
- **Sacré Bleu!:** bacon, arugula, caramelized onions, and blue cheese
- **Market Basket:** sautéed portabella mushrooms, roasted asparagus and brie cheese, topped with a mound of Frizzled Onions (page 365)
- **Loaded Baked Frittata:** ham, bacon, pan-fried potatoes, and scallions with pepper Jack and cheddar cheeses, topped with sour cream and a sprinkling of chives

Bennies from Heaven

Certain foods and the traditions connected to them help us feel connected, defined, and included. They help establish our identities. Corned beef and cabbage brings to mind the gaiety and greenness of St. Patty's Day. A glittery red box of chocolates in their tiny paper cups says it is Valentine's Day. And all over Wisconsin, Sunday afternoons revolve around mustard-slathered brats, red plastic cups sloshing with amber beer, and cheery fans wearing layers of flannel. If the Packers are up at halftime, life is good. This ritual fall activity and its specific foods and beverages help define us as Wisconsinites, filling us with a certain unarticulated state pride which we enthusiastically—some might say rowdily—share with our friends and family.

I would argue that Eggs Benedict belongs right up there with corned beef or bratwurst as an iconic food defining a moment. It evokes the feeling of gathering around a perfectly appointed table with our friends for Sunday brunch. We eat eggs or pancakes or a bowl of granola for breakfast all the time, but Sunday brunch is noteworthy, whether it is a regular, mundane Sunday repast or a one-time clinking of glasses event. Perhaps it relates to its place at the end of the weekend. The parties have ended, the workweek lies ahead, and here is a chance to have a special social moment with friends and family before life's inevitable rhythms return. Eggs Benedict is too rich and decadent to have every day, and their preparation and presentation make a statement: pamper yourself!

In its purest form, Eggs Benedict, or Benny, consists of a toasted English muffin topped with ham and a poached egg and bathed in a golden hollandaise sauce. The ingredients are mostly simple. Still, the hollandaise requires a bit of work and timing, and the eggs need to be finessed to the perfect doneness. Like a great burger, the quintessential American sandwich, what makes it tick is the quality of the parts. At Manna, we strove for perfection (always unreachable, of course) by choosing each part thoughtfully and then keeping the bar high.

The Benny Formula from top to bottom:

Hollandaise

Poached Egg

The Stuff In Between

The (Usually) Bread Base

The Garnish

The hollandaise: There is no substitute for a genuine hollandaise. It requires butter, lots of it, and egg yolks, lots of them. Perhaps you hoped to pretend otherwise, but you'll find out soon enough.

When we wanted to theme a Benny in a particular direction, we sometimes added ingredients to the basic hollandaise. For example, in the Southwestern Veggie Benny, we added a special, spicy chile-based concoction to each serving. The important thing is to create a sauce that drapes luxuriously over the eggs and whose slight tang is a counterpoint to the subtle egg flavor.

The poached egg: In my book, it must be poached to be a Benny, and the technique on page 102 helps you achieve the perfect degree of poached-ness. Choose an extra-large or jumbo egg to maximize the effect of domed yolk aglow in hollandaise.

The stuff in between: Here is where you open yourself up to possibilities and the opportunity to choose a special name for your creation. Sauté ham, peppers, and onions, and you have a Denver Benny. Top your base with some bacon and a ladleful of baked beans, and presto! You have a Blazing Saddles Benny. As you will see, the Manna varieties are a festive parade of The Stuff in Between.

The (usually) bread base: You might think the correct base here is an English muffin, and you are half right. It is part of the classic Benny definition. A purist might argue that a Benny made with anything but an English muffin is taboo, and it's fine if you buy into this premise. While many of our Bennies were indeed created with English muffins, we branched out conceptually, using a cornmeal muffin as the basis for our Southwestern Veggie Benny and potato latkes for a special Hanukkah Benny (even matzo, when the situation required it).

For much of Manna's life, we used the only good brand of English muffins on my radar. Thomas's English muffins are soft, moist, and a bit chewy. Their insides are speckled with numerous nooks and crannies to cradle butter, honey, or extra flowing hollandaise sauce. There is a *je ne sais quoi* quality about them that sets them apart from all others. For a time, Manna's bakers provided us with a delicious, house-made English muffin for the Bennies, one of the more labor-intensive projects we adopted, but the rest of the time, it was Thomas's. While it is not generally in my nature to play up store-bought products for an authentic home-cooking experience, this is one exception.

The garnish: A Benny is incomplete without its garnish, and we are not talking about a parsley sprig. The garnish should complement the In-Betweens in flavor, color, or theme. The Classic Benny is typically garnished with long, pretty spears of green asparagus, their bright colors and contrasting shapes visually balancing the plate. In fact, green is a common theme. Avocado slices, or even the drab green caper, pop against the whites and yellows of the egg and its sauce.

Benny's from Heaven

One of my recipe testers, Mark, always themed background music to his recipe testing and gave me a full report with each review. Thus, I selected him as one of my Eggs Benedict testers specifically to connect him with Harmonious Wail, a local Madison gypsy jazz group, and Maggie Delaney-Potthoff's warm-hearted rendition of an Eddie Jefferson song "Benny's from Heaven"—a clever parody on the familiar "Pennies from Heaven."

I love this song. It makes me cry whenever I listen to it (perhaps in part because it connects me to my father and our shared joy of associating the cadences of a song with wordplay in everyday language). When I latched onto the "Benny" connection, I could not hear it any other way.

Listen to the song some time on YouTube and perhaps play it the first time you make heaven-sent Bennies, reflecting on how food and music both tug at our heartstrings in the most mysterious of fashions. And in that tiny-thread sort of way, you can reconnect briefly to Manna (or to me)!

I always wanted a reason to hire Harmonious Wail for an occasion. Sharing this connection with you helps.

POACHED EGGS YOUR WAY

Makes 8 poached eggs, enough for 4 Bennies

 Start to finish in less than a half hour

Poached eggs are a wonderful thing, and not just on Bennies. The delicate, gently cooked white encapsulates the molten yolk inside. Nature's sauce! Once you're comfortable with the technique, poached eggs are great for elevating salads or even adding to a bowl of soup.

A low, wide pan is better than a deep pot for egg poaching. You can hold your hands close to the water for a gentle drop, and a larger pan also keeps the eggs better separated from one another. If you are only poaching two or four eggs, use a smaller pan.

The two challenges in poaching eggs are getting the right degree of doneness for your liking and making them look pretty. Here are the steps.

---

8 eggs, at room temperature

2 teaspoons vinegar*

1 teaspoon kosher salt

---

1. Fill a 12-inch wide, high-rimmed pan 2/3 full of water and bring to a low boil (just over a simmer, just under a full boil) over high heat. Add vinegar and salt to the water. If you do not have a large pan, you will have to poach the eggs in two batches. Too many eggs in the pan at once will drop the water temperature significantly, and the cooking times listed below may vary.
2. Crack each egg with a quick, firm rap, and then hold it close to the water. Using both hands, open the shell slowly to control how quickly the egg enters the water. Be gentle as it drops. Repeat with all the eggs.
3. Set a timer for the degree of doneness you like: 2-3 minutes for easy, 4 minutes for medium, 5 minutes for hard. Use these times as guidelines since the number of eggs in the water, and their actual size, may impact the cooking time. It's more important to know how the egg feels when properly cooked, rather than relying strictly on time. For the easy eggs, be sure the whites are completely cooked, but the yolk is still squishy. Medium eggs will have less jiggle, and hard eggs will not jiggle at all.
4. Gently remove the eggs one at a time with a slotted spoon, each time blotting the bottom of the spoon on a paper towel to wick away extra water from the egg.

*The vinegar will not flavor the eggs. Its purpose is to improve the solidifying of the whites.

HOLLANDAISE SAUCE

Makes about 1 2/3 cups, which is ample for at least 4 servings of Bennies

 Start to finish in less than a half hour

We sold extra hollandaise sauce by the tiny blue bowlful to people who could just not get enough. It was used for dipping potatoes, pouring over omelets, even for doubling down on the eggs Benedict, when our generous ladlefuls were not enough. We might have dubbed it liquid gold if that name was not already claimed by Mikey's Liquid Gold Schmaltz (pages 338-339)!

This recipe is vaguely modeled on Julia Child's classic version. Follow the technique with diligence. The butter must be brought to boiling, and you must add it slowly. If you choose to substitute fresh dill for the tarragon (or maybe add a splootch of sriracha), be our guests!

---

4 egg yolks, at room temperature

12 ounces (3 sticks) unsalted butter (no substitutions)

2 teaspoons white wine vinegar

2 teaspoons lemon juice, at room temperature

1/4 teaspoon salt

1/4 teaspoon white pepper

1/8 teaspoon cayenne pepper

1 tablespoon chopped fresh tarragon

---

1. Place egg yolks in the bowl of a food processor with the steel blade attachment. Process the yolks for about 2 to 3 minutes until they are thickened and light in color.
2. Melt butter in a microwave until just boiling (this is crucial to achieving a thick hollandaise). Immediately, and with the food processor running, slowly pour about half the butter into the yolks in a thin stream. Turn off the processor and add the remaining ingredients to the mixture. Turn the processor back on and add the remaining butter, again slowly and in a thin stream. (If the sauce is thin and runny, your butter was probably not hot enough.)
3. Ideally, use the sauce right away. If not, place hollandaise in a small metal bowl and set the bowl atop some hot (not boiling) water in another, larger bowl. The hollandaise needs to stay warm until used, but the egg yolk may set if it is too warm.

CLASSIC EGGS BENEDICT

Makes 4 Bennies

 Project Alert! May require multiple stages or overnight preparations—read through before proceeding

Assemble the Benny described in this recipe, and you have the classic, namesake version. Make a small change, like substituting bacon for ham, and it is still a Benny but no longer classic. How far can you stray from the original and still call it eggs Benedict? Pretty far, it seems, if you Google the variations. Apparently, you can pour some hollandaise on a quiche and call it a quiche Benedict. Or make deviled eggs, drizzle them with hollandaise, and call them deviled eggs Benedict.

Well, pish posh! Do as you will and call it a Benny, but here is where I draw the line: a poached egg must be involved, and it must be draped in hollandaise. After that, name it what you want and consider it a variation of the classic. Some of the Manna variations are described in the next pages.

A fully assembled, ready-to-eat eggs Benedict is a simple recipe in multiple parts. Each part is easy, but pulling it all together requires timing, and you will most likely welcome a second pair of hands (i.e., necessary). If you have a crowd for breakfast, ply them with mimosas and let them know you will bring out the Bennies as they are finished.

Since timing is so important, assemble and organize as many parts as possible before you begin. Read the steps closely beforehand, and think it through. Then, ready-set-cook!

For the Asparagus Garnish

12 spears of asparagus, ends trimmed

1 large clove of garlic, minced

1 tablespoon olive oil

1 small pinch of salt

For the Benny Parts, to Have at the Ready

4 Thomas's English Muffins

Softened butter

About 8 ounces thinly sliced ham (preferably from the bone), or Canadian bacon slices

8 eggs at room temperature

1 recipe Hollandaise Sauce (page 103), parts ready for last-minute assembly

Paprika (optional)

Advanced Preparation

1. For the asparagus: Heat a medium sauté pan over medium-high heat. Toss asparagus with the garlic clove, oil, and salt. When the pan is hot, add the asparagus and cook, turning often with tongs, for about 3 to 5 minutes, depending on their thickness. When they are done they should be crisp-cooked, and neither limp nor soft. As soon as they are done, remove them from the pan to a plate and set aside.
2. Halve the English muffins and lightly spread each half with butter. Set aside.
3. For the poached eggs and ham: Get a large pan ready for poaching the eggs, as described in the recipe on page 102. Have the eggs nearby in a bowl, ready for cracking, and have the ham ready on a plate.
4. For the hollandaise: Get all of the ingredients for the hollandaise recipe prepared and ready to be quickly assembled.

Here We Go (deep breath)

1. Bring a round of mimosas to your guests.
2. Turn on the egg water and bring to a boil. Once it reaches a full boil, turn it down slightly so it continues to simmer while you do other things.
3. Place a large griddle pan over two burners and turn the heat to medium-low.
4. Make the hollandaise sauce per the recipe, and keep warm while finishing the eggs Benedict.
5. Set the English muffin halves buttered side down on the heated griddle, and let brown while finishing the dish.
6. Heat a medium sauté pan to medium, add the ham, and allow to heat through. Turn the heat to low and keep the ham warm until you are ready for it.
7. Poach the eggs (page 102) to the desired degree of doneness. As you remove them from the water, blot off any extra water with a paper towel.
8. And now, at last! Set two grilled muffin halves on a plate, grilled side up. Top each with some ham, then the poached eggs. Ladle the hollandaise over the eggs, allowing it to drip down onto the muffin. Place three spears of asparagus decoratively on the plate, dust with paprika if you so desire, and serve.
9. Phew! More mimosas! Big one for you.

MUCH-LESS-CLASSIC EGGS BENEDICT (THE MANNA VARIATIONS)

Makes 4 Bennies

 Project Alert! May require multiple stages or overnight preparations—read through before proceeding

These variations require the same flurry of activity as when assembling the Bennies and benefit from two pairs of hands.

Be the star of your own party and make one of the supercalifragilistic variations of the classic Benny. Or dream up your own. The variations summarized below follow the Benny Formula on page 100. Refer to the Poached Egg (page 102) and Hollandaise (page 103) recipes as you go.

Southwestern Veggie Benny

We worked hard to offer creative and enticing vegetarian alternatives. Here, the ingredients, colors, and flavors of the Southwest are reflected in our veggie version of eggs Benedict. It is a far cry from the classic, bearing only the poached eggs and a jazzed-up hollandaise sauce. In fact, it found a calling with many a meat eater.

Hollandaise: kicked up a notch with a bit of heat, such as sriracha

Poached eggs: traditional

The stuff in between:

- A layer of refried beans spread directly onto the base
- Sliced onions and mixed red and green peppers sautéed in oil with a minced clove of garlic, seasoned with salt and pepper

The base: a not-too-sweet, home-baked cornmeal muffin, split in half, buttered and cut side grilled

The garnish: avocado slices and a few tortilla chips

Jack Benny

On Mother's Day, we served sweet, colorful, pretty, light, and festive foods. But on Father's Day, we brought on the meat, and our Jack Benny embraced all that is Dad (in the most stereotypical sense of the word). For a while, this version was a mainstay on the regular menus. The flavors were big, and the meat was ample. It is a perfect recipe for using up leftover brisket.

Hollandaise: traditional

Poached eggs: traditional

The stuff in between:

- Manna's Red Wine-Braised Beef Brisket with a little of its sauce (pages 340-341)
- Frizzled Onions (page 365)

The base: Thomas's English muffin

The garnish: crispy fragments of bacon, sprinkled on top

Houston Street Benny

Houston Street—pronounced How-stun—in New York City is an east-west, two-mile thoroughfare that acts as a dividing line between the upper, grid-like portion of the city and the smaller, neighborhood-like sections of lower Manhattan. Two celebrated restaurants on Houston still beckon visitors worldwide: Russ & Daughters (opened in 1914) and Katz's Deli (opened in 1888). Both retain their local (and well-aged) charm, having served the nearby immigrant Jewish community in the early 20th century. The Houston Street Benny is a nod to the role Russ & Daughters played in bringing smoked fish excellence to its community.* Much lore surrounds the experience of waiting patiently in line at the tiny retail store, then watching as the experienced employees slice your lox in front of you, paper thin, from one of several varieties on display in the case. It is a quintessential Jewish experience.

Hollandaise: traditional, but substitute fresh dill for the tarragon

Poached eggs: traditional

The stuff in between:

- Slices of Nova lox, the best you can get your hands on
- Sliced fresh tomatoes

The base: Bialys (pages 314-315) or substitute a bagel or English muffin

The garnish: sliced avocados, a sprinkling of capers, and a sprig of fresh dill

Hannukah Benny

Even though this Benny made an appearance only once a year as a Hanukkah special, it is worth a mention because it is so good. It is not unlike the above Houston Street Benny, yet it is a very different eating experience. The potato latke base, fried to a proper crispness and combined with the other Benny ingredients, is heavenly.

Hollandaise: traditional

Poached eggs: traditional

The stuff in between:

- Slices of Nova lox, the best you can get your hands on OR
- A vegetarian version—slices of sweet potatoes roasted with olive oil and minced garlic

The base: Potato Latkes (pages 344-345)

The garnish: spears of roasted asparagus

*The story of Russ & Daughters, as a family business and New York institution, is told beautifully and with love in the book *Russ & Daughters: Reflections and Recipes from the House That Herring Built* by Mark Russ Federman, a grandson of the original owner.

Quiche Me

Manna's quiche was truly unrivaled—if we do say so ourselves. Originally created for breakfast at the inn, quiche quickly became popular as a catering item at both breakfast and cocktail parties. When Manna first opened, quiche was our one eggy entree. But it soon became so off-the-charts popular we chose it as the logo for our T-shirt: a slice of quiche on a plate with the invitation "Quiche Me." (And a few astonishing statistics about ingredient use and production were on the back.)

In our first couple months of business, we made quiche the old-fashioned way (the way you get to make it at home), in a traditional deep-dish quiche pan with a removable bottom. But we had only 12 pans, and every day we would laboriously empty and refill them, scurrying to keep up with the rapidly growing demand. One day, in desperation, we discovered the perfect disposable (yet reusable) aluminum pan to help us streamline production, allowing us to ramp up quiche production by orders of magnitude.

What makes these quiches so exceptional? I was never much for the taste or texture of baked eggs, and it is perhaps from my aversion, that this filling-laden, dairy-forward quiche evolved. The crust itself was flaky, and the custard was particularly luxurious and silken, made with the best our dairy state cows have to offer—cream, cream, and cream and, of course, cheese. The quiches were deep and wide, allowing a greater ratio of filling to crust. And the fillings were creatively crafted and generously portioned, so each forkful was packed with flavor.

We were constantly asked the question: "Which quiches don't have any onions?" The correct answer was none. People asked because they did not like onions. Yet onions provide a background note necessary to bring out the quiche's flavors, as salt is necessary to bring out flavors in most savory foods. When properly sautéed, onions are not noticeable, but a lack of onions makes the filling less interesting. Onions, alas, cannot be left out.

For some holidays and special weekends, quiche production dominated the cafe, moving like The Blob into every corner of our operations, and became a logistical challenge that affected every person at Manna. In the front-of-house, staff answered a steady stream of calls, wrote up orders, and kept track of the dwindling and ever-changing inventory on countdown sheets prepared by Rachael, our quiche maven. Rachael directed from behind the scenes, planning which quiche fillings to make and how many of each, then portioning and cataloging them for subsequent bakeoffs. Tony, the baker, provided his Tony-perfect crusts, and Rachael baked off quiches not just for preorders but also extras for walk-in customers and enough for our in-house daily quiche by the slice. Quiche-mania reached its apex between Thanksgiving and Christmas, when the staff bartered heatedly for square inches of cooler space to store them, and fluttering Post-Its in their neon pinks and electric greens helped us keep the orders straight. Boxing, labeling, and organizing took place in the wee hours on the day of pickup. And then—blink—everything disappeared by two o'clock that afternoon. It was a wild ride for a few weeks, and we loved it. Despite the sometimes nightmarish feel of keeping it all straight, the satisfying teamwork was its own reward.

In 15 years, we made about 50,000 quiches, the equivalent of about 250,000 (20,000 dozen) eggs, 10,000 gallons of cream for the filling, and 9,000 pounds (4 1/2 tons) of butter for the crusts. In case you were wondering.

A Few Quiche Tips for Creating Your Own:

- Manna's quiches were big and deep, and that was part of their allure. We used a deep pan that measured ten inches wide by two inches deep, and we filled every cubic inch it held. Our quiche was substantial and crave-able, and we hope you make it as described. The crust recipe suggests several possibilities for your home version.
- When planning your filling, be sure to include onions! (See note on opposite page.)
- Use about 8 ounces of cheese and 8 ounces of meat.
- For vegetables that you prefer to eat with a bit of crispness, such as broccoli or asparagus, cook them minimally when making the filling. They will spend nearly 1 1/2 hours in the oven and do not need much more than a quick sear to bring out their flavor. Otherwise, you will be eating a quiche full of veggie mush.
- For vegetables that retain a lot of water, like spinach or mushrooms, be sure to cook the water out before using them. If not, that moisture will seep into the custard, and the result will be a watery, sloppy filling rather than a luxurious, creamy one.
- You can freeze quiches, but beware that veggie quiches tend to give off water during the freeze-thaw process, also resulting in a juicy, watery quiche when reheated.
- Rewarm quiche with foil covering the top to avoid over browning.
- If you know in advance how many servings you plan to cut the quiche into, it is best to pre-score the cold quiche before reheating. That way, you will not shatter the crust or smoosh the filling, both of which are delicate when heated.

QUICHE CONSTRUCTION

Makes one 10-inch, deep-dish quiche, yielding 6 large to 10 small servings depending on slice size

Project Alert! May require multiple stages or overnight preparations—read through before proceeding

There is no good way to say it. This quiche is going to take a little time. I am not saying this to be discouraging, but more as a heads-up. Instead of thinking about the time involved, think about your friends gathered around your dining room table with a beautiful bowlful of raspberries, a warm coffeecake, and steaming pots of French press coffee. Your friends are clamoring for you to hurry up. You're ready to bring out your centerpiece quiche, take off your apron, and dig in. It's payoff time!

You will find recipes for crust preparation, custard proportions, and a bunch of favorite fillings on the following pages. Once you have these components ready to go, come back to this page for instructions on assembling and baking your masterpiece and how to reheat it for serving. The finished quiche will keep nicely in the fridge for five days.

Most of the time involved in making quiche is taken by one of the quiche components spending quality time in the oven or fridge. Your actual hands-on time will comprise about 30 minutes making the crust, 10 minutes making the custard, maybe 30 minutes making the filling, and an extra few minutes at the end assembling the parts and popping the quiche into the oven.

A sea of quiche.

Below is an overview of the quiche-making process. (Each part—crust, custard, and filling—can also be made a couple of days ahead of time.)

Day 1

Make and bake off the crust.

While crust is baking, make the filling and prepare the custard.

Add filling and custard to the crust, then bake the quiche.

Cool quiche completely and refrigerate overnight.

Day 2

Score quiche into serving portions and rewarm.

Have Ready

One fully baked Quiche Crust (page 113)

One recipe of Quiche Custard (page 112)

One recipe of your choice of filling (pages 116 to 123)

To Assemble and Bake (Day 1)

1. Preheat the oven to 325 degrees. Line a baking sheet with a parchment pan liner and set aside.
2. Set the crust onto the baking sheet. Place filling into the crust and spread it about with your fingers, breaking up clumps so that the custard will flow through it easily.
3. Pour custard over the filling. The amount of filling and custard combined should reach the level just below the top of the crust. (Don't overfill. If it overflows, it can be challenging to remove it nicely from the pan.) If you come up short, swirl a bit more cream into the mix. Depending on your pan size, there may be extra custard, which you could use to whip up a nice spaghetti carbonara for supper.
4. Using your fingers again, gently wiggle them about in the filled quiche, distributing the filling and custard together evenly to avoid clumping of the filling and pooling of the custard.
5. Set the baking sheet with quiche in the oven. Bake 50 minutes, then rotate the pan 180 degrees. Bake an additional 20 to 30 minutes, until the quiche is puffed and golden in the center and is just set (the center should not have a wet wiggle). If your oven runs hot and the quiche seems too brown on top after the first 50 minutes, lightly crimp some aluminum foil over the top for the last part of the baking.
6. Remove the quiche from the oven and let it cool completely in its pan, then refrigerate uncovered. Ideally, it should refrigerate overnight to give the quiche a chance to fully set up, then be reheated for serving the next day. If you want to eat the quiche the same day it is made, let it cool for at least two hours, as the custard will be fragile and may not hold well when you try to lift the first piece from the pan. At Manna, we let quiches chill overnight, then removed them from the pan the next day before reheating, as described in the next steps. I prefer this strategy.

To Reheat and Serve (Day 2)

7. Preheat the oven to 325 degrees.

8. Remove the quiche from the fridge, and warm the bottom and sides of the pan gently on a stovetop (just enough to loosen the quiche from the pan). Invert the quiche onto a plate or baking pan, then re-invert right side up onto another baking pan.

9. Score the quiche into the number of desired serving pieces (8 large or 12 smaller) by cutting into the crust to just below the rim and then scoring lines about 1/4 inch deep across the top of the quiche. (Scoring makes serving much easier. If you do not pre-score the quiche, it may be difficult to cut through the hot, delicate crust without shattering it and making a mess.)

10. Cover the top with aluminum foil, then place in the oven for 45 minutes. Let cool 5 to 10 minutes before serving.

QUICHE CUSTARD

Makes enough for one 10-inch deep-dish quiche

 Start to finish in less than a half hour

People used to tell us they just wanted something "light" for breakfast, so they'd order a slice of quiche. But as the folks at Chocolate Shoppe say, "If you want nutrition, eat carrots." Yeah, Manna's quiche philosophy was more like that. The fillings are delectable, and the crust tender-buttery, but the custard and ample cheese elevate the quiche to stardom.

5 large eggs
1 3/4 cups half & half
1 3/4 cups heavy cream
1/2 teaspoon salt
1/4 teaspoon pepper

Beat eggs well in a medium bowl. Add remaining ingredients and mix until well combined. The custard is now ready for quiche assembly.

QUICHE CRUST

Makes one 10-inch deep-dish quiche crust

Allow 2 hours for dough preparation, chilling, rolling, and blind-baking

 Hands-on time less than an hour (additional cooking or chilling times involved—read through before beginning)

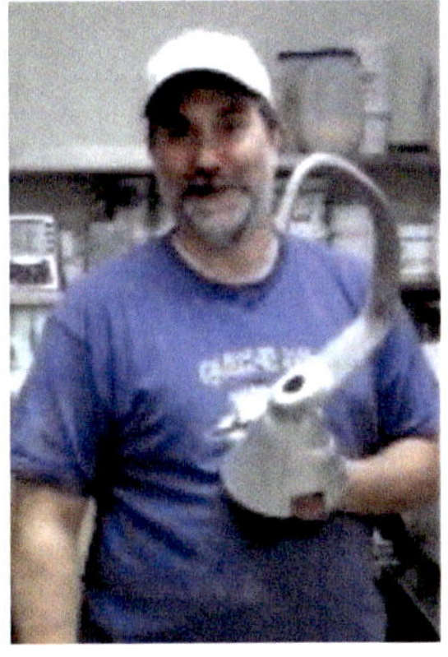

Tony.

Like a good loaf of bread for sandwiches, the crust should play a starring role in a quiche. Tony, a baker at Manna from day one, was king of the quiche crust (among many other things), turning out about 75 of them on an average week for Rachael, the queen of quiche production. We called his crusts Tony-perfect—tender and giving as you sank your fork into that first bite, with plenty of crumbly, flaky plushness to compliment the lavish filling within. In fact, "Tony-perfect" became part of the Manna vernacular—the ultimate compliment.

Quiche crusts, like most pastry crusts, require practice, patience, and adherence to a few basic rules: (1) Keep your ingredients nice and cold to prevent the shortening or butter from blending into the fabric of the dough (you are aiming for a "layering effect" such as in mica—not a combining effect, such as in cookie dough). (2) Handle the ingredients as little as possible with your hands to minimize warming the dough. (3) Work quickly, kneading the dough just enough to hold it together (an overworked dough will be tough and lack flakiness). I knead dough only with the heel of my hand, which is cooler and drier than my palm.

This crust recipe—along with the quiche filling and custard recipes on the following pages—assumes that you will be using one of the following pans: a deep-dish, 11-inch quiche pan with a removable bottom; a 2-inch-deep, 10-inch-round cake pan; or a 10-inch springform pan. If you have none of these and need to use a regular pie plate, you will have leftover everything unless you cut back on the proportions by about 1/3 to 1/2.

You will need 4 to 5 pounds of dried beans, lentils, or pie weights for the blind baking in Step 10.

---

2 1/2 cups flour

1/2 teaspoon salt

4 tablespoons (2 ounces) shortening (such as Crisco), chilled, cut into 1/2-inch cubes

6 tablespoons (3 ounces) cold butter cut into 1/2-inch cubes

1 cup ice water (leave the ice in until you are ready to use the water)

---

1. Mix the flour and salt in a food processor. Add shortening and butter and pulse in short bursts until small butter-flour pebbles the size of corn kernels have formed in the mixture.
2. Turn the mixture into a metal bowl. From your cup of ice water, measure out 8 tablespoons and sprinkle it over the flour mixture, all the time tossing with a spatula, until a dough forms. If the dough seems too dry, toss in a little more water, a few drops at a time. The final dough should just hold together when squeezed and be neither crumbly-dry nor tacky-wet.
3. Lightly flour a work surface, and turn the dough out onto it. Knead once or twice with the heel of your hand to pull it together. Pat the dough into a ball and flatten it slightly to create a disk or puck shape. Wrap the puck in plastic, then roll the wrapped puck gently on its edges, as if rolling a tire. This will help round out the puck and create even edges. Refrigerate the puck for at least an hour (up to overnight).
4. Preheat the oven to 350 degrees. Grease your chosen baking pan. (If it is a springform, make sure it is assembled.)
5. Fifteen minutes before you are ready to roll the dough, remove it from the fridge. Set it onto a lightly floured surface and dust the top lightly with flour. With a rolling pin, roll the dough to about 1/8-inch thickness or into a circle about 14 inches in diameter. Roll with even pressure, turning the dough about a quarter-turn from time to time to help promote a uniform shape. Trim off a small amount of dough from the edges of the crust and reserve it for later patching, if needed.
6. Fold the dough in half to create a semi-circle. Gently set the dough into your prepared pan with the fold in the center, then unfold the dough to fill out the pan. Make sure the dough is centered in the pan before continuing.
7. Gently press the dough into the bottom corners of the pan, where the bottom meets the sides. Then press the dough into the sides of the pan, filling the grooves nicely if you are using a quiche pan. You should have extra dough overhanging the side, which you can now fold back over to the inside of the pan, thus doubling up on the upper portion of the crust. (A springform is generally 3 inches high—a bit higher than what you want for this crust. If you are using one, let the dough initially come close to the top of the pan, then fold it over on itself. Your doubled-up rim, or top edge of the crust, should now be about 1/2 to 1 inch below the top of the springform sides.) Press the doubled-up dough together well so that everything sticks together, then press a little extra at the top of the rim to extend the side crust up over the top edge by just a bit. This will help keep the custard from sloshing over. Finally, use your fingertips to touch up the rim of the crust so it looks tidy all around.
8. Check the crust carefully for cracks or tiny holes, and if needed, use bits of the reserved dough for patching. If you don't do this, the custard filling will ooze out during baking, causing the quiche to stick to the pan and then run the risk of ruining it when you de-pan it. Reserve any extra dough until the initial baking is done, in case more patching is needed.
9. Line the crust with a piece of aluminum foil large enough to come up past the top rim. Fill the foil to the top with lentils, dried beans, or pie weights. Place the crust in the oven and bake for 20 minutes. This is the "blind bake," which will partially cook and set the crust in place so it will not fall.

10. Remove the crust from the oven and remove the aluminum liner with beans. Check once more for holes or cracks and repair with reserved dough, if necessary. Prick the bottom of the crust with a fork to minimize puffing. Return the crust to the oven and bake another 10 to 20 minutes. The final crust should be lightly golden on the sides and look just barely baked in the middle. Let it cool completely. The crust is now ready for use in quiche assembly.

BACON, ONION, AND SWISS QUICHE FILLING

Makes enough for one 10-inch deep-dish quiche

 Start to finish within an hour, give or take

The hands-down favorite quiche was this riff on a Quiche Lorraine, full of smoky bacon and onions caramelized to a medium hue, cradled in creamy custard. Even if you were full and couldn't eat one more bite, you did anyway. It was that kind of addicting.

---

12 ounces raw bacon, chopped into 1/2-inch pieces (more, if you are a shameless snacker)

2 medium onions (about 12-16 ounces total), peeled, halved and thinly sliced

1/4 cup dry white wine

1/2 teaspoon dry rosemary, crushed to a powder

4 ounces Swiss cheese, grated (about 1 1/4 cups)

4 ounces Parmesan cheese, grated (about 1 cup)

---

1. Heat a medium skillet over medium heat. Add chopped bacon and sauté, stirring frequently, until crisp. Remove bacon from the pan with a slotted spoon and drain on paper towels. (Avoid eating too much of it yourself, or your guests will be sorry.)
2. Drain all but 2 tablespoons of the bacon grease from the pan, then return the pan to the stove. Add onions and cook, stirring frequently, until they become a bit golden. Turn the heat down to medium-low and continue cooking for 30 to 40 minutes until the onions have taken on a caramel hue. Turn up the heat to high, add the white wine and cook until the liquid is gone.
3. Remove the pan from the heat, stir in rosemary, and let the mixture cool. When completely cool, mix in the reserved bacon (if you left any!) and the two kinds of cheese.

HAM, CARAMELIZED ONION, AND BRIE QUICHE FILLING

Makes enough for one 10-inch deep-dish quiche

 Hands-on time less than an hour (additional cooking or chilling times involved—read through before beginning)

This is a festive quiche that Manna often made for special occasions, but when demand for it grew, we made it part of the regular rotation.

---

2 tablespoons butter

2 medium onions (about 12-16 ounces total), peeled and thinly sliced

3 tablespoons dry white wine

6 ounces brie cheese, rind left on

1 teaspoon minced garlic

1/4 teaspoon pepper

8 ounces high-quality unsliced ham, cut into 1/4-inch cubes (about 2 1/2 cups)

---

1. Melt butter in a medium sauté pan over medium heat and add sliced onions. Cook until onions begin to soften. Turn heat to medium-low and cook for 40 to 60 minutes until onions are caramelized. About halfway through the cooking, stir in the white wine. Stir frequently, and adjust heat if needed to keep onions from burning.
2. While onions are cooking, prepare the brie. Cut the cheese into 1/2-long strips that are 1/2-inch wide. Set the strips on a parchment-lined pan and freeze for 1 hour. Remove from the freezer and immediately dice into 1/2-inch cubes. Keep the brie cubes cold until you're ready to add them to the filling (this will prevent them from softening and clumping together).
3. When the onions have finished cooking, stir in garlic, pepper, and ham, and cook the mixture for 3 to 4 minutes. Remove from heat and let cool completely.
4. Stir in chilled brie cubes until well incorporated.

SAUSAGE, MUSHROOM, SPINACH, AND FETA QUICHE FILLING

Makes enough for one 10-inch deep-dish quiche

 Start to finish in less than a half hour

Choose an excellent sausage for this quiche. Fraboni's sausage, here in Madison, is without rival. I am not always this brand-loyal, but the Fraboni's folks have a special touch. I have specified sausage links in the recipe. I like how they caramelize a bit as they brown, and there is something about the "bite" of a link sausage due to its thin casing. Also, it holds its shape nicely, rather than crumbling into tiny bits the way bulk sausage does. That said, you can use bulk sausage and any brand you prefer.

5 ounces frozen spinach, thawed

8 ounces Italian sausage links (about 2 links)

8 ounces button mushrooms, sliced (about 3 cups)

1/2 teaspoon minced garlic

1/4 teaspoon salt

1/4 teaspoon pepper

5 ounces feta cheese (about 1 1/4 cups) coarsely crumbled and kept chilled until ready to use

3 ounces shredded Monterey Jack cheese (about 1 cup)

1. Place spinach in a colander and squeeze well to remove excess water.
2. In a medium sauté pan over medium heat, cook sausage links until well browned and cooked through. Let drain on a paper towel, and when cool enough to handle, dice into 1/2-inch pieces. Reserve drippings in the pan.
3. Over medium heat, sauté mushrooms and garlic in pan drippings until all the liquid from the mushrooms has evaporated, and they start to brown. Add cooked sausage, spinach, salt and pepper and mix well. Let cool completely.
4. Gently mix in cheeses, making sure feta crumbles do not get too small.

BROCCOLI, SUN-DRIED TOMATO, AND CHEDDAR QUICHE FILLING

Makes enough for one 10-inch deep-dish quiche

 Start to finish in less than a half hour

It can be challenging to keep vegetables from overcooking in a quiche, which bakes for nearly 1 1/2 hours. For this broccoli quiche to be its best, sauté the broccoli only briefly, so it is still crisp before the quiche is baked off.

---

1 tablespoon butter

1 small onion (about 4 ounces), diced

1/2 teaspoon minced garlic

1/4 cup dry white wine

3 tablespoons sun-dried tomatoes in oil, drained and thinly julienned

8 ounces broccoli florets and stems, cut into 3/4-inch pieces (about 3 cups)

1/4 teaspoon salt

1/4 teaspoon pepper

2 ounces cream cheese (1/4 of an 8-ounce package), cut into 1/2-inch pieces

8 ounces grated cheddar cheese (about 2 1/2 cups)

---

1. In a medium sauté pan over medium heat, cook onions in butter until they start to brown, then add garlic and cook for 1 minute.
2. Turn heat to medium-high and add wine. Cook until liquid is reduced to 1 tablespoon.
3. Add sun-dried tomatoes and broccoli to the onion mixture. Season with salt and pepper and cook for 1 to 2 minutes. Broccoli should be bright green and remain crisp and undercooked.
4. Turn off heat, add cream cheese pieces to the pan and let soften. Stir to blend in cream cheese and let the mixture cool completely.
5. When the mixture is cool, mix in the grated cheddar.

CHILE RELLENOS QUICHE FILLING (AKA SOUTHWESTERN OMELET FILLING)

Makes enough for two 10-inch deep-dish quiches or filling for six omelets

 Start to finish in less than a half hour

Chorizo, a spicy pork sausage, comes in two varieties. Spanish-style chorizo is a cured and seasoned product, hard like pepperoni, with smoky flavors redolent of paprika. It is often sliced and eaten as a part of a charcuterie board. Mexican chorizo is an uncooked sausage whose flavor is defined more by chili spices. It must be cooked before it is eaten. This filling is based on the Mexican style. Chorizo is the dominant flavor in the dish, which is intensified by chiles and mellowed, if only a bit, by the mildness and creamy texture of potatoes. Although its flavors are strong, its spiciness does not overwhelm.

This big, bold filling has many applications. In a quiche, its assertive flavors are gentled by a creamy custard, but in an omelet (where it gained a devoted following at Manna), the savory chorizo flavors dominate. It is also at home nestled into a split baked potato or made into an open-faced, grilled sandwich, dripping with melted cheese or layered into a big bowlful of nachos.

The filling freezes well. Portion it as you like, and have it available at a moment's notice for an impressive brunch dish, lunch base, or hors d'oeuvres component.

1 large or several small red potatoes (about 8 ounces total), diced very small (1/4 inch)
2 teaspoons minced garlic
Canola oil

1 package (12 ounces) Mexican-style chorizo
1 medium onion (6 ounces) diced small
1 can (7 ounces) mild or medium chopped green chiles
1 1/2 tablespoons bottled hot green salsa (preferably Mrs. Renfro's)
Also needed if the filling will be used for quiche:
16 ounces grated Monterey Jack cheese (about 5 cups)

1. Preheat the oven to 400 degrees and line a sheet pan with parchment paper. In a bowl, toss together the diced potatoes, garlic, and just enough oil to lightly coat the potatoes. (There is no need to salt the potatoes, as there is more than enough saltiness in the chorizo.) Spread the potatoes on the prepared sheet pan and roast for about 12 to 15 minutes until they are golden and fully cooked. Stir the potatoes once during roasting. (Keep a good eye on them so they don't get too dark and dried out.) Let cool.
2. While the potatoes are roasting, heat a medium sauté pan over medium-high heat. Add chorizo to the pan and cook, breaking up the clumps until the fat has fully rendered and the meat resembles cooked ground beef. Remove from the heat and drain the meat in a strainer. Discard the fat.
3. Return the pan to the stove, now over medium heat. Add 1 tablespoon oil to the pan, then add the onions. Cook onions, stirring occasionally, for about 10 to 15 minutes until they are softened and golden brown. Stir in chiles, green salsa, and cooked chorizo and cook a few more minutes. If there is extra oil, let the mixture drain one more time, then stir in the potatoes at the end.
4. If you're using the filling for quiches, cool it completely, then mix in the cheese. Divide into two portions. If you are only making one quiche, the other portion will freeze well.
5. For all uses, the filling can be used right away or frozen.

RED PEPPER, MUSHROOM, LEEK, AND CHEVRE QUICHE FILLING

Makes enough for one 10-inch deep-dish quiche

Start to finish in less than a half hour

The decadence of this quiche derives from the generous amount of chèvre, and the use of leeks in place of onions.

---

1 1/2 tablespoons butter

1 1/2 cups thinly sliced leeks (white part only)

2 1/2 cups sweet red pepper, cut into 1/2-inch dice (2-3 peppers)

8 ounces button or cremini mushrooms, sliced thin (about 2 1/2 cups)

2 tablespoons dry white wine

1/4 teaspoon salt

1/4 teaspoon pepper

2 ounces cream cheese (1/4 package), cut into 3/4-inch pieces

6 ounces chévre, crumbled into 3/4-inch pieces, well chilled until ready to use

---

1. In a medium sauté pan on medium-low heat, sauté leeks and red peppers in butter until partly soft. Increase heat to medium, add mushrooms and cook until all the liquid from mushrooms has evaporated and mushrooms begin to brown. Stir in white wine and cook until liquid is gone. Season with salt and pepper.
2. Remove from heat and add cream cheese to the pan. When it has softened from the heat, stir it into the filling. Let the mixture cool completely, then gently stir in the chèvre. Try to retain little clumps of chèvre rather than letting it mix into the filling until smooth.

ARTICHOKE AND FOUR-CHEESE QUICHE FILLING

Makes enough for one 10-inch deep-dish quiche

 Start to finish in less than a half hour

This was our longest-running and most popular vegetarian quiche. You can use any mix of cheese you like—various combinations will each taste a little different.

---

1 tablespoon butter

1 small onion (about 4 ounces), diced

1 cup sweet red pepper, diced into 1/4-inch pieces

1 can (15 ounces) artichoke hearts, drained, patted dry with a paper towel, and coarsely chopped

1/4 cup fresh or frozen peas

1/4 teaspoon salt

1/4 teaspoon pepper

2 ounces grated Swiss cheese (about 2/3 cup)

2 ounces grated Parmesan (about 1/2 cup)

2 ounces grated Monterey Jack cheese (about 2/3 cup)

2 ounces grated provolone (about 2/3 cup)

---

1. In a small sauté pan over medium heat, sauté onions and red peppers in butter until golden. Remove from heat.
2. Mix artichokes and peas into onions. Season with salt and pepper, and let cool completely. When the mixture is cool, stir in the grated cheeses.

Oatcakes and Friends

My friend Holly did not eat or even like pancakes. One day on a lunch date, she confessed this to me apologetically, as though saying so was a personal affront to my livelihood. I thought nothing of it at the time, but several weeks later, an e-mail arrived from Holly out of the blue. She had met another friend for breakfast at Manna and felt that she owed it to me to try the oatcakes despite her dislike, both as a kindness and to find out what the hubbub was all about. It was, she wrote, a life-altering moment on the pancake front. Manna's oatmeal pancakes can do that to a person. They have a magical allure that is difficult to explain, and once people try them, they are forever under the spell.

This one recipe, made thousands of times since its discovery, was a key reason guests returned over and over to The Collins House. So at Manna, we named them Collins House Oatmeal Pancakes, and they became an iconic menu item—a seemingly ordinary plate of pancakes that became extraordinary. I originally stumbled across the oatcake recipe in an old *Bon Appétit* magazine, referred to as Swedish Oatmeal Pancakes. We found this amusing and baffling since Swedish pancakes are thinner and more crepe-like. But it was a hit. Thank you for this gift, *Bon Appétit!* (Or, in Julia mode, thank you, and "bon appétit!")

At The Collins House, we took pride in our interesting variety of pancakes. In addition to oatcakes (the most popular), we served buckwheat banana, upside-down pumpkin sticky cakes, "surprise" pancakes with a mix of grains—the list goes on. But when we got to Manna and made these delicious "varietal" pancakes as weekend specials, our customers continued to order only the oatcakes. After a time, we phased out weekend pancake specials, and for most of our years offered only oatcakes and buttermilk cakes.

Oatcakes are healthful and filling (in a good way). The ratio of oats to flour in the recipe is 4:1, and because we used whole rolled oats, the batter had to soak for at least 45 minutes to absorb the liquid before it could be used. This soaking softens the oats, leaving just enough texture to give the cakes substance and just enough lightness to let the diner enjoy a plateful. They are soft, moist, and have an alluring whisper of vanilla.

Like any good pancake, oatcakes pair beautifully with Wisconsin maple syrup, one of the most expensive ingredients we carried (and served as freely as tap water). Never did we even consider using anything but the real deal, always from local Wisconsin folks. Even if you normally use maple-flavored pancake syrup at home, you should get a special (I would even say beautiful) jar of real Wisconsin maple syrup to set aside just for The Collins House/Manna oatcakes. It makes all the difference.

Note: For general advice about mixing pancake batter and cooking pancakes, see page 129.

COLLINS HOUSE OATMEAL PANCAKES (AKA OATCAKES)

Makes about 10 pancakes

 Start to finish within an hour, give or take

And without further ado...

---

2 ever-so-slightly rounded cups of whole rolled oats (not quick-cooking)

1/2 cup flour

2 tablespoons sugar

1 teaspoon baking powder

1 teaspoon baking soda

1/4 teaspoon salt

2 eggs

2 ounces (1/2 stick) butter, melted and cooled a little

2 ever-so-scant cups of buttermilk

1 teaspoon vanilla extract

---

1. Combine dry ingredients (oats through salt) in a medium bowl.
2. In a separate medium bowl, beat together the eggs and melted butter until emulsified. (See page 129 for more about emulsification.) Stir in buttermilk and vanilla until well mixed. Add in dry ingredients and use a whisk to mix them well. (Contrary to the advice dished out in "Bringing Out the Best in Your Cakes" on page 129, oatcake batter should be mixed thoroughly until it's free of lumps.)
3. Let the batter sit for a minimum of 45 minutes. Longer is okay. Whole rolled oats need time to absorb the batter, so they will not be chewy.
4. Heat a cast-iron skillet (preferable) or other heavy-duty sauté pan on medium-low heat. When hot, lightly butter or spray with cooking spray. Pour 1/3 cup batter onto the griddle for each pancake, leaving at least an inch or more between pancakes. When bubbles start to form on the top of the pancakes, and the edges are just getting dry, flip the cakes and let cook another few minutes until done in the center. Check cakes as they are cooking, and adjust the heat so they do not brown too quickly.

Fun with your Oatcakes

Here's an oatcake starter kit. As always, serve up your memories or do your own thing!

Granola Crunch Cakes

For these, you will need a batch of Manna Granola (page 139). After measuring out the batter onto the griddle, spread each pancake out just a bit. Sprinkle some granola over the pancakes, and that's it. Finish cooking as per the oatcake instructions, then serve the pancakes granola-side up.

Funky Monkeys

Stir some chocolate chips into your oatcake batter, then cook as directed in the recipe. (Or, sprinkle chips onto each cake and gently fold them in with the handle end of a spoon.) When pancakes are hot off the griddle, spread peanut butter on each one so it becomes melty. Slice bananas over all. And though it seems like overkill, don't forget the syrup!

Celebrate with Berries!

Roll these out for New Year's Day brunch, Veterans Day, graduation, or July 4th—any brunch or breakfast that begs for a red, white, and blue moment. Stir some blueberries into the oatcake batter and cook as described. Top with more blueberries and raspberries and a big blob of whipped cream. Then go overboard with a few berries for garnish, or chocolate shavings.

And for the Millennial in You...

Cook up any leftover batter into a few more pancakes, then cool the finished pancakes, cover, and refrigerate. The next day cook up some bacon (or sausage patties). Warm the pancakes on a low power setting in the microwave for a minute, and heat a griddle over low heat. Make a breakfast sandwich with the meat of your choice, a slice of cheddar, and maybe an over-easy egg. (My millennial son would insist on adding sriracha.) Grill on the griddle until the cakes are reheated and cheese has melted. Serve maple syrup on the side for optional dipping. (Lindsay, our last kitchen co-manager at Manna, was the queen of oatcake leftovers. When we were cleaning at the end of a Sunday shift, she would quietly visit a corner of the counter and cook up leftover cakes into little bitty waffles for future secret meals.)

"Everything Else" Cakes and A Few "Misfit Recipes"

On the following pages are a few pancake recipes for your consideration, all from The Collins House collection. The buttermilk cakes are the best of their kind that I know. If you crave a basic pancake or have small children with single-minded food tastes, this is your recipe. Two other favorites were buckwheat banana and cornmeal honey cakes. If French toast is more your thing, the Fantasy Sticky Bun French Toast recipe is included on page 136. It is the sweet and sticky equivalent of the quiche recipe, made with tons of everything you don't want to know about, and cooks up into a custardy, blissful mouthful.

Because not everything fits neatly into a chapter, I have include a few miscellaneous recipes—three mandatory and one whimsical—to round out the breakfast/brunch chapter. There are a few things you won't want to miss, including granola and our two great potato sides. The oatmeal recipe is a nod to my dad's somewhat unorthodox idea of breakfast. It is a recipe where the story takes center stage, and returns this cookbook to its origins.

Bringing Out the Best in Your Cakes

Mixing: The general song and dance for pancake making: mix dries, mix wets, mix dries and wets. Yes, and also:

Mix the wet portion of the batter by first emulsifying the melted butter with the eggs, then adding the remaining wet ingredients to this mix. **Emulsification** is the process of binding together ingredients that would not normally bind, and in the process making them thicker. With pancakes, if you do not first bind the butter to the eggs, the melted butter may congeal into globs in the buttermilk, forming numerous little clots that do not distribute nicely through your batter.

When combining the wets and the dries, do so gently using a whisk. An overmixed pancake batter will not be as tender or fluffy as one in which you blend the ingredients only as much as needed. Instead of "beating," use the whisk to "fold" the ingredients together. The final batter may look a bit lumpy—not perfectly smooth and satiny.

Griddle temperature: The surface temperature of your griddle should be between low and medium. Too high, and the cakes will get too brown before they cook in the middle. Too low, and they will remain pale, and may overcook before you think they are ready to turn. Check the cakes as they cook, and adjust the heat as necessary.

Flipping the cakes: Pancakes are ready to flip when the edges are just beginning to look a little dry, and the center is showing air bubbles popping up in the still-wet batter. (The bubbles are telling. If you flip before they appear, the cakes will splatter when they plop back down on the pan. If the bubbles show but the center batter has dried out, you have not turned them soon enough.) Once flipped, they will only require another minute or two to finish. Note that the cooking time on side one is longer than on side two.

Tricking out the batter: If you want to add ingredients, do it the moment you drop the batter on the griddle. If I add something like chocolate chips to a pancake, I will use a spatula or spoon to gently spread a bit of batter over that ingredient. This way, when I flip the pancake, the ingredient is protected from the direct heat of the griddle and will not get crispy or burnt.

BUTTERMILK PANCAKES

Makes 10 pancakes

 Start to finish in less than a half hour

Pancakes for Breakfast, by Tomie dePaola, is an engaging picture book for preschoolers. It has no words, so you have to make up the story as you flip through the pages. It tells of a little old lady in a cabin in the woods, determined to make herself a big stack of pancakes for breakfast, and she goes to considerable lengths to do so. It is, as most children's books are, about many things on many levels. For me, one of them is the warm memory of how a tall stack of pancakes and locally produced maple syrup beckons, as if at the end of a rainbow. I "read" this book to my toddler son, Josh, who then developed his own particular patter to accompany my telling (using the only words he spoke at the time—"all gone" and "more"). We always laughed knowingly at our punchlines. Find a copy, and share it with your kids, or your kids' kids.

These are my pot-of-gold pancakes. The recipe is deceptively simple, but the proportions are perfect. They are best washed down with a crunchy chomp of bacon.

---

1 1/2 cups flour

2 tablespoons sugar

2 teaspoons baking powder

1/2 teaspoon baking soda

1/2 teaspoon salt

1 egg

2 tablespoons butter, melted and cooled a little

1 1/2 cups buttermilk

1 teaspoon vanilla extract

---

1. Combine dry ingredients (flour through salt) in a small bowl.
2. In a separate medium bowl, beat together the egg and butter until emulsified. Stir in buttermilk and vanilla until well mixed. Gently add in dry ingredients with a whisk until well incorporated but still a little lumpy looking. Do NOT overmix, or the cakes will be a little tougher (less fluffy and delicate).
3. Heat a cast-iron skillet (preferable) or other heavy-duty sauté pan on medium-low heat. When hot, lightly butter or spray with cooking spray. Measure 1/3 cup batter onto the griddle for each pancake, leaving at least an inch or more in between pancakes. When bubbles start to form on the top of the pancakes and the edges are just getting dry, flip the cakes and cook another minute or two until done in the center.

Lemon Loves: A Buttermilk Pancake Variation

Lemon curd is for lemon lovers like chocolate ganache is for chocoholics—a luxurious indulgence by the spoonful. Lemon curd features prominently in our Triple Lemon Cake (page 331), but here it is used to bridge warm, airy buttermilk pancakes and sweet, colorful berries. A clear departure from the usual maple syrup-drenched pancakes, these are a lemon aficionado's daydream.

To make Lemon Loves you will need to make Lemon Curd (pages 331-332). Since it freezes well, you can have it around all the time.

Then, after you've dropped some Buttermilk Cakes (page 130) on the griddle, toss some fresh blueberries on top and cook them into the cakes. When cakes are ready, place them on a plate lavished with more fresh blueberries and sliced strawberries, and serve with ample lemon curd for spreading or dipping—whipped cream, too, if you're feeling your oats.

Jacob the oatcake wrangler.

BUCKWHEAT BANANA PANCAKES

Makes about 12 pancakes

 Start to finish in less than a half hour

Collins House guests were frequent beneficiaries of this fragrant pancake, but for some reason, they never made it to the Manna menu. So here they are—a must-try. The banana flavor is gentle, and the mix of flours offers a subtle wholesomeness to the recipe. Garnish your plate with enough slices of banana so you can have one with each bite. Toasted pecans and blueberries are happy additions too.

---

1 cup unbleached white flour

1/2 cup whole wheat flour

1/2 cup buckwheat flour

2 tablespoons sugar

4 teaspoons baking powder

1 gently rounded teaspoon baking soda

1/2 teaspoon salt

2 eggs, beaten

4 tablespoons butter, melted and cooled a little

3/4 cup mashed, overripe banana (1 1/2-2 bananas)

1 1/2 cups buttermilk

1/4 cup milk

1/2 teaspoon vanilla extract

---

1. Combine dry ingredients (flour through salt) in a small bowl.
2. In a separate medium bowl, beat together the egg and butter until emulsified. Whisk in bananas, buttermilk, milk, and vanilla until well mixed. Gently add in dry ingredients with a whisk until well incorporated but still a little lumpy looking. Do NOT overmix, or the cakes will be a little tougher (less fluffy and delicate).
3. Heat a cast-iron skillet (preferable) or other heavy-duty sauté pan on medium-low heat. When hot, lightly butter or spray with cooking spray. Measure 1/3 cup batter onto the griddle for each pancake. When tiny bubbles form in the center of the pancakes and the edges are set, flip the cakes and cook another minute or two until the center feels set. Serve topped with sliced bananas or blueberries and warm maple syrup.

CORNMEAL PANCAKES

Makes about 10 pancakes

 Start to finish in less than a half hour

A little bit of cornmeal can be transformative. In these pancakes, the cornmeal proportion is just right to give the cakes a bit of texture and crunch without being heavy. Imagine downing them while sitting on the painted wood porch of a bed and breakfast in the foothills of the Blue Ridge Mountains, with a creek burbling gently in the distance and a fiddle tune playing mournfully over the next rise. Except, here we are in subzero Wisconsin, so let's instead conjure up the indoor porch at The Collins House, overlooking the frozen expanse of Lake Mendota, with a fire crackling nearby.

This pancake riffs on our basic buttermilk cake recipe by swapping some cornmeal for flour and using honey or maple syrup for its sweetening.

---

1 cup flour

1/2 cup medium yellow cornmeal

2 teaspoons baking powder

1/2 teaspoon baking soda

1/2 teaspoon salt

1 egg

1 tablespoon honey or maple syrup

2 tablespoons butter, melted and cooled a little

1 1/2 cups buttermilk

---

1. Combine dry ingredients (flour through salt) in a small bowl.
2. In a separate medium bowl, beat together the eggs, butter, and honey (or maple syrup) until emulsified. Stir in buttermilk until well mixed. Gently add in dry ingredients with a whisk until well incorporated but still a little lumpy. Do NOT overmix or the cakes will be a little tougher (less fluffy and delicate).
3. Heat a cast-iron skillet (preferable) or other heavy-duty sauté pan on medium-low heat. When hot, lightly butter or spray with cooking spray. Measure 1/3 cup batter onto the griddle for each pancake, leaving at least an inch or more in between. When bubbles start to form on the top of the pancakes and the edges are just getting dry, flip the pancakes and cook another minute or two until done in the center.

GLUTEN-FREE BUCKWHEAT PANCAKES

Makes 10 pancakes

 Start to finish in less than a half hour

Shirley was one of those customers who ordered the same thing, day after week after month. Her predictability was something you thought you could trust, almost to the extent that you got her order ready without asking. Except occasionally, she would throw a wrench into your well-intentioned plans. For years we had served these pancakes without variation to our gluten-free customers, until one day Shirley, itching for something new, asked if we could turn them into blini-like crepes, thin and flat. And once we tried them, it became the new only thing she would order.

Below is the recipe for our traditional gluten-free buckwheat pancakes. See the following page for Shirley's Blinis.

---

1 1/2 cups buckwheat flour

1/2 cup brown rice flour

1 1/2 teaspoons baking powder

3 tablespoons sugar

1/2 teaspoon salt

1/4 teaspoon cinnamon

1 egg

3 tablespoons butter, melted and cooled a little

2 1/4 cups buttermilk

1 teaspoon vanilla extract

1/4 cup sugar mixed with 1/2 teaspoon cinnamon

---

1. Combine dry ingredients (buckwheat flour through cinnamon) in a medium bowl.
2. Whisk egg with melted butter. Add buttermilk and vanilla and whisk to incorporate.
3. Gently add dry ingredients to wet ingredients and mix gently with a whisk until well incorporated but still a little lumpy looking. Do NOT overmix or the cakes will be a little tougher (less fluffy and delicate.
4. Heat a cast-iron skillet (preferable) or other heavy-duty sauté pan on medium-low heat. When hot, lightly butter or spray with cooking spray. Moderately sprinkle cinnamon sugar onto the butter, where you will be placing the pancake batter. Measure 1/3 cup batter onto the sugared areas of the griddle for each pancake, leaving at least an inch or more in between pancakes. When bubbles start to form on the top of pancakes, and the edges are just getting dry, flip the cakes and let cook another minute or two, until done in the center. Serve at once.

SHIRLEY'S BLINIS

Makes about 24 blinis

To make these the Shirley way, follow Steps 1 through 3 in the Buckwheat Pancakes recipe on the preceding page, but then add milk (about 1 1/2 cups or a little more of whole or 2% milk for an entire recipe) to thin the batter. When the batter is at the proper consistency, it will form a fairly thin crepe when poured into the hot pan. It may take a bit of experimentation to get it just so.

Heat a 6-inch nonstick skillet or crepe pan over medium heat. When the pan is fully heated, lightly butter it, then pour just enough batter so that when you rotate the pan to spread it, you have a very thin layer. Cook on one side until golden brown on the bottom and mostly dried out on the top, then flip and cook on the other side about 1 minute more (the second side need not brown). Slide onto a plate and repeat with the remaining batter, using a dab of butter in the pan with each new crepe. The blinis can then be rolled with your choice of filling, such as more cinnamon sugar, jam, Nutella—go wild. Also, they can be stacked and frozen. (I like to freeze them four to a pack, making two crepes each for two people.)

FANTASY STICKY BUN FRENCH TOAST

Makes enough to soak bread for 4 servings
(short prep time, but needs an overnight soak)

 Hands-on time less than an hour (additional cooking or chilling times involved—read through before beginning)

"Picture yourself in a boat on a river."

I believe this dish evolved from a daydream such as one the Beatles sang about, wherein every component is decadent and luxurious. Fantasy Sticky Bun French Toast might have started as a menu item reserved for Valentine's Day and New Year's Eve, but somehow it became the everyday French toast. Be careful what you dream for.

The custard recipe below works for sticky buns as well as any other sturdy bread that likes to sop up some liquid. It is an overnight technique so that you can soak your bread on a Friday night and arise Saturday morning, pad to your kitchen in your PJs and snugglies, and have breakfast ready in a flash. The overnight soak produces a French toast with a rich, silken, custardy inside. You can certainly lighten it up a bit by substituting milk for the heavy cream, but it will not have the same indulgent quality.

---

3 tablespoons sugar

1/2 teaspoon cinnamon

1/8 teaspoon nutmeg

6 eggs

1 1/2 cups heavy cream

1 1/2 cups half & half

1/2 teaspoon vanilla extract

2 tablespoons rum

4 Sticky Buns (pages 254-255), cut horizontally into thirds OR substitute

8 thick slices of Challah (pages 309-311), preferably not fresh OR

8 thick slices of pumpkin cranberry bread OR

Any other thick-cut, not-too-airy bread of your choice (If it's too light and fluffy, like Wonder bread, it will fall apart. The bread needs structure to stand up to the custard.)

Optional Toppings:

Sliced strawberries

Whipped cream

Chocolate Maple Syrup (below) or regular maple syrup

---

1. Mix sugar, cinnamon, and nutmeg.
2. Beat the eggs in a medium bowl. Add the sugar mixture to the eggs and beat until the sugar has dissolved.
3. Add heavy cream, half & half, vanilla, and rum. Mix well.
4. Pour the mixture into a pan large enough to hold your bread slices. Place slices atop custard and allow to soak up custard on one side for about 1/2 hour. Carefully flip the bread with a spatula, cover the dish and refrigerate overnight.
5. Heat a skillet over medium-low heat until thoroughly hot. Butter the skillet and add the slices of French toast. Cook for 8 to 10 minutes on one side, then flip and cook another 4 to 6 minutes. Check partway through cooking to make sure the skillet is not too hot, and adjust if necessary. To check for doneness, press down on the center of the French toast with a spatula. If uncooked custard oozes out, continue to cook until it does not.

CHOCOLATE MAPLE SYRUP

Makes 1 heaping cup

1 cup maple syrup (preferably local to your state)

2 tablespoons unsweetened cocoa powder

2 tablespoons butter

A pinch of salt

Mix all ingredients in a small pot. Heat, whisk, cool, and store. Keep refrigerated, but serve gently warmed.

GRANOLA

Makes about 2 pounds or about 7-8 cups

 Hands-on time less than an hour (additional cooking or chilling times involved—read through before beginning)

Whenever granola was baking at Manna, I'd come running, drawn by the intoxicating fragrances of cinnamon, toasting nuts, and vanilla. When the batch had cooled on the pans, and before the granola was mixed with the dried fruits, I'd find a perfect, golden-brown nugget—crunchy and not too sweet. It was hard to stop munching. Feel free to substitute your favorite nuts or dried fruit. Add flaxseeds if you like. Toss in chocolate chips for the kids! Just be sure to add these at the end after the granola has fully cooled.

Granola is often eaten alone but also has many uses as an ingredient, from a crunchy component in tall parfaits layered with local yogurt and fresh berries to a baked-on topping for the Granola Crunch Cakes (page 127).

---

2 3/4 cups whole rolled oats

3/4 cup shredded sweetened coconut

1/4 cup sunflower seeds

1/3 cup chopped walnuts, untoasted

1/2 cup slivered almonds, untoasted

1 teaspoon cinnamon

3 tablespoons honey

3 tablespoons brown sugar

1/3 cup vegetable oil

1/2 teaspoon vanilla extract

1/3 cup raisins

1/3 cup dried cranberries

1/3 cup chopped dates

---

1. Preheat the oven to 325 degrees. Line two sheet pans with parchment paper and set them aside. Regular cookie sheets will not work well because their lack of sides will allow the granola to fall off. If you do not have parchment, you can grease the pans well.
2. Combine the first six ingredients (oats through cinnamon) in a large bowl and mix thoroughly by hand. Mix together honey, brown sugar, vegetable oil, and vanilla, and add to dry ingredients. Using your hands to mix will help distribute the sticky liquid portion evenly over the grains, nuts, and seeds. In this case, a rubber spatula does not work as well.
3. Spread the mixture onto sheet pans and bake until golden brown. Stir the granola and rotate the pans about every 8 minutes during baking so it will brown evenly. Total baking time will be 40 to 50 minutes, give or take a few minutes, but keep an eye on it. Deep golden, hinging on brown, is ideal. Too dark, and it will pick up a bitterness.
4. Cool granola completely, then crumble it by hand. Be sure to leave some inviting small chunks for easy snacking. Stir in the dried fruits or any other additions after the mixture has cooled so that these ingredients retain their moistness and chew factor.
5. Store granola in an airtight container for 2 months or more. (If it is still crunchy, it is still good.)

The perfect granola color.

CHEESY POTATO HASH

Fills one 9 x 9-inch baking pan, yielding 9 medium pieces cut 3 x 3 inches

 Start to finish within an hour, give or take

Carrie Carlson, our long-time kitchen manager, did many things to make Manna's kitchen a well-oiled machine, and this hash was one of the plans she successfully hatched to ease the burden on the line cooks while getting the food out faster. While delicious and wildly popular, our pan-fried potatoes required oven-roasting as well as constant stove-top attention, and occupied multiple cooks in different areas. They were a constant thorn in our sides. Carrie thought a baked hash might be easier all around, and right she was. Too right, perhaps. In taming one monster, she created another, albeit gentler, monster. One line cook's lightened load became our prep cook's nightmare when the cheesy hash rose to the top of the charts during weekend brunches. (It took weeks to scale up production to meet the demand!)

This hash is a creamy-dreamy-gooey-cheesy potato casserole, with crisp edges giving way to plump potato-y forkfuls. Made in regular household proportions, it is no nightmare at all. Great for breakfast, as a side with roasts, or leftovers right out of the fridge, reheated or cold.

Béchamel Sauce

2 tablespoons butter

1/4 cup chopped onion

2 teaspoons minced garlic

3 tablespoons flour

1 1/4 cups milk

1/2 cup heavy cream

1 teaspoon dried thyme

1/2 teaspoon salt

1/8 teaspoon ground black pepper

Cheesy Hash

Butter or cooking spray

1 bag (30 ounces) frozen shredded potatoes, thawed, with excess water squeezed out

1 recipe Béchamel Sauce, above

3/4 cup shredded medium cheddar cheese

1 teaspoon salt

1/2 teaspoon pepper

3/4 cup grated cheddar cheese for topping

---

1. **For the béchamel sauce:** Melt the butter in a medium saucepan over medium-low heat. Add onions and garlic and cook, stirring occasionally, until onions have begun to soften, about 5 minutes. Add flour and cook for 3 minutes, stirring occasionally.
2. Increase heat to medium and gradually add milk and cream to the saucepan, whisking well after each addition to keep lumps from forming. Cook until the béchamel just begins to boil, whisking often. Turn off the heat and mix in thyme, salt and pepper. Let cool until you're ready to finish the hash.
3. **To assemble the cheesy hash:** Preheat the oven to 375 degrees and grease a 9 x 9-inch baking pan.
4. Place the shredded potatoes in a bowl with béchamel sauce, 3/4 cup cheddar cheese, salt and pepper, and mix well. Place hash in prepared pan, and pat evenly into place.
5. Top the hash with the remaining 3/4 cup cheddar cheese and cover the pan with aluminum foil. Bake in the preheated oven for 30 minutes. Remove the foil and bake for an additional 15 minutes. If the cheese needs a little extra crisping, place the pan under a broiler for a few minutes. Remove from oven and let sit 10 minutes before serving.

PAN-FRIED POTATOES

Serves 4 HUNGRY to 8 dainty people

 Project Alert! May require multiple stages or overnight preparations—read through before proceeding

These little potato nuggets are crisp on the outside, creamy on the inside, with garlic permeating the mix. Manna's pan-fried potatoes were parboiled, marinated, roasted, and pan-fried, and there was no cheating if you wanted that perfect bite. At the end of each weekend service, the leftover pan-fried potatoes were piled high onto a white stoneware serving platter and, accompanied by a bowl of our spicy Russian dressing, were set out for staff to munch on like a big communal bowl of popcorn. After eight hours of a crazy Sunday brunch, nothing tasted better.

Both potato type and chunk size are important in this recipe. Russet potatoes do not have the same consistency as reds. They will be mealier and will fail to crisp up in the same way red potatoes do. Too small of a dice will produce a chewy potato piece, and an overly large chunk will be plenty potato-y but hard to crisp up in the same way.

---

2 1/2 pounds red potatoes, cut into 3/4-inch chunks (about 8 cups)
1 tablespoon plus 3/4 teaspoon salt, divided
2 tablespoons olive oil
2 tablespoons vegetable oil
1/2 teaspoon ground black pepper
2 teaspoons minced garlic

For Final Cooking:
Additional oil for sheet pan
2 teaspoons additional minced garlic

---

1. Fill a soup pot with cold water. Add potatoes and 1 tablespoon of the salt. Bring to a boil over high heat, then reduce heat to a simmer and cook until the potatoes are just barely done, about 10 minutes. (Taste for doneness.) Strain potatoes and let cool.
2. Mix cooled potatoes with olive and vegetable oils, the remaining 3/4 teaspoon salt, pepper, and garlic. Let marinate for at least 1 hour or up to overnight.
3. Preheat the oven to 375 degrees and lightly oil a sheet pan. Spread potatoes on the pan and roast for 20 minutes, stirring halfway through. Remove from the oven and cover until ready for the final cook in Step 4.
4. Heat a large sauté pan on medium-high heat. When plenty hot, add oil and garlic to the pan, then immediately add roasted potatoes. Stir-fry the potatoes until the outsides are as crisp as you like them. Serve immediately.

TED'S OATMEAL "NAPOLEON"

Serves 1

Start to finish in less than a half hour

My earliest food memory was of my father (Ted) making this oatmeal. I think I was two years old. I relished those moments spent with him, watching the simple joy he found in preparing and anticipating this dish he so loved. I find it fitting that my professional life ultimately revolved around oatmeal pancakes. It is entirely possible that the name of the dish derives from my father's sense of self-importance and grandeur. I never knew, but it certainly fits the man.

Dad, Dr. Spaet, Ted—
a man of depth and gusto.

My mother made oatmeal, too, only with milk—never water. Once when I was three, on a trip from my home in New York to visit my grandmother in Madison, I was served oatmeal cooked in water. I cried and cried.

As an adult, steel-cut oats are my go-to for a bowl of oatmeal, partly for their superior nutrition and partly because of their toothsome texture. But for this recipe, stick with rolled oats, which produce a creamier bowlful.

1/2 cup whole rolled oats, not quick-cooking or steel-cut

1 cup milk, the higher the butter fat, the better

2 teaspoons brown sugar

1 pinch of salt

2 teaspoons unsalted butter

1 scoop of your favorite vanilla ice cream (scoop size to match your appetite)

2 teaspoons cognac, the best you have around

---

1. Place the oats and milk in a small pot and bring to a simmer over medium-high heat. Reduce heat to medium low and continue to cook about 5 more minutes, stirring, until oatmeal is creamy and cooked through.
2. Remove from heat and stir in brown sugar and salt.
3. Place steamy oatmeal in a lovely stoneware bowl and top with butter. As the butter melts, swirl it into the oatmeal.
4. Scoop ice cream atop the oatmeal and drizzle the cognac around the sides.

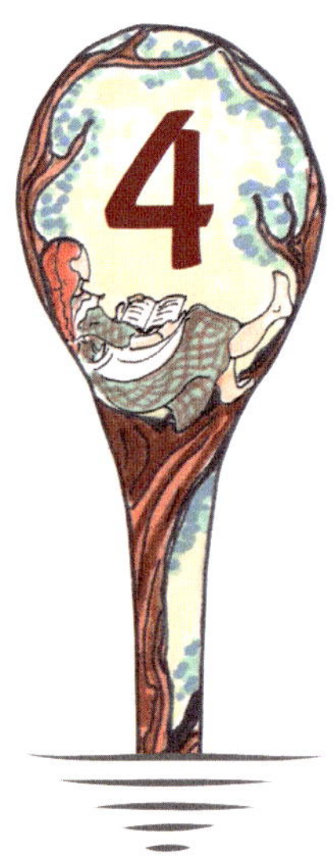

Lunch

If a plate of eggs and hash browns is synonymous with the American breakfast, then a hearty sandwich and soup is what surfaces in our mind when lunchtime rolls around. Although we might instead choose a leafy salad filled with nutritious roughage and fewer calories, a sandwich is what our upbringing and acculturation tell us we want.

Manna's breakfast roots took hold at the B&B, but lunch stemmed from our years of corporate catering. The orders came from small offices ordering in for a meeting as well as large companies holding seminars or training sessions for hundreds of people. We also hosted on-site meetings at the inn, where Madison business folks would hold private retreats, gazing at the sailboats breezing past while creating sandwiches to their liking, from a sandwich buffet that for years defined our catering and informed our choices at Manna.

We developed a core of wisdom from our luncheon catering customers that informed our choices at Manna: Carnivores prefer poultry over all other meats. A majority of people prefer white bread to all other bread. Vegetarians appreciate creativity and are grateful when they can build a sandwich with more than just cheese, lettuce, or a smear of hummus. Thoughtful presentation leaves a lasting memory. Fresh, house-prepared food does not go unnoticed.

Over the years, our lunch menus remained fairly consistent, though every so often we would change them to accommodate waning tastes or update with fresh ideas. We served a daily special or two to keep things interesting for adventure seekers. But as much as people like to try something new (or say they do), we discovered in the end that they tend to order their favorite menu items, sometimes every day. Menu change is all fine and well, but you'd better not take away anyone's favorite dish.

Navigating this Chapter

At Manna, kitchens and coolers held an assemblage of components, or diverse building blocks, that line cooks could quickly access to prepare sandwiches or salads to order. They included ingredient bins, portions of cheeses and meats, assorted squeeze bottles of sauces and condiments, and so on. Along with the line cooks, but more behind the scenes were production cooks who toiled over those batches of sauces and dressings, roasting and slicing those meats and preparing everything else that ensured service could run smoothly.

Translating a restaurant kitchen into a restaurant cookbook has its challenges, as this chapter illustrates. Welcome to the world of from-scratch restaurant cookery, where not just every dish, but every component of every dish, is a recipe unto itself. For example, the Medi-Wrap sandwich (page 183) comprises five distinct recipes, which likely seem daunting for a home cook. This chapter is organized to help with that.

The first part presents what I think of as a "deconstruction" of the sandwiches (or platters)—a series of recipes for the individual parts. Following a few recipes for some of the core "proteins," you will find recipes for the many "building blocks" from which our menu items were constructed. Any of these may be used in any way you like to make your own creations. The more parts you want to make and keep on hand, the more flexibility you will have to re-create Manna sandwiches or design your own masterpieces.

Following the building blocks are a handful of recipes (more like formulas) for popular sandwiches and salads "reconstructed" as the menu items they once were. The sandwich descriptions cross-reference all their components, including the building blocks. From these two approaches to the sandwiches—in their individual parts and then described as they had appeared on the menus—I hope your toolbox will be adequately filled for an inspired future of sandwich creativity.

Finally, after all that seemingly complicated work of making a simple sandwich, the chapter concludes with recipes for delicious sandwich accompaniments—a few side salads and a number of soups. Have fun!

The "Meats"

I include quotation marks in this section's title because the more accurate term for it is "Proteins," a more all-inclusive heading that includes meats, fish, bean- or legume-based items, and eggs. But what a soulless term!

We rarely served cold-cut meat (save for some ham), believing that convenience did not outweigh quality. For example, from the beginning, we used beef tenderloin for our roast beef, marinating it overnight and roasting it to a juicy, seductive medium rare. As the centerpiece of many a business meeting, wedding, or holiday table since we began catering, that meat alone contributed greatly to our success. A few favorite protein recipes follow.

A Note About the Brisket

I have included Manna's brisket recipe as part of a focused collection of Jewish foods for the Manna soul in the "Jewish Fridays" chapter on pages 340-341.

The Art of the Sandwich

I love watching my husband, Mike, craft a sandwich for himself. Before my eyes, his own private Picasso emerges. First, he selects his bread—for him, the focus of the entire experience—and decides which meats and cheeses he is in the mood for. Then he scours the fridge and freezer for interesting building blocks—spreads or ingredients that we have squirreled away for just these moments, like jalapeño pesto; caramelized onions; harissa; bacon jam; or bright, multi-colored cherry tomatoes from the end-of-season farmers' market, roasted to an intense sweetness with garlic and chili pepper flakes. Sometimes he adds a final touch like thin slices of banana pepper, maybe a spoonful of aioli, or a crown of green leaf lettuce, for the crisp cool balance it provides. He assembles his masterpiece with passion, fussing over ingredient placement, always grilling the bread, and making sure that the cheese bubbles in the broiler just so. And he's right—his sandwiches are always better than mine!

CHICKEN SHAWARMA

Makes about 6 servings

 Start to finish in less than a half hour

This is the chicken used in our shawarma platter, but it is a versatile base for all sorts of meals. At home, we make wrap variations, serve it as a component of a Buddha bowl, or add some extra veggies and toss it with pasta. It is especially great for low-carbing it (cook up a bunch and leave it in the fridge for snacking).

Seasoning MIx

1 tablespoon turmeric

1 1/2 teaspoons salt

2 teaspoons coriander

1 teaspoon cumin

1 teaspoon black pepper

1 teaspoon white pepper

1 teaspoon cayenne

1/8 teaspoon cinnamon

1/8 teaspoon allspice

1 tablespoon olive oil

1/2 cup plain yogurt

2 pounds boneless, skinless chicken breasts, cut into 3/4-inch cubes

Vegetable oil for frying

1. Combine all seasoning ingredients (turmeric through allspice) in a medium bowl. Thoroughly coat the chicken pieces with the seasoning mix.
2. Mix oil and yogurt in a small bowl. Add to seasoned chicken and toss together, making sure all pieces are thoroughly coated. Marinate for one hour, or store marinated chicken in the freezer for up to 3 months.
3. To cook chicken, heat a sauté pan or wok over medium-high heat with vegetable oil. Stir-fry the chicken pieces in batches (do not crowd the pan) until no longer pink, but still juicy, about 5 to 8 minutes.

JAMAICAN JERK CHICKEN

(One Marinade and Two Cooking Techniques)

Makes 1/4 cup marinade, enough for 4 to 6 six-ounce servings of chicken

 Start to finish in less than a half hour

The roasted, sliced jerk chicken we used for sandwiches in our catering rivaled the beef tenderloin in popularity. It was our standard preparation for cold chicken, and the sauce later became the basis for hot sandwiches at Manna. The flavor is unique, a particular amalgam of spicy Scotch bonnet peppers, garlic, and other spices. It can be fiery hot, but even if you are averse to heat (I am not so tolerant myself, these days), you can still enjoy the flavors of this sauce through judicious use. That is, don't let the scary word "spicy" keep you from trying it, because its flavors are wonderful on their own.

I have presented two ways to cook jerk chicken. Both use the same marinade. The stovetop method is a quick stir-fry, with the meat cut into small chunks. Because chunks offer more surface area for the sauce to cling to, this version tends to be a bit spicier. The oven version takes a little longer but is hands-free. The breasts cook while you do other things and are then sliced into strips for serving.

The marinade below also goes beautifully with shrimp, fish, and pork.

Marinade:*

2 tablespoons oil

1 tablespoon Walkerswood Hot and Spicy Jerk Seasoning (or other wet jerk sauce—not a dry rub)

1 tablespoon lemon juice

Mix together the marinade ingredients in a small prep bowl. Then use as much or as little as you like, depending on your personal preferences. (Allow 2 to 3 teaspoons of marinade for every 6 ounces of chicken. The lower amount produces an average heat level.)

*Once opened, the Walkerswood Seasoning will keep in the refrigerator for many months. The prepared marinade will keep for several weeks.

Chicken

24 ounces boneless chicken breasts (four 6-ounce breasts)

To cook the chicken, choose one of the following methods:

Stir-Fried on the Stovetop

1. Cut the chicken into 1-inch cubes. Mix the cubes with 2 teaspoons or more of the marinade for every 6-ounce breast.*
2. Set a medium sauté pan over medium-high heat and add a bit of oil. When hot, add the chicken pieces and stir-fry until done, about 5 to 7 minutes.

Roasted in the Oven

1. Preheat the oven to 400 degrees.
2. Coat each chicken breast with 2 teaspoons jerk marinade.* Place the breasts in a roasting pan and set in the oven. Roast until the center is still juicy but no longer pink, about 20 minutes.
3. Let the breasts sit on a cutting board for 5 minutes, then slice against the grain into 1/4-inch-thick slices.

*You may want to experiment to find your level of spice tolerance. Two teaspoons of the sauce will make the chicken average-spicy.

A Plug for Walkerswood Jerk Seasoning

Walkerswood Jerk Seasoning is one of the few prepared products I enthusiastically recommend. At Collins House, we ordered the seasoning wholesale in bright red buckets, but by the time we got to Manna, the company no longer sold it wholesale. Alas, it was a Woodman's trip every few weeks to keep our stock of jerk flowing. Woodman's always seems to carry it, and you can find it online as well. Walkerswood is replaceable, of course, but the jerk flavor will not be Manna's jerk flavor.

MARINATED ROAST TENDERLOIN

Makes enough for sandwiches for a small crowd of 8-12 people (needs to marinate overnight)

 **Project Alert! May require multiple stages or overnight preparations—read through before proceeding**

Sharon James turned 50 in 1991, and her husband Chuck wanted to surprise her with a party. He lined up The Collins House for the catering and planned a special menu, most of whose specifics are lost to Father Time. But included on her buffet was this beef tenderloin, marinated overnight, roasted rare, and sliced into medallions that were presented in elegant, overlapping slices on a silver platter, accompanied by an Apple Horseradish Sauce (page 164).

Chuck was beside himself with the stress of planning and pulling off the surprise, so you can imagine his reaction that evening when a Collins House staff person backed our catering van into his brand new BMW. (Perhaps you can imagine my reaction, too.) This was in the early days of our catering operations when every new customer had great potential as word-of-mouth advertising. We were eager to make a good impression and thought of it as our role to make the catering process smooth and stress-free. This was not the approach we had in mind. But the tenderloin carried the day. (Of course, our prompt, repair-related customer service efforts didn't hurt, either.) The tenderloin went on to become a signature item for our catering business, and that moment became, as they say, the beginning of a beautiful friendship.
For more than 25 years we would cater Sharon's festive Christmas gatherings, where the tenderloin, joined on the buffet by our quiche (and always the Mint Melts)—pages 298-300, became an annual highlight for her guests.

The recipe is simple but incredibly delicious. What probably made it so special to our customers is that it was unusual to use the tenderloin cut of beef for ordinary lunch sandwiches. The apple horsey sauce sealed the deal.

Marinate the meat overnight, the day before you want to roast it.

---

2 tablespoons olive oil

1 tablespoon minced garlic (2-3 large cloves)

1 teaspoon salt

1/2 teaspoon pepper

3/4 teaspoon dried rosemary, crushed to a powder

One whole tenderloin (2 1/2-3 pounds), silver skin removed (page 362)

---

1. In a small bowl, mix together all the ingredients except the tenderloin.
2. If you like, trim off about 2 to 3 inches from the narrow end of the beef. You can freeze the narrow end for other uses (or sear it in a pan and make steak and eggs for breakfast). Leaving it on is fine too, but the resulting sandwich slices will be small and perhaps overcooked.
3. Once the meat is ready to go, coat it with the marinade. Wrap the meat tightly in plastic and refrigerate overnight. It can also be frozen in the marinade for several months.
4. Remove the meat from the fridge (or defrost to fridge temperature) and set it on a roasting pan. Preheat the oven to 375 degrees.
5. Place the meat in the oven and roast until an instant thermometer registers 135 degrees when inserted into the thickest part of the meat. Start checking the temperature after about 25 minutes. The time will vary depending on the thickness of your roast and its temperature when it goes in the oven.
6. Remove the roast from the oven and, if you're using it for sandwiches, let it cool completely. Then cover and chill it. (It will cut more easily if it is chilled.) It can also be eaten hot, with a big bowl of mashed potatoes and some roasted asparagus.
7. For cold sandwiches, slice the meat as thinly as you can. For hot "platter meat," slice 1/8 to 1/4 inches thick.

Bread Matters

A top-notch sandwich is the product of top-notch ingredients, and it all starts with the bread. Since the beginning of Collins House Catering, this has been an important mantra for our business. At Collins House, we baked our own breads and roasted our own meats. Initially, we had ZERO experience in professional catering but a firm belief in our cooking, baking, and customer service skills, so off we went. It was a grassroots but professional approach to the whole thing. My catering partner, Jarno, made the daily bread based on whatever called to her that day ("I feel like wheat bread with a bit of honey today."), and that is what the client got. Sometimes, we would receive a call from a regular customer, specifically requesting the bread they had at their last catered affair. Jarno would chuckle and scratch her head, trying to remember what she made. But at Manna, where the same people came in with regularity, each day's bread had to be the same. So we ultimately formalized our Collins House bread recipes and added a few new ones from the Manna bakers, presenting a lineup that best complemented our sandwiches.

ROASTED GARLIC HUMMUS

Makes 2 cups

 **Start to finish in less than a half hour**

Caramelized onion hummus. Olive tapenade hummus. Spicy three-pepper hummus. The list goes on and demonstrates the versatility of what was once just "hummus," a simple dip/spread of Middle Eastern origins. Manna's version adds roasted garlic for a subtle, sweet-nutty component to the standard flavor profile.

If you want to use hummus as a sandwich spread, do not add too much extra liquid, or it will ooze off the edges of the bread and go "splootch" on your lap. But if you use it as a dip for veggies, you may want it a bit softer. This is a have-it-your-way recipe.

One can (15 ounces) garbanzo beans, drained and rinsed

4 large garlic cloves, peeled and roasted (page 359)

1 clove garlic minced, not roasted

1/4 cup tahini, or more to taste

2 tablespoons lemon juice, or more to taste

2 tablespoons water or more for thinning

2 tablespoons olive oil

1 teaspoon cumin

1/8 teaspoon cayenne pepper

1 teaspoon paprika

1 teaspoon salt

1/8 teaspoon black pepper

1. Place all the ingredients in the bowl of a food processor fitted with a steel blade. (You can also use an immersion blender.) Process for 2 minutes, scrape down the sides of the bowl, then continue to process until creamy and smooth. The longer you go, the more silken it will become.
2. Taste for balance of flavors and consistency. Hummus is easily adjusted to be a bit tangier (more lemon juice), thicker or thinner (more or less water), or richer in tahini flavor.

Building Blocks (aka Sandwiches Deconstructed)

Sometimes it takes but one out-of-the-ordinary ingredient to elevate a meal and etch it in one's memory. Arugula pesto pops with its nutty, distinct flavor. Bacon-onion jam provides a deeply contrasting, salty-sweet punch to delicately-flavored slices of turkey. Building blocks come in many varieties, from the meats, cheeses, and other protein components, to the sauces and dressings that flesh out a sandwich's (or salad's) ideas.

On the top shelf of my freezer (and in every narrow shelf on the door) is a cascade of tiny portion cups, each labeled in permanent marker with a word or an initial distinguishing one portion cup from the one next to it. (For recommendations on using portion cups as storage containers, refer to the discussion on page 154.) Some of the items are always there (e.g., caramelized onions, jalapeño pesto, chicken stock reduction), and when they run low, I replenish them, just as I might a jug of oil or a bottle of soy sauce. These are my building blocks, and I reach for them as I would any spice or flavoring. But the nifty part is that they are homemade, and as such, they give me the satisfaction of knowing precisely what went into making them. There are no preservatives. The salt level is just to my taste. And, because I know how much time and energy went into their making, I have a certain respect and appreciation for each ingredient as I cook with it.

The building blocks included in this chapter represent the many bins and squeeze bottles that lined the Manna kitchen every day, from dawn to dusk. The batch sizes were large, the hours for their making long, yet once lined up in their duck-rows, chilled, unwrapped and waiting, it took but minutes to assemble a sandwich or platter. A slice here, a spoonful there, a crumble over the top, and voila! Sounds easy, doesn't it? The answer is yes and no.

It takes a couple of hours to make caramelized onions, but don't let that deter you. The value of having these on hand as part of your pantry is well worth the time. You can make a batch to last you months. At Manna, we made 30 pounds at a time, but you might only do two pounds. We made house dressing to doll up hundreds and hundreds of side salads a day (plus more for other purposes), using a massive immersion blender. You will make a tiny batch with a whisk. The following recipes are the groundwork for the menu items that use them, and they make their appearances throughout the rest of the lunch chapter. They are here because they defined the sandwiches from Manna, but their uses extend far beyond that.

Plastic Portion Cups (for storage)

My home cooking relies on a freezer full of ingredients that I use in small amounts, including many of the building blocks described in this chapter. I also keep handy portions of fresh lemon or lime juice that I squeeze just for this purpose, or stock reductions for making sauces. Small plastic portion cups, with lids that snap tightly into place, make storage neat, organized, space-efficient, and convenient. (While I am not an advocate for increased plastic use—we wash out our Ziploc Bags and let them drip dry, and bring mesh silicone bags to the store for our vegetable shopping—this is one exception. You can wash and reuse these too as long as you don't ruin them in the microwave!)

It was because we ran a restaurant that these little storage containers came to our attention for home use. You can buy them by the sleeve (a sleeve of cups and a separate sleeve of matching lids) at any restaurant supply store or online. We use 1 ounce (2 tablespoons), 2 ounces (4 tablespoons), and 5 ounces (about 2/3 cup). These assorted sizes give us flexibility when deciding how to freeze an item, with consideration to how we will use it when we defrost it.

BACON JAM

Makes about 2 1/2 cups

 **Hands-on time less than an hour (additional cooking or chilling times involved—read through before beginning)**

Bacon jam is sweet and salty, tangy and sticky, both pedestrian and luxurious. We spread bacon jam on our brisket melt sandwich, but the jam has many applications. Use it to doll up an ordinary grilled cheese sandwich for a weekday repast. Serve it alongside a nice liver pate with plain crackers. Give it center stage as a spread for crostini on New Year's Eve, when decadence defines the evening. Or eat it, sparingly, with a spoon.

While this project is easy enough to accomplish, it does require some time for the onions to caramelize and the jam to come together.

1 1/2 pounds bacon, diced into 1/2-inch pieces
2 medium onions (about 12 ounces), diced
1 tablespoon minced garlic
1/2 cup cider vinegar
1/2 cup packed brown sugar
1/4 cup maple syrup
3/4 cup brewed coffee

1. Heat an 8-inch sauté pan over medium heat and add diced bacon. Cook until crisp, stirring often. Remove bacon from the pan with a slotted spoon and drain it on a paper towel. Leave the bacon drippings in the pan.
2. Add onions to the pan (the pan will be full) and sauté over medium heat until a little soft and translucent, about 10 minutes. Reduce heat to medium-low and continue cooking until the onions are caramelized, 1 1/4 to 1 1/2 hours. Stir every 10 minutes or so, and check the heat to make sure the onions do not burn before caramelizing. When they are done they will have shrunken considerably and will be a deep golden to brown color.
3. Add remaining ingredients to the onions, including cooked bacon, and simmer on low until thickened, another 30-plus minutes. Let partially cool.
4. Puree 1/3 to 1/2 of the mixture in a mini food processor or with an immersion blender. Add puree to the rest of the cooked ingredients and combine thoroughly. Let cool completely, then portion and freeze.

CARAMELIZED ONIONS

Makes 1 cup

Hands-on time less than an hour (additional cooking or chilling times involved—read through before beginning)

Caramelized onions offer an unexpected sweet note to the savory dishes they grace, but you can't just whip up a little batch each time you crave them. It takes around two hours to properly caramelize onions, and the final product barely resembles the original. Ten cups of raw, tear-inducing white onions slowly transform, under your watchful eye, into one cup of deep, dark, intensely flavored ribbons. They are distinctly sweet and have lost any hint of their initial sharpness—another food entirely, it seems. Since the cooking time is long, it is worth making these onions in a large batch and freezing them, so you only have to do it once in a while.

Cook them into scrambled eggs. Schmear them on toast. Adorn your sandwiches with little forkfuls. But go easy—with their flavor so concentrated, a little goes a long way.

The following recipe will result in about one cup of caramelized onions. Portion them into 2-tablespoon or 1/4-cup amounts and freeze the precious bundles for future culinary adventures. They will be on the freezer shelf waiting to turn your roast beef sandwich from ordinary to extraordinary shortly after you hit defrost on the microwave.

2 1/2 pounds yellow onions, peeled, halved, and sliced very thin (about 10 cups)

1/4 cup vegetable oil

1 1/2 teaspoons sugar

1 1/2 teaspoons red wine vinegar

1. Heat a medium skillet with high sides over medium heat. When hot, add the oil and then the onions. Cook the onions, stirring well every few minutes so that they cook evenly. During this stage, they will be giving up their water, a process that will be finished when all the water has cooked off. Adjust the heat down a bit, if necessary, so the onions do not brown, but they should stay at a good simmer for this step. (Allow 30 to 60 minutes.)
2. When the onions have become translucent and the extra water has cooked off, reduce the heat to medium low. They may have taken a light golden hue at this stage, a good sign that they are coming along nicely. Sprinkle sugar over the onions and continue to cook, stirring often.

3. Keep a good eye on the onions. Eventually, they will turn a deep caramel color, but you do not want them to "brown" from the cooking. There is a difference between "browning" in the pan and caramelizing, which happens as the sugars begin to change their molecular structure. Find a heat where they will cook slowly for about another 60 to 90 minutes without burning or browning from the pan heat. (Do not turn up the heat to hurry the process along.)
4. When the onions are golden brown and beginning to truly caramelize, add the vinegar to the pan and stir well. The vinegar will provide a counterpoint to the pure sweetness of the onions. Continue cooking until the onions are fully caramelized. The process is done when the onion pieces look like small, tawny interlaced ribbons with a jam-like consistency.
5. Let the onions cool completely, then portion and freeze.

TROPICAL FRUIT SALSA

Makes 3 cups

 Start to finish within an hour, give or take

Two recipes in this book, the Jamaican Chicken Sandwich and Marvel's Passion Salad, are partly defined by this exotic tropical fruit salsa. As with other fruit-based salsas, it goes well with roasted meats, especially spicy ones, and simple fish preparations.

Choosing ripe and fragrant fruit will make a big difference in the outcome. Frozen tropical fruit medleys work well, but read the ingredient list first. Bananas or berries are not flavors you want to include.

---

2 tablespoons vegetable oil

1 medium red onion finely chopped (about 1 cup)

1/2 medium sweet red pepper finely chopped (1/2 cup)

1 tablespoon finely grated ginger

1 cup finely chopped ripe papaya

1 cup finely chopped fresh or canned pineapple

1 cup finely chopped ripe mango

1/4 cup cider vinegar

1/4 cup packed brown sugar

2 teaspoons curry powder

1/2 teaspoon red pepper flakes

---

1. Heat the oil in a medium saucepan over medium heat. Add the red onion and sauté until softened, about 10 minutes. Add the red pepper and ginger and sauté, stirring often, until the peppers are softened, about 10 minutes.
2. Add the fruits, vinegar, brown sugar, curry powder, and red pepper flakes. Simmer, stirring occasionally, until the liquid has reduced to a thick syrup, about 30 minutes.
3. Puree a quarter of the cooked fruit mixture with an immersion blender or mini food processor. Return the puree to the pan and stir to combine with the remaining salsa.
4. Cool salsa completely, then portion and freeze.

ROMESCO SAUCE

Makes about 3 cups

 Start to finish in less than a half hour

Romesco is a classic sauce from the Spanish town of Catalonia, used to dress up simply prepared fish and seafood. It is so good it is worth finding different uses for it. At Manna, it popped brightly from beneath the layers of fresh veggies and multigrain bread, turning our Sunshine Dreamin' sandwich into a hearty, savory meal.

---

1 cup almonds, toasted until golden brown (page 363)

1 thick slice of white bread

1 tablespoon minced garlic

1 teaspoon red pepper flakes

Pinch of salt

Pinch of pepper

3 medium red peppers (about 1 1/4 pounds), roasted (page 360)

1/3 cup red wine vinegar

1/3 cup olive oil

---

1. Process almonds and bread in a food processor for 30 seconds. Add garlic, seasonings, roasted red peppers, and vinegar. Puree until smooth.
2. With the machine running, add oil in a slow, thin stream. Check for seasoning, then portion and freeze.

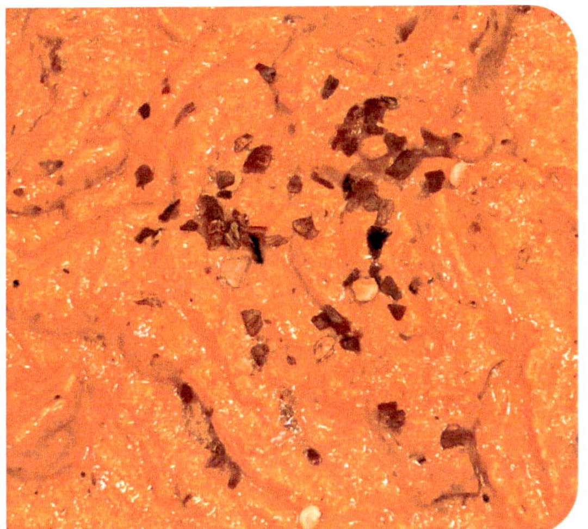

PESTO AND SONS

Start to finish in less than a half hour

If you call it "pesto," you usually refer to the thick sauce made from lots of fresh basil, garlic, pine nuts, Parmesan cheese, and olive oil. But from here, the imagination takes hold, and other ingredients may step in for the basil, resulting in intensely flavored, versatile sauces.

At Manna, pestos were mostly used as spreads for sandwiches, and for our catering customers, we created many a pasta salad or canapé with a pesto component. (See page 198 for Pasta Salad with Poblano Pesto.) Pestos provide an efficient way to preserve the bounty of summer and have many applications. Swirl pesto into a risotto, or spoon it atop a steamy baked potato. Use it as a simple accompaniment to grilled fish.

Here are a few to choose from, starting with the classic basil variety. Traditional pesto calls for pine nuts, but because they are expensive and their flavor is overwhelmed by the other ingredients, we substituted walnuts with no ill effect.

Classic Basil Pesto (yields about 1 1/4 cups)

1 cup packed fresh basil

1 1/2 teaspoons minced garlic

1/3 cup walnuts or pine nuts toasted and chopped (page 363)

1/2 cup Parmesan cheese

1/2 cup olive oil

Salt and pepper to taste

Arugula Pesto (yields about 1 1/4 cups)

1 cup packed fresh arugula

1/2 teaspoon minced garlic

1/4 cup walnuts, toasted and chopped (page 363)

1/2 cup Parmesan cheese

1/2 cup olive oil

Salt and pepper to taste

Roasted Poblano Pesto (yields a scant cup)

6 ounces poblano chiles, or 1 large, roasted (page 360)

1 small jalapeño chile, roasted (page 360)

1/2 bunch cilantro, trimmed and roughly chopped

2 cloves garlic, peeled and roughly chopped

1/4 cup grated Parmesan cheese

1 1/2 tablespoons lemon juice, or more to taste

3 tablespoons olive oil

Salt and pepper to taste

1. For all of the above pesto varieties, place all of the ingredients except the oil, salt and pepper into the bowl of a food processor. Blend for 1 minute, then drizzle in the oil while the processor is still running. Scrape down the bowl, add salt and pepper, then give the food processor a final whirl.
2. Use immediately or store refrigerated or frozen.

ROASTED GARLIC CREAM CHEESE

Makes about 2 cups

 Start to finish in less than a half hour

Use this delicious spread in wraps as a rich and creamy component in place of sliced cheese. It creates a different sandwich experience. It can also be swirled into scrambled eggs, mashed in with potatoes, or spread onto slices of ham and rolled up for a quick, high-protein snack.

8 ounces cream cheese

1/4 cup roasted garlic (page 359)

2 tablespoons half & half

1/8 teaspoon salt

1/8 teaspoon black pepper

Combine all ingredients in the bowl of a mixer fitted with a paddle. Mix on medium speed for 2 to 3 minutes until smooth and spreadable. It should keep for a couple of weeks in the fridge.

GARLIC ROASTED CHERRY TOMATOES

Makes 1-2 cups

 Start to finish in less than a half hour

At late summer farmers' markets, nothing commands my attention more than the overflowing boxes of red, yellow, orange, and purple cherry tomatoes. I can't help myself. I buy oodles of them every week and then get to the task of adding these autumn-hued gems to my freezer building blocks.

Roasted cherry tomatoes have a sweet, tomato-y intensity that provides a punch to many things—soups, pasta dishes, risottos, sandwich toppings. Or make a pesto-like spread out of them. (I never have, but it sure sounds good!)

2 pints assorted cherry tomatoes

1/2 teaspoon red pepper flakes

2 teaspoons garlic, minced

1/4 teaspoon salt

1/4 teaspoon black pepper

1-2 tablespoons olive oil to coat the tomatoes

1. Preheat the oven to 425 degrees. Line a sheet pan with a piece of parchment paper, and lightly grease the parchment.
2. Quarter the larger cherry tomatoes and halve the smaller ones. Toss in a bowl with the rest of the ingredients, then spread the mixture out on the pan.
3. Roast the tomatoes until they are speckled with darkish brown spots and appear partially shrunken, about 12 minutes or longer.
4. Remove from the oven and cool, then portion into bags or small jars and freeze, if not using immediately. (It is best to portion them into quantities you would use since they freeze together into a solid mass.)

ROASTED RED PEPPER RELISH

Makes 2 cups

 Start to finish in less than a half hour

Slather this tangy relish over burgers or use it as a condiment for roast pork or chicken, as we did for catering. At Manna, it appeared in the Peter Wrappit (page 185), providing a snappy pop to the gentle collection of veggies and garlic cream cheese spread.

1 1/2 pounds (3-4 large) red peppers, roasted (page 360) and cut into 1/4-inch dice

1 1/2 tablespoons olive oil

3/4 cup chopped onion

1 teaspoon finely chopped garlic

2 tablespoons cider vinegar

1 tablespoon sugar

1/8 teaspoon dry mustard

1/8 teaspoon cayenne pepper

1. In a medium saucepan over medium heat, add the oil and onions and sauté until the onions are soft. Add the peppers and garlic and continue to cook for 2-3 minutes.
2. Combine the vinegar, sugar, dry mustard, and cayenne pepper in a small bowl, then add to the pan with the peppers and onions and cook until most of the liquid has evaporated. Let cool before using. Store refrigerated or frozen.

APPLE HORSERADISH SAUCE

Makes about 1 cup

 **Start to finish in less than a half hour**

Once, in an otherwise friendly review, our Tenderloin Triumph sandwich was referred to as "dry as dust." Well, no wonder. During our catering years, our roasted tenderloin was served with abundant amounts of this apple horseradish sauce. Our corporate luncheon catering was in demand because of it. However, at Manna, when we first discussed how to present the sandwich to our customers, the nervous Nellies on our staff felt we should put the sauce on the side to avoid offending people who didn't like it. I always felt strongly that a sandwich was meant to be offered up how WE felt it was meant to be crafted, and if customers didn't like it, they could request a modification. I lost this battle but ultimately won the war. After that less-than-flattering review, we designed our sandwiches to be perfect as described, and if customers wanted to change them, be our guest!

This horsey sauce is easy to make and goes well with most sandwich meat, especially beef or ham. It is a horseradish sauce for horseradish haters. The apple, onion, and cider vinegar bring sweetness and gentility to the harshness of the horseradish, and a generous dollop is often not enough.

1/3 cup prepared horseradish, measured then drained

1/4 cup mayonnaise

1 1/2 tablespoons cider vinegar

1 1/2 tablespoons Dijon mustard

1 teaspoon sugar

1/2 teaspoon salt

1 pinch cayenne pepper

Half of a medium apple, cored but skin left on, grated

2 1/2 tablespoons grated red onion

Whisk all ingredients together in a stainless-steel bowl. Chill and store.
It will keep at least 1 week.

GARLIC AIOLI

Makes about 1 cup

 Start to finish in less than a half hour

Aioli is jazzed up mayonnaise. Basic mayo is an emulsification of egg yolks and oil, and an aioli includes garlic and sometimes other flavors. Use this sauce as you would a mayo on sandwiches, and you will have kicked your sandwich up a notch or three. It will keep 1 to 2 weeks in the fridge.

2 egg yolks

1 teaspoon lemon juice

2 teaspoons water

2 teaspoons crushed garlic

1/4 teaspoon salt

3/4 cup canola oil

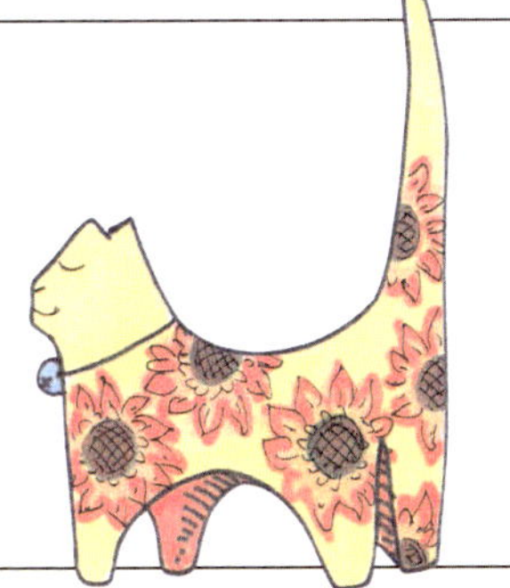

1. Combine all ingredients except canola oil in a small but deep bowl. (You can also do this in the bowl of a mini food processor, but the volume of ingredients is too small for a full-sized food processor.)
2. Drizzle in the oil in a thin stream, all the while beating with a whisk to emulsify the aioli. The mixture should be thick and smooth.

HOUSE DRESSING

Makes about 1 1/2 cups

 **Start to finish in less than a half hour**

Often when a restaurant features a house dressing, it is a statement, a signature menu item so good that no other choices are needed. Such was the case with this dressing, used on our side of greens. Although we did keep a Ranch dressing and a simple balsamic vinaigrette available for people who needed other options, this dressing was in a class of its own. It joined the A-list of Manna recipes, keeping company with such luminaries as the oatcakes and the pumpkin chocolate chip muffins.

This amazing little recipe was first introduced to us by a former Collins House staffer and caterer, Scott Perkins, now a design historian at Fallingwater (a famous Frank Lloyd Wright-designed home in Pennsylvania). One feature that makes it so versatile is its creaminess, which comes, in the absence of any dairy, from the egg-oil emulsification. My younger son, Ike, who normally tells me I can leave him important recipes in my will, insisted he have this one the moment he had a kitchen of his own.

Be patient when drizzling in the oil, and you will be rewarded with a silken dressing. Make it at least one or two hours ahead of use, allowing the flavors to marry and mellow a bit, but don't keep it longer than a week in the fridge.

---

1 egg

1/3 cup white wine vinegar

1/4 teaspoon sugar

1/4 cup Dijon mustard

2 teaspoons minced garlic

1/2 teaspoon salt

1/2 teaspoon pepper

1 cup vegetable oil

2 teaspoons minced, packed fresh basil

---

1. Place all the ingredients from the egg through the pepper in a food processor. Blend for 1 minute.
2. With the food processor running, add the oil in a slow, thin stream until the dressing is emulsified. Add basil at the end and blend for 30 seconds more.
3. This dressing will keep for at least 5 days in the fridge.

RUSSIAN DRESSING

Makes about 1 1/2 cups

 **Start to finish in less than a half hour**

Russian dressing isn't supposed to be spicy, but this one is just a bit. For a few of our customers, the spiciness was a deal-killer, but for most people, it was what made the Reuben. And the Monte Christo. And the leftover pan-fried potatoes at the end of a busy day. When Manna closed its doors in 2020, someone asked if we would sell a gallon of it.

This dressing keeps at least a couple of weeks.

---

2 tablespoons dill pickle, finely minced

1 tablespoon grated onion

1 teaspoon prepared horseradish

1/2 teaspoon Worcestershire sauce

1 1/2 teaspoons pickle juice

1 teaspoon lemon juice

1 tablespoon roughly chopped parsley

1 cup mayonnaise

1/4 cup sour cream

1 to 1 1/2 tablespoons sriracha chili sauce (to taste)

Mix all the ingredients in a bowl. (That's it!) It'll keep at least a couple of weeks in the fridge.

CILANTRO DRESSING

Makes about 1 1/2 cups

 Start to finish in less than a half hour

This excellent dressing is healthful and versatile. It is thick and creamy from the pureed avocado and yogurt and has no added oil. We used it for the quinoa salad, but it would make an excellent dressing for meats or fish or salads.

1/2 cup mashed avocado (about 1 medium avocado)

2 tablespoons chopped green bell pepper

2 tablespoons chopped onion

1/2 teaspoon minced garlic

1 teaspoon minced serrano or jalapeno pepper

1 teaspoon salt

1 packed cup cilantro leaves, roughly minced

1 tablespoon white wine vinegar

2 teaspoons fresh lime juice

2/3 cup plain yogurt

2 tablespoons water

Place all ingredients in a food processor or blender and blend until smooth. Let sit for an hour or two before serving to let the flavors blend and mellow. Refrigerate for up to a week.

CHIPOTLE LIME DRESSING

Makes about 1/2 cup

 **Start to finish in less than a half hour**

A little of this smoky/spicy dressing goes a long way. Be sure to add it in small increments to your dishes. You can always add but never subtract.

2 chipotle peppers from a can with adobo sauce (don't rinse)

1 garlic clove, minced

1/4 cup lime juice

1 teaspoon sugar

1/4 teaspoon salt

1/4 teaspoon pepper

1/2 cup olive oil

Place all the ingredients except the oil in a mini food processor or blender, and blend well. Drizzle in the oil while mixing. Stores for a couple of weeks in the fridge. (This dressing can be frozen.)

FETA DRESSING

Makes about 1 cup

 Start to finish in less than a half hour

A thick, creamy dressing with Middle Eastern/Mediterranean origins that works on salads, as a dip for veggies, and as an accompaniment to the Chicken Shawarma that prompted its creation (page 147).

1/2 cup mayonnaise

1/4 cup plain yogurt (not Greek)

2 teaspoons lemon juice

1/4 teaspoon lemon zest

1 small clove garlic, minced

1 tablespoon minced parsley

1/2 teaspoon cumin

1/8 teaspoon cardamom

1/4 teaspoon black pepper

Pinch of cayenne pepper

1/4 cup feta cheese, crumbled, but not too fine

Mix all ingredients except feta in a bowl and whisk well. Add feta at the end and stir it in with a spatula. Refrigerate for at least a week.

SEXY DRESSING

Makes about 1/2 cup

 **Start to finish in less than a half hour**

I love this simple vinaigrette. It has a bit of sugar, a splash of spice and is considerably more interesting than a basic balsamic dressing. At one time, it graced our Sexy Salad, a bed of greens all a-tumble with avocado, candied pecans, juicy red strawberries, and bits of salty bleu cheese. If you ever need a change of pace from our house dressing, let this vinaigrette flirt with you.

1/4 cup olive oil
1/4 cup raspberry vinegar
1/2 tablespoon balsamic vinegar
1 tablespoon sugar
1/4 teaspoon hot sauce
1/4 teaspoon cinnamon
1/4 teaspoon salt
1/8 teaspoon pepper

Mix all ingredients together well in a jar with a lid, and shake it, shake it, shake it. It will keep a long time at room temperature or in the fridge.

Sandwiches from the Menu, Reconstructed

A restaurant production cook's job is to ready the pantry with building blocks, much like the ones presented in the previous section, so that the line cooks have them in easy reach for quick assembly. The production cook may have six large projects to accomplish over an eight-hour shift, and as long as he completes them in that time frame, his day is a success. The line cook's job, in contrast, is to make sandwiches or craft salads from a huge array of building blocks quickly, efficiently, and accurately—snap snap snap. Within that same eight hours, four line cooks might process hundreds of plates of food, in batches of four or eight or ten, in about ten minutes for a batch. At home, when you open your fridge and pull out the makings of a sandwich, you become your own line cook, except that your time is your own.

Many favorite sandwiches from Manna menus have been "reconstructed" on the following pages. Every component you would find in one of those sandwiches is listed in "The Parts," right down to their lettuce leaf and smear of mayo. Any component that is a building block recipe is cross-referenced to the page that recipe is on.

The *how-to* of making the sandwiches is written more loosely here than in other recipes in the book. It's more about guidance or tips or observations and less about weights and measures and dice sizes. My goal was to bring these sandwiches to life with their stories and lore while providing the specifics a former customer would need to re-create a favorite memory. So often, our customers asked for a sandwich by name but then made changes to suit their preferences. I imagine you will do the same here, whether you were a longtime regular or a newbie to Manna food.

Note: Each reconstruction recipe makes one sandwich. I have deliberately left out quantities for each part that goes into a sandwich because you should assemble it in any way you like as your own sandwich creator. Also, it feels silly to specify "one leaf of lettuce," or "4 ounces of meat," or "2 tablespoons of dressing." While such specificity is crucial in a restaurant setting for portion control purposes and sandwich consistency, those rules don't apply here.

"ONLY IN WISCONSIN" BRISKET MELT

This sandwich is sort of a Jewish-Wisconsin fusion food. Melted cheese curds, practically our state food, are an adornment, but Manna's red wine-braised beef brisket takes center stage. This is a hearty sandwich, dripping with gravy six hours in the making, and it requires a sturdy bread to support it. At Manna, we served it on grilled challah slices.

The Parts

Melted or softened butter for grilling the bread

Challah Bread slices (pages 309-311)

Red Wine-Braised Beef Brisket (pages 340-341), warmed in some of its gravy*

Cheese curds, sliced

Bacon Jam (page 155) or cooked bacon slices

Frizzled Onions (page 365)

To Prepare One Sandwich

Butter and grill two slices of challah in a pan on medium-low heat until crisp and golden. Place warmed brisket over one slice of the bread. Top with cheese curds and slide under a broiler for a few minutes to get the curds melty and bubbly. In the meantime, spread the other grilled bread slice with some bacon jam (or use cooked bacon slices). When the curds are melty, remove the bottom half from the oven and top with a small handful of onion frizzles. Cover with the top half, and enjoy. Extra napkins are encouraged.

Sandwich Tips

Bread Base: Challah is a nice choice, not just because it fits the Jewish bill, but because it is a gentle-tasting bread sturdy enough to support the gravy, yet doesn't distract from the strong flavors of the sandwich. When grilled, it goes all crisp on the outside while staying soft inside.

*Brisket: When you slice beef brisket for an entree, there will invariably be some scraps and shreds that don't hold together in neat-looking pieces. We used these extras for the sandwich. Slices or scraps—it's all good. But if you slice the brisket specifically for sandwiches, slice it thin. Thicker slices make for nice mouthfuls at the end of a fork, but in a sandwich they can make for awkward bites.

TENDERLOIN TRIUMPH

Bitter, spicy horseradish is not for everyone—myself included, but with two exceptions. At Passover, bracingly hot horseradish is slathered atop gently flavored ovals of gefilte fish, and to me, the two seem made for each other. (This is possibly because, in Jewish households, you eat this combination more or less from birth.) I never eat plain horseradish at any other time of the year. But in the horseradish sauce used here, the root's attention-grabbing quality is tamed by other ingredients, and the result is a new profile with prominent apple flavor and a gentler horseradish side note.

Tenderloin makes wonderful cold-cut meat. It is lean yet flavorful, and because it is a long, slender cut of meat, it more fully takes on the flavors of its marinade. Roasted rare, cooled and thinly sliced, it is an elegant base for sandwiches. In 35 years of catering, and at Manna, it was the only beef we used for this purpose.

This sandwich shines because of the beef and the amazing apple horseradish sauce. If you're looking for a menu item a little more sophisticated than a sandwich, serve the tenderloin sliced and laid out in graceful, overlapping slices on a beautiful platter. The batch of horseradish sauce you serve with it will disappear in no time.

The Parts

Rustic French roll or halved baguette

Marinated, Roast Tenderloin, thinly sliced (pages 150-151)

A leaf or two of leaf lettuce

Apple Horseradish Sauce (page 164)

To Prepare One Sandwich

Pile the tenderloin onto your bread, spoon on the horsey sauce, and top with lettuce. The sauce is wet and juicy, so no mayo is needed.

THE SPICY CATRINA

Catrina was the sister of my first kitchen manager, and she joined us at Manna not long after we opened. This sandwich was her creation. We named it not just for her but also in memory of the victims of Hurricane Katrina, which hit New Orleans the month we opened, bringing some staff our way.

Many people like spicy foods. At least millennials do (especially millennials who work in restaurant kitchens). Young or old, though, people who enjoyed a bit of fire with their sandwich gravitated to the Spicy Catrina. As at any good Asian restaurant, this sandwich can be one, two, or three peppers strong by adjusting the amount of jerk marinade used in preparing the chicken.

The Parts

Jamaican Jerk Chicken (pages 148-149)

Melted or softened butter for grilling the bread

Ciabatta or rustic French rolls, halved

Classic Basil Pesto (pages 160-161)

Fresh tomato slices

Crisp-cooked bacon slices

Pepper Jack cheese slices

To Prepare One Sandwich

Prepare the chicken according to one of the techniques in the jerk chicken recipe.

While the chicken is cooking, butter and then grill the bread halves buttered side down in a pan or on a griddle over medium-low heat. When crisp and golden, spread the top half with pesto, and when the chicken is cooked, set it on the bottom half. Top the chicken with tomatoes, then bacon and finally cheese. Set the bottom half under a hot broiler until the cheese is bubbly. Add the top half and grab a few napkins. You'll need them.

CLASSIC REUBEN

Like brothers and sisters, Reuben and Rachel sandwiches share a genetic core, yet their personalities are as different as siblings can be.

While some think of a Reuben as the quintessential Jewish sandwich, it is not quite so, since the sandwich mixes meat (corned beef) and dairy (Swiss cheese), a forbidden combination in the world of kosher. More genuinely Jewish would be a hot corned beef sandwich on rye with a schmear of mustard. This basic sandwich can be made ethereal by piling it with thin-sliced house-cured corned beef and serving it, still steaming, with crisp, cool kosher dills on the side.

And that's exactly the way Katz's Deli does it. Katz's, the famous Jewish delicatessen on Manhattan's lower east side, offers not just an eye-popping sandwich but an experience to match. Long lines, crowded tables, and impatient counter staff slicing the meat to order contribute to a sense of chaos that somehow feels meant to be.

A Reuben, then, is a thoroughly tricked-out corned beef sandwich full of complexity and intrigue. Pungent sauerkraut, creamy Russian dressing, and nutty Swiss cheese are added to the piles of thinly sliced corned beef, and the concoction is grilled to crunchy-on-the-outside, drippy-on-the-inside glory—what's not to love? (Unless you are one of those sauerkraut haters, like Mike, in which case move on to the Rachel!) Reubens are a cornerstone sandwich of any deli or sandwich restaurant worth its mustard.

Manna's classic Reuben has several defining characteristics: Pratzel's corn tzizel rye bread, a lean house-cured corned beef, and a slightly spicy Russian dressing.

The Parts

Melted or softened butter for grilling the bread

Swiss cheese slices

Corn Tzizel Rye Bread slices (pages 312-313)

Lean corned beef from the brisket, thinly sliced

Sauerkraut, well drained

Russian Dressing (page 167)

To Prepare One Sandwich

Butter the bread slices on one side. Place the cheese on the unbuttered side of one half. Grill both halves of the bread until crisp and lightly browned in a pan over medium-low heat.

While the bread is grilling, heat a second pan over medium heat. Pile the corned beef in one pile and the sauerkraut in another. Use tongs to toss each in its own pile, so they get steamy and heated through. When the corned beef is ready, transfer it to one of the bread slices. Quickly toss the kraut with some of the Russian dressing, and pile that on top of the corned beef. Place the second bread slice on top and press down lightly. Remove the finished sandwich from the pan to a cutting board, halve the sandwich on a diagonal and serve with a dish of extra Russian dressing for dipping.

CLASSIC RACHEL

This almost-as-famous variation of the Reuben is a compromise sandwich that's as good as its counterpart. For the sake of all the eaters out there who don't eat red meat, the Rachel substitutes roast turkey for corned beef and coleslaw for sauerkraut. (You either love or hate sauerkraut, and while I fall on the love side, I know sour, fermented cabbage is not for everyone. Yet I love the Rachel almost as much for the sweet/salty, cool/warm combination of a crisp slaw with good meat.)

The Parts

Melted or softened butter for grilling the bread

Swiss cheese slices

Corn Tzizel Rye Bread slices (pages 312-313)

Roasted turkey breast, thinly sliced

Generously heaped coleslaw

Russian Dressing (page 167)

To Prepare One Sandwich

Butter the bread slices on one side. Place the cheese on the unbuttered side of one half. Grill both halves of the bread until crisp and lightly browned in a pan over medium-low heat.

While the bread is grilling, heat a second pan over medium heat, and warm up the turkey. When it's hot, transfer it to one of the bread slices and top it with coleslaw. Drizzle on a little Russian dressing. Place the second bread slice on top and press down lightly. Remove the finished sandwich from the pan to a cutting board, halve the sandwich on a diagonal and serve with a dish of extra Russian dressing for dipping.

GRILLED HAM AND GOUDA

This was one of the original sandwiches at Manna, made in part to showcase our caramelized onions. For a time, we substituted Havarti cheese, but what an outcry! The loudest and most persistent complaining came from my son, who accused us of having ruined his favorite sandwich. Back came the Gouda.

The Parts

Melted or softened butter for grilling the bread and searing the spinach

Corn Tzizel Rye Bread slices (pages 312-313)

Caramelized Onions (pages 156-157)

Sliced aged Gouda cheese

Ham (a good-quality deli version), thinly sliced

Fresh spinach leaves, de-stemmed and left whole

Salt

To Prepare One Sandwich

Butter two slices of bread on one side. Spread a thin layer of caramelized onions on the unbuttered side of one of the bread slices and top the onions with the sliced Gouda. Then grill both bread slices, buttered side down, in a pan over medium-low heat until golden and crisp.

While the bread is grilling, heat a second pan over medium heat and warm the ham. Transfer the ham to one of the grilling bread slices, then melt a teaspoon of butter in the empty pan. Add a large handful of spinach and a tiny pinch of salt. Toss the spinach with tongs until it is wilted, then set it atop the ham. Place the second bread slice on top and press down lightly. Remove the finished sandwich from the pan to a cutting board, halve the sandwich on a diagonal and serve with a dish of extra Russian dressing for dipping.

JAMAICAN CHICKEN SANDWICH

Sweet, cool tropical fruits and spicy Scotch bonnet-based jerk chicken vie for attention in this assemblage. Definitely a case of opposites attracting.

The Parts

Jamaican Jerk Chicken (pages 148-149) prepared using the stir-fry technique

Melted or softened butter for grilling the bread

Ciabatta or rustic French roll, halved

Tropical Fruit Salsa (page 158)

To Prepare One Sandwich

Cook the jerk chicken according to the stir-fry technique in the instructions. At the end of cooking, stir-fry a couple of spoonfuls of the fruit salsa in with the chicken.

Butter the two halves of the roll and then grill them buttered side down in a pan or on a griddle over medium-low heat. When they are crisp and golden, pile the chicken onto the bottom half of the roll and top generously with cool salsa. Place the second half of the roll on the sandwich and dig in.

TUNA MELT

Every time we reviewed and updated our menus, we looked closely at "the numbers"—the data behind whether a certain item should be pulled to make room for new and exciting creations. Someone always suggested the tuna melt should go because it was too ordinary to take up valuable real estate on a limited menu.

But it was our number one bestseller, so it stayed put. Manna's tuna melt, warm and friendly, appealed to conservative eaters, people avoiding spice, and older customers who liked simplicity, and anyone for whom tuna sandwiches evoked childhood and the real-food lunches their moms had once fixed for them. (Except my mom, who ruined tuna salad by making it with Miracle Whip. I'll never forget the first tuna sandwich I had at my friend Donna's house. Her mom used Hellmann's mayo, which was a life-changing revelation for me.)

During Sean's tenure as our FOH manager, he turned the tuna melt into the ultimate Jewish millennial fusion sandwich, using grilled corn tzizel rye bread and generously drizzling sriracha sauce over the tuna before grilling. I was skeptical at first, but I must admit it was pretty great.

The Parts

Melted or softened butter for grilling the bread

Ciabatta or rustic French roll, halved

Tuna salad (recipe below)

Medium cheddar cheese, sliced

To Prepare One Sandwich

Butter the two halves of the roll and grill them, buttered side down, in a pan or on a griddle over medium-low heat until golden. Spread as much tuna salad as you like on the bottom half, then top with cheese slices. Set both halves on a pan under a broiler and cook until the cheese is bubbly, then top the sandwich with the second half of the roll.

Manna's Tuna Salad

1 small can (5 ounces) white albacore tuna in water

2-3 tablespoons mayonnaise (to taste)

1/4 stalk celery, cut into 1/8-inch dice

2 teaspoons sweet red pepper cut into 1/8-inch dice

1/4 scallion, thinly sliced

Drain tuna well in a colander and press out extra liquid. Place in a bowl and mix in the rest of the ingredients, taking care to keep the tuna somewhat chunky.

BUBBE'S EGG SALAD

Egg salad seems to be such a Jewish thing, and for this reason, we called it Bubbe's Egg Salad. (Bubbe—pronounced buh-bee—means grandmother in Yiddish.) Every time we catered a luncheon spread for a bar mitzvah or some such, egg salad would be on the menu. The guests treated it more like a side salad than a sandwich filler, taking huge spoonfuls and nestling them between the noodle kugel and chopped Israeli salad.

The Parts

Challah Bread slices (pages 309-311) or other soft, gentle bread

A scoop of egg salad (recipe below)

Lettuce leaves if you must (I never understood lettuce—to me it was more distraction than complement)

To Prepare One Sandwich

Place a scoop of egg salad onto a bread slice, then top with a lettuce leaf and another slice of bread.

Manna's Egg Salad

Makes about 1 1/4 cups

My chef-son, Josh, taught me a foolproof technique for hard-boiling eggs—not so much to get them to peel more easily but to be perfectly cooked, with no ugly gray edge to the yolks. In egg salad, that gray hue is less noticeable, but when a perfectly cooked hard-boiled egg stands alone on a salad or platter, its pristine yolk is really very beautiful.

4 eggs
1 scallion, thinly sliced
1 1/2 tablespoons finely chopped sweet red pepper
2 tablespoons mayonnaise, preferably Hellmann's Real Mayonnaise
1/4 teaspoon salt
1/8 teaspoon pepper
A couple dashes of Tabasco, or more to taste

1. Place eggs in a pot with water to cover. Bring to a boil, then immediately shut off the heat and cover the pot. Set a timer for 11 minutes. After the timer goes off, immediately place the pot under cold running water and continue to fill it with fresh cold water until the water stays cold.
2. While the eggs are cooking and cooling, combine the remaining ingredients in a bowl. When eggs are cool, peel and push them through a safety grater (Equipment I Love, page 83) or coarsely chop them. Add to remaining ingredients and mix well with a rubber spatula.

EARTHY DELIGHTS (AND ITS SEQUEL: EARTH, SPIN, AND FIRE)

For a while, the grilled vegetarian sandwich we called Earthy Delights was a menu favorite: roasted asparagus spears and grilled portabella mushrooms topped with melted brie on grilled multigrain bread, spread with caramelized onions. It was a veritable garden of earthy delights, its name a joyous riff on a famous painting. (I was raised by a father who loved wordplay almost as much as he loved food.)

Somewhere along the line at Manna, we had cause to swap spinach for the asparagus and Havarti for the brie, and, happily, the new version was equally as popular. However, we did learn that when a sandwich's ingredients change, its name must, too, or you will never hear the end of it. (Customers can be very loyal to food!) So I renamed this sandwich Earth, Spin, and Fire. The name dates me, I admit. But I love the subtle weaving of ingredient and preparation references with a fun twist (a spin, you might say) of words. I love secrets just as much as food and wordplay, so we rarely explained the significance of our menu item names, aiming to provide the guests with a moment of delight upon discovery.

The Parts

Melted or softened butter for grilling the bread

Multigrain Bread slices (pages 316-317)

Caramelized Onions (pages 156-157)

Portabella mushrooms, sliced and seared in olive oil with a dusting of salt

Asparagus spears roasted with a bit of garlic, olive oil, and a dusting of salt

Slices of brie cheese

To Prepare One Sandwich

Butter the bread slices. Spread one slice of the bread with a thin coating of caramelized onions and grill both bread slices, buttered side down in a pan over medium-low heat. Layer the mushrooms, asparagus, and cheese on top of one of the bread slices. Slip the bread with toppings under a broiler until the brie is melted. (Brie melts quickly, so keep an eye on it.) Top with the remaining slice of bread.

For the Earth, Spin, and Fire Variation

Replace asparagus with spinach that has been quick-seared in a little butter and salt, and sub Havarti for the brie. Or use another kind of green vegetable and another kind of creamy cheese, and call the sandwich anything you want!

THE MEDI-WRAP (AND A BARB VARIATION)

Every lunch restaurant needs a basic hummus sandwich. And while we loved a good hummus sandwich as much as the next guy, we also wanted a Mediterranean version in which the hummus was part of an ensemble rather than the star. This wrap is just that.

The sandwich has it all—crunch, creaminess, bold flavors, lots of colors, and a big dose of nutrition. Because several recipes are involved, it may seem like quite a project. One way to make the project more manageable would be to have a bunch of friends over, and if someone asks, "What can I bring?" have them bring one of the parts. Line up all the abundance, along with some flour tortillas, and have your guests build their own. Small-sized wraps will work, but the 12-inch round, flying saucer-sized wraps that restaurants use will best accommodate all the ingredients involved.

The Parts

Flour tortillas (10- or 12-inch) white or spinach

Roasted Garlic Hummus (page 152, or use store-bought)

Curried Couscous Salad (page 197)

Israeli Tomato Cucumber Chopped Salad (page 199)*

Cilantro Dressing (page 168)

To Prepare One Sandwich

Warm the wrap briefly in a microwave or in a pan on the stovetop. (A warm wrap will roll up better.) Spread hummus on the wrap, then top with a layer of couscous salad and a layer of chopped salad. Spoon dressing on top. Begin to roll up the wrap, keeping it snug as you go. When 1/3 of the way done, fold the sides over the ends, then continue rolling until the wrap is complete. Use your hand to keep the sides of the wrap tucked in as you roll. Place seam-side down, and cut in half diagonally.

For a Barb Medi-Wrap: Cook up some Chicken Shawarma (page 147) or 4 to 6 ounces of seasoned chicken meat. Add to wrap on top of the couscous salad.

*You can skip making the full-blown salad and substitute just the chopped tomatoes and cucumbers, but at the very least add a squeeze of lemon juice

SUNSHINE DREAMIN'

I'm not a vegetarian, but I do love a good sandwich centered on vegetables—something more than a few bland layers of inoffensive cucumbers and out-of-season tomatoes with a slice of cheese for show. Something with flavor and grit. The Sunshine Dreamin' is a ramped-up cold veggie sandwich that addresses the valid grievances of vegetarians, for whom menu items sometimes seem but an afterthought. The romesco sauce, in all of its boldness, transforms the experience.

So much is going on in this sandwich, yet nothing gets lost. Every component has a distinct texture, and the flavors range from bold to gentle.

The Parts

Multigrain Bread slices (pages 316-317)

Avocado slices, lightly salted

Tomato slices

Havarti, Monterey Jack, Gouda, or other soft, gentle cheese, sliced

Thin slivers of red onion

Alfalfa or other sprouts

Romesco Sauce (page 159)

To Prepare One Sandwich

Place a layer of avocado slices on a slice of bread. Continue adding layers in the order above until you have added the sprouts. Then spoon on the romesco. When you lightly press another bread slice on top, the orange-red romesco will act as a beautiful edible glue, cementing all those errant veggies in place and giving visual pop to the sandwich.

Sandwich Tips

Bread Base: Multigrain bread adds to the healthfulness here. Its earthiness and texture complement the gentler flavors of the vegetables while standing up to the bold sauce.

Avocados: Avocados are bland by themselves but suddenly come alive when salted. It is like night and day. Even if there are other salty ingredients nearby, the flavor of the avocados benefits from direct salting.

PETER WRAPPIT

Peter is a naughty bunny who steals vegetables, as every backyard bunny ought to. This wrap was playfully named in his honor. It conceals a gardenful of crisp fresh veggies that Peter would surely have enjoyed, bound together with garlic-roasted cream cheese. You'll like it, too. It is easy, refreshing, and adaptable to what you have in the fridge or garden. Admittedly, this sandwich is full of many building blocks that need to be made. I loved this sandwich and present it here as a concept as well as a recipe.

The Parts

Flour tortillas (12- or 10-inch) white or spinach

Roasted Garlic Cream Cheese (page 161) or softened plain cream cheese mixed with a sprinkle of garlic powder

3-4 roasted asparagus spears cut into 1-inch segments

About 2 cups mixed field greens

1/3 cup coarsely grated carrot

1/3 cup shredded red cabbage

House Dressing (page 166)

Roasted Red Pepper Relish (page 163)

Frizzled Onions (page 365)

To Prepare One Sandwich

Gently warm the wrap (it will roll more easily when warm). Spread it with a thin but noticeable layer of the cream cheese. In a medium bowl, toss together the asparagus, field greens, cabbage, and carrots. Add enough house dressing to lightly coat the greens, and toss the mixture. Place greens mixture onto the wrap and top with 3 to 4 tablespoons of the red pepper relish. Finally, add a small handful of frizzled onions. Begin to roll up the wrap, keeping it snug as you go. When 1/3 of the way done, fold the sides over the ends, then continue rolling until the wrap is complete. Use your hand to keep the sides of the wrap tucked in as you roll. Place seam-side down, and cut in half diagonally.

Other Good Fillers

Fresh raw beets, peeled and grated

Alfalfa or other sprouts

Cucumber, peeled, seeded, and diced

Broccoli stems and/or florets, grated

Platters and Entree Salads

I love creating a themed lunch platter. For me, this means assembling a collection of ingredients that have some commonality—culinary, cultural, or seasonal—and then giving the dish a name that evokes the theme. Platters tell a story. They can transport you to a special place or time—a picnic in the French countryside or a sunset repast on the coast of a small Mexican village. They can also carry personal meaning. The French Country Picnic recipe on the following page became a meaningful story in our family's lives.

The following recipes also incorporate some of the building blocks from the previous section.

Chicken Shawarma Platter.

SHAWARMA PLATTER

Makes a platter for 1 (multiply it for any number of servings)

When they were in their early 20s, my two sons traveled to Israel together as part of the Birthright Israel program, whose goal is to encourage young Jewish folks to experience Israel. Of the many high points on this trip, and a memory that stays strong, is the ubiquitous chicken shawarma sandwich. Made from seasoned meat, roasted gyros-like on rotisseries, authentic shawarma is exotic and alluring. The boys made it their goal to find the best shawarma in Israel. Since their return, nothing in this country lives up to their memories. But isn't that how it always goes?

This shawarma is not *that* shawarma, but my sons' stories planted a seed in me to fashion a platter around the flavors of Middle Eastern cuisine. The chicken, marinated in lively spices and sautéed, nicely complements our Medi-Wrap (page 183) and works well in a stir-fry with other vegetables, served over rice. Best yet, it freezes beautifully, marinated but not yet cooked.

1/2 cup Curried Couscous Salad (page 197)

1/4 cup Roasted Garlic Hummus (page 152)

1/2 cup Israeli Tomato Cucumber Chopped Salad (page 199)

A handful of mixed field greens

1/4 cup Feta Dressing for the greens and for dipping the chicken (page 170)

2 teaspoons vegetable oil

5-6 ounces Chicken Shawarma (page 147)

Pita Bread wedges, warmed (pages 318-319)

---

1. On a large plate or small serving platter, arrange the couscous, hummus, chopped salad, and greens as you please, leaving a place to set the chicken. Both the couscous and hummus can be placed directly onto the platter rather than in separate little bowls, allowing the different parts to flow together harmoniously. The feta dressing should be in a tiny ramekin or bowl of its own.
2. To cook the chicken, heat a small sauté pan over medium-high heat with 2 teaspoons of vegetable oil. Add the chicken and stir-fry until just done, about 4 to 6 minutes.
3. Set cooked chicken on the plate. Serve the platter with warm wedges of pita bread on the side.

FRENCH COUNTRY PICNIC

Makes a platter for 1 (multiply it for any number of servings)

This platter was originally designed to be reminiscent of an afternoon under a shady tree in the Loire Valley, complete with a bottle of wine, cows dotting the adjacent pasture, and a timeworn chateau just visible on the horizon, where a thunderstorm is brewing. I once shared just such an afternoon with my late sister Linda during a trip where we biked the French countryside, eating more incredible brie cheeses than we knew existed. However, the story behind this platter was superseded by another great story detailed in the accompanying sidebar. Both stories fill my heart.

The proportions described below are for one, so multiply as needed. For serving, you will need an oversized plate or a small platter, as the assemblage needs a lot of space.

---

5 spears of asparagus

Olive oil

1 small clove garlic, minced

Salt and pepper

One 6-ounce chicken breast, cut into 3/4- to 1-inch cubes

3 long slender wedges of an excellent brie cheese

1 hard-boiled egg, halved lengthwise (cooking instructions on page 181)

A handful of mixed field greens

Wedges of tomato, preferably heirloom, or a small handful of assorted cherry tomatoes

Pitted Niçoise olives (as many or as few as you like)

House Dressing (page 166)

1/4 cup Garlic Aioli (page 165) in a tiny ramekin or decorative bowl

Baguette bread in thick slices

---

1. Toss the asparagus spears with a teaspoon of olive oil and the minced garlic until evenly coated. Heat a medium-sized sauté pan over medium-high heat, and when hot, lay the asparagus spears out in a single layer. Sprinkle a tiny pinch of salt over the top. Sauté the asparagus, turning the spears over occasionally so they become lightly browned but remain crisp-cooked, about 3 to 5 minutes depending on the thickness of the spears. Do not let them get too soft. As soon as they are ready, remove them to a plate so they won't continue to cook.
2. Reduce the heat to medium, and in the same pan add 1 teaspoon oil. When hot, add the chicken pieces, sprinkle with salt and pepper, and cook, turning once or twice until they are just done, about 4 to 6 minutes.

3. To assemble the platter, use your imagination and have fun arranging the ingredients, each in its own space except for the olives, which you can scatter over everything.
4. The aioli may be spread on the baguette or used as a dip. Make a mini sandwich or savor each ingredient. Drizzle some house dressing over the greens and tomatoes, Enjoy your visual presentation as much as each bite. The platter pleases on many levels.

Love Story

My son Ike began work at Manna in his early teens, a time in his life when his journey into adulthood had taken some dark, difficult turns. But just before freshman year of high school, he met Ashley, and the desire to win her over compelled him to clean up his act. Ike begged us to hire Ashley too, and during their tenure together at Manna, we (parents and staff alike) looked on wistfully as the astonishing relationship of these two 15-year-olds unfolded. It was a relationship defined by gentleness, mutual respect, and a tenderness more often witnessed in couples who have spent a lifetime together.

Each day after school, the romance slowly gained momentum over an order of the French Country Picnic platter. I cherish the memory of the two of them sitting at the counter, nibbling bites of asparagus and chicken, lost in quiet, private conversation like an old married couple (except that the talk was likely of math tests, soccer practice, and fantasy football). Ashley, in particular, had a limited palate and tended to balk at trying new foods, but Ike encouraged her to create mini sandwiches from all the parts, and through his coaching, her food tastes blossomed. The two of them brought out the best in each other.

For their rustic barn wedding, Ike begged me to re-create this platter in a buffet-friendly format. ("You expect ME to cater your wedding?" I was incredulous, but he meant the Manna crew—phew!) But what had begun as a composed platter serving one had now morphed into a huge buffet spread serving 125. Thus, we felt the need to post directions for the wedding guests, helping them experience the vision that brought Ashley and Isaac together in the first place.

SOUTHWESTERN QUINOA MIX

(For lunch salads or breakfast bowls)
Enough mix for 8 main-course servings

 Start to finish within an hour, give or take

This delicious mix—gluten-free and vegan at its core—is used as the basis for a warm Southwestern-focused lunch platter and can easily become a breakfast entree (although no longer vegan) with the addition of some over-easy eggs. The quinoa mix itself freezes beautifully. Make a large batch and portion it into individual serving amounts. (Note that it remains vegan as long as you do not add proteins nor use the accompanying cilantro dressing.)

Quinoa Mixture

1 1/4 cups quinoa

2 1/4 cups water

1/4 teaspoon salt

One can (14 ounces) black beans, drained and rinsed

1 1/2 cups corn, either fresh off the cob (2 ears) or frozen and defrosted, briefly pan-sautéed

1 large sweet red pepper, diced (about 1 1/2 cups)

6 scallions, thinly sliced

1/2 cup gently packed cilantro, chopped

1 tablespoon chili powder

2 teaspoons cumin

1 teaspoon smoked paprika

1 1/2 teaspoons garlic powder

1 1/2 teaspoons onion powder

1/4 teaspoon chipotle chili powder

For Finishing the Quinoa and Serving

Vegetable oil

Chipotle Lime Dressing (page 169)

Sweet potato slices tossed with a bit of oil and minced garlic, then roasted in a 400-degree oven until lightly browned and cooked through, 10 to 15 minutes

Avocado slices

Additional fresh corn or black beans

Cilantro leaves for garnish

Tortilla chips on the side

Cilantro Dressing (page 168)

Optional additions: slices of roasted chicken breast (lunch) or two over-easy eggs (breakfast)

1. **To make the quinoa mix:** Rinse the quinoa well and place it in a small pot with water and salt. Bring to a boil, turn down to lowest heat, cover and cook for 15 minutes. Turn off the heat. Drain away any excess water and let cool with the cover on. When quinoa is cool, add in the remaining mixture ingredients (black beans through chipotle chili powder). The mix may be used at this point, chilled for later use, or frozen in serving-size quantities.
2. **To prepare single servings of quinoa bowls:** Heat oil in a sauté pan over medium heat. For each serving, add 1 1/2 cups of quinoa mix to the pan, along with 1 tablespoon chipotle dressing. Stir-fry the mix until heated through, and add more dressing to taste, if desired.
3. Portion the quinoa mix into wide, shallow bowls for serving (or create a single presentation in a larger bowl). Top with slices of roasted sweet potatoes and slices of avocado. Sprinkle on more corn or black beans, if desired. Add slices of roast chicken for lunch or dinner or over-easy eggs for brunch, if desired. Sprinkle on a few cilantro leaves. Serve cilantro dressing on the side (or go vegan and use more of the chipotle dressing instead) and garnish the plates with tortilla chips.

CONCERTS ON THE SQUARE COUNTRY TURKEY SALAD

Makes 8 cups (about 5-6 servings)

 Start to finish in less than a half hour

For many years, Collins House Catering was an "approved" caterer for providing box lunches to sell at Concerts on the Square (Madison's signature summertime music series). It was a thrilling time to be a caterer, and from that experience, we had an early notion that we would enjoy serving a larger public at a later time. But it was not without its challenges. Customers would call in preorders each week, and there was always a steady number of walk-ups to our stand. We would prep all the food the day before and assemble hundreds of box lunches on Wednesday mornings. But there was often a threat of rain, which made some weeks a bit tenuous. Nonetheless, the enormous effort of prepping, cooking, and assembling the orders in this short time span was a weekly high.

The country turkey salad is a perfect picnic meal—refreshing and easy to eat. It followed us to Manna, and now, hopefully, beyond.

Honey Curry Dressing

1 teaspoon minced garlic

1 egg

2 tablespoons honey

2 tablespoons cider vinegar

1 1/2 teaspoons Dijon mustard

1 teaspoon dry mustard

1 teaspoon curry powder

1 teaspoon ground coriander

1/2 teaspoon allspice

3/4 cup canola oil

Salad

1 pound roast turkey, cut into 3/4-inch cubes

3/4 cup diced celery (1/2-inch dice)

3/4 cup diced smoked Gouda cheese (1/2-inch dice)

2 medium apples, cored but not peeled, cut into 1/2-inch dice

4-6 ounces mixed field greens

About 3/4 cup candied pecans (see sidebar, next page)

1. For the dressing, place all ingredients except for the oil in a food processor with a steel blade and blend for 20 seconds. With the machine running, add canola oil in a slow, steady stream until the dressing is thick and creamy.
2. Toss the dressing with the turkey, celery, Gouda, and apples in a bowl until well coated. Serve on a platter or individual plates over a bed of mixed field greens, and sprinkle pecans on top.

Pecans from Heaven

For the best candied pecan on the planet, look no further than your own backyard. Fortune Favors, previously called Nutkrack is an incredible crisp, sweet, nutty experience, and this salad is the perfect place to try these nuts if you haven't already. They are made here in Madison by a company founded by Eric Rupert, a one-time Ovens of Brittany baker, L'Etoile chef (and my then 13-year-old son Josh's first professional cooking instructor)!

MARVEL'S PASSION SALAD

Makes a platter for 1 (multiply it for any number of servings)

Marvel, one of our early Manna FOH employees, was a woman of twinkling laughter, loving kindness, and a compulsion to serve people. (She was my neighbor as well, and everyone in the area knew her. Everyone.) Marvel had the gift of drawing the crank out of people—of turning a needy customer into a smiling, grateful one.

And she was passionate about her food. One day she thought up this salad for herself, intending to enjoy a healthful lunch in a sea of bakery treats. Customers leaned over her shoulder to ask what she was having, and before you knew it, the salad was on our menu, where it stayed for years. Long after Marvel left Manna to join her daughter in business, her bright presence lived on in this dish.

The Tropical Fruit Salsa featured in our Jamaican Chicken Sandwich defines this salad and provides its finishing touch.

---

3 tablespoons vegetable oil

One 6-ounce filet of tilapia, walleye, or lake trout

Cornmeal (enough to coat filet) seasoned with salt and pepper

A large plateful of mixed salad greens

1/4 cup shredded red cabbage

1/4 cup shredded carrot

Half of an avocado, sliced

A handful of cherry tomatoes, halved

1/4 cup Tropical Fruit Salsa (page 158)

2 tablespoons Chipotle Dressing (page 168)

---

1. Heat the vegetable oil in a small sauté pan over medium-high heat. Coat the fish fillet in the cornmeal, shaking off the excess. Sear the fish for about 3 minutes on each side.
2. Toss the greens, cabbage, and carrots together and set them on a serving plate. Top decoratively with avocado and cherry tomatoes, and place fish on top. Add a healthy dollop of fruit salsa to the platter, and serve with chipotle dressing on the side.

Salads on the Side

Once, at a small, locally-owned co-op restaurant off the interstate in Youngstown, Ohio, I had the side salad of my dreams—an understated dish I will forever remember. It was a simple salad of thinly julienned kale flecked with quinoa, dotted with dried cranberries and toasted pecans, and dressed just so with a vibrant lemon-honey-Dijon vinaigrette—the perfect yin and yang of sweetness and bite. I would drive 500 miles for that salad.

There is no reason a side salad should be an afterthought. While the ones in this chapter may not be destination-wedding dishes, they make for some darn good eating, alongside sandwiches, soups, and entrees. You might even drive 500 miles for them.

A note about Manna's house salad:

There's no recipe in this book for Manna's house salad, only one for its dressing on page 166. For our signature side salad, just toss your favorite greens with the dressing and serve.

TWO-POTATO SALAD

Makes about 6 cups

 **Start to finish in less than a half hour**

Never ones for same-old, same-old, we offered a potato salad of a different color. In it, sweet potatoes and red potatoes cozy up together with a kicky mayo-based dressing. A hint of spice, a bit of crunch, and a whiff of herb give this salad plenty of character.

---

1 pound sweet potatoes, peeled and cut into 3/4-inch cubes

1 pound red potatoes, unpeeled and cut into 3/4-inch cubes

Dressing Ingredients

1/2 cup mayonnaise

2 teaspoons cider vinegar

2 1/2 tablespoons medium-hot green salsa (we love Mrs. Renfro's brand)

1 tablespoon minced fresh tarragon

1/2 teaspoon salt, or more to taste

4 scallions, thinly sliced

2 stalks celery, diced into 1/4-inch cubes

---

1. Place sweet potatoes in one pot and red potatoes in a second pot. Fill both pots with water to cover the potatoes and add 2 teaspoons salt to each pot. Place pots on the stove and bring water to a boil. Cook potatoes until tender but not overcooked, about 10 minutes. (Note that the time is an estimate, as they will likely be done at slightly different times.) Drain in a colander and allow to partially cool.
2. While potatoes are cooking, mix together dressing ingredients and set aside.
3. When the potatoes have cooled enough to handle, add them to the bowl with dressing and mix until well incorporated. Be gentle so as not to mush the potatoes. Chill before serving.

CURRIED COUSCOUS SALAD

Makes about 6 cups

 **Start to finish in less than a half hour**

Save for the Wisconsin-friendly addition of dried cranberries, this recipe was an Ina Garten original. We put it on the menu on day one, and it stayed to the end. It is wonderful in so many ways. The flavors are subtle yet complex, the textures are varied, and the overall effect is one of lightness. Though an ideal accompaniment to a sandwich, it still shines on its own.

---

1 1/2 cups dried couscous

1 tablespoon butter

1 1/4 cups boiling water (measured after boiling)

1/4 cup plain yogurt

1/4 cup olive oil

1 teaspoon white wine vinegar

1 teaspoon curry powder

1/4 teaspoon turmeric

1 teaspoon salt

1/2 teaspoon pepper

1/2 cup carrot, peeled and coarsely grated

1/2 cup lightly packed minced parsley

1/2 cup dried cranberries

1/4 cup slivered almonds, toasted

2 scallions, thinly sliced

1/4 cup red onion, finely diced

---

1. Place couscous in a large bowl with butter. Pour the boiling water over the couscous. Cover bowl tightly with plastic wrap and allow the couscous to soak for 5 minutes. Fluff couscous with a fork to separate granules and let cool.
2. Whisk together yogurt, olive oil, vinegar, curry, turmeric, salt and pepper. Pour mixture over couscous and mix gently but thoroughly.
3. Add the carrots, parsley, cranberries, almonds, scallions, and red onions. Toss mixture well and taste for seasoning.

PASTA SALAD WITH POBLANO PESTO

Makes 4-5 cups

 Start to finish in less than a half hour

Although catering customers liked to order pasta salads for buffets, their event guests didn't seem excited about eating them. At Collins House Catering, we developed this simple but offbeat pasta salad to perk their interest. It is an excellent use of roasted poblano pesto and has a bit of a Southwestern spirit.

1/2 pound bowtie or penne pasta

2 teaspoons olive oil

1/3 cup diced sweet red pepper

3 scallions, thinly sliced

1 cup corn, either fresh off the cob or frozen and defrosted, briefly pan-sautéed

1/3 cup pitted black olives, sliced

1/2 cup cherry tomatoes, halved or quartered

1/2 cup grated Parmesan cheese

1/4 cup Roasted Poblano Pesto (page 160), or more to taste

Salt and pepper

1. Cook pasta in a pot of boiling water until al dente (per package instructions). Drain, and toss with the olive oil, to keep the pasta from sticking together.
2. Combine remaining ingredients in a medium bowl and mix well, then toss in the pasta. Add additional pesto or additional olive oil if needed. Add salt and pepper to taste.

ISRAELI CUCUMBER TOMATO CHOPPED SALAD

Makes about 2 cups

 Start to finish in less than a half hour

This crisp, cool chopped salad is a classic Israeli preparation and often accompanies shawarma or hummus. We served it as a stand-alone salad on catered buffets of Jewish food and as a side component on our Middle-Eastern dishes at Manna. It is refreshing and versatile.

1 tablespoon olive oil
1 tablespoon lemon juice
1/4 teaspoon salt
1/8 teaspoon black pepper

1 cup cucumber, unpeeled, seeded and cut into 1/2-inch dice
1 cup seeded and diced tomato (Cherry tomatoes are nice too, but don't bother seeding them!)
1/4 cup finely diced red onion
1/4 cup medium-packed minced parsley

In a small bowl, mix olive oil, lemon juice, salt and pepper. Place remaining ingredients in a medium bowl and toss with the olive oil mixture. Taste for seasoning.

Soup

Max was an older gentleman who came daily to Manna during our first year, unfailingly clad in a thick, oversized red plaid flannel shirt. After ordering his customary bowl of soup, extra hot, he would shuffle into the back room, quiet and alone. Every day we delivered his soup, and every day he sent it back with the complaint that it was not hot enough.

Restaurants must keep their hot foods at 160 degrees for health safety reasons, so we did. But apparently, this was not hot enough for Max, who one day, after weeks of complaining, derailed our first kitchen manager, Orianna, with an angry diatribe. She was a soft-spoken and even-tempered gal, and after shedding a few tears, she heated a bowl of soup to boiling on the stove and carried it out to him herself.

A warm and curious friendship ensued. Orianna learned about Max's lost ability to sense heat, and Max learned of Orianna's gentle spirit and caring touch. Every day Orianna would personally deliver Max his hot, hot bowl of soup until we noticed one day that he had not been around in a while.

Soup has the power to soothe and heal like almost no other food. Manna's collection of soups was lengthy, since every soup cook had the freedom to create. Our collection evolved over the years. Lukas, last in the line of fabled soup chefs, kept a faded notebook crammed with a mishmash of perfectly typed recipes, folded up clippings, and stacks of scrap paper filled with ingredient lists but devoid of instruction or even recipe names. Only matzo ball soup was served with regularity on Jewish Fridays, but if a customer asked when, for example, mushroom barley soup would next appear on the menu, the request would be passed to Lukas. He was always delighted by these indirect kudos, and we made sure to let the customer know at least a week ahead when it would appear so that they could plan their visit accordingly.

Culling the list for this cookbook was itself a creative challenge. I solicited input from former customers and made sure to include a couple of my favorites (mulligatawny, for one).

To make the best soup, use a rich, genuine homemade stock. A store-bought product will do in a pinch and produce a perfectly suitable soup. But the level of salt and the canned or preserved flavor imparted to a purchased product will always intrude.

I have included our recipe for chicken stock herein, which is essential to our Matzo Ball Soup (that recipe is in the "Jewish Fridays" chapter on pages 336-337) and other soup recipes in the book. I've also included a basic veggie stock recipe for cooking vegetarian soups. Other stocks—primarily beef or seafood—are easy to make, but since I did not need them for this cookbook, they are not to be found here.

At left: Mulligatawny Soup, page 208

CHICKEN STOCK

Makes about 12 cups
(little initial effort, lots of stovetop time and an overnight chill)

 Project Alert! May require multiple stages or overnight preparations—read through before proceeding

Oy vey! A hundred cooks, a hundred different chicken stock techniques. What's a soup bubbeleh to do? This is a pretty basic stock-making technique, producing a deeply rich soup that can be eaten as is, or chock full of matzo balls, or in any recipe calling for chicken stock. Just remember that if you choose to add fresh herbs to your stockpot, the soup will taste like the herb, as will all the recipes you use it in.

Be sure to save the congealed fat from this stock, as per Steps 4 and 5 below. It is an essential ingredient for Matzo Balls, pages 336-337.

4-5 pounds chicken backs and necks, or one roasting chicken, at least 5 pounds

1 large unpeeled onion (10 ounces), quartered

2 unpeeled medium carrots, cut into chunks

2 large stalks of celery, cut in chunks (or substitute the top quarter of the celery with the leaves)

1/4 bunch of parsley

1 bay leaf

2 teaspoons whole peppercorns

1 tablespoon salt

Water to cover

---

1. Place all ingredients in a stockpot. Add water to cover by about an inch—no more. Bring to a boil over high heat, at which point a grayish-brown bubbly foam will float to the surface. Skim this off a few times with a slotted spoon or strainer until the foam stops forming. Reduce heat to low so that the stock simmers at a slow bubble (one or two bubbles every couple of seconds).
2. Leave the stock to simmer for 5 to 6 hours uncovered. In the beginning, you may need to adjust the heat to keep the simmer slow. Once you have the simmer rate controlled, you are free to read, shop, throw balls for your dog, or otherwise enjoy the day.

3. At the end of the cooking time, turn off the heat and let the stock sit on the stove for another hour. Place another large pot or bowl in your sink, and strain the stock into it, pressing on the solids to extract all the stock. (Mike forgot the bowl once, and his entire pot of soup went down the drain. Don't do that at home.) If you used a whole chicken, you can remove and reserve the parts to turn into a (somewhat bland) chicken salad or feed the dog.
4. Place the stock in the refrigerator overnight. The next day, remove the congealed fat from the top and set it in a small saucepan. If you like, reheat the stock, and strain it one more time with a fine-mesh strainer to remove small particles. Taste the stock and add more salt as needed.
5. **Save the fat!** Heat the saucepan with the fat in it over medium heat, and let the fat simmer until you no longer see steam rising from it. (The steam is extra liquid, and when it no longer rises, your fat should be pure.) Let cool for 10 minutes, then strain the fat through a fine sieve into a small jar. This can be stored in the fridge for a few weeks or in the freezer for a long time.

Portioning "Fool's Gold" for future matzo balls, see "A Schmaltz Obsession," page 339.

Reducing Chicken Stock into Glace de Volaille

Chicken stock is easily frozen for future use, but if you don't have a big freezer, you can reduce it to make glace de volaille, the culinary term for chicken stock reduced to a syrupy consistency. It takes up little freezer space and can easily be reconstituted back into stock. It is the one building block my freezer is never without.

Here's how it works: Once the stock is finished, strained, chilled, and defatted, measure the amount of stock you have in cups, and divide that number by eight. For example, 16 cups of stock divided by 8 equals 2 cups. That 2-cup amount is the final volume you are aiming to produce.

Bring the measured stock to a rapid boil and let it reduce until it gets close to the final volume. At this point, the reduction happens quickly and can go from "not quite there yet" to "almost gone" in minutes. The length of time it takes to reduce the stock will vary depending on how much you have to begin with, how high the heat is, and the size and shape of the pot, so keep a good eye on it. (I typically make around 28 cups of stock, which reduces to 3 1/2 cups in about 1 1/2 to 2 hours.)

The resulting concentrate is the intense, flavor-packed reduction called glace de volaille. It is the homemade equivalent of bouillon cubes. If you do not have plastic portion cups (see page 154 for more information), a good way to portion is to measure 1/4-cup increments into muffin tins. Chill the tins until the demi-glace sets (i.e., becomes jelly-like due to the concentration of collagen). Then remove the jelly "pucks" and wrap them individually in plastic wrap. A 1/4-cup portion will reconstitute with 1 3/4 cups of water into 2 cups of stock. (If I only need a cup of stock, I cut one of the frozen pucks in half.)

VEGETABLE STOCK

Makes 8-10 cups

 **Hands-on time less than an hour (additional cooking or chilling times involved—read through before beginning)**

Just as with chicken stock, using homemade vegetable stock in vegetarian soups provides a richness of flavor not achievable by using just water. And veggie stock by itself can have that same "chicken soup for the soul" effect. Dianne, one of my recipe testers, was assigned this stock recipe during a difficult time in her life, and she discovered in the course of tasting it that she loved the broth on its own. She made batches to keep in her fridge and heated it in mugs in the afternoons for its delicious and soothing effects. A good vegetable broth can stand alone.

Homemade veggie stocks can be filled with all the nutrition your refrigerator has to offer. Kitchens scraps such as mushroom stems, carrot peelings, or potato skins are great additions to a simmering pot. Manna's vegetable stock was pretty basic so that its background flavors enhanced soups without imparting any specific or unwanted flavors. (Asparagus, for example, may add a noticeable flavor.) But you can add any veggie scraps or herbs that you have on hand, including fresh garden herbs. Just bear in mind that veggies like broccoli or Brussels sprouts or fennel bulbs, which have a distinct flavor of their own, will influence your stock's flavor. Neutral is generally better in stock recipes.

As with all stocks, veggie stock can be made in large batches, reduced, and stored in your freezer.

---

1 large (1/2 pound) onion, quartered

3-4 carrots (1/2 pound), coarsely chopped

4 stalks celery, coarsely chopped

1/4 bunch of parsley

2 teaspoons whole black peppercorns

2 teaspoons salt

10 cups cold water

---

1. Place all the ingredients in a stockpot and cover with 10 cups of water. Set over high heat and bring almost to a boil. Reduce heat and let simmer gently on low heat for 3 hours.
2. Strain the stock, pressing down on the veggies to extract their juices. Discard the vegetables and cool the stock completely.
3. The stock can be used immediately or reduced and frozen for later use (see instructions for reducing Chicken Stock on page 204).

JOSH'S STEAK CHILI

Makes about 10 cups

 Hands-on time less than an hour (additional cooking or chilling times involved—read through before beginning)

My son Josh created this chili one day for a chili cook-off. As a teenager (and even now as a professional chef), Josh preferred the experimental to the classic, and for this challenge he wanted a chili with no beans. Instead, he used hominy, made from dried whole corn kernels that have been treated with alkali, which gives the chili its pozole-like character. He also wanted to improve on mundane ground beef, so he substituted steak. Josh won that cook-off, and others, with this recipe and solidified his budding reputation in our neighborhood as a driven young chef-to-be.

This is not a classic chili, so if you are looking for a bowlful of ground beef and pinto beans in chili-rich tomato sauce, this isn't it. But it was the only chili ever served at Manna, from Labor Day through Memorial Day. (And while we did not serve it in the dog days of summer, people asked for it anyway!)

---

4 slices bacon, chopped
1 1/2 pounds beef sirloin, cut into 1/2-inch cubes
1 small onion (about 4 ounces), chopped
1 small green pepper (about 4 ounces), seeded and chopped
1 small sweet red pepper (about 4 ounces), seeded and chopped
1 tablespoon minced garlic
2 1/2 tablespoons chili powder
1 tablespoon ground cumin
1 teaspoon ground coriander
1/2 teaspoon red pepper flakes
1/2 teaspoon dried oregano
1/4 teaspoon cayenne pepper
1 can (28 ounces) petite diced tomatoes, with juices
1 can (14 ounces) tomato puree
2 cups beef stock (store-bought or homemade)
1 can (14 ounces) white hominy, drained and rinsed
Salt to taste, if needed

Optional garnishes: grated cheddar cheese, sour cream, finely chopped red onions

---

1. Cook bacon in a medium sauté pan over medium heat until crisp. Remove bacon with a slotted spoon to a paper towel and reserve. Leave drippings in the pan.
2. Increase heat to high and add sirloin to pan in batches (do not crowd the pan). Brown on all sides, then remove meat and reserve.
3. Reduce heat to medium. Add onions, peppers, and garlic to the pan and sauté until vegetables are almost soft. Stir in spices and let heat a minute or two until fragrant.
4. Transfer mixture to a soup pot. Add tomatoes, tomato puree, and stock, then bring to a boil, reduce heat and simmer for 45 minutes. Add hominy to chili and let simmer for another 15 minutes. Taste and adjust seasoning with salt, if needed.
5. The chili may be eaten right away, or for better flavor, chill it overnight and reheat the next day. Serve in bowls and offer the optional garnishes as accompaniments.

MULLIGATAWNY SOUP/STEW

Makes about 10 cups

 **Hands-on time less than an hour (additional cooking or chilling times involved—read through before beginning)**

When I was a little girl, my father took me to a restaurant in Skaneateles, New York, called The Krebs. My memories are of big platters of food coming to our table, family style, and of this soup. Almost 60 years later, I can still taste its sweetly curried, creamy redolence, its delicate morsels of chicken and rice, and my own innocent awe and happiness. That evening, when offered a choice of dessert, I asked for another bowl of the soup. I have yet to find the Krebs' recipe for this soup, and since my memory of it dimmed over time, this recipe is a bit of a hybrid—a cross between the flavors I've reminisced about and the one that Lukas, our soup chef extraordinaire, created.

Mulligatawny originated in India and became a popular soup in Great Britain. It has many versions, some of which are more brothy and soup-like, and others are thicker and more ingredient-laden, like a stew. This recipe is somewhere in between and helps bring me back to a deeply etched moment of my childhood.

---

1 tablespoon vegetable oil

2 pounds skin-on, bone-in chicken thighs (about 6 large or 8 average)

Salt and pepper

1 tablespoon sesame oil

1 tablespoon vegetable oil

1 medium yellow onion (6 ounces), peeled and chopped

1 tablespoon minced fresh garlic

1 tablespoon grated fresh ginger

1 1/2 teaspoons sugar

1 tablespoon garam masala

1 1/2 teaspoons ground coriander

1 teaspoon turmeric

1/8 teaspoon cayenne

1/2 teaspoon salt

2 medium tomatoes (12 ounces), finely diced (or one 14.5-ounce can petite diced tomatoes, drained)

4 cups Chicken Stock (page 202-203)

1 medium sweet potato (8 ounces), peeled and diced to 1/2 inch

2 medium russet potatoes (12 ounces), peeled and diced to 1/2 inch

1 can (15.5 ounces) garbanzo beans, drained and rinsed

1 cup heavy cream

1 cup coconut milk

1/2 cup slivered almonds, toasted (page 363)

Cooked white rice for serving, optional

Additional toasted slivered almonds for garnish, optional

---

1. Preheat the oven to 425 degrees. Line a baking sheet with a parchment pan liner. Rub 1 tablespoon vegetable oil all over the chicken thighs, season lightly with salt and pepper and set on prepared pan. Roast thighs for 40 minutes, then remove and let them cool completely. When chicken is cool, remove the skin,* remove meat from the bones, and dice meat into 1/2- to 3/4-inch chunks. Reserve.
2. While chicken is roasting, heat sesame and vegetable oils in a stockpot over medium heat. Add onions and cook for about 10 minutes, until translucent and beginning to brown. Add garlic and ginger and cook another 2 minutes. Add sugar, garam masala, coriander, turmeric, cayenne, and salt, and stir to coat veggies with the seasonings.
3. Add tomatoes, chicken stock, and both types of potatoes to the pot. Bring to a boil, reduce heat to medium-low, and simmer uncovered for 40 minutes.
4. While the soup is simmering, combine heavy cream and coconut milk in a medium saucepan and simmer until reduced to 1 cup. (Cream boils up and over easily, so keep an eye on it and adjust heat accordingly.) In a blender, grind 1/2 cup toasted slivered almonds until fine, then blend in cream mixture until smooth. Set aside.
5. Strain the soup into a bowl. Place about half of the solids into a food processor with about 1 cup of the liquid (or use an immersion blender), and puree until perfectly smooth. Return the soup to the pot along with the pureed veggies and the unpureed solids.
6. Stir in the cream/almond puree and simmer for 5 minutes. Add the diced chicken meat and garbanzo beans to the soup pot and heat through. If desired, serve the soup over rice and garnish it with the toasted almonds.

*For a delicious snack, crisp the chicken skin in the hot oven for 5 to 8 minutes, then enjoy it while you continue cooking.

AFRICAN PORK AND PEANUT SOUP/STEW

Makes about 10 cups

 Start to finish within an hour, give or take

More soup than stew, this savory, spicy dish nonetheless fills you up like a main course, needing only a warm loaf of bread and a refreshing salad to round out the meal.

---

1 tablespoon sesame oil

1 whole pork tenderloin (about 1 1/4 to 1 1/2 pounds), cut into 1/2- to 3/4-inch cubes

1 medium onion (about 6 ounces), peeled and diced small

1 large green pepper (about 6 ounces), seeded and diced medium

1 can (14.5 ounces) petite diced tomatoes

1 teaspoon minced garlic

1/2 teaspoon curry powder

1/2 teaspoon ground coriander

1/2 teaspoon ground cumin

1/4 teaspoon red pepper flakes

1/2 teaspoon ground ginger

1/4 teaspoon cinnamon

1 bay leaf

1/2 teaspoon salt

1/3 cup creamy peanut butter

3 tablespoons tomato paste

4 cups Chicken Stock (pages 202-203)

2 tablespoons minced cilantro

Optional garnishes: cilantro leaves and crushed peanuts

---

1. Heat a large soup pot over medium-high heat, then add sesame oil. Working in batches so you don't overcrowd the meat, add pork to the pan and stir-fry until lightly browned. Add onion and green peppers and sauté a few minutes until vegetables start to soften. Add canned tomatoes, then all of the seasonings. Reduce heat to medium and cook for 15 minutes, stirring occasionally.
2. Whisk peanut butter and tomato paste into 1 cup of the chicken stock until smooth. Add this mixture along with the remaining stock to the soup, bring to a simmer, reduce heat to medium-low, and let simmer for 30 minutes. Stir in cilantro.
3. Serve in bowls with optional garnishes.

SPLIT PEA WITH HAM

Makes about 8 cups

 **Hands-on time less than an hour (additional cooking or chilling times involved—read through before beginning)**

When deciding which soups to include in this cookbook, I asked Manna Facebook followers to weigh in. I was surprised when this one came up. Not because I thought it was a bad soup, but because I didn't think people liked peas, split or otherwise. I didn't, due to a childhood pea trauma.

Linda Barnstead's mom forbade her to come out and play unless she finished her peas, so I sneakily finished them for her. I can still see those menacing canned peas in their little Pyrex bowl. Later that evening, I fell ill with what was probably the flu, and those peas came back to haunt me. The association was so strong that I could not look a pea in the eye well into my adulthood. That included the pots of split pea soup my father hovered over, for he cherished this soup.

I didn't taste the split pea soup at Manna for a long time, assuming that my childhood pea memory would come back and bite me. But one day I did, and it was as cathartic and liberating as a good session of psychotherapy. It was delicious!

---

1 cup split green peas

2 strips bacon, diced

1 small ham hock*

1 small onion (about 4 ounces), diced

1 stalk celery, diced

1/2 teaspoon minced garlic

6 cups Chicken Stock (pages 202-203)

1 medium russet or Yukon Gold potato (about 6 ounces), peeled and chopped

1 small bay leaf

1/4 teaspoon black pepper

10 ounces cooked pit ham (ham trimmed from the bone), in 1/2-inch dice (about 3 cups)

A little salt, if needed

---

1. Rinse split peas under water until the water runs clear.
2. In a stockpot over medium heat, cook the bacon until crisp. Remove bacon and reserve, but leave cooking grease in the pan. Add ham hock to the pan and sear until the edges turn brown, then remove and set aside. Add onion and celery and sauté until the onions are softened and transparent but have not browned. Add garlic and sauté for 1 minute.
3. Add stock, potatoes, rinsed split peas, ham hock, bay leaf, and pepper and bring to a simmer. Allow soup to simmer 1 1/2 to 2 hours until peas are breaking apart. Remove the ham hock, cool it, remove any meat, cut it into a small dice, and set aside. Remove the bay leaf.
4. Puree the soup in a blender or food processor or with an immersion blender. Return soup to the pot and add cooked bacon, pit ham, and meat from the ham hock. Taste for salt level (the ham and ham hock are salty to begin with, so you may not need any additional salt). Rewarm before serving.

*Ham hocks can vary in how much meat they have on them. If yours is particularly meaty, you may prefer to hold back on some of the diced ham in the soup. This soup does err on the meaty side.

TOMATO BISQUE

Makes about 9 cups

 Hands-on time less than an hour (additional cooking or chilling times involved—read through before beginning)

This beautiful, bright tomato bisque is luxurious and satisfying. The soup's tomato base is combined with a cream reduction sauce, and the resulting marriage balances the acidity of the tomatoes with the silkiness of cream. (You can adjust the proportions of cream and half & half, or substitute some milk if you find the soup too rich.) Garnish it with chives or float some homemade croutons on top. Have a great loaf of bread at the ready, rewarmed in the oven, with some soft butter nearby.

Soup Base

3 tablespoons vegetable oil

1 medium onion (about 8 ounces), chopped

1 tablespoon minced garlic

3 stalks celery, trimmed and diced

2 teaspoons fresh thyme (or 1/2 teaspoon dried)

1 bay leaf

1 teaspoon salt

1 can (6 ounces) tomato paste

Two 28-ounce cans diced tomatoes, including liquid

Cream Reduction Sauce

2 tablespoons butter

1/4 cup chopped onions

1 teaspoon dried basil

1 small bay leaf

1/8 teaspoon cloves

1 cup half & half

1 cup heavy cream

1 tablespoon sherry

1/2 teaspoon salt

1/4 teaspoon white pepper

Optional garnishes: minced chives, homemade croutons, julienned fresh basil

---

1. **To make soup base:** Heat oil in a soup pot over medium heat. Add onions, garlic, and celery and sauté until onions are translucent. Add thyme, bay leaf, salt, and tomato paste, and stir until tomato paste is incorporated into the onion mixture. Add diced tomatoes, turn heat to high, and bring the soup to a boil. Reduce heat and simmer slowly for about 1 hour. Turn off the heat and remove the bay leaf.
2. **To make cream reduction:** Melt butter in a medium saucepan over medium heat. Add onions and sauté until translucent. Add all the remaining ingredients (except garnishes), increase heat to high, and bring to a boil. Reduce heat to medium low and simmer slowly for about 45 minutes, stirring occasionally and adjusting heat if necessary to prevent the sauce from sticking to the bottom of the pan, or burning. The sauce will reduce and thicken a bit.
3. **To finish the soup:** Puree tomato soup base in batches until smooth. Strain the cream reduction through a sieve directly into the tomato base, and stir well to blend. Taste and add more salt and pepper as needed.
4. To serve, rewarm the soup and ladle into bowls. Garnish with chives, croutons, or basil.

CARROT GINGER SOUP

Makes 8 cups

 Start to finish within an hour, give or take

There is no mistaking the origins of this soup, a brightly-hued puree which, not minutes earlier, was a bunch of fat, crisp carrots sitting on your countertop. The recipe is based on just a few simple components and produces a beautiful, silky, subtly flavored soup. Feel free to jazz it up with more ginger or perhaps even a pinch of cayenne. And while any carrot will do, ones from your garden, or a summer market, are noticeably superior in flavor and will contribute to an even better bowlful. The soup would make a lovely light luncheon entree, accompanied by a small salad and, of course, crusty bread.

2 tablespoons butter

1 large or 2 smaller onions (about 10 ounces total), peeled and chopped

2 tablespoons grated fresh ginger

5 cups Vegetable Stock (page 205)

2 1/2 pounds carrots, peeled and coarsely chopped

1 1/2 cups heavy cream

1/2 cup orange juice

1/4 teaspoon salt

Optional garnish: minced chives

1. Melt butter in a large pot over medium heat. Add onions and ginger, and sauté until onions are translucent.
2. Add vegetable stock and carrots, increase the heat and bring to a boil. Then reduce the heat to a simmer and cook uncovered for 30 minutes. Strain the soup, then puree the strained solids in a blender. Add some of the hot stock as needed to help the carrots become liquified. Add puree back into the stock.
3. Stir in the cream, orange juice, and salt and heat through. Garnish each serving with a sprinkling of chives.

RED LENTIL SOUP

Makes about 8 cups

 Start to finish within an hour, give or take

Lentil soup was its own sub-genre at Manna, so it was hard to choose a favorite. This one has a lovely autumn hue from the red lentils and gentle, savory simplicity. Plus, it is vegan and healthful. It appeals to devotees of lentil soup and is a friendly invitation to the uninitiated.

1 cup red lentils

4 cups water

1 large onion (about 8 ounces), chopped

2 tablespoons vegetable oil

1 tablespoon minced garlic

1 1/2 tablespoons grated fresh ginger

1 1/2 teaspoons cumin

1 1/2 teaspoons ground coriander

1/2 teaspoon turmeric

3 cups Vegetable Stock (page 205)

One 14-ounce can petite diced tomatoes

1/2 teaspoon salt

1/2 teaspoon ground black pepper

Optional garnish: a dusting of turmeric

1. Rinse lentils under cold water until water runs clear. Place them in a medium pot and add 4 cups water. Bring to a boil and cook lentils until tender, about 15 to 20 minutes. Drain and reserve.
2. In a large soup pot, sauté onions in oil over medium heat until translucent. Add garlic and ginger and cook for 2 minutes. Add cumin, coriander, and turmeric and cook for about 2 more minutes.
3. Add lentils, stock, and tomatoes. Bring to a simmer, cover, and cook until lentils are tender, about 30 minutes.
4. Puree 1/3 of the mixture, then recombine with the rest. Add salt and pepper.
5. Serve each bowlful with a dusting of turmeric, if you like.

MUSHROOM BARLEY SOUP

Makes about 8 cups

 **Hands-on time less than an hour (additional cooking or chilling times involved—read through before beginning)**

Jody Flatt, an early Collins House Catering employee, brought us this cherished family favorite straight from her mother's recipe box. She remembers how, in her childhood, her older brother intensely disliked barley, while her younger brother would not touch mushrooms, both claiming allergies in their defense. Each sibling would laboriously separate out the parts they disliked, resulting in one bowl of broth with only barley and one with only mushrooms. Jody left The Collins House for a long, fruitful career in cancer research. But still passionate about cooking professionally, she eventually opened a catering business. (And in a full-circle kind of way, she came back to us as a recipe tester for this book!)

This soup, tweaked ever so slightly from Jody's version, is perfect for one of those Wisconsin winter days when the wind rattled windows and children charged home early from school, eager to jump into growing piles of drifted snow (and when the happiest critter in the house was a Bernese mountain dog, who had a love of sub-zero temperatures and blizzards coursing through her veins).

1/2 cup pearled barley, rinsed
1 cup water

2 ounces (1/2 stick) butter, divided
1 medium onion (6 ounces), chopped
2 large or 3 medium carrots, peeled and chopped
1 medium russet potato (6 ounces), peeled and chopped
12 ounces button or cremini mushrooms, sliced
3 tablespoons chopped parsley
1 clove minced garlic
4 cups Chicken Stock (pages 202-203) or Vegetable Stock (page 205), divided
2/3 cup half & half
1 tablespoon lemon juice
1/2 teaspoon salt
1/2 teaspoon pepper

8 ounces assorted wild mushrooms, such as shiitake, crimini, or oyster, de-stemmed and sliced

3 tablespoons sweet sherry

1/2 cup sour cream

Optional garnishes: paprika, minced chives, sour cream

---

1. Rinse barley under cold water until the water runs clear. Place barley in a small pot, add 1 cup of water and bring to a boil. Reduce heat to low, cover tightly, and cook for 40 minutes. Turn off heat, remove the lid, and set aside.
2. Melt half the butter (2 tablespoons) in a stockpot over medium heat. Add onions, carrots, and potatoes and cook until softened, 10 to 15 minutes. Add button (or cremini) mushrooms, parsley, and garlic and let cook until the mushrooms have lost all of their liquid. Season with salt and pepper, then add about a third of the stock. Gently simmer the soup, covered, for 10 minutes. Turn off the heat.
3. Puree the soup using an immersion blender or in batches in a blender. Return the puree to the pot and add remaining stock, half & half, lemon juice, salt and pepper.
4. In a separate medium sauté pan, cook the remaining wild mushrooms in the remaining 2 tablespoons of butter over medium-high heat. Once the mushrooms have given up their water and begin to brown, deglaze the pan with sherry. When the sherry has cooked out, add the mushrooms to the soup pot, along with the cooked barley.
5. Before serving, rewarm the soup and garnish with sour cream, chives, and paprika.

From the Bakery

Every morning we unlocked the doors at Manna for the early birds, people on their way to work, or just early risers who had a hankering for a still-warm sticky bun or a sunrise muffin. The display of pastries, lined up like soldiers, was a thing of beauty—a sight that few people saw because the selection was quickly depleted. "Give me that one in the back row, on the right," a customer might instruct. "That one has more streusel." And so it would go, with staffers slipping hand-picked scones into bags or juggling big boxes with an array of pastries.

Every customer had a decided favorite, and woe-be-us if that item was already sold out by the time they arrived. Many learned the lesson that a quick phone call would guarantee we'd save one of their favorite muffins, and would even call a day ahead just to be sure. The chocolate chip cookies kept Craig happy through his last years and even followed him home when he could come in no more. The bakery was a source of joy for customers and staff alike. Every now and again, a server would deliberately break a muffin in half or crumble a cookie with a falsely sheepish, "Oops," and then share chunks with everyone. We liked to call it quality control.

For a smallish cafe, we put out a lot of bakery, both in quantity and variety. There was something for everyone. In addition to the usual suspects—muffins, croissants, scones, cookies, cakes, and pies—we offered a proud lineup of gluten-free pastries, a smattering of traditional Jewish favorites—even a vegan cake, a glittery gem hidden in plain sight atop the bakery case. And there was nothing that was not from scratch, including gluten-free biscotti to inform our gluten-free pie crusts and homemade toffee for the Annie Oakley cookies. The list was long, the labor intensive. Every one of us, even the skinniest, put on a pound or two in those 15 years—happily.

The bakery was something we all somewhat carelessly took for granted, though it was a magical part of the cafe. Magical because day after day, there was so much product waiting to be purchased, and it seemed to have come from nowhere. But we should have thanked every baker every day for their late-night-wee-hour toil and commitment and for literally giving us our daily bread. Some bakers came in to work at roughly the same time that you or I went to sleep at night and were often gone by the time the opening staff rolled in. They were phantoms to our customers—some of whom thought we got our bakery from elsewhere because it was always just ready and waiting. Or they assumed that I was the one who did the baking. It was hard to give credit where credit was due because we rarely saw these devoted creatures of the night. It is a shame that the bakers seldom had the opportunity to meet the customers for whom they labored.

Not all of Manna's bakers worked the graveyard shift, and those who didn't spent their days frosting cakes, filling pies, or forming hundreds of perfect rugelach. The daytime bakers laid the groundwork, stocking the freezers with unbaked cookie doughs or scones or Danish that the night crew would later bake. Their work was not time-sensitive in the same way as that of the night bakers, who were directly responsible for ensuring that each day's products were fresh and ready by opening time. But it was demanding, repetitive work, and somewhat solitary even in the presence of coworkers.

Baking for a living has a certain romanticism about it: White-toqued pastry chefs adorning tiered cakes with artful curlicues and swooshes of color. T-shirt-clad artisans sculpting crusty baguettes and multigrain boules. Intensely focused bakers expertly forming row after row of buttery, flaky croissants. But baking is not just a fragrant fantasy of caramelized sugar, rising dough, and spicy cinnamon—it is a lot of hard work and long hours. Hours of repetition, heavy lifting, kneading and forming and baking first the rye bread and next the challah, and so on, until night slowly brightens into day. Baking is physically demanding. Years spent hunched over a counter forming bread loaves or lugging and emptying 50-pound sacks of flour can take a toll on the body. And it can be a lonely job, especially if you are a social person, because baking takes a certain inner focus and often happens when no one else is around.

Yet bakers love what they do for these very reasons. Professional bakers have a passion for their work, despite the hours, despite the quantities, and despite the repetition. Baking is inherently satisfying because the final product is so delicious, smells so good, and makes so many people so happy. Bakers are creative sorts, challenged to make new goodies that suit their fancy or iron out or improve procedural kinks to make a task more efficient. And they often are solitary sorts as well, grateful for a job in which they can work alone, surrounded only by the quiet hum of an oven fan or the metered cadence of their favorite music in their earbuds. Manna's bakers were a colorful bunch, each marching to the beat of some drum or other, and their contributions were as varied as their personalities.

Two bakers, Dan and Tony, were original employees at Manna, interviewed way back when, beneath the oak leaf stencil that encircled The Collins House living room, our pre-Manna office space. Both were already seasoned veterans, attuned to the rhythms of night baking and experts at creating, troubleshooting, and turning recipes for 12 into recipes for hundreds. They both stayed at Manna until we closed, giving direction, stability, and mentorship to those who joined them. Another long-time employee, Chris, began at Manna as a kitchen manager in the early days. He eventually turned to the bakery, where his drive, detail-mindedness, and love of baking breads helped us stay the course until the end. Sarah made the triple lemon cake a Manna icon and breathed life into hundreds of Hamantaschen every year. She took copious notes on her products—a little Sarah-diary that became invaluable reference material for all sorts of problem-solving and planning.

Almost every morning, a plate or two of crooked scones, trimmed brownie edges, or smooshed cookies would appear on a specific spot on a kitchen counter—a place reserved for all the bakery or kitchen mishaps that were not customer-worthy but that someone would gratefully gobble down in a hungry moment. Sometimes, it would be actual creations—bialys chock full of bacon and cheese or savory focaccia loaves. Thank you, bakers, for everything, including, and perhaps especially, the crumbs.

A Few Important Baking Guidelines

Conventional vs. Convection Ovens

Most recipes are written for a conventional oven and—assuming the oven is calibrated—give accurate baking times. But the baking can be uneven. A pan of muffins may be cooked on one side but still be undercooked on the other side or in the middle. Convection ovens are designed to overcome this problem and are a big help. In a convection oven, the hot air is circulated about the space by a fan or blower. The air flow reaches all areas of a pan more uniformly and thus improves the evenness of the baking.

Because it is circulating, convection heat can "feel" hotter than the oven dial indicates (just like with a wind chill factor, where it "feels" so much colder outside than your thermometer would have you believe). This characteristic can contribute to a shortened baking time compared to how long it can take at the same temperature in a regular oven. At Manna, when a recipe specified a 350-degree oven temperature, we always set the dial at 300, thus compensating for this difference. In home convection ovens, you may find that slight adjustments to the dial are necessary to mimic the correct temperature intended in a recipe.

The baking times specified in these recipes assume you're using an accurately calibrated conventional oven. If you use convection, shorten your baking time by a few minutes (more on this on the next page).

Most important of all: Know your oven! Rare is the oven that performs just as a recipe expects it to, for many reasons, including its design and craftsmanship, state of repair or disrepair, age, etc. Always use the recipe designation as a good starting guideline, then adapt it to the idiosyncrasies of your particular oven. And regardless of which type of oven you use, pay heed to the two sections below on pan rotation and baking times. Both discussions will help you coax the best out of a coffee cake, a cookie, or a loaf of bread.

Oven Etiquette for Better Bakery

Baked goods can be finicky. During the baking process, a chemical reaction is happening to create a final structure, and the process wants to happen with as little interruption as possible, especially with fragile batters like cakes or muffins. As a general rule, let products bake for about two-thirds of the total time indicated before opening the oven door. Below are a few other good oven practices:

Get in and out quickly. The longer you linger with an open door, the more the heat escapes, which can throw off baking times or even inhibit rising. If you really need to sneak a peek early on, just crack the door open and look fast!

Be gentle. If you let an oven door slam closed, all of your hard work may collapse irreversibly. Even sliding out a rack to insert a toothpick can be too jiggly at the wrong moment.

Know your oven. As mentioned in the discussion of regular and convection ovens, each oven works a bit differently. Keeping a thermometer in the oven will help you gauge whether your oven temperature is spot-on or running hotter or cooler than a recipe specifies. You can easily compensate in your baking practices if you know this.

Rotating Pans

Rotate your pans at least once during baking. It is essential in a standard oven since the hot air does not circulate, and different parts of your oven may bake unevenly. Even with convection ovens, hot spots can occur, so it is best to make pan rotation a habit. You know how frustrating it can be when a pan of cookies ends up with a mix of overly brown and still-doughy cookies! Just remember to wait until roughly two-thirds of the way through the baking process before rotating pans, and handle them gently.

Baking Times

Baking time is affected by how accurate the oven temperature is, whether the oven is convection or standard, and the material and size of your pans. As discussed above, the recipes in this book assume that you have a standard oven that's working well. In addition, they assume that you're using the pan sizes indicated. For example, if you substitute an 8 x 8-inch pan for a 9 x 9-inch pan because it is all you have on hand, your batter will be deeper, and it will take longer to bake. If you use a Bundt pan instead of a flat pan for a particular cake, the configuration of the Bundt pan will alter the baking time. Also, different pan materials conduct heat differently. Heavier pans generally conduct heat better and prevent hot spots that can mess with baking times.

Very important! Check baked goods for doneness **before** the end of the suggested baking time to ensure things are not moving too quickly. You can always bake something a few more minutes, but you cannot subtract those minutes once the bakery item is past its prime.

Greasing the Pan: Spray vs. Shortening vs. Butter

Pans typically need to be coated with some type of pan-release spray, solid shortening, or butter so that baked goods will let go easily. In the old days, we called it "greasing the pan," and we all knew what it meant, despite the term's indelicate connotations. When commercial pan spray came along, the linguistic waters seemed to muddy up, and there was no quick-and-easy way to phrase it. You can go for the environmentally incorrect (but easier to use) pan spray, or you can schmear butter or shortening with your fingers (eww, messy) or with a paper towel. (My mom used the leftover butter clinging to the waxy wrap.) I don't advocate for one over the other, but I do prefer not to repeat a lengthy instruction in every recipe. So when I say, "Grease your pans," choose your weapon!

Scraping Down Bowls

This important step should never be overlooked. When using an electric mixer, a small amount of ingredients tends to get left at the bottom or along the sides of the bowl. If they are not well incorporated, the batter won't work correctly. You may get cookies with inconsistent textures or cake batters that fall in places. And no, you can't save time and do one scrape-down at the end. Each time you add ingredients to a batter, the consistency changes, and therefore, after each new ingredient addition, the bowl should be scraped down. A good final hand mix at the end will get all the little globs still left at the bottom of the bowl. Recipes herein will simply say "scrape the bowl" when it is required.

Cubing Butter for Cutting into Doughs

Overly large chunks of butter will not cut uniformly into dough. Some pieces will remain too large, and others will be too fine. Here is a good system: Cut the sticks of butter into quarters lengthwise and lay the resulting skinny sticks out flat alongside one another. Then cut the sticks into about eight to nine pieces each, resulting in small cubes of butter that will be the perfect size for incorporating into dough.

Separating Egg Whites and Yolks

When separating whites and yolks, be CERTAIN that the yolk has not broken, or if it has, it does not contaminate the whites. If this happens, you will need to start over. Whites tainted by even the teeniest tiniest smidgen of yolk will not whip properly. I still have a nostalgic image of my mom cracking one egg at a time into a small Pyrex bowl, checking the white carefully, then transferring the single clean white to the main work bowl. In this way, if she made a mistake, she only lost one egg white and not the whole batch. (Some Jewish cooks will use this same process when cracking eggs for any purpose—separated or otherwise—to ensure that not a speck of blood contaminates the dish.)

Portioning Batters

Please refer to the discussion of portioning scoops on page 82. In the baking recipes, I refer to a portion scoop size in ounces because that is how manufacturers designate them. In liquid measurements, one ounce equals two tablespoons. Once you are dealing with solids like cookie dough or cupcake batter, that equivalency does not hold; however, it is close. A one-ounce scoop will produce, more or less, a two-tablespoon cookie portion.

Removing Cooled Bars from Pans

If you try to remove bars or cakes from their pans too soon, they may break apart, as they are fragile in their still-warm state. But if you allow them to cool fully, they are more likely to come out cleanly. It is sometimes beneficial to chill them first, as chilling will help them set more fully (a pan of bars can be completely cool but still soft and fragile). If, for whatever reason, you have chilled your bars or cake layers in their pans, then this de-panning method works well: Turn a stovetop burner on to medium heat. Hold the bottom of the chilled pan directly over the heat while moving it back and forth, up and down, for about 30 seconds (never let it sit still). Run a spatula around the perimeter of the pan, between the pan and bar (or cake), to loosen any crusty edges. Finally, invert the pan over a serving piece or another pan. This warming of the bottom will loosen the bonds of chilled butter or shortening from the pan, letting you remove your bar or cake layer easily without breaking it.

Crumb-Coating Cakes

This technique adds one quick step to the cake-frosting process and helps ensure a clean, professional look. After you've assembled your cake layers, or even for a single-layer cake, spread a small amount of frosting (just enough to provide a super thin layer) over the entire cake. Make sure it is smooth all over, then refrigerate the cake for at least 20 minutes. The thin layer of buttercream will lock in any crumbs clinging to the cake's exterior, and once it is firm, the final frosting layer can be applied without getting muddled by bits of crumbs.

Giving Buttercream a Smooth-as-Satin Finish

My friend and Collins House pastry chef, Amy, taught me this technique. Watching her finish a cake was always somewhat of a jaw-dropping experience. She would pile the frosting on the cake and give the lazy Susan a quick spin, all the while cheerfully jabbering away, her gaze often elsewhere. Her cakes were always as smooth as a freshly Zambonied skating rink, and she did it in 30 seconds or less.

You'll need hot water for this—boiling or the hottest your tap can provide—enough to achieve about a three- to four-inch depth in a glass measuring cup or a heat-proof drinking glass. Use an offset spatula (or another metal spatula with a straight edge). Dip the spatula in the hot water for 20 seconds, then smooth the frosting with the edge of the tool. Start on the sides of the cake, and each time you take the spatula away from the frosting, be sure to rewarm it in the hot water again. (The spatula must be hot at all times to achieve a smooth finish.) If you have the cake on a lazy Susan, you can slowly spin it while holding the spatula edge against it. As you spin, apply gentle pressure to the side of the cake. Where the side meets the top, apply the pressure to form a tiny rim of frosting just above the level of the cake. When the sides are smoothed to your liking, smooth out the top of the cake. The idea is to slowly rotate the cake while pulling the spatula inward, beginning with the raised rim and moving toward the center of the cake. This technique will help create a neat, crisp junction between the rim and the sides, as it smooths the top surface.

The Freezer Is Your Friend

During the recipe-testing phase of this book, we rediscovered the joy of freezing. This was not new information. At Manna, we routinely made large batches of cookies, scones, or croissants, which we froze unbaked, and then baked off daily. I suppose this had never occurred to us at home because Manna was always *there*. Now Mike and I have a freezer brimming with an assortment of unbaked goodies. When we turn into couch potatoes for some Netflix streaming at night, we can pop something into the toaster oven for a fix between episodes.

All the cookies, for example, can be made, formed, frozen in a single layer, then stored airtight for future bakeoffs (we use Ziploc bags over and over). To bake off frozen items, simply defrost them and then bake according to the recipe instructions. By making and freezing several products at home, you can have Manna variety at your fingertips.

Many products freeze exceptionally well after baking. Muffins, sticky buns, cakes, and bars will all hold up beautifully and just need to be defrosted to room temperature for serving. People may consider frozen bakery to be "not fresh," which is technically true, but preparing and baking off each item every day is not practical, or even possible, for a bakery. Yes, it can feel off-putting for customers to know they're buying defrosted cakes, but the truth is, nobody could tell the difference. At Manna, the lemon cake and lavender lime cakes, in particular, were made in batches and frozen, and you are encouraged to do the same. That way, nothing goes to waste. Note, however, that a pie with an unbaked filling, such as the Heirloom Cocoa Pie or the Pumpkin Chiffon Pie, will not hold up well in the freezer. It may become watery or change consistency.

Reheating Baked Goods—Frozen or Not—in the Microwave

Many bakery products can be gently rewarmed in a microwave without ruining the integrity of the product. But for sure, if you put a muffin in the microwave and run it on high or a minute, you will kill the muffin.

To avoid killing muffins, or any other baked goods, use the "low and slow" approach. Rewarm your products at a power level no higher than 3. Start with 30 seconds, feel them for warmth, then if needed, you can zap them again, in 20- to 30-second increments. You can always add time, but you can never take it away.

Yeast-based products in particular (croissants, sticky buns, breads) are likely to be ruined by excessive power levels, turning chewy or cardboard-like. Also, while a microwave may successfully bring them warmth, it cannot provide a crisping effect, such as you might desire with a croissant or loaf of bread. At home, we use the microwave only to take the initial freeze out of these products but then transfer them to our toaster oven for a fresh-from-the-oven experience.

If you're careful, you can even take the chill off of frosted cakes. Use a power level of 2 and heat in 20-second intervals until your dessert-for-one is just where you like it. I especially love it when a slice of cake is defrosted in this way. The cake loses its chill, becoming once again soft and moist, and the frosting gets ever so slightly melty, which I find enhances the gooey cake experience. I get my own little Barb-thrill by pushing the microwave envelope on ganache-glazed Liberty Bells (pages 276-279. While Mike scorns my cupcake, whose glaze has puddled at the base, I think it is heavenly.

A Few Bakery Ingredients Notes

- **Sanding sugar** is used to be-glitter the tops of some baked goods. It comes in coarse or medium granules and holds its shape while baking, providing a bit of sparkle and crunch to the finished product. Granulated sugar is not a good substitute, so it's best to leave your pastry unadorned if you do not have any on hand.
- **Instant coffee powder** adds intensity to the coffee flavor of a baked good without adding moisture. I am partial to the Medaglia d'Oro brand for its superior flavor and fine grain. Other brands may need to be pulverized with a mortar and pestle.
- **Vanilla and other extracts.** I strongly encourage you to choose pure extracts vs. imitation extracts or flavorings. Extracts derive flavor by allowing a product such as vanilla beans to steep for a period of time, whereas other flavorings are either diluted or synthetic. The difference is noticeable, and a poor-quality product can ruin your baked goods, providing either untrue flavors or chemical off-notes. The labels say it all.

Muffins and Scones

It was easy developing a starting lineup of breakfast pastries at Manna. For 20 years, we had cultivated a collection of muffin and scone recipes for our Collins House guests. Our specialties were in a genre of baking considered "quick," and for a time, we wholesaled them to area coffee shops and a few restaurants.

Less easy was the decision to include sticky buns, Danish, and croissants on Manna's bakery menu. These products come from "laminated" doughs, a baking genre that requires a deeper knowledge of technique and considerably more time than muffins and scones. Laminated products are made by folding layer upon layer of butter into a dough. In Manna's case, the doughs were yeast-raised, although puff pastry is an example of a laminated dough without yeast. We knew very little about the mass production of these products and felt we were in uncharted waters. Then we hired Tony, a seasoned pro who'd cut his teeth at the Ovens of Brittany and who confidently led us forward in this arena. He introduced Danish, croissants, and the beloved sticky buns (modeled after the original Ovens Brittany Bun) that we kept on the roster until we closed our doors.

A muffin is a moist, cupcake-like quick bread baked in a cup-shaped pan and served unadorned but for a light glaze or a sprinkling of streusel. Scones, in contrast, are drier, crumblier, and less sweet. Both benefit from a smear of soft butter, and both will keep you going until lunch rolls around. Muffins and scones are core to a good bakery's lineup of breakfast pastries, and both can be easily made at home. At Manna, we rotated the varieties so that everyone could have a chance at their favorites.

PUMPKIN CHOCOLATE CHIP MUFFINS

Makes 16 muffins

 Start to finish within an hour, give or take

What is it about this muffin that is so compelling? We first introduced it to Manna as a seasonal muffin in the autumn of 2005, and by January, we believed it was time to rotate in some winter options. That was a mistake. After a brief but challenging respite during which the customers lobbied us daily, and loudly, the pumpkin chocolate chip muffin returned for good and became our all-time number one bestseller, even in summer (when the chips melted in your hands as you walked out the door). And no wonder. It is as delicious as a muffin is capable of being. It is fairly dense with chocolate chips, and who doesn't love that? Or maybe we just need to be surrounded by the family comfort and nostalgic aromas of Thanksgiving all year.

The recipe is easy (no mixer needed), dairy-free (uses oil, not butter), and has stamina. (Wrapped in plastic, it stays soft and moist for nearly a week.) Enjoy!

---

1 3/4 cups flour

1 1/2 teaspoons baking soda

1/2 teaspoon salt

1/2 teaspoon cinnamon

1/2 teaspoon nutmeg

Pinch of cloves

Pinch of ginger

Pinch of allspice

1 1/2 cups sugar

1/2 cup vegetable oil

2 eggs

1 teaspoon vanilla extract

1 cup pumpkin puree

1/4 cup water

1 1/4 cups chocolate chips

Cinnamon sugar for topping: 1/3 cup sugar mixed well with 1 teaspoon cinnamon

---

1. Preheat the oven to 350 degrees. Grease a 12-cup muffin tin or line the cups with muffin liners and set aside.
2. In a medium bowl, combine the dry ingredients (flour through allspice) and mix.
3. In another bowl, combine sugar, oil, eggs, and vanilla and whisk together by hand until well combined. Add pumpkin puree and water, and whisk until smooth.
4. Mix dry ingredients into the wet batter gently, using the whisk. When the batter is almost fully combined, add chocolate chips and mix it using a rubber spatula.
5. Fill muffin tins 3/4 full* with batter. Sprinkle muffin tops lightly with cinnamon sugar, and place the muffin pan in the oven. Bake for 14 minutes, then rotate the pan and bake another 8 to 10 minutes. Test for doneness by placing a toothpick into the center of the muffin. It should come out clean. Bake longer if needed. When muffins are done, let them cool in their tins for about 20 minutes, then remove to a wire rack to finish cooling.

*Don't be tempted to overfill the muffin cups (to make 12 muffins instead of 16). The muffins will just bleed off the edges and won't look pretty. If you don't have two muffin tins, just bake off the extra batter after the first batch of muffins has cooled.

CORNMEAL RASPBERRY MUFFINS

Makes 12 muffins

 Start to finish within an hour, give or take

What a lovely tapestry of flavors and textures. The gentle crunch of cornmeal, a background note of fresh lemon zest, and tangy red raspberries popping coyly from within the folds of this golden, sweet-smelling muffin. Lest this seem like oversell, it is not. The cornmeal is present but not overly so, and the muffin is not too sweet.

You can store these for a couple of days wrapped in plastic or freeze them.

---

2 cups flour

2/3 cup medium cornmeal

1 tablespoon baking powder

1/2 teaspoon salt

6 ounces (1 1/2 sticks) butter, softened

3/4 cup sugar

2 eggs

1/2 teaspoon grated lemon zest

2/3 cup milk

1 1/4 cups frozen raspberries (do not thaw them)*

Sanding sugar (see page 226) to finish the muffins

---

1. Preheat the oven to 350 degrees. Grease a 12-cup muffin tin or line the cups with muffin liners and set aside.
2. Mix together the dry ingredients (flour through salt) in a bowl and set aside.
3. In the bowl of an electric mixer, cream butter and sugar on medium speed until well blended. Scrape down the bowl, then beat in eggs and lemon zest. Scrape the bowl again. On a low speed, add dry ingredients to the bowl in two batches, alternating with the milk, and combine well. Scrape down the bowl and give a final short mix. Using a spatula, fold in frozen raspberries gently but thoroughly.
4. Fill muffin tins 3/4 full with batter. Sprinkle muffin tops with sanding sugar. Bake for 15 minutes, then rotate the pan and bake another 10 to 12 minutes. Test for doneness by placing a toothpick into the center of the muffin. It should come out clean. Bake longer if needed. When the muffins are done, let them cool in their tins for about 20 minutes, then remove to a wire rack to finish cooling.

*You can use fresh raspberries if you like, especially if they are in season at your local market. But fresh raspberries are very fragile. You can freeze your berries first, in a single layer on a sheet pan, and they will handle much better. If you fold them in fresh and unfrozen, be extra gentle.

SUNRISE MUFFINS

Makes 12 muffins

 Start to finish within an hour, give or take

When customers asked for our most healthful muffin, we pointed them to the Sunrise Muffin, aka Morning Glory, aka Sunshine. It is packed with nutrition and is quite moist, like a carrot cake but for breakfast. The muffin itself is dairy-free and nut-free. If you want to serve it as a somewhat healthful dessert, and are not troubled by allergies, you could pipe on a lovely swirl of cream cheese frosting and top it with a whole toasted pecan.

Sunrise muffins are a good outlet for bumper crops of zucchini and carrots from your garden. Back when the muffins made their Manna debut, and as their popularity grew, we began portioning and freezing some of the components—zucchini, apples, carrots, and coconut flakes—into "packs" sized for the recipes. An acronym arose, and coincidentally the task of making these "Zac-Pacs" was assigned to a certain apprentice baker, who grated and peeled and diced and measured the ingredients. You'll never guess his name.

If you make your own Zac-Pacs, defrost them fully before using them in the recipe.

Zac-Pac

1 cup grated carrots

3/4 cup grated zucchini

One large apple (about 8 ounces) peeled, cored, and diced into 1/2-inch or smaller pieces

1/2 cup shredded sweetened coconut (lightly packed)

Muffins

1 1/3 cups flour

2 teaspoons cinnamon

1 1/2 teaspoons baking soda

1/2 teaspoon salt

1/3 cup vegetable oil

1/3 cup unsweetened applesauce

3/4 cups sugar

2 eggs

1/8 teaspoon orange extract (optional)

1 teaspoon vanilla extract

---

1. Preheat the oven to 350 degrees. Grease a 12-cup muffin tin or line the cups with muffin liners and set aside.
2. Mix Zac-Pac ingredients in a bowl and set aside.
3. For the muffins, combine the dry ingredients (flour through salt) in a medium bowl.
4. In a separate, large bowl, whisk together oil and applesauce, then whisk in eggs, orange extract (if using), and vanilla until well mixed. Stir Zac-Pac ingredients into the wet batter, then mix in dry ingredients with a rubber spatula until well blended and uniform.
5. Fill muffin tins 3/4 full with batter, and place the muffin pan in the oven. Bake for 12 minutes, then rotate the pan and bake another 8 to 10 minutes. Test for doneness by placing a toothpick into the center of the muffin. It should come out clean. Bake longer if needed. When muffins are done, let them cool in their tins for about 20 minutes, then remove to a wire rack to finish cooling.

Zac-Pac: fall harvest for your muffins.

LEMON POPPY SEED MUFFINS

Makes 12 muffins

 Start to finish within an hour, give or take

What makes this lemon poppy seed muffin stand out is the beaten egg whites, which are folded into the batter at the end. Lighter and moister than most, they have a certain elegance. Try the optional glaze if you like a bonus sweet-tart burst of lemon.

---

2 cups flour

2 teaspoons baking powder

1 teaspoon baking soda

1/2 teaspoon salt

1/4 cup poppy seeds

6 ounces (1 1/2 sticks) butter, softened

1 cup plus 2 tablespoons sugar

3 eggs, separated

Grated zest of 1/2 lemon

1 teaspoon vanilla extract

3/4 cup buttermilk

Optional finish: Confectioners' Sugar Glaze (pages 366-367, using lemon juice and finishing to a very thin consistency).

---

1. Preheat the oven to 350 degrees. Grease a 12-cup muffin tin or line the cups with muffin liners and set aside.
2. Mix the dry ingredients (flour through poppy seeds) in a medium bowl.
3. Cream butter and sugar in an electric mixer on medium-high speed for about 3 minutes until light and fluffy. Scrape down the bowl. Add egg yolks one at a time, mixing well after each addition. (Egg whites will be used in Step 6.) Scrape down the bowl. Add lemon zest and vanilla and mix to incorporate.
4. Using a low speed, add dry ingredients to the butter mixture alternately with the buttermilk, beginning and ending with dry ingredients (so three dry, two wet), and mixing gently but thoroughly after each addition. Then scrape the bowl one last time and give everything a final (but gentle) mix.
5. Use a whisk attachment on the mixer to beat egg whites in a clean, separate bowl until they hold a soft, wet peak. (They should hold their shape but not be stiff and dry). Fold 1/4 of the whites into the batter, using a rubber spatula and mixing gently but thoroughly. (This step will help lighten the batter a bit, making the subsequent folding easier.) Gently fold in the remaining whites. Do not whisk or mix with force. You do not want to deflate the air holes in the whites.
6. Fill muffin tin 3/4 full with batter and place the muffin pan in the oven. Bake for 10 minutes, then rotate the pans and bake another 6 to 8 minutes. Test for doneness by placing a toothpick into the center of the muffin. It should come out clean. Bake longer if needed. When muffins are done, let them cool in their tins for about 20 minutes, then remove to a wire rack to finish cooling.
7. If using, drizzle the confectioners' sugar glaze over the cooled muffins.

A MASTER SCONE RECIPE WITH TWO VARIATIONS

(Apricot Walnut and Chocolate Chip Orange)

Makes 10-12 scones

 Start to finish within an hour, give or take

This basic scone recipe is infinitely adaptable to your personality and cravings. Here I have offered the two most popular Manna varieties: Apricot Walnut and Chocolate Chip Orange. Both had their avid followings.

The recipe is geared for a more traditionally dry scone, although, since "dry" was generally a bad word at Manna, they are not "that dry." You can add a little extra buttermilk if you like, but that will produce a more cake-like product. ("Cake" is also a bad word in the scone realm.)

Master Scone

2 cups flour

1/4 cup sugar

1 1/2 teaspoons baking powder

1/2 teaspoon baking soda

1/4 teaspoon salt

3 ounces (3/4 stick) cold butter, cut into 1/2-inch cubes and kept chilled

1/2 cup buttermilk

1 egg

1/2 teaspoon vanilla extract

Apricot Walnut Variation

1/2 cup chopped dried apricots

1/2 cup walnuts, toasted and chopped (page 363)

OR

Chocolate Chip Variation

1/2 teaspoon grated orange zest

3/4 cup semi-sweet chocolate chips

---

1. Preheat the oven to 350 degrees. Line a baking sheet with parchment paper (or grease the pan) and set aside.
2. Mix flour, sugar, baking powder, baking soda, and salt in the work bowl of an electric mixer with a paddle attachment. Add butter cubes and mix on low until the mixture has a coarse appearance, with the butter now in irregular, pea-size bits. (If the butter becomes too well blended with the dry ingredients, your final scone will end up less tender.) Alternatively, you can use a food processor to mix the dry ingredients and then cut in the butter using the pulse button. Either way, once the butter has been properly cut in, transfer the mixture to a large bowl.
3. Beat together eggs, buttermilk, and vanilla in a separate bowl. If making the chocolate chip variation, add the orange zest.
4. Gently stir the apricots and walnuts or chocolate chips into the flour and butter mixture. Now add the wet mixture and use a rubber spatula to toss and fold it into the dry mixture until the batter is thoroughly combined and forms a dough, but is not overmixed.
5. Scoop dough onto the prepared pan with a 4-ounce scoop (1/2-cup measure), spacing the scoops 2 inches apart. Flatten each one ever so slightly. Bake 14 minutes, then rotate the pan and bake another 8 to 10 minutes. They are done when the scone is golden around the edges, and the center, when pressed with a finger, does not yield but feels set.

OAT DATE SCONES

Makes 6 or 8 scones

 Start to finish within an hour, give or take

In The Collins House days, this scone was prominent on the list of bakery items we wholesaled to many area coffee shops. Back then, we rolled it, cut it into rounds, and drizzled it with a confectioners' sugar glaze. But at Manna, because so many products were round, we changed the shape of the oat date scone to a wedge. A few days after Manna opened, I had my first customer complaint from a woman who didn't like the new shape. She said that unless we changed it back to a round, she would not be coming back. *Sigh.* The wedge prevailed, and the scone, redolent of cinnamon and moist with dates, found its loyal following. A more recent fan was a fellow bridge player, Meg Meyer, for whom I baked a special batch the week we closed. During the months of social isolation, when we played bridge the "COVID way" (online), we made mention of the oat scone, I think, to keep the bonds of friendship strong while the pandemic raged outside.

---

1 3/4 cups flour

1 1/3 cups whole rolled oats (not quick-cooking)

1/3 cup sugar

1 1/2 teaspoons baking powder

1 teaspoon baking soda

1 teaspoon cinnamon

1/4 teaspoon cloves

1/2 teaspoon salt

6 ounces (1 1/2 sticks) cold butter cut into 1/2-inch cubes

1 cup chopped dried dates

1/2 cup buttermilk

Confectioners' Sugar Glaze (pages 366-367 using milk, and either vanilla or orange zest, and finishing to a medium consistency)

---

1. Preheat the oven to 350 degrees. Line a baking sheet with parchment paper (or grease the pan) and set aside. If you have an 8-inch springform pan, set out the side piece (but not the bottom) to help form the scones. It is not necessary, but helpful.
2. Combine dry ingredients (flour through salt) in the work bowl of an electric mixer with a paddle attachment, and mix briefly to combine. Add butter cubes and mix on low until the mixture has a coarse appearance, with the butter now in irregular, pea-size bits. (If the butter becomes too well blended with the dry ingredients, your final scone will end up less tender.) Alternatively, you can use a food processor to mix the dry ingredients and then cut in the butter using the pulse button. Either way, once the butter has been properly cut in, transfer the mixture to a large bowl.
3. Gently toss the dates into the flour and butter mixture. Now add the buttermilk and use a rubber spatula to toss and fold it into the dry mixture until the batter is thoroughly combined and just forms a dough.
4. Place dough on a work surface that has been lightly dusted with flour and knead it once or twice to bring the dough together, but do not overwork, or it will get tough.
5. If you have a springform pan, place the dough ball in the center of the ring, and pat the dough to fill out the pan, leaving the top flat and even. If you don't have a springform, just pat the dough out to a circle about 8 inches in diameter, making both the sides and top as even as you can. Use a sharp knife to cut the dough into six larger or eight smaller wedges, and set the wedges on the prepared baking sheet about an inch apart.
6. Bake scones for 12 minutes, then rotate the pan and bake another 10 to 12 minutes. They are done when the scone is golden around the edges and the center, when pressed with a finger, does not yield but feels set.
7. Remove pan from oven and let scones cool. Drizzle to your liking with Confectioners' Sugar Glaze (pages 366-367).

JAM SCONES

Makes about 12-15 scones

 Start to finish within an hour, give or take

Apologies to fans of this amazing scone who did not see it often enough in our bakery case. Surprisingly, it did not sell well enough to keep it around all the time, but not because it wasn't delicious. It was because customers put on faces of polite disappointment and ordered something else the moment they learned it contained coconut. (One of the recipe testers commented that she invited a coconut-hating friend over to help her taste her creations. Apparently, this scone made a convert of her!)

Coconut is not a dominant flavor in the recipe, but it does provide texture and a back note. The almond paste takes center stage in the scone, and the jam sets it apart.

---

4 cups flour

1/4 cup sugar

1 1/2 tablespoons baking powder

3/4 teaspoon salt

8 ounces almond paste, chilled (do not substitute marzipan)

4 ounces (1 stick) cold butter cut into 1/2-inch cubes

1 cup sweetened shredded coconut

2 eggs

3/4 cup milk

1 teaspoon vanilla extract

1/2 teaspoon almond extract

1 cup raspberry or apricot preserves, or some of each (or try your own)

---

1. Preheat the oven to 350 degrees. Line a baking sheet with parchment paper (or grease the pan) and set aside.
2. Combine flour, sugar, baking soda, and salt in the work bowl of an electric mixer with a paddle attachment.
3. Grate almond paste on a coarse grater. Add almond paste and butter to dry ingredients and mix on low speed until mixture is coarse and crumbly. Stir in coconut.
4. Beat milk, eggs, and extracts in another bowl until smooth. Add to the flour mixture and mix on low until just combined. If some dry ingredients remain in the bottom of the bowl, you can knead them in briefly by hand.
5. Use a 2 2/3-ounce scoop (about 1/3 cup) to portion the scones, and place the scoopfuls on the baking sheet. Press down to flatten slightly. Make a deep indentation in the center of each scone and place 1 to 2 teaspoons of preserves in the center. Do not overfill, as the jam will expand and bubble over during baking.
6. Bake scones for 12 minutes, then rotate the pan and bake another 10 to 12 minutes. They are done when the scone is golden around the edges and the center-most part of the dough, just outside the jam, feels set when pressed with a finger.
7. Remove pan from oven and let scones cool.

WHITE CHOCOLATE CRANBERRY ALMOND SCONES

Makes 12 scones

 Start to finish within an hour, give or take

White chocolate, almonds, and dried cranberries cry out HOLIDAYS to me, and these scones graced our bakery case from about early November until the beginning of February, when everything heart-shaped moved in. They have a bit of crunch, a handful of chewy and a welcome dose of sweet.

---

4 cups flour
2/3 cup sugar
1 tablespoon baking powder
1/2 teaspoon salt
4 ounces (1 stick) cold butter cut into 1/2-inch cubes

1 cup chopped white chocolate (baking type, not chips)
1 cup slivered almonds, toasted (page 363)
1 cup dried sweetened cranberries

2 eggs
1 teaspoon vanilla extract
1 cup heavy cream
3 tablespoons milk
1/2 teaspoon orange zest

Egg wash: 1 egg beaten with 1 tablespoon of water

---

1. Preheat the oven to 350 degrees. Line a baking sheet with parchment paper (or grease the pan) and set aside.
2. Combine flour, sugar, baking powder, and salt in the work bowl of an electric mixer with a paddle attachment, and mix briefly to combine. Add butter cubes and mix on low until the mixture has a coarse appearance, with the butter now in irregular, pea-size bits. (If the butter becomes too well blended with the dry ingredients, your final scone will end up less tender.) Alternatively, you can use a food processor to mix the dry ingredients and then cut in the butter using the pulse button. Either way, once the butter has been properly cut in, transfer the mixture to a large bowl.
3. Add white chocolate, nuts, and cranberries and mix them in gently using a rubber spatula.
4. Mix together eggs, vanilla, cream, milk, and orange zest in a separate bowl. Use a rubber spatula to toss and fold it into the dry mixture until the batter is thoroughly combined and forms a dough, but is not overmixed.
5. Place dough on a work surface that's been lightly dusted with flour, and knead once or twice until the dough holds together, but do not overwork, or it will get tough.
6. Roll the dough into a rectangle that measures about 12 by 6 inches. Cut the dough in half lengthwise to produce two pieces, each 12 by 3 inches. Using your best eyeball judgment, cut 6 triangles from each piece by zig-zagging across the dough.
7. Place scones on the baking sheet and brush each one with egg wash. Bake for 14 minutes, then rotate the pan and bake another 8 to 10 minutes. They are done when the scone is golden around the edges and the center, when pressed with a finger, does not yield but feels set.
8. Remove pan from oven and let scones cool.

EARL GREY SCONES

Makes about 10 Scones

 Start to finish within an hour, give or take

Somewhere in my travels, I tasted a scone such as this and loved it so much that I needed one for my own cafe. Baker Ella took on the challenge and created this recipe for us. It's a true "tea" scone with all the flavors and feel of an afternoon lazing away on a couch with your friends. The scone is not too sweet, and the flavors are the kind of subtle that makes your brow furrow as you identify the hints of Earl Grey and lavender. The sweet, lemony glaze graces each bite like a lemon wedge in your afternoon tea. (Don't skip the glaze. This scone relies on the sweet, tangy counterpoint.)

3/4 cup heavy cream

1 tablespoon Earl Gray tea leaves

1/8 teaspoon dried lavender buds

1/2 teaspoon vanilla extract

1/2 cup milk

4 cups flour

1/2 cup sugar

1 tablespoon Earl Grey tea leaves, finely ground in a mortar and pestle

1 tablespoon baking powder

1 teaspoon baking soda

1 teaspoon salt

6 ounces (1 1/2 sticks) chilled butter, cut into 1/2-inch cubes

Confectioners' Sugar Glaze (pages 366-367 using lemon juice and finishing to a medium consistency)

1. Preheat the oven to 350 degrees. Line a baking sheet with parchment paper (or grease the pan) and set aside.
2. Combine cream, Earl Gray tea leaves, and lavender in a small pot and bring to a simmer. Turn off heat and let the mixture steep for 15 minutes, then cool completely in the refrigerator. (You do not want any warmth to soften the chilled butter that's added in the next step.) Strain out the tea and lavender, pressing well on the solids to extract all the cream, then mix vanilla and milk into the cooled cream. Keep refrigerated until ready to use.
3. Mix flour, sugar, ground tea leaves, baking powder, baking soda, and salt in the work bowl of an electric mixer with a paddle attachment. Add butter cubes and mix on low until the mixture has a coarse appearance, with the butter now in irregular, pea-size bits. (If the butter becomes too well blended with the dry ingredients, your final scone will end up less tender.) Alternatively, you can use a food processor to mix the dry ingredients and then cut in the butter using the pulse button. Either way, once the butter has been properly cut in, transfer the mixture to a large bowl.
4. Toss the cooled cream mixture into the butter-flour mixture with a rubber spatula until the dough just holds together, then turn the dough out onto a work surface and knead once or twice to bring it together.
5. Roll out dough on a lightly floured surface to a thickness of 3/4 inch. Cut out rounds with a 3-inch cutter and set onto the prepared baking sheet. Bake for 16 minutes, then rotate the pan and bake another 10 to 12 minutes. They are done when the scone is golden around the edges and the center, when pressed with a finger, does not yield but feels set.
6. Remove pan from oven and let scones cool. Drizzle to your liking with Confectioners' Sugar Glaze (pages 366-367).

Sticky Buns and Croissants

Manna's sticky bun was our version of, and a nod to, the original morning bun, a product created at the Ovens of Brittany and so often copied that the company officially renamed it the Brittany Bun to distinguish it from its spinoffs. This singular product helped define a bakery, a restaurant, an era. Since its inception in the early 1970s, the morning bun has become a beacon of excellence for breakfast pastries, a product so simple in design and presentation yet technical in its execution. The morning bun was born in Madison during a time of change on the national food scene, an era that included the introduction of French cooking to Americans (think Julia Child and Jacques Pepin) and the dawning of local, organic, and farm-fresh philosophies. Croissants and other related pastries began to pervade bakeries, restaurants, and cafes nationwide, changing our expectations of a breakfast pastry forever. The Brittany Bun had one foot solidly grounded in French pastry techniques, the other in the sweet tooth of the American palate.

Like the Brittany Bun, our sticky bun is based on croissant dough—that leavened, layered, and rolled building block of many a fine pastry. Chilled butter, and plenty of it, is first folded over and over again—that is to say, laminated—into a rich yeast-raised dough. The swatch is rolled out, spread with cinnamon sugar, rolled up jelly-roll style, portioned, set to rise, and then baked. In the oven a gooey, caramel-y layer forms beneath the buns, which will later set into a sticky-sweet glaze. Finally, the swirly buns, still steamy from their bake-off, are rolled in more sugar, adding a sparkly finish. On your serving plate, a sticky bun's delicate exterior will shatter into mica-like shards as you unfurl its tender, yeasty coils.

Croissant dough is the basis for many pastry creations, including the classic plain croissant, an icon of simple but sophisticated elegance. At Manna, we offered chocolate or almond-filled sweet varieties and ham and Swiss or herbed Gouda options that satisfied a savory breakfast appetite. Of our many varieties, the chocolate croissant was perhaps a customer favorite, at least in part because each bore a lovely cursive "M" for Manna, written in the morning baker's unique "handwriting." Taken out to a table in the morning sunshine, the chocolate promptly melted, creating an extra-gooey treat. And while including techniques for each style of filled croissant is beyond the scope of this book, we do hope you'll give our sticky bun and basic croissant a shot.

While you're baking them, give a little salute to the Ovens of Brittany, too. Both Manna and the Ovens are gone now, but they live on in the following recipes.

BASIC CROISSANT DOUGH

Makes about 3 pounds of dough, yielding 12 sticky buns or 18 croissants

 Project Alert! May require multiple stages or overnight preparations—read through before proceeding

I have provided a classic core recipe for croissant dough and worked hard to give careful, concise instructions. For sure, some time is involved, but mostly it is not your own hands-on time. Croissant dough needs to sit and sit and sit, whether chilling between folds or slowly rising. I love that the process itself, which is both precise and methodical, forces me to slow down and enjoy the rhythms of baking, reminding me of the craftsmanship and beauty that we humans are capable of.

Once the steps are completed, you can form the dough into plain rolled Croissants (pages 250-253) or turn it into Sticky Buns (page 254-255). Here is an overview of what to expect:

Day 1 (hands-on time is less than 30 minutes)

Make the yeast dough (20 minutes)

Let partially rise, then refrigerate overnight

Roll softened butter into a ready-to-use rectangle (5 minutes), then refrigerate overnight

Day 2 (hands-on time is less than 1 hour; refrigerating, rising, and baking time is 6-plus hours)

Roll out dough once (3 minutes) and refrigerate 1 hour

Roll out dough, place butter on dough, fold to create a packet (3 minutes)

Roll out and fold initial packet (3 minutes), then refrigerate 1 hour

Roll, fold (3 minutes), refrigerate 1 hour

Roll, fold (3 minutes), refrigerate 1 hour

Roll and form final product—croissants or sticky buns (allow 45 minutes)

Rise (about 2 hours) and bake (less than 20 minutes)

You can see from the above outline that on Day 2, a good amount of time is involved (but most of it is not hands-on) to end up with a nice warm flaky pastry to eat. The baked pastries can be completely cooled and wrapped. The next morning you can simply warm them for 5 minutes in the oven to freshen and crisp the outsides and warm them through. *(Note: You may also opt to refrigerate the formed pastries overnight, then let them rise and bake them on the third day.)*

A final note: Later, in the chapter titled A few Choice Breads, you will find that all the recipes specify both weights and measures for the ingredients. Because croissant dough uses yeast and functions much like a bread in its development, I have included weights in the recipe described below. For more background, refer to "Weight vs. volume measurements," page 307.

Croissant Dough

1 1/3 cups (11.9 ounces) cold milk

2 teaspoons (0.25 ounce) yeast

2 tablespoons (0.08 ounce) sugar

1 1/2 teaspoons (0.35 ounce) salt

1 ounce butter (1/4 stick), softened

4 cups (18 ounces) all-purpose flour

15 ounces (3 3/4 sticks) butter, lightly softened (see Step 3 below)

---

1. **On Day 1:** For the dough, place milk, yeast, sugar, salt, softened butter, and flour into the bowl of an electric mixer fitted with a dough hook. Using a low speed, mix until the dough comes together. You may need to push the flour toward the center when you begin mixing to encourage it to combine. When it first comes together as a dough, stop the mixer and feel the dough. It should be soft and damp, but not sticky. After mixing a few more minutes, it will mostly come away from the sides of the bowl. Continue mixing the dough for a total of 8 minutes until it is very smooth, satiny, and elastic.
2. Remove the dough from the bowl and knead once or twice by hand to form a nice ball. Let rest for 5 minutes, then flatten the ball and pat it from all four sides to form a fat, square shape (about 6 inches square). Slip the dough into a plastic bag such as a produce bag from the grocery store. The dough should be completely and loosely covered. Let proof at room temperature until it has increased in size by about 50%, then refrigerate overnight to finish proofing. This step allows the dough to rise the first time very slowly (referred to as a retard).
3. Allow the remaining 15 ounces of butter to soften just until you can roll it. (It should be the consistency of molding clay—no softer.) The time will depend on the temperature of your room. Place the butter sticks tightly alongside one another between two pieces of parchment paper (see photos below), and using a rolling pin, roll into a square roughly 8 x 8 inches in size. Wrap the butter in plastic wrap and refrigerate overnight.
4. **On Day 2:** Line a sheet pan with parchment paper. Remove the dough from the fridge. Lightly flour the work surface and then the top of the dough. Roll the dough into a rectangle that measures about 9 x 13 inches, adding a bit of flour as needed to keep it from sticking. Place the rectangle of dough on the lined sheet pan, cover with plastic, and refrigerate for another hour.

5. While the dough is re-chilling, remove the cold, plastic-wrapped butter from the fridge and allow it to temper (slowly warm up) until it is again softened to the consistency of molding clay—a flexible mass you can pick up and handle while still maintaining its integrity. Set it aside until the dough has finished chilling. (*Note: If the butter gets too soft, re-chill it briefly, or if it is not yet soft enough, wait to take out the dough. The butter must be in this malleable stage when beginning the folding process.*)
6. Remove the dough rectangle from the fridge and place it on a lightly floured work surface so that the long side of the dough runs in front of you and the short side is perpendicular to you. Remove the butter from the parchment and set it onto one side of the dough, thus covering 2/3 of the dough and leaving 1/3 of the dough devoid of butter. The butter should almost come to the top and bottom edges of the 9-inch dough width.
7. Fold the unbuttered portion of the dough over half of the buttered side, and then fold the remaining buttered side over the top, such as you might do when folding a letter into thirds to slip into an envelope. Pinch the open ends together to seal in the butter, pat the dough into a nice squared-off rectangle, and flour the top. With a large rolling pin, roll the dough out to a rectangle that measures 8 x 16 inches, using uniform pressure to maintain an even thickness. Do not let the rolling pin roll over the ends of the dough, and use it to help maintain the rectangular shape. Fold again into thirds as described above, return it to its plastic-bag cocoon, and refrigerate for about 1 hour. You have now completed the first two folds of the process.
8. Repeat the rolling and folding two more times, each time rolling the dough into an 8 x 16-inch rectangle and then refrigerating it for one hour. After the final chilling of the dough, it is ready to be formed into either croissants or sticky buns, set to rise one last time and then baked. (Or you can chill the formed pastries overnight, then let them rise and bake them the next day. The rising time may take up to an hour longer when they are chilled.)

FORMING AND BAKING THE BASIC CROISSANT

Makes 18 traditional croissants

 Hands-on time less than an hour (additional cooking or chilling times involved—read through before beginning)

If a braided challah is the icon of a Jewish bakery, then the croissant symbolizes the wonders of French patisserie. Its simple crescent shape belies its complex layering of butter and dough. I hope that by following the techniques laid out in this recipe, you will become excited with your successes and compelled to venture into other croissant-based techniques, making your favorite fillings, forming fantastical shapes, and impressing your drooling guests.

One recipe Basic Croissant Dough (pages 247-249)

Notes on dough handling: To successfully achieve the layered effect of a laminated dough, the butter and dough must keep their distinct layers. The warmer the dough gets (the longer it is out of the fridge and handled by you), the more the butter and dough will combine, thus ruining the layering effect of the croissant. To avoid this problem, keep at least half of the dough chilled while you work with the other half; handle the dough as little as possible (and avoid touching it with the palm of your hand); and if the dough becomes too soft, throw it back into the fridge to rechill for a bit—you want it to set back up, but not become stiff. When you get to the point where you are stretching each piece of dough individually (Step 6 below), work quickly. This is the point where the dough is most vulnerable to extra heat.

1. Line two sheet pans with parchment paper and set them aside. Remove the dough from the fridge and unwrap it.
2. Set the dough onto a floured surface. Lightly dust the top with flour, then roll into a 16 x 20-inch square, always rolling evenly and with uniform pressure to help keep a clean rectangular shape. If the dough seems elastic, or does not increase in size easily, let it rest for a few minutes in the fridge so the gluten can relax.
3. When the dough has relaxed into a final 16 x 20-inch size, cut it in half so you have two halves, each measuring 8 x 20 inches. Refrigerate one half (you can gently fold it in half or thirds so it will fit in your fridge more easily), then arrange the remaining half with the 20-inch side facing you.

4. Measure across the top of the rectangle and make a mark every four inches. Now do the same on the bottom, but start 2 inches in from one side so that the marks on the bottom of the dough perfectly bisect the marks on top. Using a long chef's knife or pizza cutter, cut from the top left corner of the dough to the first mark on the bottom of the dough. Continue cutting, connecting the marks on the top and bottom of the dough, until all the dough is cut and you have nine uniform triangles, each with a 4-inch base, plus one uneven triangle at each end. Cut each of these ends into five roughly equal-sized pieces and set them aside. You will use them to bulk up the croissants when you form them, beginning in Step 7.
5. *Note: This thinly rolled dough is prone to having its butter melt, even with a minimal amount of handling, yet handle them you must! I like to refrigerate the cut triangles (you can overlap them on a plate or cutting board), then work with just one or two triangles at a time to minimize this problem.*
6. Pick up a triangle of dough, holding it by the base in one hand. With your other hand, gently stretch and elongate the triangle until its length has increased by about half. If you pull too hard, the dough will break, so be gentle and coax the length out of it carefully. Pull and stretch, but do not squeeze the dough or provide undue pressure.
7. Place the triangle back onto the work surface. Make a small cut, 1/2 inch long, in the center of the triangle base. Place a piece of the reserved dough at the base, just above the slit, and fold the base over it to encase it.
8. Gently roll the triangle up two revolutions, tugging outward as you go to slightly elongate the base (the slit will help facilitate this). Then, gently grasp the point of the triangle, and pull it away from you as you continue to roll, creating a tautness that encourages additional elongation, as well as a snug roll. When the croissant is fully rolled, place it on a sheet pan with the triangle point tucked underneath, leaving about 2 inches between each one. Curve the ends slightly inward to create the classic crescent shape. Repeat with remaining triangles of dough, and then repeat the process with the second rectangle of dough.
9. Evenly space the croissants on the sheet pan. Lightly cover or tent them with a tea towel so they don't dry out, and then let them proof until fully doubled in size (this may take 2 hours). When you touch them lightly, an indentation should remain. At this point, they are ready to be baked. (Alternatively, you can refrigerate the shaped croissants overnight, but the proofing time will be longer the next day.)
10. Shortly before the croissants have finished rising, preheat the oven to 375 degrees. When the croissants are ready, set them in the oven and bake for 10 minutes. Rotate the pan, and bake for an additional 6 to 8 minutes. The croissants should be a lovely deep golden to brown color all over. Remove from the oven and let cool on the pan.
11. Croissants may be stored a couple of days at room temperature, wrapped in plastic wrap or aluminum foil. (Take care not to wrap them so tightly that you crush their delicate flake.) They should be rewarmed in a toaster oven (or oven) rather than a microwave, which will not restore their original crispness. They will freeze well but should be defrosted before reheating.

FORMING AND BAKING STICKY BUNS

Makes 12 swirly flaky sweet and sticky buns

 Hands-on time less than an hour (additional cooking or chilling times involved—read through before beginning)

I loved it when new customers came into Manna during a busy brunch. You could always tell uninitiated customers by the way they looked around the place, owl-like, heads swiveling from counter to barista to traveling plates of food, wondering what to do, where to go, how to order, and whether they should wait. "Is this your first time here?" I would ask to help ease them into the scene. After orienting them to "our system" (which could be a bit baffling on your first visit), I would guide them through the menu choices, helping them decide on their best first meal. And off they'd go from the register, soaking it all in, full of anticipation. After a moment, I would slip a sticky bun onto a plate and ask a server to bring it to them, "compliments of Barb," to enjoy while they waited for their meal. If I was lucky, I might catch a glimpse from afar of their grateful smiles as they inhaled the aromas and savored their first bites; by the end of that first visit, they were settled into "the scene," and I knew that they'd feel as comfortable as old pros next time. I miss creating moments like these the most.

You'll need a greased nonstick jumbo muffin pan (one with 12 cups or two with 6 cups) to make these beauties. An alternative would be to bake them in large 8- or 9-ounce individual ramekins. Regular-sized muffin tins can work in a pinch if they are extra deep, but they may have an odd shape.

For Forming the Sticky Buns

Recipe for Basic Croissant Dough (pages 247-249)

A dish of water, to be brushed on dough

2 cups packed brown sugar mixed with 4 teaspoons cinnamon

For Finishing the Buns

1 cup granulated sugar

---

1. Grease a jumbo muffin tin and set aside.
2. Remove the dough packet from the fridge and set the dough onto a floured surface. Lightly dust the top with flour, then roll the dough into a rectangle that measures 18 x 24 inches. The 24-inch side should be facing you.
3. Brush the entire dough lightly with water. Use enough water so that when you top it with the brown sugar, the sugar will be moistened by the water on the bottom but still dry to the touch on top. The sugar needs the water to dissolve a bit and become gooey when baked. Not enough water, and the sugar will retain some of its crunch. You can spread the water with your hands to make sure the entire surface is covered.
4. Spread the brown sugar evenly over the entire surface of the dough, but leave an inch of unsugared dough at the top of the long side. Go all the way to the end of the other three edges.
5. Roll the dough into a tight cylinder. As you roll the cylinder, constantly pull and stretch the remaining dough away from you to make the cylinder as snug as possible. Pinch the seam well along its length so the sticky buns do not unfurl. Then plump and smooth the cylinder so that it is even and still measures 24 inches.
6. Use a ruler to mark off 2-inch lengths of the cylinder, and then, using a shape knife, cut it into 12 segments. Turn each segment on its side and set it into the greased muffin tin. When finished, place a towel over the top of the sticky buns and set it in a warm place to generously double in size. At this stage, you may refrigerate the buns overnight before the final proofing, but they will then need several hours to properly rise the next day.
7. Shortly before the sticky buns have finished rising, preheat the oven to 350 degrees. When the buns are ready, set them in the oven and bake for 20 minutes. Rotate the pan, and bake for an additional 15 minutes. Remove from the oven and let cool in the pan for 5 to 10 minutes. (They need this time for the caramelized sugar to set up and for the coils to hold their shape. But if they are left for longer than 15 minutes, they may become difficult to remove.)
8. While the buns are cooling, place granulated sugar in a medium bowl, and line a sheet pan with parchment paper. One by one, remove a sticky bun from the pan and set it in the sugar. Toss and turn the bun until it is fully and generously coated, shake off the excess sugar, and set the bun upside down on the sheet pan.
9. You made it! Eat one now before it cools completely, and celebrate your efforts.

Pies and Cakes

At the age of three, my son Ike was a sneaky little fella. Once, when my friend and Collins House pastry chef Amy had come to dinner, I noticed that I had been so busy talking that I hadn't seen or heard from Ike for a long stretch. When I called out his name, I heard the sound of his closet door rolling closed. I went upstairs to investigate and found my innocent boy hidden in his closet in his baby blue onesie, his face buried in the cake we had served for dessert—a single-layer Marzipan Torte (page 280) generously dusted in confectioners' sugar. He looked up at me with powdery white innocence, as astonished to be discovered as I was amused (although, wearing my good-parent mask, I remained stern).

I think we all have this urge, although for different, grown-up reasons, to hide from judgmental eyes with our favorite dessert and eat to our heart's content, unmindful of the calories or the sheer brashness of it. You see it in the movies all the time—the exasperated mom who pulled candy bars from her closet shoebox stash when her husband drove her crazy (*Parenthood*, 1989), or the teen gangster who lost all willpower while waiting for a girlfriend to arrive and gobbled down the whipped cream-filled pastry-shop confection he had brought for her, glancing around furtively all the while (*Once Upon a Time in America*, 1984). Desserts are our most clandestine comfort food.

The pies and cakes we made at Manna were homey and down to earth. They were designed for craving, not for beauty contests. Simple buttercream adorned the cakes, and the garnishes tended to reflect the ingredients: chocolate curls bedecked the black bottom pie, while a fine zesting of lime shimmered atop the glaze of the lavender lime cake. The Cupkopf's shiny ganache glaze was all that was needed to give this giant but unpretentious cupcake its red carpet status.

Valentine's Brunch Chocolate Chunk Streusel Coffeecake, page 283.

CRUMB PIE CRUST

Makes enough for one 10-inch, deep-dish pie

 Start to finish in less than a half hour

This easy crust comes together quickly, and there is little that can go wrong. It is also versatile in that you can choose almost any dry, crumbly cookie that complements your filling. I have listed several suggestions, but feel free to experiment.

2 level cups finely ground cookie crumbs, such as:

- Graham crackers
- Chocolate wafers
- Vanilla wafers
- Ginger snaps
- Gluten-free cookies

1/4 cup sugar

3 1/2 ounces (one stick minus one tablespoon) melted butter

1. Preheat the oven to 350 degrees. Grease a 10-inch deep-dish pie pan and set aside.
2. Mix crust ingredients together well, making sure the butter is thoroughly distributed. (Using your hands works best.) The crumbs should be evenly coated but not too buttery. If they are too wet with butter, the resulting crust, after baking, will be more crisp or cardboard-like, and less tender.
3. Place all the moistened crumbs into the middle of the pie pan and press firmly into the sides and bottom. (I like to do the sides first to make sure I have plenty to go around, then finish with the bottom. Also, make sure the crust is the same thickness everywhere. There is a tendency for the crust to be thicker in the corners, where the sides meet the bottom.) Tidy up the top rim by running your thumb around the edge, and press the miscellaneous crumbs into the rest of the crust. Depending on the pan shape and size, you may have extra crumbs, which you can sprinkle on yogurt or ice cream. (It freezes well, too!)
4. Bake the crust for 6 minutes, then cool it completely. It is now ready to use.

PASTRY PIE CRUST

Makes enough dough for one 10-inch, deep-dish pie with a top crust OR two 10-inch, deep-dish pies with no top crust

Hands-on time less than an hour (additional cooking or chilling times involved—read through before beginning)

Pie crust recipes vary greatly in the amount and type of fats used (butter, shortening, or sometimes lard). At one end of the spectrum is an all-butter crust, and for some, this is the gold standard, prized for its buttery flavor. At the other end is an all-shortening or lard crust, esteemed for its tender and flaky qualities but lacking in butteriness. In the end, you'll have to decide where you sit on this fence and make a crust whose proportions best suit you. The recipe presented here leans toward the butter.

Outside of the ingredients themselves—fat and otherwise—the best way to achieve flakiness is to keep your ingredients chilled (some people even chill the flour). In this way, the butter does not "melt" into the flour before the dough bakes, but stays separate, thus letting the pastry form into layers as it heats. Also, it's best to handle the dough as little as possible with your hands. Instead, use a rubber spatula to add in the water, and knead once or twice using only the heel of your hand (which is cooler than your palm).

Use this full recipe to make the Two-Berry Pie (pages 260-261) or any pie that requires both a bottom and top crust. Only a half recipe is needed for the Triple Chocolate Pie (pages 262-263), which has no top crust.

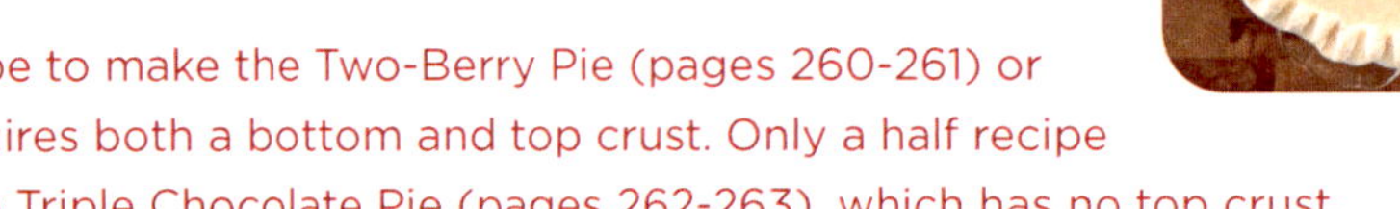

The pie dough can be made through Step 2 below and frozen for later use. Also, you can create a single-layer crust, as described in Step 7, and freeze it in the pan before proceeding with the blind bake in Step 8.

---

2 1/2 cups flour

2 tablespoons sugar

1/2 teaspoon salt

1/2 teaspoon baking powder

4 ounces (1/2 cup) solid vegetable shortening (such as Crisco), chilled and cut in 1/2-inch pieces

6 ounces (1 1/2 sticks) cold butter cut into 1/2-inch cubes

1 cup water with plenty of ice in it (you'll be using only 1/2 cup of the water)

---

1. Combine the flour, sugar, salt, and baking powder in a food processor fitted with a steel blade. Cut the chilled shortening and butter into the flour using pulses until the mixture is crumbly. You should still be able to see pebbles of butter scattered throughout the dough. Transfer to a large, wide bowl.
2. From the cup of waiting ice water, measure out 1/2 cup water (with no ice in it). Sprinkle the water over the flour-butter mixture, all the while tossing the dough with a rubber spatula. Mix until it just holds together. Dump the dough from the bowl onto a work surface, and use your hands to bring it all together (handle the dough minimally to avoid over-warming it).
3. Divide the dough in half and form each half into a ball. Flatten and shape the balls gently to form round pucks about 1 1/2 inches thick. (Here is a tip: Wrap the puck in plastic wrap, then roll it on your work surface, as though it were a wheel, for a couple of revolutions. Then lay it flat and pat it down gently—just enough to make it even. If you do this once or twice, it will produce a nice, compact puck that will roll into a much more uniform round shape, with less cracking.) Chill for at least 30 minutes (and up to 2 days).
4. Preheat the oven to 375 degrees. Grease a 10-inch deep-dish pie pan. Line a sheet pan with a parchment liner (or aluminum foil). Set it both pans aside.
5. About 30 minutes before rolling, remove one of the pucks from the fridge to soften a bit (to help prevent cracking). Dust a work surface and the top of the dough lightly with flour, then roll it out into a circle about 13 inches in diameter. If necessary, use just enough additional flour to keep the dough from sticking to the surface. Roll evenly, and turn the dough with each roll to encourage a uniform roundness.
6. Fold the dough gently in half and carefully place it into the pie pan with the folded edge in the center. Unfold the dough so it covers the pan. Press first into the corners and then up the sides to achieve a snug fit in the pan. Make sure there are no holes in the crust, and if there are, patch them with a bit of extra dough from the overhanging edge.
7. **For a two-crust pie:** At this stage, the crust is ready to be used in the Two-Berry Pie or any recipe requiring a top and bottom crust. The finishing instructions using the top half of the dough are included with the pie recipe.
8. **For a single-crust pie:** Trim the overhanging edge to within 1/2 inch of the rim, then fold the overhang over and toward the inside of the crust, thus doubling up on the thickness around the top edge.* Finish the top edge either by pinching the dough at intervals or by pressing all around with a fork. This will help seal the two layers together and give the final crust a decorative look. Set the formed crust onto the prepared baking sheet.
9. **For a "blind bake" crust (which needs to be fully baked before use, as in the Triple Chocolate Pie recipe):** Line the crust with a piece of aluminum foil large enough to come up past the top rim. Fill the foil with lentils, dried beans, or pies weights all the way to the top. Place the crust in the oven and bake for 20 minutes. This is the "blind bake," which will partly cook the crust and set it in place so it will not fall. Remove the foil and beans, prick the bottom all over with a fork, and bake the crust another 10 to 15 minutes, or until it is golden brown all over. Remove and let cool. The crust is now ready for use.

*My mom always baked up crust scraps sprinkled with cinnamon sugar for us kids to enjoy. I still do, even though I'm now making them just for myself. It would almost feel wrong not to. You should too: 375 degrees for 10 to 12 minutes!

TWO-BERRY PIE

Makes one 10-inch pie

 Hands-on time less than an hour (additional cooking or chilling times involved—read through before beginning)

Fresh out of the oven, barely cooled and still a bit runny, and scooped onto plates with two scoops of vanilla ice cream—now that is a slice of life. If you want it to look like its picture, standing tall and with no oozing, you must let it refrigerate overnight.

The pie is made with pearled tapioca, which helps it thicken and adds a pleasing, bubble tea-like texture to each mouthful.

Crust

One whole recipe Pastry Pie Crust (page 259), finished through Step 6 (unbaked bottom crust in the pan, reserved dough puck ready to roll out to form the top crust)

Cooked Blueberry Filling for Top and Bottom Layers:

1 1/2 pounds frozen blueberries

1 cup sugar

1/4 teaspoon cinnamon

1 1/2 tablespoons small tapioca pearls

1/8 teaspoon salt

Raspberry Center Layer (Uncooked):

One bag (12 ounces) frozen raspberries (kept frozen until ready to use)

2 tablespoons small tapioca pearls

1/3 cup sugar

Egg wash: 1 egg beaten with 1 tablespoon water

Sanding sugar (see page 226) to finish the crust

1. **For the blueberry filling:** In a medium-sized pot, mix half of the blueberries (3/4 pound) with sugar, cinnamon, tapioca pearls, and salt. Bring to a simmer, stirring often, and continue cooking until it begins to thicken. Add remaining 3/4 pound of blueberries and stir to combine. Let it cool completely.
2. Preheat the oven to 375 degrees. Have the bottom crust ready.
3. Place 1 1/2 cups of the cooled blueberry pie filling on the bottom of the crust. (If the filling is in the least bit warm, it will cause the butter in the crust to soften, which may lead to less flakiness.) Evenly distribute the raspberries atop the blueberries, and sprinkle the tapioca and sugar evenly over the berries. Top the raspberry layer with the remaining blueberry filling.
4. **To finish the pie:** Remove the remaining dough puck from the fridge and let soften for 30 minutes. Roll it out on a floured surface, like the first one, but into a 12-inch diameter circle. Place the dough circle on top of the pie. Trim the edges of both top and bottom crusts to within 1/4 inch of the rim of the pie pan. Press the top and bottom together gently, then tuck them underneath to create a raised border, kind of like a mini bedroll that encircles the pie. Crimp the edges decoratively and firmly all the way around the pie, either pressing with a fork or pinching with your fingers. With a sharp paring knife, score five little x's (about 1/4 inch) in the middle of the pie to let the steam escape while baking.
5. Brush the top of the pie (but not the edges) with the egg wash and sprinkle 1 tablespoon sanding sugar on top. At this point, you can either bake the pie or freeze it for later baking.
6. Bake the pie at 375 degrees for 15 minutes. Turn the oven down to 350 and bake for another 30 to 45 minutes. You can bake the pie directly from the freezer, but you will need an extra 15-20 minutes of baking time. The filling should be bubbling and the crust a nice golden brown. Let it cool. The pie will be a little soupy when it is fresh, but it will set up nicely when chilled overnight. It is best served ever so slightly warmed, à la mode.

TRIPLE CHOCOLATE PIE

Makes one 10-inch pie

 Hands-on time less than an hour (additional cooking or chilling times involved—read through before beginning)

Dan Bultman was with Manna from the day we opened until the day we closed, and for a period, he was joined by his wife, Ella, also an accomplished baker. It was a feel-good relationship for us, reflecting our core value of staff as family. Each contributed products that became part of our permanent repertoire, including Ella's Two-Berry Pie (pages 260-261), Dan's Cherry Rustic Tarts (pages 270-271), and this recipe—Dan's idea of chocolate and then more chocolate. Each layer has a different texture, depth of chocolate, and flavor, yet even with so much richness it remains cool and refreshing.

Dan and Ella Bultman together in the bakery.

Crust

One fully baked Pastry Pie Crust (one-half recipe on pages 258-259), finished through Step 8.

Chocolate Ganache Layer (bottom)

3/4 cup heavy cream

3 ounces semisweet baking chocolate, coarsely chopped

1 ounce unsweetened baking chocolate, coarsely chopped

Chocolate Pastry Cream Layer (middle)

1 1/2 cups half & half

3 large egg yolks

3/4 cup packed brown sugar

1 tablespoon cornstarch

2 tablespoons unsweetened cocoa powder

1/8 teaspoon salt

4 ounces bittersweet chocolate, coarsely chopped

1 1/2 ounces (3 tablespoons) unsalted butter

1 1/2 teaspoons vanilla extract

Chocolate Whipped Cream Layer (top)

2 1/2 cups heavy cream

5 tablespoons confectioners' sugar, put through a fine sieve

5 tablespoons unsweetened cocoa powder, put through a fine sieve

1 tablespoon vanilla extract

---

1. **For the ganache:** Bring cream to a boil over medium-high heat. Add both chocolates and stir with a whisk until the mixture is smooth. Pour into the prepared pie crust (it will be a thin layer) and set it in the fridge to cool completely while making the pastry cream.
2. **For the pastry cream:** Whisk together the first six pastry cream ingredients (from half & half through salt) in a heavy saucepan. Cook over medium heat, stirring constantly, until thick and bubbly. Then cook 1 more minute and remove from the heat. Whisk in chocolate, butter, and vanilla until the filling is smooth. Let it cool a bit, then pour it into the pie, over the ganache layer. Let it chill completely.
3. **For whipped cream and finishing the pie:** In a mixer fitted with a whisk attachment, place all the ingredients for the whipped cream. Beat on high until the cream holds its shape. Be careful not to over-whip, or it will turn to butter. Pipe the cream decoratively over the top of the pie. Serve the pie chilled. It keeps in the fridge for up to a week but should not be frozen.

DREAM TEAM PIE

Makes one 10-inch deep-dish pie

Hands-on time less than an hour (additional cooking or chilling times involved—read through before beginning)

A dessert of Olympic achievement? Maybe not, but with its graham cracker crust, vanilla custard pudding, and mousse-like peanut butter chocolate chip filling, the Dream Team Pie is a contender. Add some lightly caramelized bananas between the layers, and you just might take the gold.

This pie is a riff on a recipe from an old *Bon Appétit* magazine.

Crust

One fully-baked Crumb Pie Crust using chocolate wafer crumbs (page 257)

Vanilla Custard

2/3 cup sugar

1/4 cup cornstarch

1/4 teaspoon salt

2 cups heavy cream

1 cup whole milk

4 large egg yolks

2 teaspoons vanilla extract

2 tablespoons unsalted butter, cut in 1/2-inch pieces

Peanut Butter Chocolate Chip Mousse Filling

6 ounces cream cheese, softened

1 cup confectioners' sugar, sifted after measuring

2 teaspoons vanilla extract

2/3 cup creamy peanut butter (do not use old-fashioned or natural)

2/3 cup semisweet mini chocolate chips

2 cups heavy cream, chilled

---

1. **For the vanilla custard:** In a heavy medium pot, whisk together sugar, cornstarch, and salt until there are no lumps. Gradually whisk in heavy cream, then milk until the sugar and cornstarch are dissolved and the mixture is smooth. Whisk in egg yolks and vanilla.
2. Place the pot over medium-low heat and cook, whisking constantly, until the mixture thickens and begins to bubble. Add butter and stir until melted. Remove from the heat and pour pudding into prepared pie crust. Spread evenly with an offset spatula until even. Refrigerate until pudding is completely cool and set, at least 2 hours.
3. **For the peanut butter chocolate chip mousse filling:** In a medium bowl of an electric mixer with a paddle attachment, using low speed, beat the cream cheese and confectioners' sugar until smooth. Add vanilla and peanut butter and, using medium speed, continue beating until smooth. Stir in the chocolate chips.
4. In a separate bowl, beat the heavy cream until stiff peaks form. Be careful not to overbeat, or the cream will become butter.
5. Gently fold about a third of the whipped cream into the peanut butter mixture to lighten it. In two more batches, continue to fold in the whipped cream until smooth and homogeneous. Do not overmix.
6. **To finish the pie:** Spread the peanut butter filling evenly over the cooled vanilla filling. Refrigerate until completely chilled, and you can't wait any longer to eat it.

Craving a Black Bottom Pie?

For all of you Black Bottom Pie fans out there, despair not. All the parts are right here on these pages. Make a Crumb Pie Crust using graham crackers or chocolate wafers as your base (page 257). Top it with the Chocolate Ganache layer from the Triple Chocolate Pie (pages 262-263), and when that has set, top it with the Vanilla Custard from the Dream Team Pie (pages 264-265) and whipped cream. Voila!

MONA'S (NO, DIANA'S!) PUMPKIN CHIFFON PIE

Makes one 10-inch deep-dish pie

 Hands-on time less than an hour (additional cooking or chilling times involved—read through before beginning)

My mom made an unrivaled sour cream apple pie, but we lost the recipe. It was the only pie we ever ate at Thanksgiving because my father hated pumpkin pie, and because he tended to rule on matters such as these, pumpkin pie never made an appearance in our household. (He was also against turkey, and I can remember having spaghetti and meatballs for an occasional Thanksgiving.)

After my mom died, my father ultimately dated two women because he was lonely and wanted a companion. They both knew that to win his hand in marriage, they had to win his heart through their cooking, a truly intimidating mandate. After a couple of years, Mona became his bride. Not only could she cook, thank goodness, but she was 15 years his junior, and brought her Rolling Stones' *Sticky Fingers* album when she moved in. (I was then 15, and until I disappeared into the terrible teens, I thought she was the coolest stepmom ever.)

During this dating era, a pumpkin chiffon pie appeared as if by magic on our table, and our household was transformed in a deep and meaningful way. My father was delighted by the pie, and we were permitted, even encouraged, to discover the joy of pumpkin pie. Thanksgiving began to feel normal. Forty-three years passed before my brother-in-law popped the bubble that was my story about the pie with which Mona won my father over: It turns out to have been made by the other woman he dated, who was pretty and sweet but, in the end, too young-spirited for him.

This pumpkin pie is nothing like the one you grew up with. It is light as cotton candy, and the ginger snap crust is a spicy counterpoint to the pie's sweet gentility. Topped with whipped cream, this pie is a supremely refreshing way to wash down plates piled high with turkey, stuffing, green bean casserole, potatoes, cranberry kissel, and Parker House rolls.

Crust

One fully-baked Crumb Pie Crust using ginger snaps (page 257)

Pumpkin Filling

1 tablespoon unflavored gelatin

1/4 cup water

3 eggs, separated

1/2 cup packed brown sugar

1 1/4 cups pumpkin puree

1/2 cup milk

1/4 teaspoon salt

1/2 teaspoon cinnamon

1/2 teaspoon nutmeg

3/4 cup sugar

Whipped Cream Topping

1 1/2 cups heavy cream

1 tablespoon sugar

1 teaspoon vanilla extract

1. **For the pumpkin filling:** Mix gelatin and water together in a small bowl and set aside.
2. Add enough water to the bottom section of a double boiler so that it is not touching the top pot. If you have no double boiler, fill a medium pot about a quarter full of water. For either scenario, bring water to a boil. Mix the egg yolks, brown sugar, pumpkin puree, milk, salt, cinnamon, and nutmeg in the top of the double boiler or in a metal bowl that will mostly fit inside the medium pot without touching the water. (The sugar will be added later.) Stir the mixture constantly over the boiling water until it has thickened. (It will not get significantly thicker than it already is, but at some point, the mixture will thicken.)
3. Remove the pumpkin mixture from the heat. Add the softened gelatin and 3/4 cup sugar to the puree and whisk until dissolved and well incorporated. Cover with plastic wrap and cool to room temperature. (You can speed the cooling process in the fridge, but take care not to let the gelatin start to set. You want to incorporate the whipped egg whites in Step 4 before that happens.)
4. In the bowl of an electric mixture, or using a hand mixer, whip the egg whites until they hold firm peaks but are not dry. Fold 1/4 of the egg whites into the filling mixture until mostly incorporated, then add the remaining egg whites and fold in gently until smooth. Pour the filling into the crust, cover with plastic, and refrigerate until fully chilled and set.
5. **For whipped cream and finishing the pie:** Place heavy cream, sugar, and vanilla into the bowl of an electric mixer. Beat on high speed until the cream holds its shape, but do not over whip or it will turn to butter. Decoratively pipe or spread the whipped cream on top of the pie before serving.

HEIRLOOM COCOA CUSTARD PIE (A MANNA SHOULDA-BEEN)

Makes one 10-inch deep-dish pie

 Hands-on time less than an hour (additional cooking or chilling times involved—read through before beginning)

Some recipes have larger doses of love in them than others, and for me, this one has love spilling over the sides. When I was young, my mom made a cocoa custard which starred in several important household desserts. This recipe—a simple custard pie topped with whipped cream—was a mainstay in our home, but for me and my sister Linda, the annual highlight was a birthday cake that layered the custard with sponge cake and whipped cream—a birthday cake trifle of sorts. No matter what she made it for, whenever there was leftover custard, Mom would spoon it into a little Pyrex bowl and top it with a handful of graham cracker crumbs, just for me.

Later in my life, the pie found equal stature in my own home. It was the only dessert requested for birthdays. Sometimes our family would sit at the table around a whole, uncut pie with forks in hand (no plates). Occasionally a fresh-made pie didn't make it to a second day, and ultimately I had to make it in a larger pie pan. We called it Heirloom Pie because it felt like a family heirloom to be passed down through the generations, like a prized watch.

Crust

One fully-baked Crumb Pie Crust using graham crackers (page 257)

Custard Filling

2/3 cup unsweetened cocoa powder

1/2 cup cornstarch

1 cup sugar

Pinch of salt

4 cups milk

2 teaspoons vanilla extract

Whipped Cream Topping

1 1/2 cups whipped cream

1 tablespoon sugar

1 teaspoon vanilla extract

Unsweetened cocoa powder, optional

---

1. **For the filling:** Mix the cocoa powder, cornstarch, sugar, and salt together in a medium pot with a whisk.
2. In a separate pot, heat the milk to just under boiling. Add about 1/2 cup of the scalded milk to the dry ingredients and mix with a whisk until well-blended and there are no lumps. Then, whisk in the remaining milk.
3. Place the pot over low heat, and stir frequently. When the pudding begins to thicken, it will start to stick to the bottom of the pot, so at this point, stir constantly and with vigor to keep the pudding from clumping. Lower the heat, if necessary, to prevent sticking. The pudding is done when it has thickened and, when you stop stirring, it will bubble ever so gently. Remove from the heat and stir in the vanilla.
4. Pour pudding into the prepared crust and immediately cover the top with plastic wrap, pressing the wrap directly onto the pudding. Refrigerate until fully chilled and set, at least 8 hours but preferably overnight.
5. **For whipped cream and finishing the pie:** When the pie is fully chilled, whip 1 1/2 cups heavy cream with sugar and vanilla until it holds a peak but is not over-whipped (if it is too stiff, it becomes butter). Cover the pie completely with whipped cream either by spreading it on with a spatula or piping it decoratively with a piping bag. Finish with a light dusting of cocoa powder, if desired.

CHERRY RUSTIC TARTS

Makes six 6-inch finished tarts (multiple stages)

 Project Alert! May require multiple stages or overnight preparations—read through before proceeding

Rustic tart is another name for galette, a mini free-form pie baked on a flat pan rather than within the constraints of a pie pan. The crust is pleated or gathered around the filling in a rough-hewn way. For this recipe, the crust is made with just enough cornmeal to give it a bit of texture and character. It is a mini-pie for crust lovers.

Dmitri was a regular-like-clockwork Manna customer who seemed to live for his cherry rustic tart fix, so we set one aside for him each weekend morning, confident that he would be in. If we forgot to do this and the tarts sold out before he arrived, his look of disappointment was heartbreaking.

Cherry was the perennial favorite of the varieties, with its cheerful ruby filling oozing and bubbling over the crust's folds and cracks. Fruit fillings can be a personal preference. I was partial to the strawberry-peach variety. Feel free to make this tart using your favorite filling recipe.

Filling

1 pound frozen cherries

1/2 cup sugar

1/4 teaspoon cinnamon

2 tablespoons cornstarch

2 tablespoons water

Crust

1 2/3 cups flour

1/2 cup fine cornmeal

1 1/2 tablespoons sugar

1/2 teaspoon salt

6 ounces (1 1/2 sticks) cold butter cut into 1/2-inch cubes

2 tablespoons sour cream

5 tablespoons ice water

Egg wash: 1 egg beaten with 1 tablespoon water

Sanding sugar to finish the tarts (page 226)

1. **For the filling:** Mix half the cherries, sugar, and cinnamon in a saucepan and bring to a simmer over medium heat, stirring often. Continue to cook, uncovered, at a gentle simmer (adjust the heat if needed) for about 10 minutes to allow the extra liquid to cook down a bit. Stir in the remaining cherries.
2. Make a slurry by mixing the cornstarch and water together until smooth, then add to the fruit mixture. Bring to a boil, then simmer until the mixture has thickened. Remove from the heat and let cool.
3. **For the crust:** In the bowl of a food processor fitted with a steel blade, combine the flour, cornmeal, sugar, and salt. Add the butter and cut it into the dry mixture with pulses until it is coarse and crumbly. Place the mixture in a medium bowl.
4. Combine the sour cream and ice water in a separate bowl and mix well. Add this mixture to the dry ingredients, tossing with a rubber spatula until well combined. Place the mixture on a flat surface and knead it once or twice to bring the dough together, but do not work more than necessary.
5. Divide the dough into six equal-sized balls weighing about 3.5 ounces each. Roll the balls so they are evenly round, then press them into 1/2-inch thick disks. Pat the sides of each disk with your hands perpendicular to the surface to achieve a nicely rounded disk and with even edges.
6. **To form and finish the tarts:** Line two sheet pans with parchment paper or greased aluminum foil and set them aside. Preheat the oven to 350 degrees.
7. Roll out each disk to an 8-inch circle, using just enough flour on your surface to keep the dough from sticking. For each tart, scoop about 1/3 cup of the cooled cherry filling onto the center of the rolled-out disk. Bring a 2-inch segment of the dough's edges toward the middle of the tart and over the filling, leaving about 2 inches of the filling exposed. Continue to bring crust segments toward the center, folding or pleating the dough as you go to give it a rustic edge.
8. Brush the crust with the egg wash, being sure to cover all the folds and creases. Sprinkle the crust lightly with the sanding sugar. Set tarts onto the prepared pans and bake for 20 minutes. Rotate the pans and bake an additional 15 to 20 minutes, or until the crusts are golden brown.

FUDGE CREAM CHEESE CAKE

Makes one 9 x 13-inch cake

 Hands-on time less than an hour (additional cooking or chilling times involved—read through before beginning)

For 43 years, my dear friend Jarno hosted a "Thanksgiving for Friends" bash the Saturday before Thanksgiving. I could write a book on that event alone, filled with such stories as the annual post-meal walk through the neighborhood to replenish the wine; the annual cutthroat Risk game that ended in the wee hours, complete with trophy; the annual theme, which often involved food; and the annual chocolate dessert brought by the same couple every year. One particular year, that couple brought this cake.

It's now an old and cherished recipe to me, with its own stories to tell. One of my favorites is the many times that Jarno, her husband Gene, and Mike and I would play sheepshead until our eyes could no longer stay open. When the munchies hit, this cake would be on the table. Jarno would cut out a corner piece, and we would march down the row until arriving at the next corner piece, which Jarno quickly ferreted onto her plate. And so it went until the cake was gone, the game was won (or lost), and we felt fat and happy.

The frosting is indeed fudgy, a dark brown blanket enrobing a likewise fudgy chocolate cake, with a cheesecake filling inside. It is best eaten within a few days, if it lasts that long, but it can be frozen.

Cream Cheese Filling

2 ounces (1/2 stick) butter, softened

1 pound cream cheese (two packages), softened

1/2 cup sugar

2 tablespoons cornstarch

2 eggs

1 teaspoon vanilla extract

Chocolate Cake

5 ounces unsweetened chocolate

2 1/2 cups all-purpose flour

2 teaspoons baking powder

3/4 teaspoon baking soda

1 teaspoon salt

2 1/4 cups milk

1 teaspoon vanilla extract

5 ounces (1 1/4 sticks) butter, room temperature

2 1/4 cups sugar

2 eggs

Frosting

3/4 cup milk

6 ounces (1 1/2 sticks) butter

1 1/2 cups chocolate chips (regular baking chocolate does not work here)

3 3/4 cups confectioners' sugar, sifted after measuring

1 1/2 teaspoons vanilla extract

---

1. **For cream cheese filling:** In a food processor with a steel blade, blend the butter, cream cheese, sugar, and cornstarch until smooth. Scrape down the bowl with a rubber spatula. Add eggs and vanilla and mix until smooth. Set the mixture aside.
2. **For chocolate cake:** Preheat the oven to 350 degrees. Grease a 9 x 13-inch cake pan and set aside.
3. In a microwave-safe bowl, melt chocolate on medium power, in 2-minute intervals, until smooth. Stir after each interval. Set the chocolate aside and allow it to cool completely before using it in the batter.
4. In a bowl, combine flour, baking powder, baking soda, and salt. In another bowl, mix together milk and vanilla.

5. In an electric mixer with a paddle attachment, cream the butter and sugar on medium speed until light and fluffy. Reduce the speed to low and stir in the cooled chocolate. Scrape down the bowl, then add eggs and mix well. On a low speed, add the flour mixture in thirds, alternating with the milk mixture, until all ingredients are well incorporated. Scrape the bowl down after each addition.
6. Give the batter one final mix with a spatula. Spread just under half the batter into the bottom of the prepared pan, covering the bottom well. It is okay if it is not perfectly smooth and even, as the irregularities will give a more rippled effect to the filling.
7. Pour the cream cheese filling on top of the cake layer, spreading gently to cover the whole pan. Carefully pour the remaining chocolate batter over the top of the cream cheese layer by sweeping the batter back and forth in ribbons over the pan. (Because the cheesecake batter is a little softer than the cake batter, it takes a bit of finesse to fully cover the cheesecake and avoid batters pooling.) Use an offset spatula to finish spreading the final chocolate layer over the cheesecake layer, making sure to go to the edges of the pan.
8. Bake for about 50 minutes, then begin testing with a toothpick. A tester should come out clean of chocolate batter, although the cream cheese batter may stick. Continue baking until the cake is done, possibly 10 to 15 minutes more. Remove the cake from the oven to cool. When completely cool, de-pan onto a wire rack or transfer right away to a serving platter. Or leave in the pan, and frost directly.
10. **For frosting and finishing the cake:** While the cake is baking, place milk and butter in a medium pot and bring to a simmer. Remove from the heat, add chocolate chips, and stir with a whisk until melted.
11. Place chocolate mixture in a food processor with a steel blade. Add confectioners' sugar and vanilla. Process until smooth, scraping down the bowl with a rubber spatula at least once.
12. The frosting needs to set up to spreading consistency. It is okay to chill it to speed the process along, but stir it occasionally, and be careful not to over-chill it. When just right, it will spread easily and will hold its shape on the cake. If it is too soft, it may drip off the edges a bit. The recipe makes enough to frost the tops and sides of the cake and even have some left over to pipe a decorative border. If you frost the cake in the pan, you will have extra frosting, which freezes quite well.
13. Spread the frosting on the top and sides of the cake, and smooth it with an offset metal spatula per the instructions for Giving Buttercream a Smooth-as-Satin Finish (see page 225).

A Chef is Born

On a hot summer day in August of 1990, Josh, my eldest, turned one year old, and we celebrated with friends at The Collins House. We had made a 6-inch version of the fudge cream cheese cake for Josh, who had never eaten chocolate before. We set the cake on his high chair tray and watched his look of wonder turn into ecstasy as he wrapped his arms around the cake, pulled it toward himself, and buried his face deep in the melting chocolate. The crescendoing laughter of friends still rings in my ears.

It seems, in retrospect, that this singular moment foretold Josh's future drive to cook, and to enjoy food with relish. By the time he was two he climbed out of his crib each morning to start our coffee (doing everything but grinding the beans), and at age 11 he deboned and stuffed a whole chicken for grilling (a technique he learned at a summer cooking camp in Pennsylvania)! His career as a chef and baker in New York came as a surprise to no one—his deep and diverse knowledge of cooking and food long surpassed my own, and his expertise is tucked into my words.

CUPKOPFS AND LIBERTY BELLS

Makes about 20 regular cupcakes, or 8-9 jumbo, Manna-esque cupcakes

Project Alert! May require multiple stages or overnight preparations—read through before proceeding

Pratzel's Bakery made a one-of-a-kind cupcake, a minimalist creation whose excellence relied on two simple components. The cake itself was reminiscent of a good poundcake, moist, fine-crumbed, and sturdy. And unlike a more traditional cupcake (often a light, dry affair topped with a colorful swirl of sugary shortening-based frosting, and cluttered with garnishes), this one was simply turned upside down, a glaze of Swiss dark chocolate spilling over its top and sides. How we would have loved having that recipe for Manna, but it was not to be, and recreating it was a mystery wrapped inside an enigma.

So we made our own cupcake-like creation, a nod to that lost icon. Ours was big and bold, with a dark, moist cake that was halved, filled, and finished with a silken coat of dark chocolate ganache. It came in two killer versions: The Cupkopf boasted a thick inner layer of gooey German chocolate filling. The Liberty Bell's center was a fluffy peanut butter-buttercream of sorts, speckled with bits of crunchy toffee. This recipe offers both versions.

Note: Manna's original Cupkopf was baked in a jumbo muffin pan, which produced a dark, towering beauty of two-fork proportions. If you use one of these pans, you'll need to adjust the baking time as directed in Step 6.

This recipe looks long, but it is easier than it seems. Each part—cupcake, filling, glaze—goes quickly, and there are plenty of bowls to lick.

Cake

3/4 cup plus unsweetened cocoa powder

3/4 cup boiling water

2 ounces (1/2 stick) butter, softened

1/4 cup vegetable oil

2 cups sugar

2 eggs

2 1/4 cups sifted cake flour (measured after sifting)

1/2 teaspoon salt

1 cup buttermilk

2 teaspoons vanilla extract

2 teaspoons baking soda

Cupkopf Filling

1 cup heavy cream

1 cup sugar

4 ounces (1 stick) butter

4 egg yolks

1 teaspoon vanilla extract

1 cup pecans, toasted (page 363)

1 3/4 cups shredded sweetened coconut

OR

Liberty Bell Filling

8 ounces (2 sticks) butter, softened

2/3 cup creamy peanut butter

1 3/4 cups confectioners' sugar, sifted after measuring

1 cup marshmallow fluff

2 teaspoons vanilla extract

3/4 cup toffee bits

Chocolate Ganache Glaze

2 cups heavy cream

16 ounces semisweet chocolate (not chips), chopped

Cupcake papers or wide pastry cups for setting glazed cupcakes onto

---

1. **For cupcakes:** Preheat the oven to 350 degrees. Grease 2 nonstick muffin tins (or 1 jumbo muffin tin) and set them aside.
2. Combine cocoa powder and boiling water in a bowl and whisk until no lumps remain, then set aside to cool completely.
3. In an electric mixer with a paddle attachment, cream butter, oil, and sugar on medium speed until well combined and light—about 1 minute. Mix in the cooled chocolate on low speed, then scrape down the bowl. Add eggs, and mix well on medium speed.
4. Combine flour and salt in a small bowl. In a second small bowl, combine buttermilk, vanilla, and baking soda and mix lightly with a whisk. Add dry ingredients alternately with wet ingredients to the chocolate batter, starting and ending with the dry ingredients. Scrape down the bowl well after each addition to incorporate the ingredients, and at the end, mix by hand to ensure everything is evenly incorporated.
5. Portion batter into prepared tins, filling the cups no more than about 2/3 full. (Be careful not to overfill, or the batter will spread onto the tins, making them more fragile to handle and requiring you to trim the excess.)
6. If you're using regular-sized pans, bake the cupcakes for 10 minutes, gently rotate the pan, and bake for an additional 4 to 5 minutes. If you're using a jumbo muffin pan, bake 15 minutes, rotate the pan, and bake 4 to 5 minutes longer. The cupcakes are done when a toothpick inserted in the center comes out clean. The top of the cupcake, normally domed, will end up being its bottom, so if it seems a bit flatter than most cupcakes, that's a good thing.
7. Cool the cupcakes completely in the tins. Line a sheet pan with a pan liner and set a cooling rack over the pan. When the cupcakes are cool, carefully remove them from the tin (use a small metal spatula to loosen if necessary) and set them on the cooling rack until you are ready to fill and finish them.
8. **If you're making the Cupkopf filling:** Combine cream, sugar, and butter in a saucepan and cook over low heat until the sugar is dissolved. Place egg yolks in a bowl. Whisk 1 cup of the hot cream mixture into the yolks, then whisk yolk mixture back into the cream mixture in the saucepan. Cook over low heat, whisking almost constantly until mixture is thickened (don't let it boil). Stir in vanilla, pecans, and coconut, then refrigerate until fully chilled and set, at least 2 hours. **OR:**
9. **If you're making the Liberty Bell filling:** In the bowl of an electric mixer, beat together butter and peanut butter on medium speed until well blended. Add confectioners' sugar and mix until well combined. Scrape down the bowl and mix briefly once more. Add marshmallow fluff and vanilla and mix on a low speed, scraping the bowl down a couple of times, until well blended. Set toffee bits aside for final assembly.
10. **For glaze and cupcake assembly:** Bring cream to a boil in a small pot (keep a good eye on it so it doesn't boil over), remove from heat, and stir in chocolate until fully melted and smooth. Let it cool partially while filling cupcakes. See Sidebar for more information about properly cooling the glaze.

11. Line a sheet pan with a pan liner, and set the cooling rack of cupcakes over the sheet pan. This will allow the glaze to drip over the cupcakes without puddling and minimize the messy cleanup.
12. **To ready each cupcake for filling:** If a rounded rim or dome has formed on the top of the cupcake, trim a bit of it off with a serrated knife so the cupcake will sit flat on the pan when inverted. Then, turn the cupcake upside down, slice it in half crosswise and leave it on the pan with the trimmed side on the bottom (the final creation is upside down from how it baked).
13. Separate the two halves of the cupcake and spread a generous amount of your chosen filling on the bottom half (about 1/4 cup for the standard-sized cupcake), keeping the filling within the edges of the cupcake. (If you're making Liberty Bells, sprinkle 1 tablespoon of toffee bits on top of the filling.) Then set the remaining half on top. Do your best to arrange the halves to be well aligned. Repeat for all the cupcakes.
14. When the glaze is ready, pour about 3 tablespoons over the top of each cupcake. Let glaze run down the sides of the cupcakes, covering as much as possible but also leaving some cake and filling peeking through. The best way to do this is to portion out a scant 1/4 cup of glaze, then slowly pour the glaze in a circular motion over the top of the cupcake, close to the rim, letting it "drape" over the sides.
15. Let the glaze set while the cupcakes are on the rack. Slide a metal spatula under each one, and transfer to a pastry cup (or flattened cupcake paper) to hold it. The cakes may be eaten right away or refrigerated, but be sure to bring them to room temperature for serving. You can also refrigerate them until well set, then wrap each individually in plastic and freeze.

A Note About Glaze

There is a short window of time when the glaze is at its peak viscosity for finishing the cupcakes. If it is too runny, it will run right off the cake, and what remains will be thin and disappointing. If it is too thick, it won't drape down the sides like a robe of satin. (Instead, it will need to be spread with a spatula to cover the cupcakes, and then it will look lumpish and sullen.) Keep a close eye on the cooling glaze, stirring it occasionally. When it is just right, it will be viscous but pourable. If it gets too thick, you can rewarm it a tad. It takes a little practice, so have patience.

MARZIPAN TORTE

Makes one 10-inch round, single-layer torte

 Start to finish within an hour, give or take

Here is the cake of Ike-in-the-closet fame (see Pies and Cakes introduction, page 256). Its single layer is deeply fragranced with almond paste, and its crumb is moist and dense. It stands alone, needing no frosting, just a dusting of confectioners' sugar to gussy it up. This cake made frequent appearances at catered events, and on several occasions, it served as an elegant, off-the-beaten-path wedding cake. Concentric tiers of decreasing size were layered one on top of the next. The cake was generously dusted with confectioners' sugar, and raspberries cascaded lavishly down the side and around the base with a flower here and there for a finishing touch. Each serving was surrounded by a vanilla bean creme anglaise and drizzles of fresh raspberry sauce.

Technically, this cake is made with almond paste, an ingredient made of ground almonds and sugar. Marzipan is similar—perhaps more evocative—but has additional ingredients that allow it to be molded in different ways. The two are *not* interchangeable. But calling the cake "Almond Paste Cake?" Not so much.

---

6 ounces (1 1/2 sticks) butter, softened

12 ounces almond paste, grated or cut into 1/2-inch pieces

1 cup plus 2 tablespoons sugar

4 eggs

1/2 teaspoon vanilla extract

1 1/2 tablespoons brandy

1 cup plus 2 tablespoons flour

3/4 teaspoon baking powder

Confectioners' sugar for dusting the top

Raspberry Sauce for serving

---

1. Preheat the oven to 350 degrees. Grease a 10-inch round cake pan (a springform will work too) and set aside.
2. In the bowl of an electric mixer with a paddle attachment, cream the butter and almond paste on medium speed until smooth. Add the sugar and mix well. Scrape down the bowl.
3. Add the eggs, vanilla, and brandy and beat on medium speed until smooth, scraping the bowl once. Combine the flour and baking powder and add to the bowl. Mix on a medium speed until just well combined. Give a final mix with a rubber spatula to ensure a uniform batter.
4. Spread the batter into the prepared pan. Bake the cake for 30 minutes, then test for doneness. The cake is done when a toothpick inserted in the center comes out clean. Bake longer if needed.
5. Cool the cake completely. To serve, dust lightly or generously with confectioners' sugar by shaking the sugar through a sieve over the cake. Serve the cake with some of the raspberry sauce on the plate. (The cake is also very good alone.)

RASPBERRY SAUCE

Makes about 3/4 cup

7 ounces frozen raspberries, thawed to room temperature

1/3 cup sugar

1 to 2 tablespoons orange liqueur, such as Grand Marnier (optional)

Puree raspberries, sugar, and orange liqueur (if using) in a food processor until well blended and smooth. Strain through a sieve, pressing on the solids to extract as much liquid as possible. Store refrigerated for a week, or freeze.

This simple sauce has multiple applications. Drizzle it on ice cream, swirl it into cheesecake batter, or craft cocktails with a burst of fresh summer flavors. We used it to give our raspberry mimosas a beautiful hue and fragrance.

SOUR CREAM COFFEE CAKE (WITH TWO VARIATIONS)

Makes one 10-inch Bundt Cake

Hands-on time less than an hour (additional cooking or chilling times involved—read through before beginning)

Warm-from-the-oven sour cream coffee cake found its way to the plates of umpteen overnight guests at The Collins House B&B over the course of 20 years. When Manna began brunch service, it became a focal point for our "Breakfast in Bed" platter. Fifteen more years it spent on the menu, nestled near the Parmesan and fresh herb scramble and graced by a bowl of mixed berries with lemon curd and whipped cream.

Featured here in two variations, the coffee cake has a buttery rich crumb and is layered just so. The streusel version (the one we served at Manna) is generously infused with vanilla. The chocolate chunk coffee cake is for when you are craving melty chocolate along with your morning coffee or for any special occasion. It is practically the only coffee cake recipe I ever use because it adapts so well to any fruit or nut or flavor.

Note: It's best to bring the chilled ingredients in this recipe to room temperature before beginning. That way, the batter will be softer and more spreadable. Also, this cake is at its most luxurious when served a little warm. At Manna, we rewarmed each slice before serving. Especially for the chocolate chunk variation, you too will be compelled to do this.

Coffee Cake

3 cups flour
1 1/2 teaspoons baking powder
1 1/2 teaspoons baking soda
1/2 teaspoon salt

12 ounces (3 sticks) butter, softened
1 1/2 cups sugar
3 eggs, at room temperature
1 1/2 cups sour cream, at room temperature
1 1/2 teaspoons vanilla extract

Variation 1: Breakfast-in-Bed Streusel

3/4 cup packed brown sugar
3/4 cup walnuts, toasted (instructions page 363)
1 1/2 teaspoons cinnamon
2 tablespoons vanilla extract mixed with 2 tablespoons water

OR

Variation 2: Valentine's Brunch Chocolate Chunk Streusel (see photo page 256)

3/4 cup sugar

2 teaspoons cinnamon

10 ounces semisweet chocolate chunks

1 cup walnuts, toasted (page 363)

---

1. **For coffee cake batter:** Preheat the oven to 350 degrees. Grease a nonstick 10-inch Bundt pan and set aside.
2. Mix dry ingredients (flour through salt) in a bowl and set aside.
3. In the bowl of an electric mixer with a paddle attachment, cream butter and sugar on medium-high for 3 minutes, until light and fluffy. Scrape down the sides of the bowl with a spatula, then beat in eggs one at a time, scraping the bowl after each egg. Blend in sour cream and vanilla on a lower speed. Then mix in dry ingredients on a low speed until well combined, using a spatula to scrape down the sides well. The batter will be thick.
4. **To assemble Variation 1*:** Mix brown sugar, walnuts, and cinnamon in a bowl. Place about 1/3 of the coffee cake batter in the bottom of the Bundt pan, then top with half the streusel. Repeat with 1/3 of batter, then the second half of streusel, then finish with the last 1/3 of batter. Smooth the top with a rubber spatula so that it is very flat and has no gaps between the batter and the pan. Pour the vanilla-water mixture evenly over the top of the batter, tilting the pan this way and that to cover it all.
5. **To assemble Variation 2*:** Mix sugar, cinnamon, semisweet chocolate, and walnuts in a bowl. Place about 1/4 of the batter in the bottom of the Bundt pan, then top with 1/3 of the streusel. Do two more layers of batter and streusel, using half of the remaining batter each time, so that there are three layers of batter and three of chocolate, with chocolate as the top layer. (Note that you only use 1/4 of the batter for the first layer because most Bundt pans are much narrower at their bottoms and widen out as they rise, so you need more batter for the wider part of the pan.)
6. **To bake both variations:** Set the pan in the center of the preheated oven and bake for about 40 minutes, then check with a toothpick at a high point in the coffee cake. It should come out clean. You can expect the coffee cake to take a total of 50 to 60 minutes, but it is good to do a first toothpick check early. When done, remove from the oven and let cool in the pan for 30 minutes. Then invert the pan and gently jiggle the cake onto a wire pan to finish cooling.

*Assembly Note: Because the batter is on the thicker side, it may be challenging to spread it over the streusel layers. For best results, portion the batter in close-together blobs around the pan. Use a rubber spatula to spread, but do so by pressing down on the spatula while rotating the pan, and DO NOT lift up on the spatula. If you do, it will pull away the streusel layer, and fixing it will be messy. Just keep turning while pressing, and the batter will spread nicely. Once you have formed a solid mass of batter, you can pick up the spatula and smooth it out.

CARAMEL APPLE CAKE

Makes one 10-inch Bundt cake

 Hands-on time less than an hour (additional cooking or chilling times involved—read through before beginning)

It's late September (maybe it's my birthday), and the newly ripened fall apples beckon from their orchards. Cider is being pressed, pies are cooling on the counter, and this coffee cake wants in. It boasts a sugary caramel glaze and a moist cake amply studded with soft baked apples—a coffee cake for the season. Bonus: The cake is easily made dairy-free. To do so, substitute margarine and dairy-free milk in the glaze. The finished cake pleases both the lactose intolerant and everyone else.

Apples

1/4 cup sugar

2 teaspoons cinnamon

1 3/4 pounds Golden Delicious apples (5-6) peeled, cored, and cut into 3/4-inch dice

Cake

1 3/4 cups sugar

1 cup vegetable oil

4 eggs

3 cups all-purpose flour

1 tablespoon baking powder

1/2 teaspoon salt

2 teaspoons vanilla extract

1/2 cup orange juice

Caramel Glaze

4 ounces (1 stick) butter (or margarine, to keep it dairy-free)

3/4 cup packed brown sugar

1/4 cup half & half (or dairy-free milk or half & half)

3/4 cup confectioners' sugar, sifted after measuring

1 1/2 teaspoons vanilla extract

---

1. Preheat the oven to 350 degrees. Grease a 10-inch Bundt pan, dust it with flour (shaking out the excess), and set aside.
2. **For the apples:** Mix 1/4 cup sugar and 2 teaspoons cinnamon in a medium bowl. Add apples and toss well to coat. Set aside.
3. **For the cake:** In the bowl of an electric mixer with a paddle attachment, combine 1 3/4 cups sugar, the oil, and eggs and beat on medium speed for 2 minutes until well blended. Scrape down the sides of the bowl.
4. In a separate bowl, sift together the flour, baking powder, and salt. In another small bowl, mix the vanilla into the orange juice. With the mixer on low speed, add the flour mixture alternately with the orange juice until combined, starting and ending with the flour. Scrape the bowl down halfway through and at the end of the mixing,
5. Fold the apples into the batter with a rubber spatula until well combined. Place the batter into the prepared pan and smooth the top with the spatula. Bake for about 50 minutes, then check with a toothpick for doneness. The cake will likely take another 10 to 20 minutes, but it's good to begin checking early to avoid over-baking it. When done, the toothpick will come out clean from the center of the cake. Continue baking, as needed, until the cake is done.
6. Cool in the pan for 25 minutes, then invert onto a wire rack and cool completely. Set the cake on a serving platter when cool.
7. **For the caramel glaze and to finish the cake:** In a small pot, melt the butter and brown sugar together and let boil for 2 minutes. Add the half & half and boil 1 minute, no more, no less. (The boiling times matter, so watch closely.) Turn off the heat and add the sifted confectioners' sugar and vanilla. Whisk vigorously until the glaze is smooth.
8. Let the caramel cool to a pouring consistency—it should be just pourable. If it is too thin, the glaze will flow over the cake too quickly, leaving just a thin glaze and pooling on the plate. If it is too thick, it will not drip down the sides on its own. Cool it to the point where it will barely drip on its own. Pour a steady stream as you turn the cake, allowing the glaze to flow over both the outside and inside of the Bundt shape.
9. The cake may be eaten while warm or after it has set. If you store it in the fridge, bring it to room temperature for eating. (The glaze will hold up if you rewarm the cake gently in a microwave.)

LAVENDER LIME TEA CAKE

Makes one 8-inch single-layer cake

 Hands-on time less than an hour (additional cooking or chilling times involved—read through before beginning)

During a pandemic, in the middle of winter, dried lavender is practically nonexistent on grocery store shelves. This did not occur to me when I sent recipes out for testing during the writing of this book. But Nicole, one of my meticulous testers, had a solution. She happened to have Earl Grey lavender tea in her cupboard, so she picked out the little lavender pieces from the tea bags one by one to make up the teaspoonful needed for the recipe! (It can be ordered on line easily enough, though in quantities that may last a lifetime.)

Eating this cake is like sitting in a hammock on a hot afternoon, sipping a margarita. Only it's a piece of cake on a plate, with tiny flecks of lime zest and speckles of purple. And it has a secret to share, whispered like a summer breeze: It's vegan.

Serve the cake at tea time or for a light summer dessert. It freezes beautifully, even when glazed.

2 cups flour

1 teaspoon baking powder

1 teaspoon baking soda

1 teaspoon salt

1 teaspoon dried lavender buds, crushed to a powder

7/8 cup white sugar (a scant cup)

1/3 cup vegetable oil

1 cup coconut milk

1 teaspoon vanilla extract

Grated zest of 2 limes

1/4 cup lime juice

Confectioners' Sugar Glaze (pages 366-367—use coconut milk and finish to a thin consistency).

1. Preheat the oven to 350 degrees. Grease an 8-inch cake pan and set aside.
2. In a medium bowl, mix flour, baking powder, baking soda, salt and lavender. In another medium bowl, whisk together sugar, oil, vanilla, coconut milk, lime zest, and lime juice. Combine the dry ingredients and wet ingredients thoroughly.
3. Pour the cake batter into the prepared pan. Bake for 45 to 50 minutes. Check for doneness by inserting a toothpick in the center of the cake. It's done if the toothpick comes out clean. Bake longer, if needed. Let cool, then remove from the pan and set it on a wire rack to cool.
4. Pour glaze over the cake while it is on the rack so that if any spills over the sides, it can drip off. Smooth the glaze with a metal spatula.

Note on the glaze: The final glaze should pour easily over the cake, leaving a thin translucent layer (not so thin that you cannot see it at all). Let it set before cutting the cake. If you wrap the cake in plastic to freeze it, take off the plastic while the cake is still frozen, as the glaze may become a bit tacky as it thaws.

Cookies and Bars

The Toll House Cookie recipe is probably the most go-to recipe I can think of, and has defined generations of household rituals. When my son Ike, of confectioners'-sugar-face notoriety (Pies and Cakes introduction, page 256), got a bit older, this was the only recipe he knew how to make, and he would always oblige us when we needed a fix. I wrote out the recipe for him on an index card so he could follow it easily; for years afterward, he assumed it was my recipe and would not use the one from the back of the package. He liked to bake the cookies to a point where, if they had been a big piece of steak, they would "still be mooing," then eat two or three in rapid-fire succession, piping hot and doughy, washing them down with—literally—a quart of cold milk. (Now married, with a house and puppy, he still eats cookies and drinks milk as if he's just walked out of a Norman Rockwell painting.)

Cookies and bars are a staple of American households, in part because they are the most basic of baking projects, often requiring just one bowl, one pan and not much time. Their batters are forgiving, and their rewards are immediate. A cake has to be frosted. A pie needs a crust, a filling, and time to set up in the fridge. In short, cookies and bars win us over because we are, at heart, a lazy bunch, and this is as easy as it gets.

A mind-numbing variety of chocolate chip cookie recipes exist. Who would think there are so many ways to reinvent this particular wheel? Nonetheless, Manna's version follows, alongside an all-American shortlist of Manna cookie/bar favorites.

Cookie Scooping

Most of the cookie recipes included in this book call for using a small scoop, shorthand for a standard 1 1/3-ounce scoop size, roughly equivalent to a rounded two tablespoons of dough. It will produce a cookie that ranges from 2 1/2 to 3 inches wide. Recipe yields are based on this scoop size.

CHOCOLATE CHUNK COOKIES

Makes about 24 cookies

 Start to finish in less than a half hour

Once upon a time, we had a chocolate chip cookie throw-down at Manna for any staff who cared to join. This recipe won! These cookies are moist in the middle, crisp on the edges, and chewy throughout. And decidedly full of chocolate. Yes, you do need another chocolate chip cookie recipe in your life.

This recipe calls specifically for chocolate chunks, though no one will complain if you use chocolate chips instead. But the chocolate chunks add character to the cookie. They're more rough-hewn and spread out a bit during the baking, resulting in a cookie that almost appears layered with chocolate, rather than punctuated with chips. The cookies feel extra chocolatey and decadent. You can buy chunks in packages, just as with chips, but if you chunk up your own from an artisanal block of chocolate, the sky's the limit on excellence.

---

2 1/3 cups flour
1 1/2 teaspoons baking soda
1/2 teaspoon salt
6 ounces (1 1/2 sticks) butter, softened
1 1/4 cups packed brown sugar
3/4 cups white sugar
2 eggs
1 1/2 teaspoons vanilla extract
2 cups chocolate chunks (see note)

---

1. Preheat the oven to 350 degrees. Line a sheet pan with parchment (or grease the pan) and set aside.
2. In a small bowl, mix together flour, baking soda, and salt.
3. In an electric mixer with a paddle attachment, cream butter, brown sugar, and white sugar on medium-high speed for 3 full minutes, until light and fluffy. (Don't skimp on the time!) Scrape down the sides of the bowl with a rubber spatula. Beat in eggs and vanilla on medium speed until just incorporated. Do not overmix. Again, scrape down the sides of the bowl.
4. Mix the dry ingredients into the batter on low speed until just mixed. Add chocolate chunks and stir with a rubber spatula to combine everything well.
5. Portion dough with a small (1 1/3-ounce) scoop onto the sheet pan, spaced 2 inches apart (they do spread). Bake for 6 minutes, then rotate the pan and bake another 4 to 6 minutes. They should be just barely set in the middle and golden on the edges. Bake them longer if needed, in increments of a minute or two. Remove the pan from the oven and let it cool.

PEANUT BUTTER RIPPLES

Makes about 18-20 cookies

 Start to finish within an hour, give or take

Thank you, Maida Heatter, for possibly the best cookie ever. This recipe, tweaked from *Maida Heatter's Book of Great Cookies*, was made famous in our businesses by our son Josh in fourth grade. Josh was a bit on the shy side, but his outgoing nature blossomed when, for a class project, he made a video of himself making this cookie in The Collins House commercial kitchen. Picture a short 9-year-old hoisting a full-sized sheet pan into giant ovens filled with rows of peanut butter batter-filled fudge cookies. He brought the cookies to school, where his teacher, Ms. Cass, was so enamored that she ordered them from Josh from then on, even through his senior year in high school. Naturally, Ms. Cass became a Manna regular, and naturally, we think of these as her cookies.

The assembly of the ripples takes a bit of time—bottom layer, middle layer, top layer—but the two doughs are easy to whip up. They are tender but firm, not crisp, not chewy.

Chocolate Dough

8 ounces (2 sticks) butter, softened

1 1/2 cups sugar

2 teaspoons vanilla extract

1/2 teaspoon salt

2 eggs

4 ounces unsweetened chocolate, melted and cooled

2 cups flour

Peanut Butter Dough

2 ounces (1/2 stick) butter, softened

1/2 cup creamy peanut butter

1 cup packed brown sugar

1/2 cup flour

---

1. Preheat the oven to 350 degrees. Line a sheet pan with parchment (or grease the pan) and set aside.
2. **For the chocolate dough:** Place butter, sugar, vanilla, and salt in the bowl of an electric mixer with a paddle attachment. Mix on medium-high until well blended. Scrape down the sides of the bowl, then beat in the eggs until mixed. Add cooled chocolate and mix on the lowest speed until combined (do not beat or overmix). Mix in the flour on low speed until just smooth. Hand mix in the end with a spatula to incorporate all of the ingredients. The final dough will be a little tacky.
3. If you only have one mixing bowl that fits the mixer, remove the chocolate dough to a separate bowl and clean the equipment to reuse for the peanut butter batter.
4. **For peanut butter dough:** Use medium speed to the cream butter, peanut butter, and brown sugar in the mixer. Add the flour and mix on low speed until well blended. This dough will be firmer than the chocolate dough, and will hold its shape when rolled.
5. **To Assemble the Cookie:** Divide the chocolate dough in half. Use an extra-small scoop (3/4, or 1 1/2 tablespoons) to portion one of the dough halves into balls. Set the balls onto the prepared sheet about 1 1/2 inches apart. Now scoop all of the peanut butter dough into same-sized balls, and flatten each ball into a 1/4-inch thick disk. Place the peanut butter disks atop the chocolate dough balls and press down to flatten these two layers slightly. Scoop the remaining half of the chocolate dough and place the balls on the top of the peanut butter layer. Then flatten just the top layer slightly. The final sandwich will be about 3/4 to 1 inch thick.
6. Bake the cookies for 6 minutes, then rotate the pan and bake another 4 to 6 minutes. When the cookies are done, the tops will just be beginning to show some gentle cracks. Let cool on the pan.

Note: The cookies can be frozen in their assembled, raw form. To bake, remove them from the freezer and let defrost on a baking pan for about 30 minutes. Then proceed with Step 6.

OATMEAL CRANBERRY WALNUT COOKIES

Makes about 16 medium cookies

 Start to finish in less than a half hour

Lenore was a long-time Manna fan who came in daily to feed her aging soul with this feel-good cookie. Frank, her devoted husband, would hold her arm and lead her, step by laborious step, to a favorite table in the sunny front room. Once Lenore was comfortably settled, Frank would come to the counter for their bakery fix, lingering for a moment of small talk with his favorite staff. Over time, we all watched Lenore's inevitable decline, and when she died, some of us attended her celebration of life. During the event, one person after another spoke of the Manna connection—of meeting Frank and Lenore there and the importance of the community feeling that enveloped everyone. We kind of knew, and yet we hardly knew at all, how Manna was the epicenter of a special sort of humanity.

---

1 1/4 cups flour
1 teaspoon baking powder
1/2 teaspoon baking soda
1/2 teaspoon cinnamon
1/2 teaspoon salt

6 ounces (1 1/2 sticks) butter, softened
1 1/2 cups packed brown sugar
1 egg
1 teaspoon vanilla extract

1 1/2 cups whole rolled oats
1/2 cup walnuts, toasted and coarsely chopped (page 363)
3/4 cup dried cranberries

---

1. Preheat the oven to 350 degrees. Line a sheet pan with parchment (or grease the pan) and set aside.
2. Mix flour, baking powder, baking soda, cinnamon, and salt in a medium bowl.
3. In the bowl of an electric mixer with a paddle attachment, cream the butter and brown sugar on high speed for 1 minute. Scrape down the sides of the bowl. Beat in the egg and vanilla on medium speed until just incorporated.
4. Add the dry ingredients to the bowl and mix on low speed until just incorporated. Scrape down the bowl again, then add the oats, walnuts, and cranberries. Mix on low until combined.
5. Portion dough with a small scoop onto the sheet pan and flatten the top just a wee bit. Bake for 6 minutes, then rotate the pan and bake another 4 to 6 minutes. The edges should be golden brown, and the center should be set. Cool the cookies on the pan.

CHAI-SPICED SNICKERDOODLE COOKIES

Makes 24-30 cookies

 Start to finish in less than a half hour

Snickerdoodle—a cookie with a nonsense name that is fun to say, but where did it come from? Theories abound, but consensus has it that the cookie is German in origin, its English name deriving from the German portmanteau *schneckennudel*, meaning "snail noodle." Schnecken is a German sweet roll that's coiled like a snail shell. The cookie has a plainer shape but, like a breakfast pastry, is buttery and cinnamon-y. Popularized in this country by people of Germanic origin, such as the Mennonites or Amish, snickerdoodles have been around a long time.

Manna made a version of the cookie as a nod to our popular house-made Chai Tea. Don't like chai? Leave out the spices. Add a little unsweetened cocoa powder to the sugar. Or cocoa powder and a bit of chili powder. Add lemon zest to the batter. Roll the cookie dough in crushed nuts instead of chai sugar. Or roll them in plain, unadulterated sugar for the sort of sugar cookie I pine for—one whose outside has just a hint of crisp but quickly yields to soft with a bit of chew.

Chai-Spiced Sugar

1/2 cup sugar

1 teaspoon cinnamon

1 teaspoon cardamom

1/2 teaspoon ground ginger

A pinch ground cloves

Cookie Dough

2 3/4 cups flour

1/4 teaspoon salt

1 teaspoon baking soda

2 teaspoons cream of tartar

1/2 teaspoon cinnamon

1/2 teaspoon cardamom

4 ounces (1 stick) butter, softened

4 ounces solid vegetable shortening (such as Crisco), softened

1 1/2 cups sugar

2 eggs

2 teaspoons vanilla extract

---

1. Preheat the oven to 300 degrees. Line a sheet pan with parchment (or grease the pan) and set aside.
2. Prepare the chai spiced sugar by combining all the ingredients in a bowl and set aside. (If you don't use it all, it keeps indefinitely.)
3. Combine the flour, salt, baking soda, cream of tartar, cinnamon, and cardamom in a bowl.
4. In an electric mixer with a paddle attachment, cream butter, shortening, and sugar on medium speed until light and fluffy, about 2 minutes. Beat in the eggs and vanilla until just incorporated. Scrape down the sides of the bowl, then mix briefly.
5. Add the dry ingredients to the mixing bowl and mix on a low speed until well combined. Scrape down the sides of the bowl and mix briefly but thoroughly.
6. Portion dough with a small scoop, and roll each portion into a ball. Roll the ball generously in chai spice sugar. (Roll once, then roll again.) Place onto the sheet pan 1 1/2 inches apart and flatten just the very top of the ball, leaving the cookie mostly round.
7. Bake for 6 minutes, then rotate the pan and bake another 6 to 8 minutes. They should be lightly golden around the edges but pale and just set in the middle. They will flatten out a good bit. Bake longer if needed. Cool the cookies on the pan.

Note: The cookies can be frozen as balls before rolling in the sugar. When you want to bake a few, remove them from the freezer and let them defrost for about 20 minutes, or until they are still a little cool but firm enough to roll easily. Then proceed with Steps 6 and 7.

MEXICAN WEDDING CAKES

Makes 20-24

 Start to finish within an hour, give or take

At first bite, this round, solid cookie seems firm and crisp, but it is a deceiving bite. As you begin to chew, it crumbles, then melts in your mouth, nutty and sweet from the confectioners' sugar you have dusted over its dome-like shape. Follow each mouthful with a sip of hot coffee. It is the sort of eating pleasure you want to enjoy alone so that you can give it your full attention.

This pretty cookie makes a lovely addition to a tray of holiday pastries, providing texture and color. We served it to guests at the wedding of Brandon, a Manna employee, and Phillip. It was a homespun affair that took place in our fireplace room after hours. Despite its name, this is not traditionally considered a wedding dessert, but it certainly plays the role well with its bridal-white dressing in powdered sugar.

---

8 ounces (2 sticks) butter, at room temperature

1/2 cup confectioners' sugar, measured then sifted

2 1/4 cups all-purpose flour

1 teaspoon vanilla extract

1/2 teaspoon salt

3/4 cup chopped pecans, toasted (page 363) and finely ground (but not turned into a paste)

1-2 cups confectioners' sugar sifted into a bowl for finishing cookies

---

1. Preheat the oven to 300 degrees. Line a sheet pan with parchment and set aside.
2. In the bowl of an electric mixer fitted with a paddle attachment, use medium speed to cream the butter and powdered sugar together until combined. Scrape down the bowl, then mix in the flour, vanilla, and salt on low speed. Mix in the pecans until the dough is uniform—it will be thick.
3. Portion the dough with a small scoop, or about a heaping 1/8 cup, onto the prepared baking sheet. The cookies should look dome-shaped, and should not be flattened. They will not spread, so you can place them as close as 3/4-inch apart if you are pressed for space.
4. Bake cookies for 15 minutes, rotate the pan, and bake another 15 minutes or a little longer. The edges will just show a hint of goldenness, and the cookie will feel set.
5. Remove the cookie sheet from the oven, and let cool for 3 minutes. Roll each hot cookie in the powdered sugar, then let sit for 5 minutes. Roll the cookies a second time in the sugar, then let finish cooling. They should be stored in a single layer in an airtight container.
6. As an alternative to rolling the cookie, you can simply sift powdered sugar generously over the top of them. While less traditional, it produces a somewhat more elegant look and will be a bit less sweet.

MINT MELTS

Makes about 36 or more half-moon-shaped cookies, 2 inches in diameter

 Project Alert! May require multiple stages or overnight preparations—read through before proceeding

This recipe almost didn't make it into the cookbook, but less than a week before the completed manuscript was to be handed off to the publisher, an unexpected encounter rescued it (see sidebar, page 301).

The mint melt is an elegant minty shortbread cookie finished with a layer of minty white chocolate ganache and a brief dip into melted dark chocolate. Because it is rolled and cut into shapes (hearts, Christmas trees, and Jewish stars were often used for the catering), the cookie can be themed for almost any occasion. Its only real drawback is that it wilts in warmer weather. (It does not hold up AT ALL at Fourth of July picnics.) At Manna, we made it in cooler weather only.

The original mint melt recipe dates back to the December 1990 issue of *Bon Appetit*. While our ingredients are more or less the same, the technique for making the cookies varies considerably. They are minty, and they do melt in your mouth, especially in summer. It just takes a little bit to get there.

For Cookie Dough

8 ounces butter, room temperature

1 teaspoon vanilla

1/2 teaspoon mint extract

2/3 cup powdered sugar, measured then sifted

2 cups all-purpose flour

For Ganache

2/3 cup heavy cream

2 1/2 tablespoons butter

12 ounces good quality white chocolate (not chips), broken into chunks

1/4 teaspoon mint extract

For Dipping Chocolate

10 ounces semisweet chocolate (not chips), chopped

1 teaspoon canola oil

Note: You will need a pastry piping bag for this project.

1. **For the cookie dough:** In the bowl of an electric mixer with a paddle attachment, cream the butter and extracts on high speed until very light, about 2 minutes, scraping the bowl once. Add powdered sugar and incorporate on low speed. Mix in the flour on low until well combined. Knead the dough once or twice, form into a ball, and flatten into a 2-inch thick disk. Wrap in plastic and refrigerate for 30 minutes.
2. **While the dough is chilling, prepare the ganache:** In a medium pot, heat cream and butter over medium-high heat until it just boils. (Watch carefully—when cream gets close to a boil, it will quickly overflow.) Immediately remove it from the heat and add the chocolate. Stir with a whisk until smooth, let cool a bit, then stir in the mint extract. Refrigerate ganache until thick but still soft enough that you can pipe it from a piping bag and have it hold its shape.
3. Preheat the oven to 350 degrees. Line two sheet pans with parchment and set them aside.
4. Lightly flour a work surface. Remove the dough from the fridge and set it onto a floured surface. Then dust the top lightly with flour. Roll dough out to a 3/8-inch thickness, using a gentle, even pressure to keep the dough thickness uniform. As you roll, occasionally dust the top lightly with flour, and flip the dough over a couple of times to discourage sticking.
5. With a 3-inch diameter cookie cutter, cut out rounds, then cut rounds in half to form half-moon shapes (or leave them uncut if you like, or choose any other simple cutter shape that is about the same size). Set the cutouts onto the prepared baking sheet as little as 1/2 inch apart (they will not spread). You can reuse the scraps (knead them together), but do not work in too much flour, or they may become too dry.
6. Bake the cookies for 6 minutes, then rotate the pan and bake another 4 to 7 minutes, depending on their size. They are done when the edges are just beginning to brown and the centers are still pale. Remove from the oven and transfer to a wire rack to cool completely.
7. Place ganache in a piping bag with a 1/4- to 1/2-inch hole cut at the end. Pipe ganache onto the back of the cooled cookies by starting at one end and moving the bag back and forth, creating a gently undulating and overlapping pattern. (You can just spread the ganache on with a knife, but it won't be nearly as refined-looking!) You are aiming for about 1/4-inch thickness of the ganache, so adjust your squeezing pressure accordingly. Leave a bit of space between the ganache and the edge of the cookie. Place the cookies in a fridge or freezer until the ganache is firm, about 20 minutes or more.

Top side, diagonal dip

Underside, showing piped ganache

8. **For dipping and finishing the melts:** Place dark chocolate in a small, microwaveable bowl and melt on medium-low power, stopping and stirring frequently so the chocolate does not burn. When melted and smooth, transfer chocolate into a bowl that is small and deep. Let the chocolate cool slightly.
9. Remove the cookies from the fridge or freezer. Grasp a cookie at one end, with the flat edge facing up. Dip the cookie into the melted chocolate so the cookie is half-dipped on the diagonal (from the endpoint diagonally across the fat part of the cookie). Lightly shake the cookie to let extra chocolate drip off, then lightly wipe the edge of the cookie across the bowl rim to minimize the extra chocolate.
10. Place the cookies ganache side down onto a baking sheet lined with parchment, and refrigerate until set. At this point, the cookies can be condensed, overlapping, onto a pan and covered with plastic wrap. The cookies can be frozen for a month or refrigerated for a week. They are best eaten at room temperature. Note that once they are unwrapped, moisture in the air will settle onto the dipped chocolate, first beading up a bit and ultimately drying out in a way that will leave the cookie a bit less glossy than when first dipped. But that's okay.

This Cookie Says It All

Our next-door neighbors' landscaper and his wife had been living temporarily in the neighbors' house for a few months, and while we had seen them in passing, they were unknown to us (or so we thought). Mike was out front planting some pretty purple annuals when a woman's voice called out, "Hey, Mike." He was initially mystified, but as Tammy, the landscaper's wife, proceeded to relate her story, the connection came into focus: The couple had married at The Collins House 18 years prior and on their wedding night, exhausted and hungry, we shared some mint melts with them. It was an experience which became for them, like our own joyous discovery of Alice Medrich's chocolate truffles, a strong and endearing memory. When they heard Manna had opened, they ordered some every year for their anniversary. And when she heard we were the Manna people, she wanted to share with us just how much this cookie meant to them, and to thank us for helping make their wedding so special. More recently, she had tried to recreate the recipe, but to no avail.

Mike ran into the house, eager to share the story with me, and at the end proclaimed, in his animated and emotional way, "This is what it's all about!" By "this," he meant everything: the years of food and service, becoming a part of people's memories, the sheer small-world nature of our lives in Madison and the surprising connections that continued to bind us. While the story was personal to Tammy, it was also one we had heard often (and never tired of hearing). But on this particular day, so close to the book's completion, it was as if she were the spokesperson for a legion of like-minded guests and customers through the years.

TRIPLE FUDGE BROWNIES

Makes one 9 x 13-inch pan

 Start to finish within an hour, give or take

This is the only pure chocolate brownie we ever made. It has no nuts because I wanted a smooth, luxurious brownie unimpeded by other annoying textures. (I also prefer creamy peanut butter!) It is dense yet tender and not at all chewy. It is very, very chocolatey. While it freezes just fine, this brownie's special, delicate quality is best enjoyed on day one (but completely cooled) or day two (wrapped well).

8 ounces (2 sticks) butter

8 ounces semisweet chocolate, chopped

2 ounces unsweetened chocolate, chopped

2 cups sugar

5 eggs

1 tablespoon vanilla extract

1 1/4 cups flour

1/2 teaspoon salt

1 1/2 cups semisweet chocolate chips

1. Preheat the oven to 350 degrees. Grease a 9 x 13-inch baking pan, line the bottom with parchment paper, and set aside.
2. Place the butter and both kinds of chopped chocolate in a microwave-safe bowl, then melt on medium power in 2-minute increments. Stir after each one, as chocolate can burn easily in the microwave. Let it cool to room temperature.
3. Place sugar, eggs, and vanilla in a large bowl and beat by hand with a whisk until thoroughly combined and smooth.
4. Add about a quarter of the cooled chocolate mixture to the egg mixture and mix well. Add the remaining chocolate and again mix until smooth and well combined. Stir in the flour and salt and mix well. Stir in the chocolate chips.
5. Place the batter in the prepared pan, being sure to leave some on the spatula for bonus enjoyment. Bake at 350 degrees for 30 to 35 minutes. To test for doneness, insert a toothpick into the center of the brownie. It should come out clean of crumbs, although it may show a bit of the melted chocolate chips. The top should feel just set, and the sides should not be hard. Remove the pan from the oven and let it cool completely. Refer to the instructions for easy pan release on page 223.

MOCHA BROWNIES

Makes one 9 x 13-inch pan

 Start to finish within an hour, give or take

This is a rich, coffee-flavored, butterscotch-like brownie with toasted nuts and chocolate chips. As it bakes, it rises but then sinks just a bit in the middle, leaving the edges a little elevated. This is as it should be, so not to worry.

The use of instant coffee adds deep coffee flavor without adding too much liquid. I recommend using Medaglia d'Oro brand instant espresso, which I find gives a superior coffee flavor. You can also use homemade espresso or very strong brewed coffee, just do not add more than 1/4 cup of liquid. However, you won't get the depth of flavor that the concentrated granules provide.

---

8 ounces (2 sticks) unsalted butter

3 1/3 cups packed brown sugar

3 tablespoons instant espresso powder dissolved in 1 1/2 tablespoons hot water

3 eggs, beaten

2 tablespoons vanilla

2 3/4 cups flour

4 teaspoons baking powder

3/4 teaspoon salt

1 1/4 cups chopped pecans, toasted (page 363)

1 1/2 cups chocolate chips

---

1. Preheat the oven to 350 degrees. Grease a 9 x 13-inch baking pan, line the bottom with parchment paper, and set aside.
2. In a medium saucepan over medium-low heat, melt the butter. Add the brown sugar and stir until dissolved. Stir in the dissolved coffee. Cool to room temperature. (Don't cheat, or the chocolate chips will melt when you stir them in!) Mix in the eggs and vanilla until well combined. Transfer the batter to a mixing bowl.
3. Combine flour, baking powder, and salt in a bowl, then stir into the butter-sugar mixture. When combined, add pecans and chocolate chips and mix thoroughly.
4. Spread batter into the prepared pan. Bake for 25 to 30 minutes, or until a toothpick inserted in the center comes out clean. Cool completely in the pan. Refer to instructions for easy pan release on page 224.

LEMONY LEMON BARS

Makes one 9 x 13-inch pan

 Start to finish within an hour, give or take

Lemon is one of those dessert flavors that people never seem to tire of, and every new product we introduced became a fan favorite. This bar had a simple shortbread base, a lemon curd-like filling, and a crumbly finish of streusel.

Crust

1 cup plus 2 tablespoons flour

3 tablespoons sugar

1/2 teaspoon salt

6 ounces (1 1/2 sticks) cold butter cut into 1/2-inch cubes

2 egg yolks

Filling

3 cups sugar

7/8 cup flour

1 1/2 teaspoons baking powder

9 eggs

3/4 cup fresh lemon juice (from about 3 or 4 lemons)

Streusel Topping

1/2 cup flour

1/2 cup sugar

A pinch of salt

2 ounces (1/2 stick) cold butter cut into 1/2-inch cubes

---

1. **For the crust:** Preheat the oven to 350 degrees. Grease a 9 x 13-inch baking pan, line the bottom with parchment paper, and set aside.
2. In a food processor with a steel blade, blend flour, sugar, and salt to combine. Add chilled butter and mix with pulses until the mixture resembles coarse meal. Add the egg yolks and mix with pulses until the dough begins to clump. Do not overmix.
3. Press the dough into the bottom of the prepared pan, spreading it uniformly and firmly. Bake for about 10 minutes, or until lightly golden.
4. **For the filling, topping, and assembly:** In a bowl, whisk together the sugar, flour, and baking powder until well combined. Add the eggs and whisk until well combined, then add the lemon juice and whisk again until well combined. Pour the filling into the baked crust. Bake for 30 minutes until the filling is barely set and still a bit tacky on top. (This is just the first part of the baking time.)
5. While the bars are baking, prepare the streusel. Combine flour, sugar, and salt in a food processor with a steel blade. Cut in the butter with pulses until the mixture resembles coarse meal but still has small lumps.
6. After the 30-minute bake, evenly sprinkle the streusel over the top. Bake for an additional 5 to 10 minutes, then cool completely. Refrigerate at least 4 hours, or until the filling is well set. Refer to instructions for easy pan release on page 223.

Amy testing Lemony Lemon Bars in Copenhagen.

A Few Choice Breads

This section offers but a peek into the vast world of bread baking by presenting a few recipes that were, in essence, the building blocks of our business. Sandwiches are quite literally built on bread, and we very much believed that a sandwich built on average bread would never be more than average itself. We want you to bake the breads from Manna because nothing rivals a home-baked loaf of good bread—the deeply satisfying experience of kneading, forming, baking, and eating it fresh. And since all of our sandwiches were crafted with these particular loaves, you can now make a Manna Reuben at home. Use any old rye bread, and you can still call it a Reuben, but make it with slices of your own, hand-crafted corn tzizel rye bread and be transported.

Numerous books have been written on bread baking, and there is much science behind its nuances. You need to consider so many things: ambient temperatures, moisture levels in the atmosphere, the activity of the yeast, starting temperatures of ingredients. Some people spend a lifetime searching for bread's holy grail, just as some aspire for a perfect ten on the uneven bars. But mastering bread basics is within anyone's reach, and my husband Mike is, ironically, a poster boy for just that.

Mike was born and raised in a kosher Jewish bakery, teething on bagels in infancy and developing his lifelong habit of clutching a wedge of bread in his left hand (the better to push food onto a fork or mop up a plate). He absorbed flour through his very pores, yet did not even attempt to bake his own bread until his first month of retirement after the café closed, when he was going through withdrawal from Manna bread. His first loaf out of the oven was a joy to behold, if a bit on the homely side, but he gained confidence with each passing attempt. Now he makes sure he bakes and stocks the freezer each week with his favorite breads to keep his carbohydrate addiction well fed. Mike's early bread-baking experiences came in handy as I crafted the recipes included here.

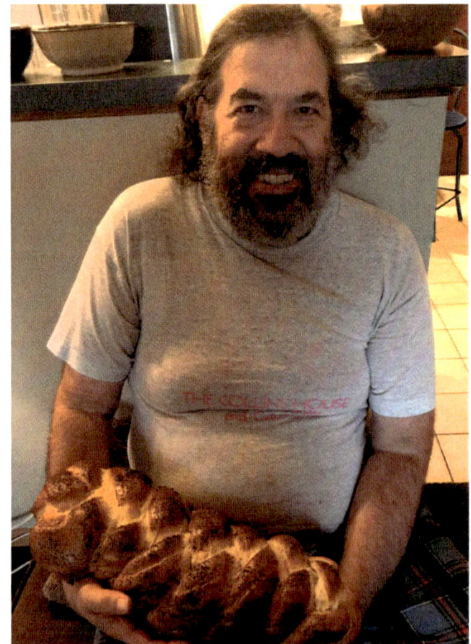

Mike proudly displaying his first loaf of bread... ever!

By understanding a few basics about the art and science of baking a yeasted dough, you can quickly move from following the rules to following your intuition. You can tell by your home's thermostat whether the dough will rise in 45 minutes or 1 1/2 hours. By sticking your fingers deep into the dough, you will know if it has too little or too much flour. In short, you can turn from the cookbook to your senses to tell if your loaf is on track for success.

Mixing the dough takes about 20 minutes, and then it rises while you walk the dog. Shaping the dough takes about 10 minutes, and then it rises again while you read on the porch. The bread gets a final pampering, maybe a quick egg wash or a roll in cornmeal, and it goes in the oven to bake. Now you grab a beer to reward yourself (and pull out the butter to soften as long as you're in the fridge). The point is, once you get the hang of it, bread baking will not intimidate you; it will liberate you! Every loaf of bread, even one you've made dozens of times before, is unique. And when you open the oven door, you'll have the gratification of beholding the treasure inside. It never gets old.

Much science goes into producing a loaf of bread in terms of the correct ratio of flour to moisture, how long it's kneaded, how long it proofs, and how long and at what temperature it bakes. Here are some pointers and guidelines for the recipes:

- **Weight vs. volume measurements:** The bread recipes in this book include both weight and volume measures. Measuring by weight is a more accurate and scientific approach, resulting in more consistent loaves with predictable hydration. By weighing ingredients, you can greatly reduce the margin of error. Still, baking is also intuitive. I bake by the feel of the dough, and the instructions here are written to help you learn that feel. If you do not own a scale, you can let your hands guide your judgment of whether a dough has too much or too little flour.

- **Yeast:** I use active dry yeast is, which is most commonly available. Other yeasts, such as instant or fresh, work a bit differently and have subtle taste differences. So many variables, including the yeast, affect how a bread loaf will turn out. By consistently using the same type and brand, you will develop a certain trust in how that product will work for you.

- **Bread flour:** Unless otherwise specified, the white flour called for in the following recipes is bread flour, which contains more gluten than all-purpose flour, thus contributing more elasticity to the dough. I recommend King Arthur flours for all baking.

- ***Using your senses*:** Learning the feel of a good loaf takes practice, and the biggest crime is adding too much flour. There is a tendency to think that if the dough is sticking to your fingers, it needs more flour. Not necessarily so. It is difficult to articulate something that is best evaluated by feel, but here is a shot at it: Initially, the dough will be too wet and stick to everything like wet rubber cement. It will have a glossy appearance as well. As you add more flour, the stickiness becomes manageable, and the gloss starts to dull. But be patient and don't add flour too quickly. As the dough is kneaded and the gluten develops, it will strengthen the dough, making it less sticky. When bread dough is just right, it should form a ball as you knead it by hand but still have a tackiness if you press your fingers into it. If you were to let it rest on the table, it would need to be scraped up to loosen it, but once you started kneading again, it would form that nice ball. Once you manage to not over-add flour, you will get a nice moist loaf. Too much flour dries out the bread, and the resulting loaf, while tasty when still warm, will dry out and get old more quickly.

- **Correcting for over- or under-hydrated bread doughs:** If a dough is too sticky, the correction is easy—add more flour, bit by bit, until a good consistency is achieved. But if you have already added too much flour, you can still correct the error. Simply add small amounts of water in increments to the dough. It won't incorporate as quickly and easily as adding flour would, but be patient, and it will work its way in. (You could also toss in a dusting of flour to the bowl. This may seem counterintuitive, but adding the flour helps the water to incorporate. Otherwise, your dough ball may slip-slide around in the bowl like a wet balloon.)

- **Rising time:** I do not like to give strict rising times for bread since so many factors must be considered, including the starting dough temperature and ambient temperature, as well as the actual ingredients in the bread. (Sugar makes things go faster and salt slower. High-fat doughs are slower to rise, potato dough faster.) As a general rule, allow about 45 minutes to an hour for an average rise under average conditions. BUT:

  The most important thing is to watch for a doubling of the dough or loaf size. Apart from hydration, temperature is the number one factor that will affect bread. Yeast is a living organism, and like all living things, it thrives in a certain temperature range. Dough rises best between 75 and 80 degrees. It is important to consider your environment. In the middle of a Wisconsin winter, it is unlikely to be above 70 degrees inside, and dough in a cooler environment will take longer to proof. Mike uses many tactics when our house is cold: setting the dough in a ray of sunshine or next to a heating vent and then cranking up the heat, or sometimes placing the bowl in the oven (oven turned off!) along with a bowl of boiling-hot water. (The steam helps create a warm environment, and the oven helps provide an insulated space.) Finally, if you know it will be cooler where your dough is proofing, you can use warmer water than you normally would—up to about 115 degrees. If it's hotter than that, you'll risk killing the yeast.

  On the flip side, a warmer environment can cause the dough to rise so quickly that you barely have time to get in that dog walk. On a warm summer day, be prepared to check in on your dough often. An over-risen dough can lose its ability to rise a second time and may produce a flatter final loaf. Also, the dough needs time for the bread's flavor to develop, and a dough that rises too quickly may taste a bit "yeasty." On days such as these, slowing the rise in the fridge may be a good idea.

  In short, the most important thing is whether the loaf looks doubled. Start watching it after about 45 minutes to an hour, the average time under average conditions, and you will have a sense of how much longer it might yet take or if it is ready for the next step.

- **When is my loaf done?** The most common way to check for doneness is to pick up the loaf and give the bottom a quick knock—*thump, thump*—with your fingertips. The knock should sound hollow rather than flat, and it takes a couple of times to know what to listen for. If you are unsure, insert a thermometer in an inconspicuous seam near the center of the loaf. The internal temperature should be between 190 and 200 degrees. Once you're comfortable with how the temperature range "sounds," you'll no longer need the thermometer.

If you are new to bread baking, take your time and follow these recipes carefully. In the end, you can puff out your chest in yeasty pride as you share the joy of your beautiful loaf.

CHALLAH

Makes 1 large or two small loaves

 Hands-on time less than an hour (additional cooking or chilling times involved—read through before beginning)

Many breads symbolize the cultures they arise from—the French baguette, the Ethiopian flatbread injera, filled steamed buns from China, chewy fry breads from the Navajo, to name a few. Jessamyn Waldman Rodriguez's beautiful cookbook, *The Hot Bread Kitchen Cookbook: Artisanal Baking from Around the World*, tells a compelling story of immigrant women, their homeland breads, and forging a life in America by learning the trade of bread baking.

I would argue that challah is one of the most iconic of all. The loaf is a beautiful intertwining of bread strands, like the people it belongs to, whose traditions are woven together. The earthy hues of gold and deep brown speak to the warmth and comfort of the weekly Shabbat meal, when Jewish families all over the world gather to find nourishment and renewed spirituality around the dinner table. Challah is a kind of manna.

Manna's challah was a classic version: eggy, sweet, soft, and fragrant. We baked it into individual sandwich rolls or tall, proud loaves for slicing. Of course, on Fridays we formed it into the traditional poppy seed-sprinkled braid. At Jewish Holiday times, we shaped it into a coil, or "foigle," with and without raisins. Challah is a richer bread dough than plain white bread and thus more noticeable when part of a sandwich. Its sweet notes can complement the salt in, say, tuna salad quite nicely. If you bake a loaf and have any day-old around, challah is a classic go-to bread for French toast.

1/4 cup (2 ounces) warm water (80-90 degrees)

1 scant tablespoon active dry yeast

1 1/4 cups (10 ounces) whole milk, warmed to 80-90 degrees

2 ounces (1/2 stick) butter, melted

3 tablespoons honey

1 large egg

2 large egg yolks

1 1/2 teaspoons salt

4 to 5 cups (22.6 ounces) all-purpose flour (not bread flour), or more as needed

Egg wash: 1 egg beaten with 1 tablespoon of water

2 tablespoons poppy seeds or sesame seeds (optional)

---

1. In a small bowl, stir yeast into the warm water. Let sit for 5 to 10 minutes until the yeast begins to foam, indicating that it is active.
2. In the bowl of an electric mixer fitted with a dough hook, mix together all of the ingredients, including the proofed yeast, but not the flour. Mix on low speed for a minute to combine the ingredients.
3. Add about 4 cups of the flour and mix on low speed until all the flour is incorporated. Continue to add flour in half-cup increments until the dough comes together as a damp ball. It should feel a bit tacky, and a little should stick to your fingers. Continue to let the dough hook mix and knead the dough for about 3 minutes. On a medium speed, a good dough will come away cleanly from the sides of the bowl, even though it will feel tacky when touched. (If the dough comes together as a ball that does not stick to the bowl and does not stick to your hands, it has too much flour.)
4. Place the dough onto a floured surface and knead for about 5 to 10 minutes until it is smooth and satiny. Add a little flour as needed, but be careful not to add too much. When you work the dough, it should just barely come away from the work surface to form a ball. If you touch it with your fingertips, it should have some tackiness. The dough may stick a bit to your fingers. It should not, by any means, feel dry. Form the dough into a ball and set it into a lightly oiled bowl. Cover with a damp towel.
5. Allow the dough to double in size (see Rising Time on page 308). Remove the risen dough from the bowl onto a work surface and gently deflate it. If you are making two loaves, divide the dough in half using a sharp-edged knife, then gently form each half into a rough ball. Cover with a towel and let rest for 10 minutes. From here on, handle the dough gently, and do not knead at all. Once you knead the dough, it will cause the gluten to toughen, or "tense up," and will make working with it more challenging.
6. Line a sheet pan with parchment paper. Preheat the oven to 350 degrees if your oven is convection or 375 degrees if you do not have convection.

7. To form the dough into a braid, cut the dough into three equal pieces. (If you are making two smaller loaves, then follow these instructions for each half.) Roll out each dough piece into a strip about 18 inches long (for the one large loaf) or 14 inches long for each of the two smaller loaves. As you roll each strand, gently taper it from the center toward the ends so that the center of the strand is slightly wider and the ends narrower. Lay the strips alongside each other, and pinch them together at one end. Place the pinched end furthest away from you and the open ends close to you.
8. To start, pick up the left-hand strand and cross it over the center strand. The left-hand strand is now the new center strand. Next, cross the right-hand strand over the center strand so that it becomes the new center. Continue alternating left and right strands over the current center strand until you have reached the end of the dough. Pinch together the end nubs after braiding. Tuck the pinched ends underneath the loaf, and then plump the loaf a bit so that the center is rounded and full, and the width drops off toward the ends. (Got it?)
9. Place the braided dough on the baking sheet lined with parchment paper, cover with a damp towel, and let rise until the dough is almost doubled in size. This may take a little less time than the first rise since the dough is now active and eager for a nice long sit in the sauna!
10. Generously brush the risen loaf with the egg wash and sprinkle with poppy seeds or sesame seeds, if you like. Bake for 20 minutes, then turn the pan and bake another 20 minutes. (The smaller loaves will take a little less time—15 minutes/turn/15 minutes.) The loaf should be golden brown. When the loaf is done (see When Is My Loaf Done? on page 308), let cool on a wire rack.

Jarno and Josh baking bread.

CORN TZIZEL RYE

Makes 1 large loaf (sourdough needs to prepped a day ahead)

 Project Alert! May require multiple stages or overnight preparations—read through before proceeding

Pratzel's Bakery was a St. Louis institution started by Max Pratzel, who immigrated to the U.S. at the turn of the 20th century. And for just shy of 100 years, this singular kosher bakery was near and dear to St. Louis's expansive Jewish population. My husband, Mike, a third-generation Pratzel, grew up in the bakery, helping his dad with deliveries by day, and packing away a loaf of this corn tzizel rye bread each night at dinner. The bread became an icon of the café, too.

Manna's Reuben sandwiches featured this rye and were a case in point for one of our guiding principles: An excellent sandwich begins with excellent bread. The rye is sourdough-based and slightly chewy, with a final roll in cornmeal that gives it its unique character. To make it, you'll need a sourdough starter, which takes about a week to develop. (But then you can keep it indefinitely, with proper feeding, and the older it gets, the better it gets.) The King Arthur website provides a good set of instructions for making a starter.

Note: You'll need to feed the starter the night before you make the bread, then the next day, bring it to room temperature and measure it when you begin the loaf. We feed our starter twice a week with all-purpose flour, but we feed it with rye flour on the day before baking the rye bread. We think of it as a rye starter.

1/4 teaspoon active dry yeast

1/4 cup (2 ounces) room temperature water (70 to 80 degrees)

1 1/4 cups (10 ounces) room temperature water (70 to 80 degrees)

1/2 cup (3 1/2 ounces) sourdough starter (see note above)

1 tablespoon plus 2 teaspoons caraway seeds

2 teaspoons (.4 ounce) salt

2/3 cup (2.8 ounces) medium rye flour

3 1/2 to 4 cups (17.6 ounces) bread flour, divided

Oil for a dough bowl

1 cup medium cornmeal for finishing the loaf

---

1. In a small bowl, stir yeast into the warm water. Let sit for 5 to 10 minutes until the yeast begins to foam, indicating that it is active.
2. In a mixer fitted with a dough hook, mix the 1 1/4 cups water, sourdough starter, activated yeast, caraway seeds, and salt. Add the rye flour and 3 cups of bread flour. Mix on medium-low speed for a couple of minutes. Continue adding flour in small amounts, as needed, until the dough mostly comes away from the sides of the bowl but is still a bit sticky. Let the machine continue to work the dough for about 5 minutes.
3. Transfer the dough to a lightly floured surface and knead it until it comes together in a ball but is still a bit tacky to the touch. Place the ball into a lightly oiled bowl and cover with plastic.
4. **Folding and rising the dough:** Let the dough sit for 15 minutes after setting it in the bowl. Remove the dough, flatten it somewhat, fold it into thirds envelope-style, and then return it to the bowl. Repeat this process two more times so that there is a total of three 15-minute rests and three folds. After the last fold, return the dough to the bowl and allow it to rise until doubled in bulk (see Rising Time on page 308).
5. **Forming the loaf:** Remove the risen dough gently from the bowl and set it on a work surface. Pat it into a thick rectangle (about 8 x 6 inches), then roll it into a tight cylinder. Fashion the cylinder into a loaf with slightly tapered ends, like an official NFL regulation football sitting with a flat bottom on a pan—Go Pack Go!
6. **Finishing the loaf:** Line a sheet pan with parchment paper and sprinkle the parchment with a little cornmeal, where you will be placing the loaf. Place 1 cup of medium cornmeal in a shallow pan. Wet your hands well with tap water, and pat the loaf all over to thoroughly moisten it. Roll the wet loaf in the cornmeal, making sure to cover all sides amply. Place the loaf on the prepared sheet pan, cover with a kitchen towel, and rise until almost doubled in bulk.
7. **Getting ready to bake the loaf:** Halfway through the final rise, preheat the oven to 400 degrees. Place a cast-iron pan in the bottom of the oven. When the oven is fully preheated, fill a 1-cup measuring cup about half full with tap water. Then score the risen loaf with a sharp knife or razor by making 3 diagonal cuts on the top, each about 2 inches long and 1/2 inch deep. Place the cup of water and readied loaf within easy reach of the oven.
8. Now, in one rapid set of motions, open the oven door, pour the water into the cast iron pan, set the loaf on the rack, and close the oven door. (Beware of the sudden burst of hot steam. Oven mitts are a good idea here.) Quickness is important to minimize how much steam escapes the oven. This technique gives the bread one final lift and a great crust.
9. Once the loaf is in, immediately lower the oven temperature to 350 degrees. Bake for 15 minutes, then, working quickly, rotate the pan and close the oven door pronto. Bake another 20 minutes. When the loaf is done (see When Is My Loaf Done on page 308), let it cool on a wire rack.

BIALYS

Makes 1 dozen bialys

 Hands-on time less than an hour (additional cooking or chilling times involved—read through before beginning)

Bialystok, Poland, was home to a small, close-knit Jewish community, now no longer in existence, whose legacy included this humble eponymous little roll. The soft-crisp-chewy round is known for its center dimple, which is traditionally filled with an onion-poppy seed mixture. In the old days, long lines would form outside bialy bakeries, as customers waited to get their bialys straight from the hot brick ovens and eat them at their best. Indeed, if the bialys had already cooled by the time they got to the door, some patrons would just walk away!

The bialy reminds us of the strong ties that exist between bread and cultures. At Manna, we recreated this little gem with a nod to authenticity, as explored by Mimi Sheraton in her small volume *The Bialy Eaters: The Story of a Bread and a Lost World*. Through it, we shared a lost piece of our own culture and re-emphasized the importance of great homemade bread in our lives.

Bialys are at their best when they still have their original oven heat wafting from them. If you don't eat them the day you make them, freeze them right away to preserve their integrity. You will need to toast them after freezing, but you will be glad you saved them. Our freezer is never without its bialy stash.

Bread

1 1/4 teaspoons active dry yeast

1/4 cup (2 ounces) room temperature water (70 to 80 degrees)

1 3/4 cups (14 ounces) room temperature water (70 to 80 degrees)

6 1/4 cups (28 ounces) bread flour

2 teaspoons salt

Oil for the dough bowl

Onion Poppy Seed Filling

1 tablespoon canola oil

1 medium (about 6 ounces) onion, peeled and finely diced

1 teaspoon poppy seeds

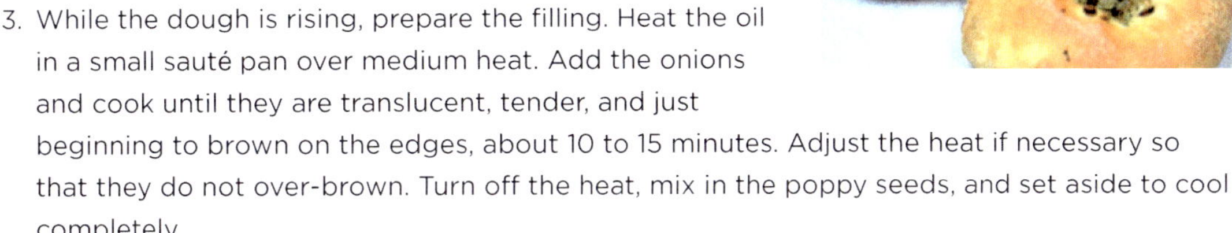

1. In a small bowl, stir yeast into the water. Let sit for 5 to 10 minutes until the yeast begins to foam, indicating that it is active.
2. Fit a mixer with a dough hook, and add the proofed yeast, remaining water, flour, and salt to the work bowl. Mix on low speed for a minute to combine the ingredients. The dough will be stiff but should not feel dry. Increase the speed to medium and continue to knead the dough for 5 to 10 minutes until smooth and satiny. Form the dough into a ball and place it in a lightly oiled bowl. Cover with a damp towel and set in a warm area to double in size (see Rising Time on page 308).
3. While the dough is rising, prepare the filling. Heat the oil in a small sauté pan over medium heat. Add the onions and cook until they are translucent, tender, and just beginning to brown on the edges, about 10 to 15 minutes. Adjust the heat if necessary so that they do not over-brown. Turn off the heat, mix in the poppy seeds, and set aside to cool completely.
4. Line two sheet pans with parchment paper and set them aside.
5. After the dough has doubled in size, divide it into 3.5-ounce pieces (or divide equally into 12 balls). Roll each piece into a smooth ball shape and place it on the lined sheet pan. After all the balls have been formed, cover them with a light towel and place them in a warm area to rise again.
6. Before moving to Step 7, allow the balls to fully double in size, but about 10 minutes before this time, preheat the oven to 500 degrees.
7. **Read this step through thoroughly before forming bialys**. Start by flouring your hands. Very gently (so as not to deflate it), lift a ball of risen dough by sliding your fingers underneath, from both sides. The ball should now be cradled atop your fingers, still in its round form and not deflated. Using your thumbs, gently create a deep indentation in the center of the ball. Rotate the dough in your hands, always keeping your thumbs in the center and using them to widen the indentation as you rotate the dough. That is, press the dough outward from the inside, using only your thumbs. Do not press the edges or the outside of the dough directly—just the center, pushing outward. The indentation should not go all the way through. Rather, the formed bialy should appear as a hole-less donut with a deep, 2-inch-wide basin in its center. The outside diameter of the bialy should be about 4 inches. Set each finished bialy onto the prepared baking trays and keep covered with a lightweight towel as you form the remaining bialys.
8. Once all the bialys are formed, spread a heaping teaspoon of the onion-poppy seed filling into each indentation.
9. Immediately place the trays of bialys in the oven. Bake them for 6 minutes, rotate the pans, and bake for another 4 minutes. They are done when they begin to take on a brown hue, as if blushing. Eat them as hot as you are willing.

MULTIGRAIN BREAD

Makes 1 large loaf

 Hands-on time less than an hour (additional cooking or chilling times involved—read through before beginning)

Our first bread baker was Sara, a fellow Madison north sider who nurtured this bread recipe into adulthood. Solid, moist, complex with flavor but simple in stature—it was wonderful in every respect. The presoaked seeds and grains bring a subtle, agreeable texture to the bread. We formed this rustic bread into a traditional round boule shape for sale to customers but baked it into giant long loaves for kitchen use, where we needed a uniform slice size for sandwiches. Customers often asked for the bigger, less-polished loaf for the same reason.

This multigrain loaf relies on a soaker mix—a presoak, if you will—of the whole grains that go into it. Soaker mixes pre-soften the hard grains, making them easier to chew (yet still leaving some toothsome texture to the bread). If you want to bake this bread regularly, you can make large batches of the dry ingredients for the soaker, then measure out 3.8 ounces (about 3/4 cup plus 2 tablespoons) of your mix for each batch of bread.

This recipe should be started the day before you want to use it.

Seed-Grain Soaker Mix

3 tablespoons (.75 ounce) whole rolled oats

2 tablespoons (.75 ounce) millet

3 tablespoons (1 ounce) flaxseed

3 tablespoons (0.33 ounce) wheat bran

3 tablespoons (1 ounce) sunflower seeds

1/4 cup plus 2 tablespoons (2.8 ounces) boiling water

Bread Dough

3/4 cup (6 ounces) very hot tap water

1/2 cup (4 ounces) buttermilk

3 tablespoons (1.25 ounces) packed brown sugar

4 teaspoons (1 ounce) honey

1 tablespoon (.35 ounce) active dry yeast

1 1/2 cups (6.7 ounces) wheat flour

1 3/4 cups (7 ounces) bread flour

2 teaspoons (.35 ounce) salt

Oats for finishing the loaf

---

1. Start the soaker at least 2 hours (or overnight) before beginning the bread dough. Mix all the dry soaker ingredients together, then pour boiling water over them and stir to combine. The grains will absorb all the water and become softened. Don't be tempted to add more water, as it will alter the moisture proportions in the loaf. Set aside.
2. **For the bread:** Fit a mixer with a dough hook, and add the hot water, buttermilk, brown sugar, and honey to the work bowl. (The goal is to end up with a final liquid temperature of no more than 105 degrees. If it is too hot, let it keep cooling, but if it is not hot enough, it will still work—it will just be off to a slower start.) Then stir in the yeast. Allow yeast to proof until it begins to foam, indicating that it is active, about 5 to 10 minutes. Add the soaker and mix to combine on a low speed.
3. Add both flours and salt to the bowl and mix on medium-low speed for 5 minutes. Increase the speed to medium and mix another 3 minutes. The dough should be moist and pliable but not sticky. Turn the dough onto a lightly floured surface and knead by hand briefly for about a minute.
4. Grease a large bowl and place the dough in the bowl. Cover and let rise until doubled in bulk (see Rising Time on page 308). Remove the dough from the bowl, deflate it with a gentle press, and pat it into a 12 x 6-inch rectangle. Fold the dough over on itself envelope-style. Repeat the folding process twice more, return the dough to the bowl seam side down, and rise again until doubled.
5. Grease a 9 x 5-inch loaf pan. (If you do not have a loaf pan, the bread will bake up just fine on a sheet pan as a free-form loaf. In this case, line a sheet pan with a pan liner.) Remove the dough from the bowl. Gently pat the dough into an 8 x 8 inch square, then tightly roll up the square into an oblong shape. Tuck in the seams at either end, and plump and shape the loaf to fit the loaf pan. Generously brush the top of the loaf with water, then press oats into the top. As the dough rises, the oats will spread out and provide a nice finish to the loaf. Alternatively, form the dough into a round shape that looks like a baseball cap minus the visor. Likewise, wet this with water, roll the top in oats, and set it on the sheet pan. For either formation, let the bread rise until doubled.
6. About 15 minutes before the dough has finished rising, preheat the oven to 400 degrees. Use a very sharp knife or razor blade to make three 1/4-inch-deep diagonal slash marks on top of the loaf. Place loaf in the oven and bake for 25 minutes, then rotate the pan and bake another 15 to 20 minutes. When the loaf is done (see When Is My Loaf Done? on page 308), let it cool on a wire rack. If baking in a loaf pan, let rest in the pan for 20 minutes, then remove to a wire rack to finish cooling.

PITA BREAD

Makes 12 pita pockets

 Hands-on time less than an hour (additional cooking or chilling times involved—read through before beginning)

Pita bread, almost more than any other bread (except for maybe a Navajo fry bread, which is my idea of heaven on earth), is a tremendous pleasure to make, especially for bread newbies. It is a simple and friendly dough to craft, handles easily when forming the little loaves, does not need a second rising, and bakes in six minutes flat. Even after years of making this bread, I never cease to be surprised and gratified when I open the oven door and am rewarded by these poofy pitas, which hold their shape long enough for you to inhale their beauty, and which then quickly deflate, leaving their secret pockets intact, awaiting your spectacular fillings. Mike and I can't help but eat a couple straight from the oven, spread with butter, before dinner is ready.

This recipe uses some whole wheat flour, but if you prefer, you can leave it out. I like the character the bread gets from using just a little.

1/4 cup (2 ounces) warm water (80-90 degrees)

1 scant tablespoon active dry yeast

1 3/4 cups (14 ounces) warm water (80-90 degrees)

2 tablespoons honey or brown sugar

1 1/2 teaspoons salt

3/4 cup whole wheat flour (3 ounces)

3 1/4 to 4 1/4 cups (14.6-19.1 ounces) all-purpose flour, or more as needed (don't use bread flour)

---

1. In a small bowl, stir yeast into the warm water. Let it sit until the yeast begins to foam, indicating that it is active, 5 to 10 minutes.
2. In the bowl of an electric mixer fitted with a dough hook, combine the proofed yeast, water, honey or brown sugar, and salt. Add the whole wheat flour and 3 1/4 cups of the all-purpose flour, and mix on low speed until all the flour is incorporated. Continue to add flour in half-cup increments until the dough comes together as a damp ball. It should feel a bit tacky, and a little should stick to your fingers. Continue to let the dough hook mix and knead the dough for about 3 minutes on medium speed. A good dough will come away from the sides of the bowl, even though it will feel tacky when touched. (If the dough comes together as a ball that does not stick to the bowl and does not stick to your hands, it has too much flour.)

3. Place the dough onto a floured surface and knead until the dough is smooth and satiny, about 5 to 10 minutes. Add a little flour as needed, but be careful about adding too much. When you work the dough, it should just barely come away from the work surface to form a ball. If you touch it with your fingertips, it should have some tackiness. The dough may stick a bit to your fingers. It should not, by any means, feel dry. Form into a ball and put the dough into a lightly oiled bowl. Cover with a damp towel.
4. Allow the dough to double in size (see Rising Time on page 308). Remove the risen dough from the bowl onto a work surface and gently deflate it. Divide the dough into 12 roughly equal pieces (they need not be perfectly even, but using a scale, if you have one, will help them be uniform). Form each piece into a ball, and cover the balls with a towel to rest for 15 minutes.
5. Line two sheet pans with parchment paper. (Depending on the final size of the rolled pita, only three or four will fit on a pan at a time. So even with two pans, you will need to bake in batches.) Preheat the oven to 450 degrees.
6. Dust a work surface with flour, then dust one of the pita balls with flour as well. Using a rolling pin, roll the ball out, turning it frequently to keep a uniform round shape until it is between 1/8 and 1/4 inches thick (no more—width matters here) and about 7 to 8 inches across. Set the pita on the pan, and repeat with as many pitas as will fit (they can be close but not touching on the pan). Always keep the unrolled balls of dough covered.
7. Immediately place the pan (or pans) in the oven and bake for 6 minutes. While the pita is baking, set a kitchen towel out on a flat surface, where you can transfer the baked pita to cool.
8. When the timer bings and you open the oven door, you will be greeted with a magical surprise. In 6 short minutes, the flat disks will have ballooned into poofy pita pillows, with just a hint of golden brown to their tops and bottoms. They are done! (It is okay if they are not brown. In fact, you don't want them too brown, or they quickly become brittle after cooling.)
9. Remove the pan from the oven and, using tongs (or wearing oven mitts), transfer the pitas to the kitchen in a single layer. (When the pockets deflate, they give off hot steam, so handle them carefully.) Cover with another kitchen towel and let cool. This way, the towels absorb the steam released as they cool, and the outsides will stay soft rather than dry out. After they have cooled completely, they can be stored in plastic bags or frozen.

Gluten-Free Baked Goods

The gluten-free recipes here are separated from the rest of the bakery recipes. After all, the two shouldn't touch! For those of you who need or desire gluten-free baked goods, you have arrived at a happy place. For those of you who do not have such needs, please don't go anywhere. We worked hard to make this collection of bakery items indistinguishable in flavor and texture from their gluten-full counterparts. Sometimes they are even better. You'll see.

When we opened Manna, there was nothing gluten-free in our bakery lineup, perhaps because there was never a call for it at The Collins House, so it was not in our area of expertise. And gluten-free just wasn't on the radar at the time. But soon, the requests began to trickle in, causing our bakers to quake in their kitchen clogs. Some of them said that gluten-free baking was best left to people who specialized in it. It was not our bailiwick, and we should stick to what we knew. Others felt we were over-diversifying our offerings. And besides, they argued, how big of a market could there really be for gluten-free bakery? But customers continued to ask, and after a time, it seemed downright neglectful not to pay heed to their requests.

Fast forward a few years. The bakers had chilled a bit on the idea that "gluten-free" was not in their vocabulary. Rather than feeling as if they were spending extra labor to make six people happy, they realized there was significant demand for their goodies. We'd gone from having a bakery case devoid of gluten-free baked goods to devoting an entire shelf to them.

A product labeled gluten-free carries the stigma that it will be of lesser quality (just as, conversely, anything labeled "kosher" tends to be thought of as better quality), which is not always true. Our solution? While we needed to label all of the gluten-free products for people who needed to know, we used the abbreviation GF and put it *after* the item's name, thus giving prominence to what was most important—the product itself. When people saw the stately layered lemon cake in the display case, it was the cake that mattered. And when they tasted it? Well, that myth about gluten-free came tumbling down.

Our gluten-free bakery lineup included four rotating muffins, three rotating scones, three amazing cookies, a bread, and several pies and cheesecakes, all led like a proud mother duck by the lemon cake. It was a collection carefully curated to please bakery lovers on both sides of the gluten divide. The collection that follows includes many of the faves.

All-Purpose Gluten-Free Flours (A Cautionary Note)

These flours are not all created equal. Different manufacturers have different blends, which will affect baking outcomes in different ways. In particular, a GF flour blend that already has xanthan gum in its mix can impact recipes that call for xanthan gum as a separate ingredient, adding more thickening power than intended. When a recipe called for all-purpose gluten-free flour (some use brown rice flour or tapioca flour), we used Bob's Red Mill exclusively. One time we changed brands, and everything suddenly turned out differently (and not in a good way). Just sayin'. If you bake gluten-free often, it is a good idea to use the same brand all the time, so your outcomes will be consistent.

CHEWY PEANUT BUTTER COOKIES (GF)

Makes 12 cookies

 Start to finish in less than a half hour

Like Forrest Gump's feather, this gluten-free peanut butter cookie floated into the hands of the Bob's Red Mill folks from a customer of theirs and ultimately blew our way. It was the third in our triple crown of champion gluten-free cookies, running neck and neck with the Annie Oakleys and Chocolate Truffles.

---

2 cups creamy peanut butter

2 cups packed brown sugar

2 eggs, lightly beaten

2 teaspoons vanilla extract

2 teaspoons baking soda

1/4 cup gluten-free all-purpose flour (see boxed discussion on page 320)

---

1. Preheat the oven to 350 degrees. Line a sheet pan with parchment paper (or grease the pan) and set aside.
2. Place all the ingredients in the bowl of an electric mixer fitted with a paddle. Mix on medium speed for two minutes, then scrape down the bowl with a rubber spatula and mix another minute.
3. Portion dough with a small scoop onto the sheet pan, leaving about 1 1/2 inches between cookies. Flatten the cookies to about 1/2 inch (they do not spread much), then make a crisscross mark on the top of the cookie with a fork. Bake for 6 minutes, then rotate the pan and bake another 4 to 6 minutes. The cookies are done when the tops are just set. Remove from oven and let cool. This is one of those few cookies in the world that is probably more delicious fully cooled.

ANNIE OAKLEY COOKIES (GF)

Makes about 20 cookies

 Start to finish in less than a half hour

This cowgirl cookie holds its own among the big boys. It is chock full of, well, everything—oats, coconut, chocolate, pecans, toffee. Plus a variety of gluten-free flours. If you do not normally stock a pantry full of the latter necessities, maybe now is the time.

3/4 cup brown rice flour
1/4 cup potato starch
3 tablespoons tapioca starch or flour
1/2 teaspoon xanthan gum
1 teaspoon baking powder
1 teaspoon baking soda
1 teaspoon cinnamon
1/4 teaspoon salt

3 ounces (3/4 stick) unsalted butter, softened
1/2 cup granulated sugar
1/2 cup packed brown sugar
1 egg
1/2 teaspoon vanilla extract
1 cup whole rolled oats
2/3 cup shredded sweetened coconut, toasted (page 364)
3/4 cup semi-sweet chocolate chunks
2/3 cup chopped pecans, toasted (page 363)
2/3 cup chopped toffee

1. Preheat the oven to 350 degrees. Line a cookie sheet or sheet pan with parchment paper and set aside. (If you do not have parchment, lightly coat the pan with cooking spray or butter.)
2. Mix together the dry ingredients (brown rice flour through salt) in a medium bowl and set aside.
3. In the bowl of an electric mixer with a paddle attachment, cream the butter, sugar and brown sugar on medium-high until light, about 3 minutes. Scrape down the bowl and mix again briefly.
4. Add the egg and vanilla and mix on medium speed until smooth. Scrape down the bowl. Add the flour mixture to the butter-sugar mixture and mix on low speed until combined. Add oats, coconut flakes, chocolate chunks, pecans, and toffee, and again mix on low until just combined. Give a final mix by hand to incorporate the ingredients from the bottom of the bowl. The dough will be thick.
5. Portion the dough with a small scoop onto the sheet pan, leaving 1 1/2 inches between blobs. Form the blobs into a ball shape, rather than flattening them, as they will spread a good deal on their own. Bake for 6 minutes, then rotate the pan and bake another 5-7 minutes. The cookies should be a light golden brown all over, with the center just barely set. They may be irregular in shape and will have darker patches winding throughout from the melted toffee. Cool on the pan.
6. The cookies may be frozen unbaked. Thaw them to room temperature before baking.

CHOCOLATE TRUFFLE COOKIES (GF)

Makes about 14 cookies

 Start to finish in less than a half hour

These cookies taste just like the name implies. The outside has a hint of crispness, giving way to a rich, soft, truffle-like filling. The milk accompaniment is optional, but you'll want it!

1/4 cup brown rice flour

3 tablespoons potato starch

1 1/2 tablespoons tapioca flour

1/2 teaspoon xanthan gum

1/2 teaspoon baking powder

1/2 teaspoon salt

2 1/2 cups semisweet chocolate chips for the dough

3 tablespoons unsalted butter

3 eggs

3/4 cup sugar

2 teaspoons vanilla extract

2/3 cup additional chocolate chips (the coffee-flavored ones are amazing in this recipe)

Optional accompaniment: 1 pint cold milk (whole, 2%, or skim)

---

1. Preheat the oven to 350 degrees. Line a sheet pan with parchment paper (or grease the pan) and set aside.
2. Combine the brown rice flour through the salt in a bowl and set aside.
3. Place 2 1/2 cups chocolate chips and butter in a microwave-safe bowl, and melt using medium power, in 2-minute intervals. Stir after each interval. The mixture should be smooth and free of chocolate lumps. Let partially cool.
4. In the bowl of an electric mixer with a paddle attachment, beat eggs, sugar, and vanilla on medium speed until light in color and somewhat thickened, about 2 minutes. Add melted chocolate-butter mixture to egg-sugar mixture and beat on medium-low speed until smooth. Scrape down the sides of the bowl, then mix in the dry ingredients on low speed until well combined. Stir in 2/3 cup chocolate chips with a spatula and incorporate well.
5. Portion dough with a small scoop onto the sheet pan, leaving about 1 1/2 inches between blobs. Pat the tops down ever so lightly, but do not flatten the cookies. Bake for 6 minutes, then rotate the pan and bake another 4 to 5 minutes. The cookies are done when the tops are just set. The cookie's surface will begin to appear a bit cracked and dry, like the desert in a drought. This is as it should be. Remove from the oven and let cool for 10 minutes.

BANANA CHOCOLATE CHIP MUFFINS (GF)

Makes 12 muffins

 Start to finish within an hour, give or take

This muffin was among the many products made by Ana, a Latina woman who spoke almost no English when she began working in Manna's kitchens. She reminded me of another woman who had worked as a housekeeper at The Collins House, Vicki , who was from Nepal and spoke no English whatsoever. Both women were driven by a strong work ethic and the desire to learn and grow in their jobs, and we did our best to support them by finding ways to bridge the communication gap (including the life-saving Google Translate). Ana proved to be an excellent cook, but her real passion was baking, and in time she moved into the bakery, initially learning basics like muffins, scones, and cookies by watching what the bakers did and writing out her own recipes. She soon took ownership of more complicated projects, such as making our weekly supply of English muffins. I was so impressed with Ana's self-motivation that I tracked down a bread baking book that presented recipes in English and Spanish, so she and the more seasoned bakers could "talk baking" together. Ana, like Vicki, ultimately took ESL classes, and as their language skills grew, we had the delight of getting to know them, as if for the first time.

Everyone loved these gluten-free muffins for their ample banana flavor and fine, poundcake-like crumb. The mini chocolate chips, which could easily enough be replaced with regular chocolate chips, contributed to their pleasing, speckled appearance.

Muffins

1 cup brown rice flour

1/3 cup almond flour

2 tablespoons plus 2 teaspoons potato starch

1/2 cup sugar

1 teaspoon baking soda

1 teaspoon baking powder

1 teaspoon xanthan gum

1/2 teaspoon salt

1 cup mashed, overripe bananas (about 3)

1 egg

5 ounces (1 stick plus 2 tablespoons) butter, melted and cooled

2/3 cup mini chocolate chips

Streusel

2/3 cup packed brown sugar

1/3 cup gluten-free all-purpose flour

1/4 teaspoon cinnamon

1 ounce (2 tablespoons) cold butter, cut into 1/2-inch cubes

1. Preheat the oven to 350 degrees. Grease a 12-cup muffin tin or line the cups with muffin liners. Set them aside until ready to use.
2. Combine dry ingredients (rice flour through salt) in a medium bowl.
3. In the bowl of an electric mixer with a paddle attachment, beat the bananas and egg on medium speed until well blended. Add in the dry ingredient mixture on low speed, pour in the melted butter, and continue to mix on low until smooth. Scrape down the sides of the bowl once or twice to incorporate all the ingredients, then stir in the chocolate chips.
4. To make the streusel, combine all the ingredients in a food processor and pulse until the mixture is in coarse, small lumps.
5. Scoop the muffin batter into prepared tins, filling them about 3/4 full. Crumble streusel topping over the muffins. Bake for 14 minutes, then rotate the pan and bake another 8 to 12 minutes. Test for doneness by inserting a toothpick into the highest, most central part of the muffin. It should come out clean. Allow muffins to cool for 20 minutes in the pan, then transfer them to a wire rack to finish cooling.

BLACKBERRY ORANGE MUFFINS (GF)

Makes 12-15 Muffins

 Start to finish within an hour, give or take

Maybe there was orange zest in the batter at one time, but apparently, the bakers at Manna used lemon zest instead. The bakery case label always read Blackberry Orange Muffins, and the gaffe went unnoticed by all. Even Fred, a regular customer and gluten-free bakery connoisseur, who ordered four of these and four banana chocolate chip muffins every Friday, never made a peep. I decided to leave the name of this muffin intact. But just to be sure, I included lemon and orange zest in the ingredient list, with the option to go either way.

1/4 cup Bob's Red Mill all-purpose gluten-free flour (see boxed discussion on page 320)

1 cup brown rice flour

1/2 cup potato starch

1/2 cup tapioca flour

2 teaspoons baking powder

1/2 teaspoon baking soda

1/2 teaspoon xanthan gum

1/2 teaspoon salt

1 teaspoon cinnamon

Pinch of nutmeg

1/2 cup white sugar

1/4 cup packed brown sugar

4 ounces (1/2 stick) butter, melted and cooled

2 tablespoons vegetable oil

2 eggs

1/2 cup sour cream

3/4 cup buttermilk

Grated zest from half a lemon or orange

1 teaspoon vanilla extract

1 1/4 cups fresh or frozen blackberries (keep frozen until used)

Sanding sugar (see page 226) to finish the muffins

---

1. Preheat the oven to 350 degrees. Grease a 12-cup muffin tin or line the cups with muffin liners. Set aside until ready to use.
2. Combine dry ingredients (gluten-free flour through nutmeg) in a bowl and mix well.
3. In the bowl of an electric mixer with a paddle attachment, cream together the two sugars, butter, and vegetable oil for about a minute, scraping the bowl once. Beat in the eggs, then sour cream, buttermilk, lemon or orange zest, and vanilla. Scrape down the sides of the bowl once or twice to incorporate all the ingredients. Add the dry ingredients to the wet mixture, mix on low speed first, then increase the speed to medium and beat until smooth.
4. Gently fold in blackberries by hand, and mix until they are well distributed. (If the blackberries are especially large, halving them first while still frozen distributes them better in the batter.)
5. Scoop muffin batter into prepared tins, filling about 3/4 to 7/8 full. Sprinkle each muffin with 1/2 teaspoon sanding sugar. Bake for 14 minutes, then rotate the pan and bake another 8 to 10 minutes. Test for doneness by inserting a toothpick into the highest, most central part of the muffin. It should come out clean. Allow the muffins to cool for 20 minutes in the pan, then transfer them to a wire rack to finish cooling.

RASPBERRY OAT SCONES (GF)

Makes 12 scones

 Start to finish within an hour, give or take

This gluten-free scone is traditional as scones go—crumbly, oaty, and not too sweet—plus the raspberries provide a nice pop. A few mini chocolate chips would make an indulgent addition.

---

1 cup brown rice flour
1/3 cup potato starch
1/3 cup tapioca flour
1/3 cup sugar
1 tablespoon baking powder
1/2 teaspoon baking soda
1/2 teaspoon cinnamon
1/2 teaspoon xanthan gum
1/2 teaspoon salt
5 ounces (1 1/4 sticks) cold butter, cut into 1/2-inch cubes
1 1/3 cups whole rolled oats

1 egg
1/2 cup buttermilk

3/4 cup frozen raspberries (keep frozen until used)

---

1. Preheat the oven to 350 degrees. Line a sheet pan with parchment paper (or grease the pan) and set aside.
2. Place the first nine ingredients (brown rice flour to salt—do not include oats) in the bowl of a food processor. Process for 15 seconds. Add the butter to the dry ingredients and pulse until the mixture is crumbly, then pulse in the oats once or twice. Move the ingredients from the food processor to a medium bowl.
3. In a separate bowl, beat together egg and buttermilk.
4. Add the frozen raspberries to the dry ingredients and toss briefly, then pour in buttermilk mixture and toss with a rubber spatula until well combined. You may need to knead once or twice to bring dough together, but do not overwork it. Raspberries are fragile.
5. Scoop the batter onto the prepared pan using a 2-ounce scoop or 1/3-cup measuring cup, and flatten slightly. Bake for 12 minutes, then rotate the pan and bake another 10 to 12 minutes. They are done when the scones are golden around the edges and the center, when pressed with a finger, does not yield but feels set.

TRIPLE LEMON CAKE (GF)

Makes one 9-inch four-layer cake (several components and several stages of preparation/chilling—can be made in 1 half day or over 2 days)

 Project Alert! May require multiple stages or overnight preparations—read through before proceeding

This cake, adapted from a recipe by Annalise Roberts from epicurious.*com* (November 2005), was the star of the Manna gluten-free bakery lineup. As with many of our products, the only reason you knew it was gluten-free was that its name said so. It is hands down one of the best cakes I have ever eaten, and I am not a lemon-forward kind of gal. Having a slice is almost like eating a trifle. The lemon-zested cake layers are soaked and oozy with bright, fresh lemon curd. The cake is finished with a buttercream bursting with yet more lemon flavor.

At Manna, we'd dollop the lemon curd atop mixed berries as a jazzed-up fruit accompaniment to brunch entrees. Lemon curd was also the crowning highlight of the Lemon Love Pancakes (page 131). The cake itself, minus the lemon zest, is an excellent basic gluten-free white cake—moist and flavorful. It would make a good core cake recipe for other gluten-free creations (maybe a nice peach compote between the layers).

This cake freezes quite well, as do its separate components. Make the curd in bulk and use it whenever you're feeling a little tart and sassy!

Lemon Curd

3 large eggs

4 large egg yolks

1 cup sugar

Pinch of salt

1 tablespoon cornstarch

2/3 cup fresh lemon juice

1 tablespoon grated lemon zest

2 tablespoons butter, cut in 1/2-inch pieces

2 tablespoons heavy cream

Cake

2 1/2 cups brown rice flour

1/2 teaspoon salt

1 tablespoon baking powder

1 teaspoon xanthan gum

1 cup milk (whole or 2%)

1 cup canola oil

1 teaspoon vanilla extract

1 tablespoon finely grated fresh lemon zest

2 cups sugar

4 large eggs

Lemon Buttercream

12 ounces (3 sticks) unsalted butter, softened

5 cups confectioners' sugar

1/3 cup fresh lemon juice

1 tablespoon finely grated fresh lemon zest

---

1. **For lemon curd:** In a medium-sized heavy-duty saucepan, whisk eggs, egg yolks, sugar, and salt together. Dissolve the cornstarch in lemon juice, then add lemon juice and zest to the egg mixture. Cook over medium-low heat, stirring constantly, until thickened and pudding-like (about 8 to 10 minutes). Remove from the heat, press through a strainer into a medium bowl, and stir in the butter pieces and heavy cream. Refrigerate until completely cooled and ready to use.
2. **For lemon cake:** Place an oven rack in the middle of the oven and heat the oven to 350 degrees. Grease two 9-inch round by 2-inch-high cake pans, and line the bottom of each pan with a round of parchment paper (you can make cutouts from the rectangles).
3. In a medium bowl, mix together the brown rice flour, salt, baking powder, and xanthan gum until well combined. In another bowl, mix together the milk, canola oil, vanilla, and lemon zest until thoroughly combined.
4. Place the sugar and eggs in the bowl of an electric mixer with the paddle attachment, and beat on medium speed until combined, about 1 minute. Reduce the speed to low. Add the flour mixture alternately with milk mixture, starting and ending with the flour mixture, and mix until well combined. Scrape down the sides of the bowl at least twice during the mixing.
5. Divide the batter evenly into the two cake pans and bake 35 to 40 minutes. They are done when a toothpick inserted in the center comes out clean. Cool the cakes in their pans for about 10 minutes, then invert them onto wire racks to finish cooling. Refrigerate the cake layers for at least 2 hours. This will make them firmer and less fragile for the assembly. If you refrigerate cakes overnight, wrap them in plastic.

6. **For lemon buttercream:** Place the butter in the bowl of an electric mixer and beat on high speed for 1 to 2 minutes until light and fluffy. Turn off the mixer, scrape down the bowl, and add confectioners' sugar, lemon juice, and lemon zest. To begin the final mixing, turn the mixer on and off quickly a few times to let the confectioners' sugar start to incorporate with the butter without poofing out of the bowl. Then increase the speed to high and beat for 3 minutes, scraping the bowl down at least once.
7. **To assemble the cake:** Use a long, serrated knife to halve each cake layer horizontally. You will have four cake layers.
8. Put a bottom layer on a serving plate, and place the plate on a rotating cake stand, if you have one. Spread half of the lemon curd on this bottom layer. Spread a second cake layer with some of the buttercream (about 1/4 thick), and place it carefully atop the first layer. Set a third cake layer atop this and spread it with the remaining lemon curd. Finally, place the last cake layer on top. Make sure the layers are stacked in a nice, even pile. Refrigerate the assembled cake before frosting. A firm cake frosts more easily.
9. Crumb-coat the cake (page 225), then frost the top and sides of the cake with most of the rest of the buttercream (page 332). Pipe decoratively around the rim and bottom with the remaining buttercream. The cake may be refrigerated for six days or frozen for at least two months.

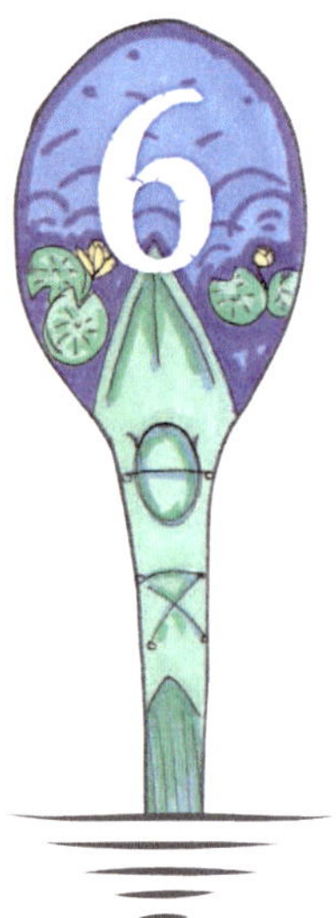

Jewish Fridays: Manna's Culinary Soul

In developing Manna's opening menus, we knew that on Fridays, we would feature the traditional foods of our culture—challah, matzo ball soup, beef brisket—as a small and symbolic way of highlighting the importance of our Jewish backgrounds to our largely non-Jewish community. The Jewish Shabbat, which begins on Friday night before sundown and ends the next day at sundown, is a special time of rest and reflection, so we honored this moment by offering the traditional foods of a Shabbat meal to our customers. Fridays were also a time to remind ourselves of our Jewish core values, which included the joy of kibitzing with our neighbors and supporting social justice causes, as well as breaking bread together.

Over time, many traditional Jewish foods and cultural symbols wove their way into Manna's fabric. We served potato latkes during Hanukkah, fried addictingly crisp in a vegetable oil/schmaltz blend. Mike cooked up matzo brei (a Jewish French toast, kinda sorta) during Passover and took special pride in joining the kitchen staff to do the cooking himself. I thought of him as the bearer of our Jewish food torch, and in time the cooks absorbed his Jewish ways (from his "oy gevalts" to his faithfully crafted matzo balls). A small part of each of them became Jewish, too! Rugelach, a flaky rolled pastry from the kitchens of Eastern European bubbes (and another universal Jewish food that bound the international Jewish diaspora), became a favorite staple in the bakery. And the bialys, of course, brought to life parts of our ancestry lost to the Holocaust.

If you looked about the cafe at our collection of tchotchkes (knickknacks), you'd see plenty of subtle nods to our heritage: a giant, dreidel-shaped cookie jar perched high on a shelf above the baristas and tiny wooden dreidels tucked here and there. We lit candles for Hanukkah and even held a Passover Seder in the back room.

This chapter gathers together the Jewish recipes we made at Manna, and the stories that bring alive our passion for cooking them. It distills the disparate parts of Manna into a meaningful whole, reflecting the passion with which we ran our business. A soup recipe in the Soup Chapter would be just another great recipe, but included in this section it has context. These are foods that simmered and crackled and steamed up our home kitchens long before they made their way to you. Everything about them defines us, defines Manna, and defines what we all meant to each other. Read the stories, cook the foods, and carry with you your own smidgen of Jewishness.

Challah: Food For Thought

Manna's challah recipe has been nestled appropriately into the bread chapter (pages 309-311), surrounded by words and guidance on bread baking techniques. But challah had an important place on Jewish Fridays at the cafe, so it's fitting to make a note of it in this chapter, too.

Golden braided challah is not just a beauty to behold nor a universal symbol of the importance of bread in culture. It is also a joy to bring to life. The dough is a creamy yellow color, rich with eggs, and smells as subtly sweet as it will later taste. It is smooth and satiny—a pleasure to knead. Forming the braids is a loving act, and the egg wash and poppy seed finish are like a final touch on an artist's work.

Much symbolism is attributed to this sacred loaf, from the number of braids meant to reflect the twelve tribes of Israel to interweaving ideas and culture. When the loaf awaits, fresh from the oven on your dinner table, the swells of the braids beckon you to pull them off and eat them warm—no knife necessary. The shape of the loaf encourages you and your loved ones to break bread together.

MATZO BALL SOUP

Makes 6-7 servings of soup, each with 2 large matzo balls

 Hands-on time less than an hour (additional cooking or chilling times involved—read through before beginning)

"Floaters" are light, fluffy matzo balls that melt irresistibly in your mouth. "Sinkers," on the other hand, are dense and have a noticeable chew factor. Which side are you on? The lines are drawn as if between the Cardinals and the Cubs, and in this analogy, the Cardinals win hands down. That is to say, at Manna, floaters ruled.

There are numerous recipes out there for matzo balls, but why would anyone want to look further than the back of the Manischewitz matzo meal box? Our recipe adheres to this classic with one major exception: We substitute properly rendered chicken fat (aka Mikey's Liquid Gold Schmaltz) for vegetable oil. It makes all the difference in the world.

Matzo Balls

4 eggs

1/4 cup Mikey's Liquid Gold Schmaltz, melted (pages 338-339), or "second-rate" chicken fat saved from making stock (see Step 5 of Chicken Stock page 203)

1 cup Manischewitz matzo meal (substitute another brand at your own risk—not all matzo meal is created equal)

2 teaspoons salt

1/4 cup chicken stock

3 quarts water

1 tablespoon kosher salt

Soup

8-10 cups Chicken Stock (pages 202-203)

2 medium carrots, peeled and thinly sliced

2 cups shredded or cubed chicken meat, either saved from making the chicken stock or cooked fresh from roasted chicken thighs

8 cooked chicken gizzards, cut into quarters (optional, perhaps, for some, but in Mike's mind it isn't matzo ball soup of it doesn't have gizzards))

Matzo balls from the recipe above

Salt and pepper to taste

---

1. **For the matzo balls:** In a medium bowl, beat the eggs and stir in the melted schmaltz. Add the matzo meal and 2 teaspoons salt. Stir until well incorporated. Add the chicken stock and continue to stir until the mixture becomes a thick slurry. Cover the bowl with plastic film and refrigerate for at least 30 minutes.
2. Fill a 4-quart or larger pot with 3 quarts of water, add kosher salt, and bring to a boil. Wet your hands with cold water. Scoop out about 1 1/2 tablespoons of the matzo ball mixture with a spoon, and roll it around gently with your hands to form a ball about 1 1/2 inches in diameter. Plop the ball into the boiling water. Repeat until all the mixture is used. Using a large wooden or slotted spoon, make sure the balls are not sticking to the bottom of the pot. Cover the pot tightly, lower the heat just enough so the water doesn't boil over, and boil for 40 minutes. Do not open the lid to peek at the balls during cooking. Make sure water is at a constant rolling boil. You should see steam coming out from under the lid.
3. When the balls are done, remove them from the cooking pot with a slotted spoon and place them in the pot of chicken soup you will be serving. (Or, if the soup is not ready, place the matzo balls in a pot of clean, warm water and keep warm until ready to serve.) These matzo balls will be nice and fluffy and truly amazing (if you didn't peek during simmering, and if you used Mikey's Liquid Gold Schmaltz, that is).
4. **To finish the soup:** Bring the chicken stock to a boil. Add carrots, chicken pieces, and gizzards if using. Turn down to a low simmer and allow the carrots to cook until tender. Taste and add salt and pepper if needed. Add the matzo balls, heat through, and serve.

MIKEY'S LIQUID GOLD SCHMALTZ

Makes 16 ounces of rendered fat, plus gribenes

 **Hands-on time less than an hour (additional cooking or chilling times involved—read through before beginning)**

Mike may be fanatical about his matzo balls, but his true passion lies with the process of making schmaltz (rendered chicken fat) and then using it everywhere (especially in the matzo balls). He relishes scenting our house with burbling onions and melting chicken fat and waits like a restless child for the moment when he can get at the gribenes (pronounced gree-buh-niss). These are Jewish chitlins of a sort—the crunchy bits left over from the rendered fat. Mike mostly eats these like popcorn, but he also uses them as a delicious addition to scrambled eggs, mashed potatoes, or like onion frizzles in a sandwich. Sometimes he even invites our Jewish friend Jarno over, so they can hover over the bowl together like two kids sneaking a treat when their mother isn't looking. Food author Michael Ruhlman brings this singular ingredient to life in his small volume *The Book of Schmaltz*, a loving ode to simplicity, culture, and tradition.

You need a lot of chicken fat and skin to produce schmaltz, so each time you prepare chicken for cooking, trim off the extra blobs and bits of skin and fat. Freeze these bits in a container, to which you can keep adding more blobs. After a time (depending on how often you eat skin-on chicken), you will have accumulated enough to make a batch of schmaltz. Once rendered, you can store it in the freezer indefinitely. In addition to its use in matzo balls, it imparts a subtle but perceptible flavor to roasted vegetables or fried potatoes and is essential for excellent Matzo Brei (pages 348-349). Use it whenever you feel a little Jewish or want to impress (and surprise) your Jewish friends.

Note: Choose an old or banged-up pot for this recipe. The fat becomes browned, the onions caramelize as they cook, and it all does a really good job of creating a crusty mess on the bottom of the pan. It will clean up okay, but this is not a task for your pretty cookware.

---

2 pounds chicken fat and skin pieces, partially frozen

Water, enough to cover the chicken fat and skin

1 tablespoon kosher salt

1 1/2 cups chopped onions

---

1. Cut the chicken fat and skin into small pieces, about 1/2 inch to 1 inch in size. Place them in a large pot (see note above) and cover them with water. Add the salt and stir.
2. Bring the water to a boil over high heat. As it starts to boil, you will see some foam (or "schaum," if you are being Jewish about it) rising to the top. This foam is sort of murky

looking, with big bubbles, and contains some of the impurities you want to get rid of. Use a strainer to remove as much of it as possible. It may take a few times before the foaming stops.

3. Let the pot of water-fat continue to cook at a medium boil for about 30 minutes, then add the onions to the pot. Stir and continue to boil. Every 15 minutes or so, scrape the bottom of the pot with a heavy-duty metal spatula to keep the onions and fat from burning.
4. The goal is to boil off all the water, with only rendered fat and bits of skin and onion remaining. Partway through the process, the bubbles will begin to get smaller, and when you notice this, turn the heat down so that the contents are at more of a brisk simmer than a boil. From here on, check and stir more frequently. You want the solids to turn a deep golden color but not burn. At the end, the mixture will once again start to foam on top, but the bubbles will be more like a fine, whitish foam.
5. Remove the pot from the heat, let the mixture cool for a few minutes (it is very hot, so be careful), then strain the rendered fat through a sieve into a stainless steel or ceramic bowl. Let the strainer sit over the bowl for 10 minutes to allow as much fat as possible to drip through, then place the gribenes into a shallow bowl lined with several layers of paper towels. Try not to eat them all at once.
6. Let the liquid fat cool a bit more, then strain it again through a fine-mesh sieve into jars. Cool completely and cover jars. The schmaltz will keep in the refrigerator for several weeks, or you can freeze it indefinitely.

A Schmaltz Obsession

If you were to open our home freezer at any given time, you would see a shelf on the door lined with gefilte fish jars, salsa jars, and olive jars full of various vintages of rendered chicken fat. (This is true of my son's small Brooklyn apartment freezer as well.) The jars with fat made using this recipe are labeled as "Liquid Gold," and Mike saves them for special occasions. But some bear the designation Fool's Gold, a jab at my meshuggeneh (crazy) husband, who thinks that the fat skimmed off the pot of chicken stock that has just simmered for six hours is not real schmaltz, but a cheap imitation—a fake! (even though this was the only fat that went into our matzo balls at Manna, and it was JUST FINE). But Mike, ever the purist, refuses to use it. I label it so he doesn't make a fatal error and ruin the balls. And when he makes fresh batches of real schmaltz, he melts the Fools Gold into it so as not to waste it, thus rescuing it from anonymity. Oy vey.

RED WINE-BRAISED BEEF BRISKET

Makes a 4-5 pound brisket, serving six or more, with leftovers for all the other uses in this book!

 Project Alert! May require multiple stages or overnight preparations—read through before proceeding

Brisket is the quintessential Jewish holiday entree, although many families serve it year-round. After it has braised for hours and hours, when the oven door is opened and the lid lifted, the beef is as yielding as soft butter.

This version was a Manna signature dish, chunky and tender, bathed in a rich sauce perfumed with red wine and slow-roasted garlic. Cooks prepped it in 70-pound batches at the end of the workday, and two people hoisted the roasting pans from the stovetop to the oven. In the wee hours of the morning, the bakers picked up the thread, removing it from the oven to cool and then wheeling it on carts into the fridge to ready the beef for the final steps of slicing, reheating, and serving. Everyone, it seemed, had a hand in brisket-making.

Braised beef brisket and spaetzle

From Labor Day to Memorial Day, this brisket was part of our "Jewish Fridays" ritual and was served with hand-made Spaetzle (page 342-343) and Brussels sprout hash. But in summer, when steamy hot braised beef was too much, we switched to barbecued brisket sandwiches topped with cool, crisp slaw. It was a lighter, more summery preparation that allowed brisket to stay on the menu. Still, each year come the end of summer, somewhere in mid-August, customers who knew the routine got restless for the real McCoy and began asking when they could expect it.

Compared to the long process we endured, making this brisket will be no trouble in your kitchen. Five pounds of meat is much easier to cook than 70 pounds. It can be made several days ahead of serving.

1/2 cup flour

1 teaspoon salt

1 teaspoon black pepper

4-5 pounds lean beef brisket, partially trimmed of its fat

1/3 cup canola oil

1 large onion (8 ounces), peeled and thinly sliced

8 cloves garlic, peeled but left whole

2 1/4 cups dry red wine (anything decent you've got sitting around)

2 tablespoons tomato paste

4 cups homemade beef stock or substitute Chicken Stock (pages 202-203)

1/2 teaspoon dried thyme

1 bay leaf

Optional: additional stock or water and cornstarch

---

1. Preheat the oven to 300 degrees.
2. Mix flour, salt and pepper, and spread it out onto a large plate. Dredge the trimmed brisket in the flour mixture, shake off the excess flour, and reserve the flour mixture.
3. Heat a large, heavy-duty roasting pan over medium-high heat. The pan should be large enough to fit the brisket and deep enough to hold all the liquids. When the pan is hot, add the oil. Once the oil is shimmering, carefully lay the brisket in the oil and sear the meat on each side to a nice dark golden brown, about 5 to 8 minutes per side. Remove meat from the pan and set aside on a platter. (If the brisket is too long to fit in your pan in one piece, cut it in half against the grain and sear each piece separately.)
4. In the same pan but over medium heat, add onions and garlic and cook until golden, about 10 minutes. Add the remaining flour from the dredge and stir for 2 to 3 minutes to make a roux. Slowly add red wine while whisking, bring to a boil, then reduce heat to medium-low and simmer for 20 minutes or until the wine has reduced and the sauce has thickened a bit. Stir in tomato paste, beef stock, thyme, and bay leaf, then carefully add the brisket to submerge it in the liquid.
5. Bring the sauce to a boil, then cover the pan with a tight-fitting lid. If you do not have a lid, wrap the top tightly in aluminum foil. Place in the oven, and let braise for 6 to 8 hours.
6. Test the beef with a fork. It should be fall-off-the-bone tender (even though there is no bone). Fish out the bay leaf. Let brisket partially cool with the lid off, then refrigerate overnight with no lid.
7. The next day, remove the brisket from the fridge. Skim off any accumulated fat from the top of the sauce, and remove the brisket from the sauce to a large cutting board.
8. Slice the brisket against the grain into 1/4- to 1/2-inch slices. (Thinner is better for sandwiches, thicker for a dinner entrée, but whatever you prefer is fine.*) Lay the slices into an oven-proof serving dishing, overlapping them slightly.
9. In a medium saucepan, bring the sauce to a simmer over medium heat. If it seems too thick, add a little stock or water to thin it out. If it seems too runny, mix 1 tablespoon cornstarch with 1 tablespoon water, and whisk this into the simmering liquid. Adjust the sauce as necessary to achieve the consistency you like. Once the sauce is finalized, pour it over the sliced beef. Cover the dish with a lid or foil and reheat the brisket in a 350-degree oven for 45 minutes. At this point the brisket may be stored in the fridge for several days before serving.

Note: Save the crumbled scraps for use in sandwiches or on the Jack Benny (pages 106-107).

*Any extra brisket freezes beautifully.

SPAETZLE

Makes about 7 cups, enough for 6 ample portions

 Start to finish in less than a half hour

Manna's Red Wine-Braised Beef Brisket (pages 340-341) and spaetzle are a perfect culinary marriage. The compact, diminutive egg dumplings make an ideal vehicle for other thick, rich sauces of Eastern European descent, too. They remind me of the Hungarian food my father loved to make, paprika-red dishes finished with a swirl of sour cream. Since my maiden name was Spaet, I somewhat irrationally feel a nostalgic link to home whenever I make spaetzle.

Spaetzle batter is easy to whip up but cooking the little dumplings requires a bit of finesse. The biggest challenge may be finding a gadget around your house to form them easily into the right size and shape. Consider investing in a spaetzle maker. It won't be expensive, and it's built to do the job. I love homemade spaetzle so much that it is worth having this single-use item around. The one pictured here slides back and forth across the gadget's holes, creating dumpling pieces of perfect and uniform size. At Manna, we used a pan with similarly sized holes. At home, you could use a flat, hand-held grater with very large holes. If you don't have the right gadget, you can snip off tiny pieces of dough with scissors. Just keep dipping the scissors in water to prevent sticking. Spaetzle makers can be found online through Amazon or other specialty food sites.

---

3 1/2 cups flour

1 teaspoon salt, plus additional salt for the boiling water

1 large pinch nutmeg

1 large pinch paprika

4 eggs, beaten

1 1/3 to 1 1/2 cups water, divided

1 tablespoon butter

---

1. Place flour, 1 teaspoon salt, nutmeg, and paprika in a large bowl and mix well.
2. Make a well in the center of the flour and pour in the beaten eggs and 1/2 cup of the water. Mix by hand with a wooden spoon until the dough is well mixed, adding additional water to achieve a thick dough, like a brownie batter that needs to be scraped into the pan, not poured. (If the batter is too thick, it will be hard to work with and will not come through the holes nicely. If it is too thin, it will come through the holes in long stringy pieces and have a mushiness to the bite. Perfect spaetzle will seem a bit al dente.)
3. Bring a pot of salted water to a boil. Place spaetzle maker or large-holed grater over the water, and, working in batches, grate batter into the water. For each batch, stir with a spoon so the dough does not sit in one spot. After about 2 minutes, when the water has come back to a boil and the spaetzle float to the surface, they are done. Remove spaetzle with a slotted spoon to a colander to drain. Repeat with the remaining batter. When all spaetzle are cooked, mix in the butter and serve.

Note: Before you sit down to dinner, clean out your spaetzle maker thoroughly. Otherwise, the batter will harden onto it like spackling compound.

POTATO LATKES

Makes 12 pancakes

 Start to finish in less than a half hour

Potato latkes, or pancakes, are too delicious to be slated for a once-a-year occasion. They are a classic delicacy made during Hanukkah, a Jewish holiday that celebrates the miracle of the oil that burned for eight days, instead of just one day, when the Jews reclaimed their temple from the Greeks in a long-ago time (really short version of the story). In addition to lighting a menorah for eight days, foods eaten during this time are generally fried in oil. Latkes and *sufganiyah* (jelly doughnuts) are the most traditional and well known of these.

Here again, we see aficionados divided down the middle. As with sweet vs. savory noodle kugels or floater vs. sinker matzo balls, this time the division is over the best way to eat latkes. Should you down these crispy-hot delicacies with sour cream or applesauce? (Or plain?) When you make latkes, offer both!

At Manna, we fried up our latkes for a few special occasions other than Hanukkah. Sometimes we substituted them for the English muffin base for eggs Benedict, with slices of Nova lox replacing the ham. (There was also a vegetarian version that featured slices of roasted sweet potato instead of lox.) And, it's no surprise that it was always Mike in the kitchen, grating, wringing out, and frying 100 pounds of potatoes (and snacking all the way).

I think of latkes as a much better hash brown patty—in a different class altogether. They are a perfect accompaniment to roasted meats or can be a meal unto themselves.

For this recipe, you will need a large (10- to 12-inch) sauté pan, preferably cast iron.

1/3 cup matzo meal or bread crumbs

1/3 cup flour, or more as needed

1 teaspoon salt

1/2 teaspoon black pepper

2 to 2 1/2 pounds russet or Yukon Gold potatoes, peeled and set in cold water until ready to use

1 medium to large onion (about 8 ounces), peeled and left whole

1 egg

Vegetable oil for frying, about 1/3-1/2 cup total (add some schmaltz, or rendered chicken fat, for added flavor)

Applesauce or sour cream for serving
(at Manna we dolled them up with caramelized apples)

---

1. Combine matzo meal or bread crumbs, flour, salt and pepper in a small bowl.
2. Grate the potatoes with a coarse grater, by hand, into a medium bowl. Take a small handful of the grated potatoes, squeeze as much water out of them as possible, and then place the potatoes into a medium bowl. (Keep squeezing! The more water you can wring out, the crispier the latkes will be.) Continue with handfuls of grated potatoes until all have been well wrung out. By the end, the muscles of your hands should feel spent! (Once the potatoes are peeled, and especially after they have been grated, they will start to discolor, so work quickly to finish the grating and get them mixed in with the other ingredients.)
3. Grate the onion into the bowl with the grated potatoes. Add the flour mixture and egg to the potatoes and mix until all the ingredients are well incorporated. If the mixture seems too wet, add a little more flour.
4. Heat the sauté pan on medium to medium-high heat and add the oil. When the oil is hot, take a small amount of the potato mixture (a scant 1/2 cup) and make a patty in your hands that is as flat as you can make it without having it fall apart. The patty does not need to be perfectly round. Little slivers of grated potato poking out of the edges make for nice crispy tidbits.
5. Place the latkes carefully in the hot oil until the pan is filled. Leave a bit of space around each latke so they are not touching, thus allowing the edges to become crisp. As they cook, check the latkes to make sure the heat is not too high. The potatoes need time to cook through. If they become too dark too quickly, they can burn, so adjust the heat, if necessary.
6. When deep golden brown (about 5 to 6 minutes), flip the latkes and press down with a metal spatula to flatten slightly. Continue to cook on the second side until golden brown and cooked through, another 4 to 5 minutes. Remove from pan with a spatula and set on paper towels to drain. Serve immediately with your choice of accompaniments.

NOODLE KUGELS: A YIN AND A YANG

Makes one 9 x 13-inch casserole

 **Hands-on time less than an hour (additional cooking or chilling times involved—read through before beginning)**

Noodle kugel is the Jewish second cousin, once removed, to mac and cheese. The difference is that kugels tend to be more like a bread pudding, to the extent that they are not drenched in a cheese sauce but are firmer, cutting into neat squares that hold their shape on your plate. The two varieties included here came from decades of catering to the Jewish community in Madison. Like matzo ball soup, kugel is one of those comfort foods for which every Jewish home has a favorite recipe. And as with matzo ball soup, battle lines are drawn. In this case, though, it is not over the question of sinkers vs. floaters, but of sweet vs. savory.

In the Pratzel household, a sweet kugel was unheard of, and for many of the catering years, our customers had only the one choice—the cheesy version passed down from my stepmother, Mona. Her original index card is still taped in my recipe notebook, its blue ink blurry and faded from years of use. Then along came Nicole, a Jewish friend and neighbor from the other side of the preference line, who served up her sweet version of kugel at a Rosh Hashanah gathering of neighborhood Jews. I was an instant convert, and from then on, our catering audience had the choice between the two. The eternal feud between sweet and savory lives on.

Kugels can be frozen unbaked and can go directly from the freezer to the oven. You will just need to add an extra half hour or more to the baking time and keep them covered for the first 30 to 45 minutes of baking.

Savory Custard

3 ounces (3/4 stick) butter, melted

8 ounces (1 package) cream cheese, gently warmed in a microwave

1 1/2 pounds cottage cheese

4 large eggs, lightly beaten

8 ounces cheddar cheese, grated

Salt and pepper to taste

OR

Sweet Custard

4 ounces (1 stick) butter, melted

2 cups sour cream

1/2 pound cottage cheese

1 cup sugar

6 eggs, lightly beaten

2 teaspoons vanilla extract

1/8 teaspoon cinnamon

For either version: 1 pound broad egg noodles

---

1. Grease a 9 x 13-inch casserole dish and set aside. Preheat an oven to 375 degrees.
2. Whether you are making the savory or sweet version, mix all the ingredients for the custard until well combined.
3. Bring a large pot of lightly salted water to a boil. Boil the noodles until they're almost done, but still have a little toothsomeness in the center, about a minute less than the package directions specify for al dente. They will finish cooking in the oven, absorbing the sweet or savory goodness from the custard that bathes them. Drain the pasta and return it to the pot.
4. Add the custard mixture to the hot cooked noodles and mix well. Pour the mixture into the prepared pan and smooth the top.
5. Bake for 45 minutes, uncovered. The kugel is ready when the top turns an inviting golden brown, and the stray bits sticking out are a bit crisp.

MATZO BREI

Makes 1 large or 2 smaller servings

 Start to finish in less than a half hour

Often referred to as Jewish French toast (which it isn't, but it sounds good), matzo brei (rhymes with fry) is a distant cousin, thrice removed, to the custardy, maple syrup-drenched brunch favorite. The only similarity is that both are dipped in an egg mixture before being fried. Matzo is the flat, cracker-like bread served during Passover. Eaten alone, it is the epitome of plain. Passover lasts for eight days, and since matzo is the only type of "bread" allowed, people became creative in elevating it to something delicious, even craved. Matzo brei is one of those creations.

The cooked brei is typically served plain or with applesauce. Another variation is simply to sprinkle on cinnamon sugar, which is how I was served real French toast growing up.

---

2 eggs

Salt to taste

4 cups very warm water

2 whole squares of matzo

1-2 tablespoons Schmaltz (pages 338-339) or vegetable oil, or ideally a combination of both

---

Serving Suggestions

Applesauce (for the children)

Caramelized apples (Manna's grownup apple variation)

Cinnamon sugar (because I'm my father's daughter)

Maple syrup (because Mady, Josh's fiancé, had a good suggestion, and duh ... Wisconsin)

Plain (mostly my purist husband)

1. In a wide, shallow bowl, beat the eggs and add salt to taste. In a separate wide and shallow bowl, pour in the warm water.
2. Break each piece of matzo into about 6 to 8 pieces and place in the warm water. Turn it often until the matzo just begins to soften. It should no longer be hard but should not get mushy.
3. Remove the matzo from the warm water and place it in a strainer to drain the excess water. Then, place the soaked matzo in the beaten eggs and turn the matzo several times to ensure it all gets coated.
4. In a large skillet over medium heat, add the schmaltz or vegetable oil. When the pan is very hot, add the matzo, one piece at a time, filling up the entire skillet in a slightly overlapping single layer. If there is any egg left in the bowl, drizzle it over the matzo. Lightly salt the brei all over.
5. Let cook until the matzo is a nice golden brown on the bottom, about 5 to 7 minutes. Turn the entire matzo over with a spatula in one piece. Cook on the second side for another 3 to 4 minutes.
6. Serve hot out of the pan with your favorite topping (or not) and enjoy. Chag Sameach! (Happy Passover!)

RUGELACH

Makes 18 two-inch rugelach

 **Project Alert! May require multiple stages or overnight preparations—read through before proceeding**

Rugelach (pronounced roo-guh-lakhhhhh) is a classic Jewish pastry comprising a rich, lightly sweetened dough rolled up with nuts, fruits, chocolate, or other fillings. They're like tiny, sugary strudels. Rugelach originated in Europe but became popular wherever the Jewish diaspora landed, always evolving slight variations wherever they went. If you visit bakeries that make rugelach, each version will appear a bit different in size or shape, in dough type or fillings.

Despite its association with Jewish culture, rugelach is a universal symbol of food for the soul and makes frequent appearances at important gatherings, Jewish and otherwise. It is common to bring rugelach to a shiva, the traditional seven-day mourning period for a Jewish person who has died. Rugelach often graces the pastry table at a ritual bar mitzvah celebration (ours certainly did). And it has become a trendy choice for a house gift to bring to the boss's Christmas party.

The rugelach fillings below are fairly traditional. You would find them in any Jewish bakery worth its muster. But rugelach can be a playground for creativity. Our fillings included apple butter and pumpkin butter in the fall, and on Valentine's Day, chocolate raspberry was a favorite. Fill them as you will, but remember that the purists (the same people who only order bagels in New York and NEVER have anything more than pepperoni on their pizzas) may rib you a bit!

I have tasted many rugelach in my day. Every time I see them in a Jewish bakery or deli case, piled deep in a giant glass jar or laid out in row after sugary row, I buy some—I can't help myself. And yet, I am often disappointed. I have yet to try a rugelach better than these, which are the gift, once again, of Julia Child's book *Baking with Julia*. Her dough contains both cream cheese and butter, providing an opulent depth. And our technique for rolling and baking is spot-on. At Manna, we offered a variety of fillings and cut the rugelach into plump pillows. (A typical rugelach is maybe an inch or two wide and sold by the pound. Ours were three long inches and sold individually!)

Dough

8 ounces (2 sticks) butter, softened

8 ounces cream cheese (1 package), softened

1/4 teaspoon salt

1/4 cup sugar

2 1/4 cups flour

Filling and Finishes (each makes enough for one batch of rugelach)

Chocolate-Prune Filling

1 cup canned prune filling or homemade prune butter

2 tablespoons cinnamon sugar (see below)

1/2 cup mini chocolate chips

For the topping: 2 ounces semisweet chocolate, melted (to be applied after baking)

OR

Apricot-Almond

1 cup apricot jam

2 tablespoons cinnamon sugar (see below)

1/2 cup finely chopped toasted almonds

For the topping: 1/4 cup finely chopped toasted almonds

OR

Poppy Seed-Walnut

1 cup poppy seed filling or homemade poppy seed butter

2 tablespoons cinnamon sugar (see below)

1/2 cup very finely chopped toasted walnuts (almost, but not quite ground)

For the topping: poppy seeds

A Few Additional Finishing Components

Cinnamon sugar: 1/4 cup white sugar, 1 tablespoon packed brown sugar, and 1 1/2 teaspoons cinnamon mixed together

Egg wash: 1 egg mixed with 1 tablespoon milk

Sanding sugar (see page 226)

1. **To make the dough:** In a mixer with a paddle attachment, cream the butter and cream cheese for 1 minute. Scrape down the sides of the bowl. Add salt and sugar and mix on medium speed until smooth. Add the flour and mix on low until all ingredients are well incorporated.
2. Turn the dough out onto a lightly floured work surface. Form the dough into a rectangle about 1 1/2 inches thick (its dimensions don't matter at this point). Pat it this way and that with your hands so the rectangle has straight edges and is even all around. This will help ensure even rolling at the next stage. Wrap the dough in plastic wrap and refrigerate until completely chilled, at least 2 hours. (At this stage, the dough may be refrigerated for 2 to 3 days or frozen for up to 1 month.)
3. While the dough is chilling, prepare one of the filling/finish combinations. (If you're making a variety of fillings, make a full batch of the ones you choose, then freeze the leftovers.)
4. **To roll and fill the dough:** Preheat the oven to 375 degrees. Line a sheet pan with parchment paper, and set this sheet pan on top of a second sheet pan with no liner. (During the initial baking, the bottom of the dough may get too dark. This technique helps prevent overbaking.)

5. Lightly dust a work surface with flour. Place the chilled dough rectangle on the flour, and dust the top with flour as well. Roll the dough into an 18 x 15-inch rectangle, with the longer side facing you. Dust with a bit more flour as needed to keep it from sticking. Trim the edges using a pizza cutter or sharp knife to form a nice clean rectangle. Cut the rectangle in half along its long dimension so that you end up with two pieces of dough, each 18 x 7 1/2 inches.

6. Spread each half of the rolled-out dough with about 1/2 cup of the jam or butter from your chosen filling. If you have a small offset spatula, use it to easily spread the thick fillings uniformly. Spread to the edges on the bottom and along the short sides of the dough, but leave about a 1-inch border at the top of each rectangle, along its 18-inch upper edge. Being careful to avoid the top border where no filling has been spread, sprinkle 2 tablespoons of cinnamon sugar on top of the filling, then top with a sprinkling of chocolate chips, almonds, or walnuts, depending on the filling you have chosen.

7. **To roll the dough with filling (read this first):** For each dough half, lightly brush some of the egg wash along the "naked" 1-inch border at the top of each rectangle. Tightly roll up the dough from the bottom such that the egg-washed top edge ends up on the bottom of the roll. Because the dough is 18 inches across, you will not be able to roll the entire thing at once. To create a uniform log, start at one end and roll about a 4-inch segment for one or two revolutions, pulling toward you a bit as you go to keep the roll snug. Then roll the next segment by the same amount. Keep rolling in segments until all 18 inches has been rolled to an even thickness. As you continue the rolling process, you will find that as the log gets fatter, it is easier to roll bigger stretches at once. Keep pulling it taut as you go to create a tight cylinder. When you are finished, the egg-washed edge should be underneath the log you have just formed.

8. Now, brush more egg wash generously along the top of the rolls, sprinkle with sanding sugar, and then sprinkle with the appropriate topping for your filling choice (*Note: The chocolate/prune filling variety should just receive the sanding sugar. The melted chocolate will be piped on the top of the rugelach after it has been baked and cooled)*.

9. **To form and bake rugelach:** Cut the logs into 2-inch lengths. You should get 9 rugelach per roll. Place the cut rugelach on the prepared sheet pan, spaced 2 inches apart.

10. Bake the rugelach for 15 minutes. Remove the bottom baking pan, rotate the pan with the rugelach, and bake for another 15 to 20 minutes. The rugelach should be a uniformly beautiful golden-brown color.

11. Let pastries cool on the pan. For the chocolate prune variety, the rugelach should be completely cool before you drizzle the tops with the melted chocolate. You can drizzle the chocolate from a spoon, or you can pipe it from a small piping bag with a small hole cut in the end. (Swish back and forth, back and forth, on a diagonal, or go to town and have fun with your designs.)

12. Rugelach can be stored in a tight container for 3 to 5 days or up to 7 to 10 days if refrigerated. They will also keep for a month or more frozen in an air-tight container.

HAMANTASCHEN

Makes 18 cookies (filling, dough, multistep assembly)

 **Project Alert! May require multiple stages or overnight preparations—read through before proceeding**

Hamantaschen are three-cornered, soft, filled cookies made for Purim, the Jewish holiday celebrating the victory of good (as personified by Esther) over the evil Haman, who wanted to annihilate the Jews. The story is told in the Book of Esther, and the cookies are full of symbolism and tradition, like so much else that is Jewish.

Every year, our family participated in the annual "H-Bake," a much-anticipated event at Beth Israel Center, the conservative synagogue in Madison. It was an extraordinary gathering of families from the congregation. High school kids took charge of production, with parents following orders! At the head of this veritable "army" was their beloved mentor (and taskmaster), Youth Director Deb—arguably the soul of the synagogue's youth community. Thousands of these beautiful cookies were assembled for an annual fundraiser during Purim. It was quite the show. Kids and their families worked together like busy bees to mix, portion, roll, fill, form, bake, organize, and box. The result was a joyous, side-by-side bonding of the Jewish community over teenage chatter, grownup reminiscence, and the warm fragrances of an ancient culture.

At Manna, we adapted the Beth Israel recipe, using butter instead of margarine. Traditional fillings would be poppy seed, apricot, or prune. I have included a less traditional but popular Manna filling—apple-date, as well as apricot, the most popular. (At Beth Israel, the untraditional fillings of blueberry or raspberry were secret, ordered only by those in the know.)

This cookie keeps its integrity well. It can be formed and frozen before baking or frozen after baking. And it keeps well at room temperature, wrapped, for several days.

Note: The hamantaschen fillings below should be made first or while the dough is chilling. They will be used chilled.

Hamantaschen Dough

3/4 cup sugar

2 cups flour, sifted after measuring

2 teaspoons baking powder

1/4 teaspoon salt

4 ounces (1 stick) butter (or margarine if you want to avoid dairy), softened

1 egg

2 tablespoons orange juice

Apple-Date Filling

One small apple, peeled and finely diced

3/4 cup packed pitted and chopped dates

3 tablespoons orange juice

1/4 teaspoon cinnamon

1/4 teaspoon vanilla extract

1/2 cup water

OR

Apricot Filling

1 cup dried apricots, coarsely chopped

Half of a 15-ounce can of apricots in light syrup, drained

1/4 cup sugar

1 1/2 tablespoons lemon juice

A little bowl of water for forming the hamantaschen

1. **To make the dough:** Sift together the sugar, flour, salt, and baking powder into the bowl of an electric mixer with a paddle attachment. On a low speed, mix in the butter, then egg, and orange juice. Continue to mix until the dough just holds together. Knead once or twice by hand, then form into a ball, wrap in plastic, and refrigerate for at least 2 hours or overnight.
2. **To make apple date filling:** Place all the ingredients in a small pot, and bring to a simmer over medium heat. Reduce the heat to low and simmer, stirring occasionally, until the apples are soft. If the mixture appears dry or sticks to the pot, add a couple of tablespoons of water as needed. Use an immersion blender or miniature food processor to coarsely chop the mixture. Refrigerate, covered, until ready to use.

3. **To make apricot filling:** Soak dried apricots in hot water for 5 minutes. Rinse until all the flour coating is gone and the water runs clear. Combine dried apricots, canned apricots, and sugar in a small saucepan and bring to a boil. Reduce heat to medium and simmer, covered, for 10 minutes, or until the dried apricots have softened. Stir in the lemon juice and remove from the heat, and cool to room temperature. Use an immersion blender or miniature food processor to blend ingredients until smooth. Refrigerate, covered, until ready to use.

4. **To form and bake the hamantaschen:** When ready to form, preheat the oven to 350 degrees. Line two baking sheets with parchment paper and set them aside.

5. Remove the dough from the fridge and let it come to room temperature. Lightly flour a work surface. Knead the dough for a few minutes by hand—just enough to make the dough smooth and malleable. Flatten the dough slightly and dust the top with flour. Roll out the dough to a 1/8-inch thickness—no thicker. As you roll, keep the work surface and top of the dough lightly floured to avoid sticking (use as little flour as possible to achieve this, so the dough does not dry out). Cut into 3-inch circles using a round cookie cutter. Gather up and reuse the scraps, but take care not to incorporate excess flour.

6. The cookie will end up with three sides—a sort of triangle—with the filling peeking out from the center. Place a heaping teaspoon of filling in the center of each circle. Dip your fingertip into the little bowl of water, then lightly moisten the perimeter of the circle. To shape the hamantaschen, gently pinch together two edges of the dough to make a point, with two sides leading away from that point. Then press the remaining rounded end toward the center, thus creating the other two sides of the triangle. Press all the seams together well, including the ends of the points, so that the formed cookie will hold together during baking. (At Beth Israel, a checker was located at each oven to make sure cookie seams were well sealed!) The dough should mostly cover the filling, but there should be about 1/2 inch of filling showing.

7. Place the cookies on baking sheets, spaced about an inch apart. Bake for 6 minutes, then rotate the pan and bake another 6 to 9 minutes. They should be lightly browned on the corners (and with only a light golden hue on the rest of the cookie). Let cool.

Use this much filling.

First pinch.

Pressing rounded end toward center,
to create three sides, three points.

Second pinch.

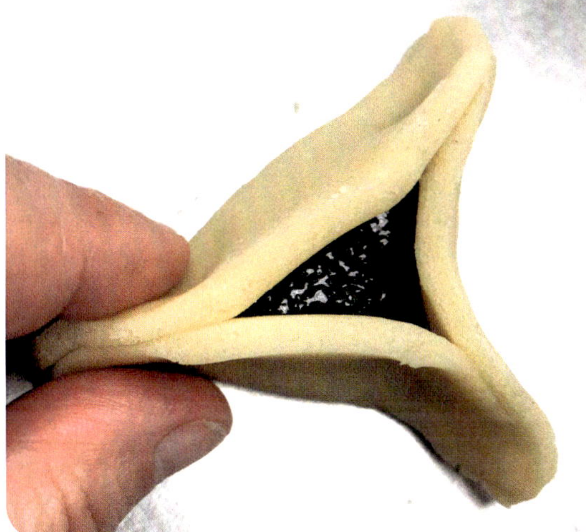

Final pinches, and shaping the cookie.

Finished cookie.

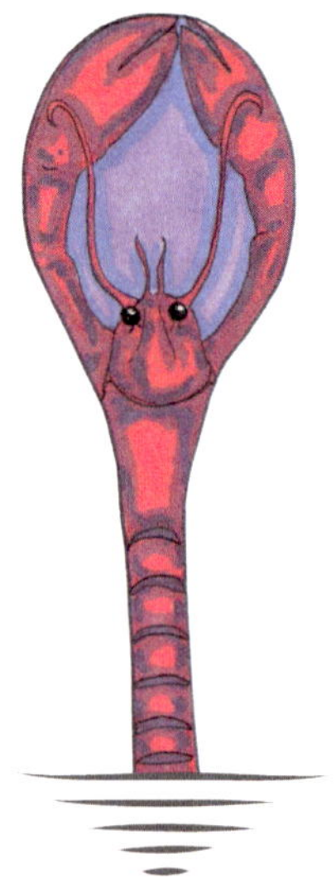

APPENDIX:

Some How-To Recipe Support

Sometimes, it takes a recipe to make a recipe. This chapter is not about making your life more complicated, but offers a few techniques and guidelines for making prepared ingredients—delicious, useful things like roasted peppers or toasted nuts, that require more than a few words of instruction.

HOW TO "ROAST" GARLIC

Start to finish in less than a half hour

Roasting garlic takes away its sharp, breath-ruining bite and leaves a nutty-sweet, soft and schmearable ingredient with a multitude of uses in its stead. By itself, roast garlic can be spread on toast and topped with sliced garden tomatoes and basil leaves—summer simplicity. Or it can be an ingredient in hummus, pesto, aioli, mashed potatoes—anywhere you would like its gentle, mellow flavor.

We once roasted garlic by wrapping it in tin foil with a bit of olive oil and setting it in a 350-degree oven for 30 to 40 minutes. This technique works fine, especially if you want to roast an entire head, still in its papery shield. (This is often done when the presentation is important: serving the whole head as part of an arrangement of other items on a plate.) But then your oven is using quite a lot of energy for this one tiny package. I prefer stovetop roasting, which is faster and more energy-efficient. You can see when it is done. Bonus: You can use the oil in other cooking, with its subtle fragrance of garlic.

One last note: If you plan to roast more than a little bit, get yourself a small bottle of peeled garlic from the store to use for this project, and roast the whole bottle's worth. You can freeze the roasted cloves and have them as an instant building block in your freezer.

Garlic cloves (as few or as many as you like), peeled and left whole

Olive oil (enough to cover the cloves)

---

1. Unless you are roasting a large amount of garlic (more than 3 to 4 cups), use a small deep saucepan. Place the cloves in it and add enough olive oil to cover.
2. Turn on the heat to medium and let the olive oil come to a simmer. Adjust the heat down so that the oil is at a very light simmer.
3. The roasting process is done when the cloves are a deep golden color and very soft. This will take about 10 to 20 minutes. Do not let them get too dark, or they will become a bit leathery on the outside.
4. Strain the cloves and save the garlic oil for later cooking. The roasted garlic can be used at once or portioned and frozen.

HOW TO ROAST PEPPERS

Start to finish within an hour, give or take

Roasted peppers are a mellow, softened version of their fresh counterpart. Roasting chars their skins, and the peppers retain a bit of that smoky flavor. If you roast peppers on your grill, they'll have extra smokiness.

Whole fresh peppers (green, red, or yellow sweet peppers, poblanos)

1. Preheat the oven to 500 degrees.
2. Place the peppers on a sheet pan lined with parchment paper. Set the pan in the hot oven and roast the peppers, turning them every 10 minutes or so. You want the entire skin of the pepper to be charred and the insides soft and steamy. It may take 30 minutes, give or take.
3. Remove the peppers from the oven and set them on a plate. Cover them with a kitchen towel and let them cool completely. (The trapped steam from the cooling peppers helps loosen the charred skin.)
4. When the peppers are cool, peel off all the skin, open the pepper, and clean out the seeds, stem, and white, fibrous tissue. The peppers are now ready to use, or they can be frozen.

Note: An alternative procedure is to char the outside of the peppers over an open flame. Turn on the flame to medium or medium high and set the peppers directly on the flame. Turn them regularly with a pair of tongs to get an even char, and when they are blackened all over, continue with Step 3 above. I like to use this technique when I have only one or two peppers to roast.

HOW TO PEEL AND SEED TOMATOES

Start to finish in less than a half hour

Maybe the first question to ask is, why peel and seed a tomato? Why not just chop it up? And the short answer is, go ahead. I do it when I feel lazy or don't care if bits of skin or tiny seeds muddle up my dish.

But peeling and seeding tomatoes is easy, relatively quick, and (I'm not sure why I say this) a somewhat cathartic and satisfying activity that appeals to my need to be methodical and efficient. I especially like doing this at the end of the summer, when the tomato harvest is at its peak. I might buy a case of tomatoes, prep them as described below, and freeze them for winter use. Then I don't have to buy canned tomatoes, and my cooking tastes all that much fresher.

Whole tomatoes of any variety except cherry

1. Bring a large pot of water to a boil.
2. Score a small "X" on the bottom of each tomato, cutting just enough to break the skin.
3. When the water is at a full boil, place as many tomatoes as will fit in a single layer, with a little float room in between each one, into the pot. Then wait about 1 minute. You want the skin to be blanched just enough so that it peels off easily, but you don't want to cook the tomato.
4. Remove the tomatoes from the pot and let them cool enough to handle. Let the water come back to a boil before adding more tomatoes to the pot.
5. When tomatoes are cooled, peel off the skins. Then, cut the tomatoes in half horizontally. With your fingers, scoop out all the seeds. Cut out the stems, then chop the tomatoes into any size you desire. Portion into jars or Ziploc bags and freeze.
6. For extra credit, save all of the seeds and juicy innards in a bowl as you work. At the end, use a fine-mesh strainer to strain out the seeds, pressing on the solids, and collect the resulting juice. You can freeze this juice as well and use it later in soups or sauces. I especially like to use it in risotto. The fresh, tangy tomato flavors of summer shine through!

HOW TO REMOVE SILVERSKIN FROM TENDERLOIN

Start to finish in less than a half hour

Silverskin is the silvery-white, satiny-smooth connective tissue that runs the length of a piece of tenderloin (beef, pork) parallel to the meat's grain. It is tough and sinewy and, left on, would give each bite a noticeable and unwelcome chewiness. It's easy enough to remove once you get the hang of it. You will need a very sharp boning knife or fish knife (one with a slight curve) to make quick work of it.

1. Set the tenderloin on a cutting board. Beginning roughly 2 inches from the wider end, insert the point of the knife just under, and snugly against, the surface of the silverskin, with the sharp edge of the blade facing toward that wide end. Slide the knife point through to the other side of the silverskin, keeping the blade snug up against it. (Because the skin is tough and sinewy, it will not break through.)
2. Once the knife is through to the other side, push it a little toward the wide end of the tenderloin until you have a free flap of silverskin. Grab hold of the flap with a paper towel to hold the slippery devil in place while you finish removing it.
3. Place the knife blade back under, and snugly against, the silverskin, this time with the sharp edge of the blade facing the narrow end of the tenderloin. Push the knife blade down the length of the silverskin until you reach the end, and the skin comes free. As you are doing so, press the blade upward and into the silverskin at a slight angle that allows it to slide along more easily and keeps it from cutting into the meat.
4. Discard the silverskin. If you like, trim off the last few inches at the narrow end to reserve for another use, such as in a stir-fry or stroganoff dish. If you roast the tenderloin, the narrow end will cook to a much more well-done stage than the wider middle. The resulting slices will be narrow and overcooked.

HOW TO TOAST NUTS

Start to finish in less than a half hour

I cannot count how many times I have thrown a batch of nuts in the oven to toast them, then gone back to binge-watching some engaging Netflix program. Suddenly, I am jolted by a strong odor, and I realize that I have just ruined the batch of nuts. Nuts toast quickly, and you should stay near your oven in restless anticipation.

I never use anything but toasted nuts in recipes. Raw nuts seem to me to be beside the point. Toasting does to nuts what salting does to food in general by bringing out their flavor. I always toast more than I need, then store the extra in a sealed jar for easy use later on.

Raw, untoasted nuts

1. Preheat the oven to 350 degrees. Line a sheet pan with parchment paper or aluminum foil. Spread the nuts out in a single layer on the pan.
2. Place the pan in the oven and set a timer for 5 minutes. Stir or toss the nuts with a spatula, rotate the pan, and set a timer for 2 more minutes. Stir the nuts again, adding another minute or two if needed, or take them out of the oven if they are done. Frequent checks are necessary to keep them from turning too dark. When they are done, they should be golden brown and have a warm, toasty aroma.

HOW TO TOAST COCONUT

Start to finish in less than a half hour

Coconut can go from not done to overdone in no time at all. On the plus side, since it goes quickly, your time spent watching it like a mother hen will also go quickly. The biggest reason is that sweetened coconut (the kind called for in these recipes) contains sugar, which can burn easily.

Shredded sweetened coconut

---

1. Preheat the oven to 350 degrees. Line a sheet pan with parchment paper or aluminum foil. Spread the coconut out in a single layer on the pan, no deeper than about 1/4 inch.
2. Place the pan in the oven and set a timer for 2 minutes. Stir or toss the coconut with a spatula and set a timer for 2 more minutes. Keep repeating this process until nearly all of the strands look toasty, with a mix of golden to medium-brown shreds, with only a few white ones. Each time you open the oven to stir, pay attention to where the hot spots are. Certain parts of the pan may get very dark very quickly, so make sure to rotate the whiter coconut into those spots.
3. Remove the pan from the oven and let it cool completely. Then you can just lift out the pan liner and pour the coconut into a jar for storage.

HOW TO FRIZZLE ONIONS (AKA FRIZZLES)

Makes about 2 cups

 Start to finish in less than a half hour

Wispy, crispy, addicting. Frizzled onions are a feminine relative to their more manly cousin, the crunchy, munchy onion ring. Dainty and elegant, frizzled onions are a habit-forming addition to the pantry, where they can be snacked on when no one is looking, or added to sandwiches or piled atop grilled steaks. They are easy to make, and they keep well.

2 large yellow onions, thinly sliced

Flour for dredging (about 1/2 cup)

1/2 teaspoon salt

1/2 teaspoon pepper

Enough vegetable oil for deep frying

1. Slice the onions very, very thinly. If you have a mandolin, this would be a good time to use it. When sliced, gently break the onions into rings.
2. Heat vegetable oil to 375 degrees in a deep fryer or a heavy-bottomed, medium-sized pot. Use enough oil to allow onions to be fully submerged when frying. (Leftover frying oil can be strained and reused.) And make sure the pot has some depth. When the onions are first submerged, the oil will bubble up, then settle back down once the moisture has cooked off.
3. Mix together flour, salt and pepper. Toss the onions in the seasoned flour, shaking off excess.
4. Place small batches of onions into the hot oil and fry until golden brown, about 2 to 3 minutes. (If you add too many onions at once, they may not fry up as crisp, since overcrowding adds too much moisture to the oil.) Stir them a bit during frying to avoid any hot spots. Also, keep an eye on them as they start to turn color. They can go from beautiful and golden to burnt in the blink of an eye. Drain fried onions on paper towels.
5. Use immediately, or store in an air-tight container for up to 2 weeks. (Line the container with paper towels to absorb any extra oil. This will help them stay crisp. If they lose some of their crispness, just reheat them in a 300-degree oven for about 3-5 minutes, then let cool.)

HOW TO MAKE A CONFECTIONERS' SUGAR GLAZE

Makes about 2/3 cup glaze

 **Start to finish in less than a half hour**

A confectioners' sugar glaze adds a crowning touch of sweetness as well as a decorative finish to many baked goods. Some people find it superfluous. For others, it's a welcome accent. Occasionally, as with the Lavender Lime Tea Cake (page 286), it is necessary. (What would a carrot cake be without its cream cheese frosting?)

Milk is the classic liquid used for this glaze, but water will make it dairy-free. Citrus juice or coconut milk can add a specific flavor to match the theme of your baked goods (coconut milk is especially nice with the Lavender Lime Tea Cake), plus they're also dairy-free.

Achieving the right consistency for your purpose can be a challenge until you have worked with it a bit and played around with liquid proportions. You may prefer a slightly thicker glaze that holds its shape or a thinner one that spreads out into a shiny, smooth layer. Sometimes, the glaze is made very thin so that all you see on your scone or muffin is a bit of glossiness. I have indicated what sort of a finish you should aim for in the recipes that use this glaze.

At Manna, the bakers made batches of the glaze with different flavor profiles, then put them directly into piping bags. The bags were stored in the fridge between uses and warmed ever so slightly in the microwave to bring them back to a piping consistency. This way, the glaze did not need to be made fresh each time, and we didn't waste a drop.

---

2 cups confectioners' sugar

3 tablespoons or more liquid (one of the following):

- Milk
- Water
- Orange, lemon, or lime juice
- Coconut milk

Optional flavor additions:

- 1/2 teaspoon vanilla extract or almond extract
- 1/2 teaspoon orange, lemon, or lime zest

Using a whisk, beat together sugar, optional flavor addition, and most (but not all) of the liquid, holding back a bit so that you have room to adjust the thickness to your needs. If your glaze needs to be thinner, add more liquid drop by drop—small changes make a big difference. If you need to make it thicker, add more confectioners' sugar. The designations below are just guidelines.

Too thick: will not pour off of a spoon but will seem more like frosting

Medium: will drizzle when swished back and forth but will retain its shape (good for scones or cookies)

Thin: will spread out fairly quickly, leaving a visible but thin solid layer (good for some cakes)

Very thin: will run off the side of products, leaving more of a lustrous finish, like shellac; the glaze itself will be less noticeable

To apply the glaze, you can simply use a spoon to drizzle the glaze, pendulum-like, over your product, which will provide a more rustic and carefree appearance to the finish. But I like placing the glaze in a piping bag, where the tiny opening at the end controls the shape and size of the drizzle, giving a more professional look.

Acknowledgments

Where does one even begin?

My friend Claire DeChristina probably thinks she had little or nothing to do with this cookbook, and in a way, it is true. But I know that she knows I'm right—she was the butterfly in this story. She once gave us a local newspaper clipping on B&Bs in San Francisco because she knew we were headed there and thought we might be interested. This random kindness unintentionally and effectively changed the course of our lives in unimaginable ways. Thanks, lady.

Manna Cafe and The Collins House B&B were all about people—inn guests, catering clients, cafe customers—and the relationships nurtured over those now-ubiquitous oatcakes. Together, for nearly 35 years, we ate, laughed, cried, celebrated, commiserated, and then ate some more. Thank you for loving the food and for including us in your lives.

It was these same people who, over the years, suggested a cookbook was in my future. In the beginning, it was a recipe request here, an encouraging noodge there, but by the time Manna was winding down, it had become a cacophonous clamor. Heartfelt thanks go out to the enthusiastic patrons who brought me to this place and reawakened my passion for writing. Sharing these recipes and memories is a natural continuation of the lives we built together—a way to stay connected.

At The Collins House, I had a wonderful staff of people-loving people who had the coffee on by 6 a.m., made infinite hospital corners, stayed up to check in late arrivals, and puttered around the kitchen, snacking on delicious morsels the caterers tossed their way. The lively catering crew cooked, plated, delivered, served, nurtured, held customers' hands, and ultimately returned "home" with hilarious stories to tell over leftovers and a beer. Oh, those were the days. Some of you are in my life still, but many more remain in the forefront of my thoughts, and I think of you often. Thanks for helping lay the groundwork, and helping us better understand just what sort of business owners we wanted to be.

At Manna, the bakers arose early; the dishwashers labored long, sweaty hours; the line cooks pounded out the orders lickety-split while the production cooks readied their soups; and the front-of-house staff smiled onward. Perhaps you've heard that restaurant life is no cakewalk, that running a B&B is not as easy as it looks. And it could not be more true. But for Mike and me, it was a deeply rewarding lifestyle lived side by side with our staff and children. I have so many staff to thank for doing this all on our behalf. I hope they know how much we cared. I'm sure we never said it enough, and maybe *this* isn't enough, but Thank You (with hugs).

Many people came out of the woodwork, for various reasons, from the time the pandemic began to the time we closed (not even four months)! Customers asked how they could help, perhaps by starting a GoFundMe page, and continued to support us by ordering food and encouraging us to hang in there. One kind soul left a $500 check for us to distribute to staff. And our amazing staff, then reduced to a barebones crew, worked their behinds off to keep up with the demand, to help keep the dream alive until the end. Thanks, Lindsay, Eric, Rachael, Jenny, Tyler, Tony, Dan, Chris, Joe, Sarah, Ana, Hannah, Steve, and Allyson. Customers and staff gave us the gift of a special kind of compassion that helped ease the pain of closing in just the right way.

I barreled into this cookbook project thinking I knew a thing or two about writing, having been a professional writer at one point in my life. But four extraordinary consultants/hand-holders/educators/critics/role models showed me just how much more I had to learn, and I am forever in their debt.

I cannot imagine how a cookbook—any cookbook—could come into existence without the considerable wisdom of Terese Allen, author of *The Ovens of Brittany Cookbook*, among many others. She is a walking cookbook Wikipedia, with answers always at the tip of her tongue. She speaks her mind, never sugar-coating a thing, always leads, encourages, and shares her knowledge freely. Thank you for every comma you subtracted (I may have added a few back in), every cheese name you capitalized, every instruction you had me laboriously cross-reference, and for all the warmth you breathed into this book. (And Terese—when first we got going on this project, you asked if you could do the book's index. Index? I hadn't so much as written a paragraph. I will forever remember your love of indexing (and the confident way in which it allowed me to envision a finished book) with a soft spot in my heart.

Michelle Wildgen—author, editor, instructor—graciously led me through the book-crafting process. Through her amazing guidance, what began as a jumble of ideas—sometimes just random paragraphs I wanted to include—became a book that made sense from beginning to end. Through Michelle, I gained a deep appreciation for the writer/editor relationship and the ability of someone else to help you see your vision. She became, to me, the kind woman in the park, taking a lost and bewildered child by the hand and helping her find her mother.

As a new and unknown author, trying to find a publisher presented many scary challenges, and I am grateful to have stumbled upon Kristin Mitchell of Little Creek Press, just down the block in Mineral Point. From the moment my first phone conversation with her ended, I knew I had found a home for this book. Kristin exuded the kind of self-confidence that the novice in me craved, and the considerable patience that I imagine publishers must need when they are pummeled with questions of minutiae—sometimes the same ones over and over again. Kristin has the gift of knowing that she doesn't need to know all the answers right away, but that when the time comes, they will present themselves. Thanks, Kristin, for letting me slow down and chill, and giving the me the courage to just enjoy watching the process unfold.

I never got a chance to meet Shannon Booth, but I was grateful to be in such capable hands. Just when I thought I had a pretty good cookbook, Shannon buffed and polished the manuscript until it shined, and once again educated me along the way. Thanks for providing a meticulousness I never knew I was missing, and helping me realize what it takes to reach that next level.

My recipe testers, eighteen in all, had to decipher my early writings, ask for clarifications, fill out questionnaires, and hunt down ingredients as they cheerfully worked to get the recipes right. I cannot thank them enough for helping me clarify every little detail, right down to the type of peanut butter (creamy or chunky). They brought so much to the table (so to speak): my long-time, cherished friend Jarno Arnovich (fellow cook, eater, and partner in catering, who tested recipes both before and after her long-overdue kitchen renovation); old Collins House staffers Deidre Buckingham and Jody Flatt; dear friends Dianne Jenkins, Nicole Resnick, Mark Dalebroux, Debbie Darien, and Ellen Barnard; Ellen Joppe, Claire Lynch, Joan Lynch, Geneva Shoemaker, and Brenda Smoody who came to me as friends of friends or family; and finally my cherished family members Bill Tetzlaff and Nancy Stitham, Stacey Tetzlaff and Eric Tetzlaff, and sons Ike and Josh Pratzel.

Before the recipes could be tested, they needed translators. Some recipes were a collection of Post-it notes. At Manna we made 75 pounds of beef brisket at a time, and all the muffins were scaled to be the size of a regulation softball. I am especially thankful to the staff who patiently answered my questions on interpretation and technique and helped reconstruct recipes to make sense for your family of four. In particular, Dan Bultman, Chris Stephens, Eric Hanson, and Lindsey Toeg gave expert guidance along the way.

Liz Parker-Dunn—long-time friend, coworker, bookkeeper, and the best "word processor" I can imagine—graciously launched the formatting of the recipes, helping to make sense of the mishmash of kitchen notes and multiple styles that was our starting point. She is one of a small handful of people in my life for whom reaching for perfection is a guiding principle in life. Thanks, Lizzie!

Emily Ranney, a former baker, brightened these pages with illustrations of the ever-beloved kitties and spoon numbers. Thanks, Emily, for your lovely drawings. They are heartfelt and mirror so poignantly many of the themes and ideas that guided the Manna experience. If you someday become a professional illustrator, I'll be the first one in line.

I conclude with a few words (okay, maybe a few too many) about my own family—not the Manna one or The Collins House one. As I have pointed out on more than one occasion in this book, my two sons are polar opposites in nearly every way except for one—they both loved Manna and were shocked when we announced its closing. And while growing up in this business affected and influenced each one differently, they are both filled with a special kind of work ethic and respect reserved for children who watch their parents toil together in business. Josh had the cooking genes, and from his earliest years was destined for chef-hood, which is where he landed. He contributed his wealth of knowledge (which certainly surpassed mine), editing my early writings and making many suggestions for additions (and quite a few subtractions). It was important to him because it was important to me, and this book has benefitted from his sensibilities.

Isaac was the non-cook of the family for most of his childhood, but as an adult, he's learned so much. I was grateful for his many curious questions during the recipe testing process, which were very much from the viewpoint of a beginner—yet every question caused me to reflect for a moment on what it was I had missed, and thus helped me better understand how to speak to a novice readership. And finally, Mike, husband, co-owner, long-time friend, and love of my life. He participated in the book as a "pretester," making sure the recipes sent to testers were at least in working order. And he listened, even during the Cardinal games, even while focused on a challenging hand of bridge, to my sentences and paragraphs, always steering me to a better place with a perspective so different from my own. He handled my year of ups and downs like a champ, and that is saying a lot!

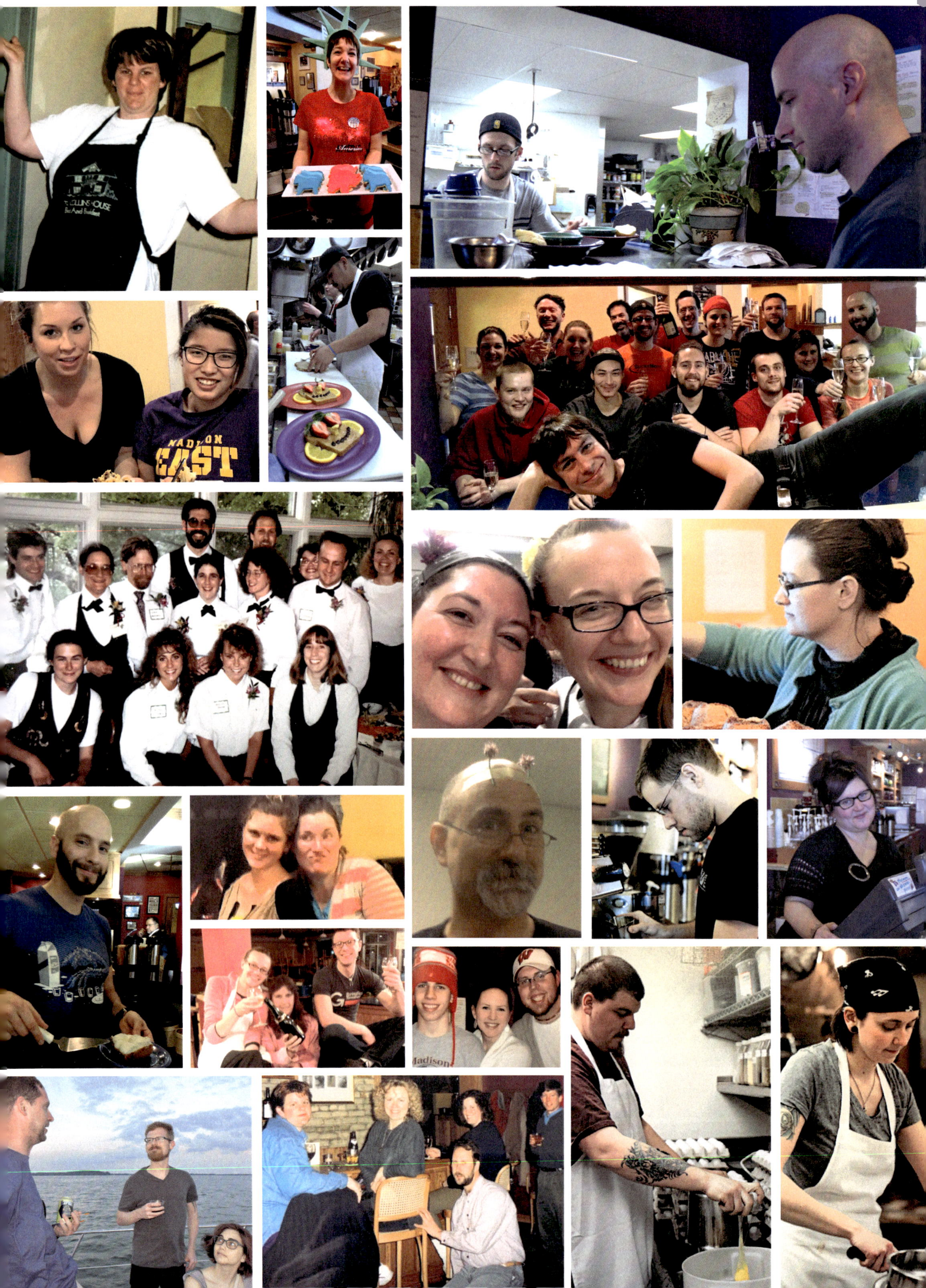
MADISON
EAST

About the Author

Barb Pratzel was a UW Journalism School graduate and science writer whose career took a decidedly sharp right turn into the world of bed and breakfasts, catering, and restaurants. Then, for 35 years she welcomed guests to her inn and customers to her cafe and bakery, all the while cultivating recipes that helped define a community. When the 2020 pandemic caused the widely beloved Manna Cafe to close, she turned once again to writing, grateful to bring her career full circle with this memoir/cookbook, the joyous result.

Barb is a New York transplant who fell in love with Madison, Wisconsin at first sight, and lives here still. She has two children deeply rooted in the ethos of small business culture, and a husband (aka business partner/lifelong companion) whose love of a loaf of bread has amply sustained her, like manna.

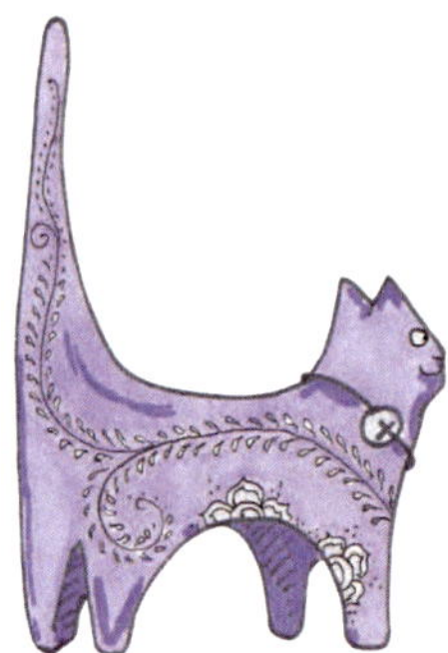

Index

Recipe page numbers are in **bold type**.

A

B

C

G

H

I

J

P

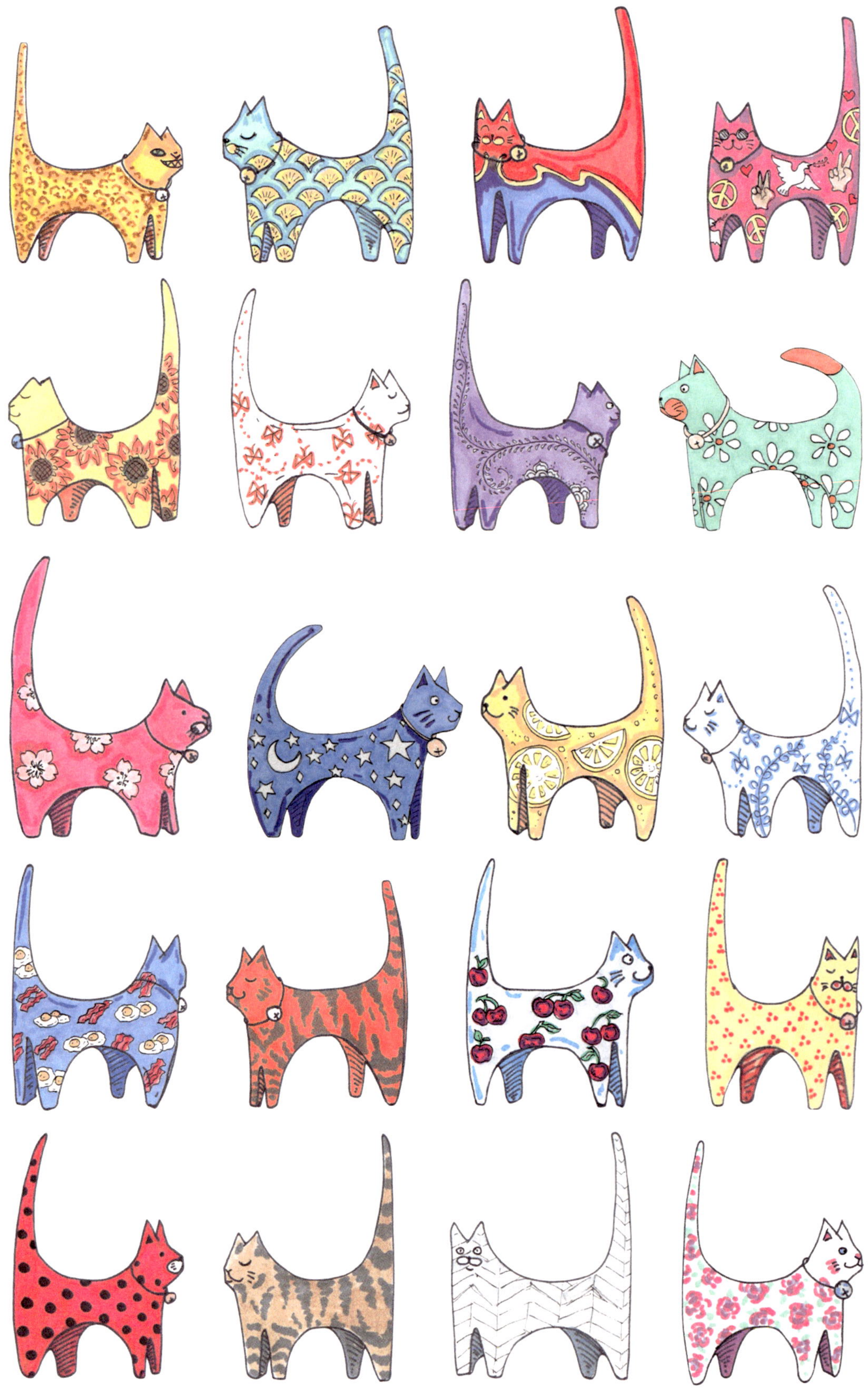

Printed in the United States
by Baker & Taylor Publisher Services